Frommer's®

Tuscany, Umbria & Florence with your family

by Donald Strachan & Stephen Keeling

WILEY
A John Wiley and Sons, Ltd, Publication

Telephone (+44) 1243 779777
Email (for orders and customer service enquiries): cs-books@wiley.co.uk. Visit our Home Page on www.wiley.com

UK Publisher: Sally Smith
Production Manager: Daniel Mersey
Commissioning Editor: Mark Henshall
Development Editor: Rhonda Carrier
Content Editor: Erica Peters
Cartographer: Simonetta Giori
Photo Research: Jill Emeny

British Library Cataloguing in Publication Data
A catalogue record for this book is available from the British Library

ISBN: 978-0-470-74988-3 (pbk), ISBN: 978-1-119-99081-9 (ebk)
ISBN: 978-1-119-97125-2 (epub), ISBN: 978-1-119-97126-9 (e-mobi)

Typeset by Wiley Indianapolis Composition Services
Printed and bound in China by RR Donnelley

4 3 2 1

Contents

About the Authors v
An Additional Note vi
Photo Credits viii

1 Family Highlights of Tuscany, Umbria & Florence 1

The Best Family Experiences 3
Exploring Together 4
Just for Children 5
Historic Sites 6
The Best Eating Options 7
The Best Accommodation 8

2 Planning a Trip to Tuscany, Umbria & Florence 9

Visitor Information 10
Money 14
When to Go 16
What to Pack 18
Health, Insurance & Safety 20
Responsible Travel 21
Essentials 22
Accommodation 27
Eating Out 31
The 21st-Century Traveller 33

3 Florence 37

Visitor Information 38
What to See & Do 48
Family-Friendly Dining 69
Family-Friendly Accommodation 76

4 Siena & the Central Hill-Towns 79

Siena 80
San Gimignano 90
Volterra 96
Arezzo 103
Family-Friendly Dining 107
Family-Friendly Accommodation 110

5 Pisa, Lucca & Northern Tuscany 113

Pisa 115
Lucca 123
Pistoia & Its Province 127
Viareggio 131
Tuscany's Far North 134
Family-Friendly Dining 136
Family-Friendly Accommodation 138

6 The Tuscan Coast: Livorno to Lazio via Elba 141

Livorno 143
The Etruscan Coast 147
Elba 149
Massa Marittima 154
Castiglione Della Pescaia 157
Parco Regionale Della Maremma 158
Monte Argentario 160
Family-Friendly Dining 162
Family-Friendly Accommodation 163

7 The Val d'Orcia, Valdichiana & Pitigliano 167

Cortona 169
Montepulciano 172
Pienza 175
Montalcino 178
Chiusi 181
Sarteano 182
Pitigliano & the Far South 184
Family-Friendly Dining 187
Family-Friendly Accommodation 190

8 Perugia, Assisi & Northern Umbria 193

Perugia 195
Lago Trasimeno 202
Assisi 205
Spello 209
Gubbio 212
Città Di Castello 214
Family-Friendly Dining 216
Family-Friendly Accommodation 218

9 Orvieto & Southern Umbria 221

Orvieto 223
Todi 228
Montefalco 230
Spoleto 232
The Far South 234
Family-Friendly Dining 237
Family-Friendly Accommodation 239

Index 241

List of Maps

Tuscany & Umbria 11
Central Florence 46
Florence Accommodation & Dining 70
Central Tuscany 81
Siena 84
San Gimignano 92
Volterra 97
Arezzo 104
Northern Tuscany 114
Pisa 117
Lucca 124
The Tuscan Coast 142
Elba 150
Southern Tuscany 168
Montepulciano 172
Northern Umbria 194
Perugia 198
Central & Southern Umbria 222

About the Authors

Donald Strachan is a London- and Italy-based journalist, writer, editor, and dad. He has written about Italian travel for publications worldwide, including *The Times*, *Sunday Telegraph*, and *Sydney Morning Herald*. He has also authored several guidebooks and travel apps on Italian and UK travel, including *Frommer's Florence & Tuscany Day by Day* (2009). To find out more, see www.donaldstrachan.com.

Stephen Keeling grew up in England, lived briefly in Latvia and spent 12 years as a financial journalist in Asia. Despite attempts to kick his gelato addiction, he has been to Italy many times—an incomparable knowledge of Tuscan Chinese restaurants formed while chaperoning a group of Vietnamese officials in 1994. Stephen has written travel guidebooks on Taiwan, Spain, Mexico and Puerto Rico, and currently lives in New York City.

Acknowledgements

Turning 70,000 thoroughly researched words into the best family guidebook to Tuscany and Umbria is a huge team effort. I'd like, once again, to thank my co-author and old friend Stephen for being generally great in every department. One day we might even find ourselves in the same region of Italy at the same time.

Many, many tourism professionals across Tuscany and Umbria provided invaluable advice and the very latest destination information.

I'd like especially to thank Roberta Romoli in Florence and Claudia Bolognesi and her staff in Volterra (yet again!). Adriana Vacca at ENIT in London was as helpful as ever. My editor Mark at Frommer's, along with colleagues Jill, Scott, and Erica, were fun to work with and professional; Rhonda Carrier's skilful text edits, and a timely suggestion of somewhere to stay in northern Tuscany, were hugely appreciated. Sue and Colin Martin were once again mega-generous in providing me with an ideal working base near Lucca, and steering me towards a superb lunch in underrated Pistoia.

Most of all, though, I'd like to thank my family. Without Lucia, Lili, and Ruby this would, quite literally, not have been the same book. Ta girls. (DS)

An Additional Note

Please be advised that travel information is subject to change at any time and this is especially true of prices. We therefore suggest that you write or call ahead for confirmation when making your travel plans. The authors, editors and publisher cannot be held responsible for experiences of readers while travelling. Your safety is important to us however, so we encourage you to stay alert and be aware of your surroundings.

Star Ratings, Icons & Abbreviations

Hotels, restaurants and attraction listings in this guide have been ranked for quality, value, service, amenities and special features using a star-rating system. Hotels, restaurants, attractions, shopping and nightlife are rated on a scale of zero stars (recommended) to three (exceptional). In addition to the star rating system, we also use **5 feature icons** that point you to the great deals, in-the-know advice and unique experiences, and amenities available. Throughout the book, look for:

FIND	Special finds – those places only insiders know about
MOMENT	Special moments – those experiences that memories are made of
VALUE	Great values – where to get the best deals
OVERRATED	Places or experiences not worth your time or money
GREEN	Attractions employing responsible tourism policies

The following **abbreviations** are used for credit cards:

AE	American Express
DC	Diners Club
DISC	Discover
MC	MasterCard
V	Visa

And the amenities:

- Airconditioning
- Baby Changing
- Babysitting
- Bar
- Breastfeeding
- Buggy rental
- Café
- Car Park
- Car Park – Free
- Car Park - Paid
- Children's Club
- Children's Menu
- Cinema
- Cots Available
- Cycle Hire
- DVD
- Fitness Centre
- Fridge
- Full Kitchen
- Games
- Golf
- High Chairs
- Internet Access
- iPod Docking
- Jacuzzi/Hot Tub/Whirlpool
- Laundry Facilities
- Lockers
- Microwave
- Minibar
- Picnic Area
- Play Area
- Pool - Children's
- Pool - Indoor
- Pool - Outdoor
- Restaurant
- Reservations
- Safe
- Shop
- Shower
- Shuttle Bus
- Snack Bar
- Spa Facilities
- Sports
- Tennis Courts
- TV
- Washer/Dryer
- Watersports Rental Equipment
- Wheelchair Access
- Wheelchair Rental

How to Contact Us

In researching this book, we discovered many wonderful places – hotels, restaurants, shops and more. We're sure you'll find others. Please tell us about them, so we can share the information with your fellow travellers in upcoming editions. If you were disappointed with a recommendation, we'd love to know that too. Please email: frommers@wiley.co.uk or write to:

Frommer's *Tuscany, Umbria & Florence With Your Family,* 2nd Edition
John Wiley & Sons, Ltd
The Atrium
Southern Gate
Chichester
West Sussex, PO19 8SQ

PHOTO CREDITS

Cover Credit: © Chris Jackson / Fotolibra

Back Cover: © Carlos Sanchez Pereyra / awl-images

All images © Donald Strachan, with the following exceptions:

Alamy: p. 132 (© Stock Italia); p. 133 (©John Warburton-Lee Photography); p. 193, p. 227 (© CuboImages srl); p. 210 (© Francesco Lacobelli).

Axiom: p. 202 (© Chris Parker).

© Lucia Santi: p. 1, p. 151, p. 174.

PCL: p. 53, p. 113 (© Brian Lawrence Images Ltd); p. 79 (© David Noble); p. 93 (© Edmund Nagele).

Photolibrary Group: p. 141 (© Cephas Picture Library Ltd); p. 185 (©Robert Harding Picture Library Ltd).

Photos to Go (Photolibrary Group): p. 5, p. 8, p. 9, p. 40, p. 50, p. 85, p. 126, p. 173, p. 176, p. 207.

TTL: p. 6 (© Stuart Black); p. 167 (© Rod Edwards).

1 Family Highlights of Tuscany, Umbria & Florence

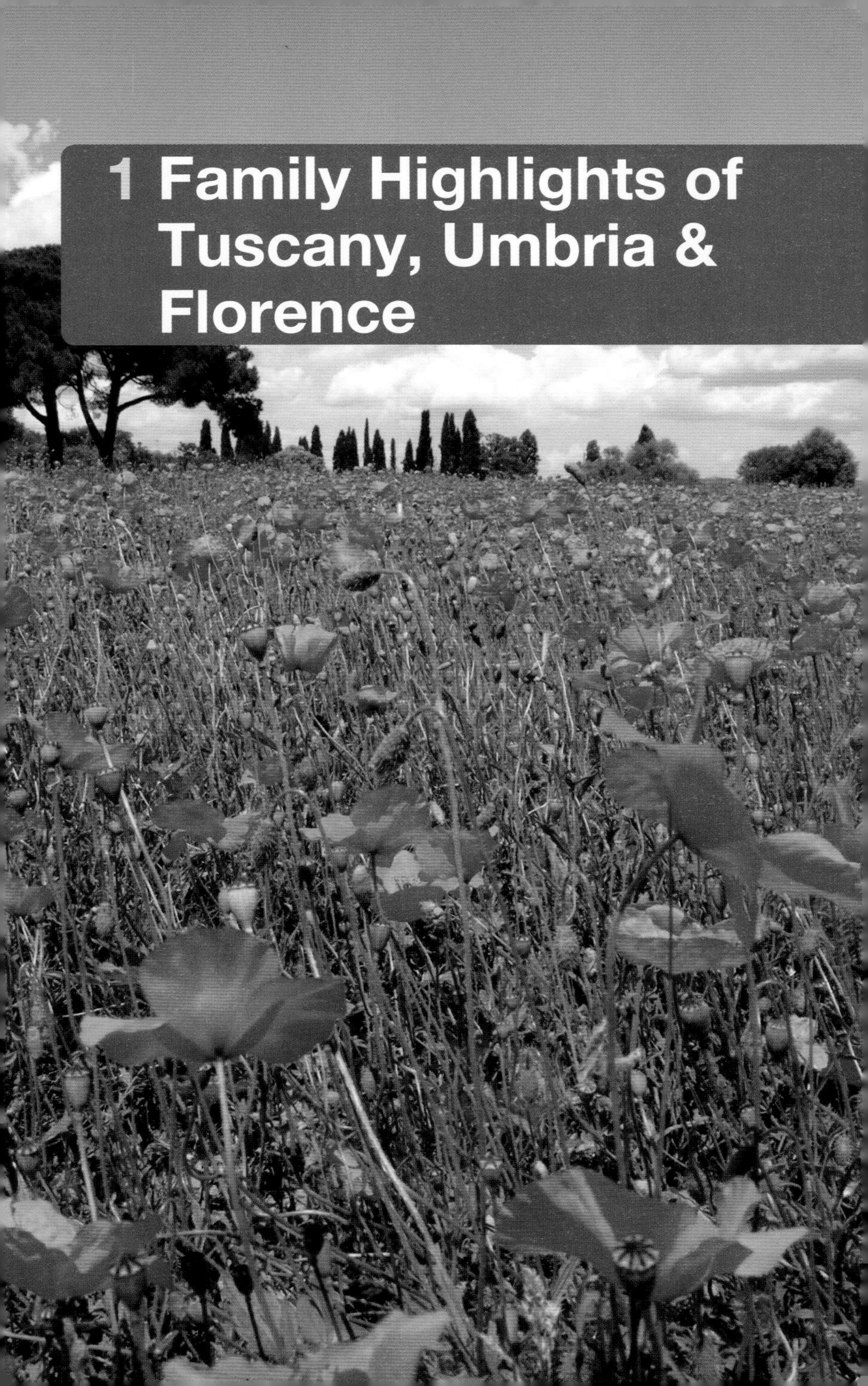

'Never an empty bed in Tuscany' is a phrase you often hear from expatriates living in this dreamy corner of central Italy. Such is the epic scenery, the rustic food and iconic wines, and the everyday beauty, that if you live here you're never short of a weekend guest. This was true when we wrote the first edition of this guidebook—and it will doubtless still be true when we reach our 20th. And it's the same in Umbria: urban, rural or beachfront, hill-town street café or rustic farmhouse, both regions have an unsophisticated, easy charm that welcomes you just as it leaves you in no doubt that this is a place apart. The lone cypress standing in the Val d'Orcia; the morning mists over the Vale of Spoleto; the sublime art and architecture of Renaissance Florence or Gothic Siena—you could *only* be here.

So, how do you begin to get the best out of Tuscany and Umbria, now you're travelling as a family? You've doubtless spotted a few guidebooks to choose from. Some of them are great—we occasionally use them ourselves. But none tell you where in Pisa to feed a toddler who can't wait until 7:30pm for the restaurants to open. Or where to change a baby close to Assisi's Basilica, how to enthuse a teen in the Lunigiana and where to take an indoor soft-play time-out near Florence's Duomo.

That's where we come in. Between us, we've lived, worked or travelled in every corner of both regions, to find places to take children that aren't listed elsewhere. We've come up with tips, tricks and custom-made itineraries to help you experience the classic sights and tastes as a family. To help you enjoy together the very best of the fun, culture and lifestyle of Tuscany and Umbria. I suppose that's partly why our previous edition was named best guidebook of the year by ENIT, the people who promote Italy to the world.

Perhaps you have one more question, and that is: are Tuscany and Umbria really for *my* family? Don't believe (all) the hype: you certainly don't need to be rich to explore and find inspiration here. Hotel prices, especially, have stabilised or even fallen a little since the previous edition. And some of the regions' best family fun costs nothing. In fact, with the right, up-to-date advice, it can be cheap to fly to central Italy, cheap to get about, cheap to eat out and cheap to stay here. When you do want to splash out, we'll suggest where and you can take it from there. Tuscany, in particular, isn't short of luxury hideouts, award-winning spas and unique rural retreats.

Then there's the art. *All that art.* We've chosen the best for you to sample and put it in context. If you don't know much about it yet, you're in the best place on earth to learn. Just remember to reward yourselves with an ice cream afterwards. Enjoy!

THE BEST FAMILY EXPERIENCES

Best Outdoor Activities
With hiking, biking and canoeing trails for all ages and abilities, the **Parco Regionale della Maremma** is the main reason to make southwestern Tuscany your base. See p. 158.

Get ready, get wet, go! Riding the rapids of the **Valnerina** is for everyone aged 4 to 74. Just don't wear your favourite shirt. See p. 236.

Best Underground & Indoor Activities Get a feel for Etruscan life, and death, at the **Tomba della Quadriga Infernale** outside Sarteano. This recent discovery was painted 300 years before Christ and is at the heart of a network of Etruscan burial sites. See p. 183.

They lay under the mud of Pisa's old harbour for 2 millennia, but now 11 Roman ships have been uncovered at the **Cantiere delle Navi Antiche di Pisa.** Watch the digging and restoration in action. See p. 118.

Seeing all 1,200 of Orvieto's caves would take half a lifetime. A 1-hour guided tour with **Orvieto Underground** takes in subterranean homes, water wells, ceramic ovens, pigeon coops, quarries, natural fridges and World War II air-raid shelters. See p. 227.

Best Museums Half-Italian, half-Scot Frederick Stibbert probably didn't intend it but his eccentric collection, now the **Museo Stibbert,** is a Florentine mini-mecca for the knights 'n' castles, Harry Potter generation. See p. 60.

For a spot of science, including Galileo's instruments, Michelangelo's compass and a medieval pharmacy, Florence's **Museo Galileo** will enthuse science-minded children of all ages. See p. 54.

Fetovaia Beach, Elba

Seven for Free

You'll be surprised at how much you can see and do in Tuscany and Umbria for nothing. These are just a few of the best.

- Wander in the footsteps of St. Francis on **Monte Subasio,** p. 208.
- Explore an **Etruscan necropolis** above the Valdichiana, p. 148.
- View fine Renaissance frescoes in **Spoleto,** p. 233, **Assisi,** p. 207, **Florence,** p. 56 and **Gubbio,** p. 212.
- Soak in the 37°C (98.6°F) **thermal springs** at Saturnia, p. 186.
- Experience the monastic calm of **Sant'Antimo,** p. 179 and **Monte Oliveto Maggiore,** p. 177.
- Process the ancient **Via Cava di San Giuseppe,** outside Pitigliano, p. 187.
- Enjoy museums such as Pisa's **Piaggio,** p. 121 and Siena's **Natural History,** p. 60.

Best Beaches There are 150 perfect beaches to choose from on Elba, so start planning now. The perfect crescents and fluorescent waters at **Fetovaia** and **Cavoli** could be the Seychelles; the rock-pools at **Sant'Andrea** offer more for little explorers than sun, sand and pedaloes. See p. 153.

Head for the massive sandy arc of the **Tombolo della Feniglia,** joining the almost-island of Monte Argentario to the mainland. See p. 161.

Best Bike Rides The tree-lined boulevards that crown **Lucca's** mighty walls are a great way to see the city for young families. See p. 123.

The gentle gradients and quiet roads around **Lago Trasimeno** are ideal tracks for an afternoon in the saddle. See p. 202.

Best Natural Wonders There isn't a view to match the 1,019m (3, 343 ft) summit of Elba's **Monte Capanne** cable-car—from Livorno to Lazio, Corsica to Capraia, Tuscany is laid out below on a turquoise carpet of Mediterranean Sea. See p. 152.

The rolling forest- and vine-clad hills of **Chianti** have inspired painters, vintners and gastronomes for centuries. In many ways, this is the spiritual heart of secular Tuscany. See p. 100.

EXPLORING TOGETHER

Best Towns & Villages Italy's spiritual heart, **Assisi,** sits on its perfect perch above Umbria's Vale of Spoleto. See p. 205.

To see **San Gimignano** at its best, stay overnight and wander the medieval heart as night falls. Rise early and catch the Collegiata in peace. See p. 90.

The gradients are insane, but the art, food, *Twilight: New Moon* appearance and wine of

Montepulciano make it an essential stop if venturing south of Siena. See p. 172.

Best Garden Laid out as pleasure grounds for Medici princes, the **Giardino di Boboli** is Florence's finest patch of tended greenery. See p. 62.

Best Castles Climb up to Cortona's **Fortezza Medicea Girifalco** to see four intact bastions and a keep, as well as unmatched views over the Valdichiana and Lago Trasimeno. See p. 171.

Montalcino's **Fortezza** kept the Sienese flag flying for 4 years after the city's defeat by Florence. It's now the only place in Tuscany where you can scramble over medieval walls and taste one of the town's 200+ Brunello wines, all at the same time. See p. 179.

Best Family Events & Festivals There's no *festa* anywhere in Italy quite like Siena's frenetic **Palio.** Held twice each summer, this ancient urban, bareback horse-race will excite visitors of all ages, if you tackle it right. See p. 82.

At **Volterra AD1398** little travellers can dress in medieval costumes and imagine Tuscan life 6 millennia ago. See p. 98.

JUST FOR CHILDREN

Best Animal Encounter Get to know the secret night-time lives of wolves, owls and lynx on a moonlight visit to **Pistoia Zoo**—but book ahead. See p. 130.

Best Attractions for Toddlers There's enchantment, imagination and some intriguing design at Collodi's **Parco di Pinocchio.** Once the maze has been conquered, make for Painting Corner or a live show. See p. 129.

When toddlers are tired of pounding the pavement, stop in at Florence's **La Bottega dei Ragazzi** play space, where you can take the weight off your feet, too. See p. 65.

Best Attractions for Teens For the grisly, gruesome and morbidly

San Gimignano

fascinating, head over Florence's Arno to **La Specola.** If the Room of Skeletons doesn't get the children, the dissected wax head and mock-ups of plague-infested Florence surely will. See p. 63.

There are no models at **Le Mummie di Ferentillo,** in the crypt of Santo Stefano—just a grisly parade of mummified corpses in a ghoulish Umbrian setting. See p. 236.

HISTORIC SITES

Best Churches Western art was born at the glorious **Basilica di San Francesco** in Assisi, the Gothic Upper Church of which houses (probably) Giotto's 28-part fresco, *The Life of St. Francis*. Downstairs is more sublime Giotto, Simone Martini, Pietro Lorenzetti and Cimabue. See p. 207.

Arezzo is the home of Tuscany's most perfect frescoes: Piero della Francesca's **Legend of the True Cross** is a giant of Western art. See p. 105.

Garish or glorious, there's nothing on the planet quite like **Orvieto's Duomo,** and don't miss some gruesome interpretations of the *Last Judgement*. See p. 225.

Essential Paintings Start at Florence's **Uffizi** (p. 52) for Duccio, Cimabue, Giotto and Botticelli's *Primavera*.

Siena's **Museo Civico** (p. 86) is a showcase for Simone Martini's *Maestà* and Ambrogio Lorenzetti's civic *Allegories*.

Umbria's top gallery, the **Galleria Nazionale** in Perugia (p. 199) houses Perugino's moving *Adoration* and Piero della Francesca's *Annunciation*, painted in precise perspective.

And don't forget Volterra's **Pinacoteca** (p. 99) for Rosso Fiorentino's *Deposition*, the first truly 'modern' work of Tuscan art.

Best Art Stops with Children There's no hushed reverence and smaller crowds at Siena's **Santa Maria della Scala,** slowly transforming itself into a series of galleries, passageways and exhibition spaces, with tons of room to get thoroughly lost. Highlights include the spooky

Basilica di San Francesco, Assisi

basement Museo Archeologico, and **Bambimus,** where paintings are hung at child height. See p. 87.

The role of art in everyday religious life is brought home at Florence's **Museo di San Marco**—especially upstairs in the frescoed cells. See p. 59.

Awe-Inspiring Architecture No building in the world is more instantly recognisable than Pisa's 12th-century **Leaning Tower.** Children need to be 8 or older to climb to the top. See p. 119.

For sheer building expertise, Brunelleschi's dome of the Florentine **Cattedrale di Santa Maria del Fiore** is peerless. Admire it for free, climb inside it, or haul yourselves up Giotto's bell-tower for the best view of all. See p. 49.

THE BEST EATING OPTIONS

Best Tuscan Treats *Bistecca numero uno*, bang in the middle of Montepulciano? It must be **Acquacheta,** where you can dig in at a fair price. See p. 187.

Montefollonico's **La Botte Piena** is a slice of rustic Tuscan heaven. They don't rush their food round here, and neither should you; see p. 188.

For Tuscany's freshest seafood, at prices you won't believe, schedule a stop in **Livorno,** for *baccalà* or *cacciucco*. See p. 143.

Best Umbrian Cooking Hanging hams, Montefalco wine and

Perfect Pizza

a dessert that uses only Perugina chocolate—you won't find a more Umbrian eatery than **Al Coccio,** in Magione's suburbs. See p. 216.

For a lazy lunch in the sun, grab a table in the family-friendly garden at **La Mulinella,** on the slopes below Todi. Children love the laid-back, spacious surroundings, and the food and wine are excellent. See p. 229.

Best Bargain Bites Cheap sit-down eats in central Florence?—it could only be **Da Rocco.** Stroll to the Mercato di Sant'Ambrogio for a local lunch, with mains at around 4€. See p. 75.

Like the barbecue you've always dreamed about, the outdoor flamegrill at **La Stalla** just outside Assisi is Umbria's best self-service. Grab a tablecloth and cutlery, find a table and prepare to be dazzled. See p. 217.

Best Ice Cream There's no shortage of choice in Florence, but **Gelateria dei Neri** edges it. See p. 74.

Back-street Siena is where we head for a taste of *pan pepato* in a cone, at **Kopa Kabana.** See p. 107.

You'll find Umbria's best *gelato* in the unlikeliest of spots, by a busy junction in Spoleto, but **Colder** is certainly worth the trip. See p. 234.

THE BEST ACCOMMODATION

Best Urban Bases A rural view 2 minutes from the centre of Spoleto? It can only be the **Hotel Gattapone,** with family suites, panoramic windows and parking on your doorstep. This is a unique treat for older children. See p. 240.

Cool, spacious family apartments within sight of Florence's Duomo don't come better than at the **Residence Hilda.** They're bookable by the night, allowing for maximum flexibility. See p. 77.

Best Country Retreats The six apartments at **Agriturismo Al Gelso Bianco** could hardly be better sited—they're close to Florence, Chianti and the Sienese hill-towns. Ask for 'Ginestra'—its terrace looks right at San Gimignano. See p. 110.

Friendly hosts, fabulous food and gorgeous grounds with plenty of space (and a pool) make **Le Torri di Bagnara** the perfect Umbrian base. These comfy apartments are just a short drive from Perugia. See p. 219.

Best Campsite Come for the views, stay for the services: **Barco Reale's** lofty perch on Monte Albano ensures panoramas from Prato to Livorno—and the site has activities during summer to keep children amused. See p. 139.

The Leaning Tower of Pisa

2 Planning a Trip to Tuscany, Umbria & Florence

The key to a successful family holiday is planning. That doesn't mean you have to decide right now where to have lunch on day 11. But you'll find that you get an enjoyable holiday, at a satisfying price, if you do some initial groundwork from the comfort of your own home (and, more pertinently, your own reliable Internet connection). Once you've arrived, your planning in advance means that everyone can hit the ground running.

One thing to remember about Italy is that **'family-friendly'** means just that. You'll find a welcome for your little ones in all museums, galleries, restaurants and hotels—in fact, just about everywhere you go. And don't fret about whether there's a children's menu or not in restaurants—waiting staff normally fall over themselves to help.

After a couple of well-planned weeks in Tuscany and Umbria, you'll all be so relaxed you won't want to come home ever again.

VISITOR INFORMATION

Before You Go

A bit of web research before the off helps separate the durum wheat from the chaff. In general, you'll find Italy fairly **web-savvy.** Every community, down to the smallest *comune,* has an easily navigable site. Many are in English (and there's always **Google Translate** for the rest).

For trip planning, start with the main *regione* tourist sites: for Tuscany, that's ***www.turismo.intoscana.it***; for Umbria, ***www.regioneumbria.eu***. Especially useful are their events and festivals search engines: plug your trip dates in to see what's on when you're there.

One level down, several *provincia* websites are worth checking. All are listed in the individual chapters that follow; among the best are ***www.terresiena.it*** and ***www.costadeglietruschi.it***. For Florence, ***www.firenzeturismo.it*** is excellent.

Specifically for children in Italy, ***www.bambinopoli.it*** is comprehensive and informative. Siena and the surrounding province are well covered by ***www.terresienabambini.it***. For general family travel advice, US travellers may find ***www.familytravelforum.com***, ***www.deliciousbaby.com***, ***www.travelsavvymom.com***, ***www.familytravelnetwork.com*** and ***www.travelwithyourkids.com*** useful. In the UK, mighty ***www.mumsnet.com*** has a travel section. Also check ***www.babygoes2.com***, ***www.takethefamily.com*** and of course ***www.frommers.com*** before setting off.

In the UK

ENIT (Ente Nazionale Italiano per il Turismo), the Italian Tourist Board, has a London office at 1 Princes Street, W1B 2AY (*020 7408 1254*). The English-language website (***www.enit.it*** or ***www.italiantouristboard.co.uk***) is a reasonable starting point.

TUSCANY & UMBRIA

In the US & Canada

The North America portal for Italy's state tourist board is ***www.italiantourism.com*** (also at ***twitter.com/enitnewyork***). The main **US office** is at 630 5th Avenue, Suite 1565, New York, NY 10111 (*212/245-5618*). **Canada's** main office is at 110 Yonge Street, Suite 503, Toronto, Ontario M5C 1T4 (*416/925-4882*).

At the Destination

See individual chapters for details of tourist offices across Tuscany and Umbria. For **Florence,** see p. 38. For **Siena,** see p. 80.

Entry Requirements & Customs

Passports & Visas

British, Irish and other EU citizens need only produce a valid **passport** or **national identity card** to be admitted to Italy. Either is acceptable. No visa is required. All other visitors must have a passport valid at least 3 months beyond the proposed stay.

Note that babies and children up to 16 not already on a parent or guardian's passport need their own child passport. These last for 5 years (3 years for under-3s in Ireland). If your child is already on your passport they can continue this way until they turn 16, your passport runs out or they need to get their own.

Allow enough time before your trip to apply for a passport; 6 weeks or more in busy periods, such as spring. Ensure that you have completed the form correctly, included the correct documentation and, most importantly, followed the strict regulations concerning photographs. These regularly hold up applications. For more information in the UK, contact the **United Kingdom Passport Service** (*0870 5210410*. ***www.ukpa.gov.uk***). Pick up application forms at your nearest passport office, any major post office or travel agencies. In **Ireland,** pick up an application form at any Garda station and most libraries. The Post Office's **Passport Express** service enables you to have the application forms and

TIP Resources for Lone Parents

One UK organisation worth contacting if you're a lone parent travelling is **Gingerbread** (*0808 802 0925*. ***www.gingerbread.org.uk***). The information on its website includes inspirational ideas for family fun and a fact sheet on holidaying as a lone parent. Membership of the **Single Parent Travel Club** (***www.sptc.org.uk***) costs £20 for life.

Be sure to ask your tour operator about single-parent discounts: camping specialist **Canvas Holidays** (*0845 2680827*. ***www.canvasholidays.co.uk***) has offered these in the past.

photos checked before posting them. Call 1679 7600 or see *www.foreignaffairs.gov.ie* for more information.

US visitors should call 877/487-2778 or consult *travel.state.gov/passport* and expect to wait 4 to 6 weeks for the routine service. The **Canadian Passport Office** is at *www.ppt.gc.ca*.

Taking Pets

EU citizens can bring cats and dogs into Italy as long as they've been issued with a **pet passport,** fitted with a **microchip** and **vaccinated** against rabies. Furry friends are not usually accepted at hotels or self-catering accommodation, so hire a villa if you can't bear to leave Fido at home. In any case, you'll have to ask the property owner for permission. See *http://ec.europa.eu/food/animal/liveanimals/pets/index_en.htm* for EU rules on the movement of animals; *www.defra.gov.uk/wildlife-pets/index.htm* explains the various UK regulations on bringing your pet back home under the **Pet Travel Scheme.**

Customs

Coming into Italy from elsewhere in the EU, you can bring tobacco products and alcohol for your own use without limit. If you're driving into Italy, you're unlikely even to be asked for your passport at the border, never mind to declare what you're carrying.

Coming home to the UK, you can bring any amount of goods for personal use, except new vehicles, mail-order purchases and more than 90 litres of wine, 10 litres of spirits, 110 litres of beer or 3,200 cigarettes. The rules for the UK and Ireland are almost identical. If in doubt, UK citizens should contact **HM Customs and Excise** (0845 0109000. *www.hmrc.gov.uk*). In Ireland, download leaflet **PN1878** from the Revenue website (*www.revenue.ie*) or call 167 44050.

US visitors should read *Know Before You Go* for the latest rules. It's downloadable from *www.cbp.gov*. Canada's rules are posted at *www.cbsa-asfc.gc.ca*.

Visiting with Disabled & Elderly Travellers

UK charity **Tourism For All** (0845 1249971. *www.tourismforall.org.uk*) produces leaflets with accessibility advice for disabled and elderly people travelling abroad. Most are available from their website and cost £3.50, but if you want to keep bang up to date, call their info line before you book. They also have online resources for anyone travelling with a disabled child. UK government website *www.direct.gov.uk/en/DisabledPeople/TravelHolidaysAndBreaks* is also packed with useful advice.

The **Owners Direct** (*www.ownersdirect.co.uk*) website allows you to search for accommodation by wheelchair accessibility, as does **HomeAway** (*www.holiday-rentals.co.uk* or *www.homeaway.com*); **Accessatlast** (01772 814 555. *www.accessatlast.com*),

TIP Keep Copies of Everything

Before you go, photocopy your passport, travellers' cheques, credit cards, itinerary and airline tickets. Carry one copy with you and leave a duplicate and your mobile number with someone back home. Cloud storage services such as **Evernote** (*www.evernote.com*) provide a useful (and free) paperless way to hold scans of important documents.

Record the **emergency phone number** for each of your credit and debit cards. You'll probably find the number on the back of your card in minuscule print. Also see 'Credit Cards', p. 34.

the one-stop shop for accessible accommodation, also recommends a property in Umbria between Perugia and Lago Trasimeno. **Accessible Accommodation** (*www.accessibleaccommodation.com*) lists several properties in Tuscany and Umbria. Italy-based **Accessible Italy** (☎ *0378 941111. www.accessibleitaly.com*) specialises in English-speaking tours of Italy, including Siena, San Gimignano, Chianti and Florence.

The national voluntary association representing disabled people in Italy is **AIAS** (☎ *06 39731704/829. www.aiasnazionale.it*). Its Florence office (☎ *055 3215145*) is at Via Leoncavallo 20. In **Spoleto** (☎ *0743 48415*), in Umbria, you'll find it at Via XXVI Marzo 1.

If you have a query relating to train travel, call the **Trenitalia disabled helpline** on ☎ *199 303060*. Staff can also reserve equipped seats for you. The website *www.bus.it* has a section dedicated to bus transport for the disabled. **Co.In Sociale** (☎ *06 7129011. www.coinsociale.it/turismopertutti.php*) lists contacts for information about guides and tour packages.

If you're heading to Assisi, *www.assisiaccessibile.it* has detailed accessibility information. Throughout the book we've noted when an attraction has disabled access—a number that's growing all the time in an increasingly accessibility-aware country.

MONEY

Currency

Italy uses the **euro** (€). A euro is divided into 100 cents, and there are notes for 5€–500€ and coins for 1 euro cent to 2€. At the time of writing, the euro–sterling exchange rate stood at 1.19€ to £1 and the dollar–euro rate at about $1.28 to 1€. For current rates and a handy converter, see *www.xe.com*. UK travellers exchanging cash to carry to Italy should check *www.travelmoneymax.com* to find the best market rates—they won't normally be from the usual high-street outlets.

Credit & Debit Cards

Major shops, restaurants and hotels accept credit and debit

cards issued anywhere in the world. **Visa** and **MasterCard** are widely accepted but **American Express** and **Diners** are usually only taken at upscale places. In smaller shops and restaurants, and isolated towns, check whether cards are accepted before buying; in many places, they're not. For lost or stolen cards, see p. 14.

If you intend using credit and debit cards while overseas, let card providers know before you go so they won't be suspicious when your cards are used abroad and refuse a withdrawal or cancel your card. Card companies are becoming increasingly zealous about this.

There's a **cashpoint/ATM** (*bancomat*) in pretty much every town; supermarkets have them as well as banks. Italy uses the **4-digit PIN** system, so if you're a North American visitor with a 6-digit code, call your bank before leaving home. You'll be charged a **withdrawal fee** each time you withdraw cash with your credit or debit card. Some debit card providers also impose a **transaction fee** every time you use your card. And on top of all that, most card issuers charge a **loading fee,** up to 2.75%, on every transaction. UK travellers can make significant savings by contacting **Moneysupermarket** (***www.moneysupermarket.com***) and applying for a credit card with a **zero loading** rate. Also, don't discount prepaid currency cards of the kind issued by **FairFX** (***www.fairfx.com***),

TIP Ways to Avoid Breaking the Bank in Italy

- **Opting for an agriturismo or a campsite** rather than a hotel is one easy way to keep tabs on your spending. Just check what kind of kitchen facilities your place has: some are limited to two electric rings and a microwave. When shopping, avoid supermarkets in resorts and tourist areas in favour of bigger stores on the outskirts of town.
- **Eating out** can be expensive, but there's no need to avoid it just because you're budgeting. Instead, visit at lunchtime and take a *menù del lavoro* ('workers' lunch'). Avoid any restaurants on a town's main piazza or tourist drag: you wouldn't expect to find value on Leicester Square or Times Square. And try to **eat DIY** once a day: buy bread, salami and a bottle of water from a supermarket and find a picnic spot.
- **Baby supplies** are pricey. If you're only visiting for a few days, bring your own. Otherwise, small packs on sale in resort supermarkets are expensive, so opt for a bumper-sized bag. And never buy baby supplies in a pharmacy but always from a supermarket.
- **Free entertainment** is out there, especially if you time your holiday right. Ask at the tourist office about local festivals, and join in the celebrations without spending a penny. Also see our 'Seven for Free', p. 4.

Getting the Children Interested

Ideas to help get children fired up for free before you leave home:

- Talk to their school about getting them an **Italian penpal** or encourage older ones to join relevant, safe **Facebook** groups.
- Get some holiday brochures and cut out pictures to make a **collage.** When you're away, try to spot images from the collage.
- Cook **Tuscan food** together using the recipes at ***www.tuscanrecipes.com***. For Italian food in general, try the BBC Food website (***www.bbc.co.uk/food***).
- Involve them in **planning** but set realistic expectations: you won't get round every church or see every important artwork.

MyTravelCash (***www.mytravelcash.com***) and others. These can be a safer and cheaper way to carry travel money overseas. **Take more than one card** with you, in case one gets lost or damaged.

> **INSIDER TIP**
> For UK travellers making a major purchase (over £100), remember that **Section 75 of the Consumer Protection Act** applies even abroad if you pay with a credit card: your card company will refund you if something goes wrong with your purchase.

WHEN TO GO

Italy is a fabulous destination all year—you don't need good weather to enjoy a visit. However, if you want to see the country at its best rather than jostle with crowds, **avoid July and especially August** (*le ferie*, holiday month), particularly on the coast. This peak season (the priciest for Tuscan hotels everywhere but Florence) is also the **hottest.** Florence in 37°C (98.6°F) with a couple of toddlers can be challenging. Furthermore, family-run shops and restaurants in the cities often close for much of August.

Winter opening hours for almost everything are shorter, and seaside resorts are likely to be deserted and/or mostly shut. Florence is surrounded by hills and so can be cold and damp in winter. Elsewhere temperatures can be chilly but are rarely bitter away from the mountains. Spring is long and temperate almost everywhere and often warm at the coast. Most **rain** falls in the autumn. Look up the weather online before you go: for Umbria, check ***www.italy-weather-and-maps.com/weather/UMB,*** for Tuscany ***www.italy-weather-and-maps.com/weather/TOS***.

A far bigger problem than weather is **crowds.** Although the countryside absorbs peak-season hordes quite comfortably, Siena (all summer) and especially Florence (June is busiest, August quieter) do not.

Prepare yourselves for **queuing** everywhere, and use the tips scattered throughout the chapters that follow to minimise the hassle. If you have the flexibility, you'll generally find Tuscany and Umbria at their best between **late March and June,** then **September to late October.** However, if it's a choice between peak season or not at all, see the advice inserted throughout the book to help navigate your way round.

Public Holidays

Offices and shops in Italy are usually closed on: **1st January, 6th January** (Epiphany, *La Befana*), **Easter Sunday** (*Pasqua*), **Easter Monday** (*Pasquetta*), **25th April** (Liberation Day, *La Liberazione*), **1st May** (Labour Day, *Festa del Lavoro*) **15th August** (Assumption, *Ferragosto*), **1st November** (All Saints' Day, *Tutti i Santi*), **8th December** (Immaculate Conception, *L'Immacolata*), **25th December** (Christmas Day, *Natale*) and **26th December** (*Santo Stefano*).

Italians are hooked on their long holiday, the *quindici giorni*, a couple of weeks around *Ferragosto* in August. Most family businesses and often entire town centres close away from tourist areas.

Family-Friendly Events

One thing central Italy isn't short of is **festivals;** even small towns have them on a regular basis. They can be great fun for families—and they're mostly free. Remember that **parking** will become difficult and hotels **expensive** and/or full around *festa* time. If you have very young children, or yours are frightened by crowds, stay away from the big festivals.

Some of the best are listed below (see relevant chapters for full details), but small village *festas* are fun too. Ask at any **local tourist office** or check the calendar on its website.

February
Carnevale Aretino Orciolaia, Arezzo, p. 103.
Carnevale, Viareggio, p. 131.

TIP Baby Stuff

The following familiar baby brands are available in Tuscan and Umbrian supermarkets: **Huggies** and **Pampers** nappies/diapers; **Johnson's** wipes and washing products; **Aptamil** and (in specialist baby shops) **Hipp Organic** powdered and liquid milk. Reliable local baby-food brands include Plasmon, Mellin and Milupa. English-speaking visitors will probably find the market for eco-friendly nappies and baby products is less developed than at home; a specialist baby retailer such as **Io Bimbo** (***www.iobimbo.it***) or a local independent is your best bet.

Devout Tuscany

What with the mesmerising scenery and rural idyll of a Tuscan holiday, there's a side that's easily missed. Every town and village, and even clubs and societies, have their own patron saint, and if you happen to be in town at the right time, you may chance upon Tuscans at prayer.

Cities such as Florence have several dates: the place goes nuts for St. John on 24th June, but lesser-known locals St. Zenobius (25th May) and St. Antoninus (10th May) are also marked. Pisa pulls out all the stops for St Ranieri (p. 117) on 17th June, whereas St. Catherine of Siena (29th April; p. 89) is one of Italy's most revered.

San Gimignano shuts down for its namesake's feast on 31st January, and again on 12th March for St. Fina (p. 93). Other fairytale hilltowns celebrate their patrons in spring and summer: Agnes in Montepulciano on 20th April, Volterra's St. Justus on 5th June and Arezzo's St. Donatus on 7th August.

March
Torciata di San Giuseppe, Pitigliano, p. 185.

April
Coloriamo I Cieli, Castiglione-del-Lago, p. 203.

May
Festa del Grillo, Florence, p. 48.
Festa dei Ceri, Gubbio, p. 213.

June
Calcio Storico, Florence, p. 48.
Giostra del Saracino, Arezzo, p. 103.
Festa di San Ranieri, Pisa, p. 117.
Gioco del Ponte, Pisa, p. 117.
Spoleto Festival, p. 232.
Infiorate di Spello, p. 210.

July
Palio, Siena, p. 82.

August
Palio, Siena, p. 82.
Volterra AD1398, p. 98.
Bravio delle Botti, Montepulciano, p. 173.

September
Festa della Rificolona, Florence, p. 48.
Giostra del Saracino, Arezzo, p. 103.
Luminaria di Santa Croce, Lucca, p. 127.

October
Sagra del Torde, Montalcino, p. 178.
Eurochocolate, Perugia, p. 197.

WHAT TO PACK

Both Tuscany and Umbria have distinct seasons, so pack appropriate clothes. You're unlikely to need more than shorts and short-sleeved tops in summer, as long as you aren't planning to eat anywhere posh or spending time in the Apennines, which can be wet and chilly almost anytime. You're expected to **dress respectfully,** with shoulders and legs covered, in all churches and cathedrals.

Packing Your Car

If you're all travelling by car, keep the following handy:

1. A cool box with drinks, snacks and fruit
2. Window-shades for the sun
3. Your child's favourite music or talking books
4. A first-aid kit
5. A box of wet wipes
6. Blankets
7. Plastic bags for motion sickness
8. A change of clothes for everyone
9. A fully charged mobile phone for emergencies (see p. 33)
10. A list of car games from the RAC website (*www.rac.co.uk/news-advice/car-knowledge/top-ten/post/2009/10/car-games/*)

Children's Kit

Beach tents When the sun shines, it really does shine, so take care not to let your little ones get **burnt.** Although a traditional parasol can be bought cheaply from a resort souvenir shop, a beach tent is more adaptable.

Swimsuits Protective swimsuits are a good idea for children who won't stay still. Zip them up in a

Calcio! The Football Season

Alongside Catholicism, Italy's other religion is football (or soccer). A trip to an Italian game is a fantastic experience. It's surprisingly easy to get tickets, too. The season runs from late August to mid-May, with one game played on Saturday evening (the *anticipo*), most on Sunday afternoons, and one on Sunday evening (the *posticipio*). The Italian league is split into four divisions: Serie A, B, C1 and C2. Florence's team rarely moves from Serie A; recent seasons have seen fellow Tuscans Siena, Empoli and Livorno yo-yoing between A and B.

Italian ticket agencies worth trying are **TicketOne** (*www.ticketone.it*) and **Booking Show** (☎ *899 030822. www.bookingshow.com*). From the UK, try **Football Encounters** (☎ *0870 7605556. www.tickazilla.com*) for Fiorentina tickets, although they're quite expensive. Or book them yourself: each club has its own selling arrangements and generally it's cheaper than buying tickets for an English Premier League or major SPL game. For Fiorentina, see p. 65; for Livorno, p. 146. You can turn up on the day and pay just about anywhere. If you're taking children, ask for a *tribuna tranquilla* (a quiet stand): you don't want to end up sitting with the *ultras*.

suit with **UV protection** and they can carry on their sandcastle building.

Lightweight pushchairs Fancy fashionable pushchairs soon become a burden in town: bring a **lightweight buggy** with a narrow wheelbase.

Portable highchairs You can't rely on restaurants providing a highchair, so bring one with you. Lightweight options include Grobag's compact 'Handbag Highchair' (a loop of fabric that secures a baby to a chair), the foldable Minui Handysitt toddler seat, and The First Years' inflatable booster. All are generally available from the usual online, catalogue or high-street retailers.

HEALTH, INSURANCE & SAFETY

Medical Insurance

Travellers to Italy who are resident within the EU need to carry their **European Health Insurance Card** (EHIC) as proof of entitlement to free/reduced-cost medical treatment abroad. The easiest way to apply for a card from the UK is online (***www.ehic.org.uk***); alternatively, call *0845 6062030* or get a form from a post office. EHIC forms only cover *necessary* medical treatment so are not replacements for travel insurance policies (see below).

US visitors should consider more comprehensive travel medical cover. Try **MEDEX** (*410/453-6300*. ***www.medexassist.com***) or **Travel Assistance International** (*800/821-2828*. ***www.travelassistance.com***).

Travel Insurance

UK Visitors

When choosing travel insurance, read the small print of your home or credit card insurance carefully to check whether it covers you for lost cards, luggage, cancelled tickets or medical expenses. If not, opt for an **annual multi-trip policy** if you travel abroad at least twice a year. **Moneysupermarket** (***www.moneysupermarket.com***) compares prices and coverage across a bewildering range of single- and multi-trip options.

US Visitors

Get estimates from **travel insurance comparison site** ***www.insuremytrip.com***, or call them on *800/487-4722*.

Staying Healthy

Take copies of **prescriptions** in case a family member loses his/her medicine or it runs out. Note the **generic name** too, in case local pharmacists are unfamiliar with the brand. Take an extra pair of any contact lenses or prescription glasses.

If your child has an illness that needs swift and accurate treatment (such as epilepsy, diabetes, asthma or a food or sting allergy), **MedicAlert** (*www.medicalert.org.uk*) provides bracelets or necklaces engraved with an ID number and details of the medical condition. The number of a 24-hour emergency line is also engraved on the disc; this accepts reverse charge calls to access specific medical details from anywhere in the world and in more than 100 languages.

In any medical emergency, call ☎ *118*.

Safety

Italy is a safe destination for children, especially away from the crowds. Walking through any town, you'll spot front doors left ajar while owners have popped out to chat to a neighbour. But **common sense** is still required. Make sure to lock cars and apartments. Don't leave valuables in sight in your car: store them in a safe at your hotel or apartment reception. In resorts, don't leave belongings in view by a pool or on the beach. And make sure you have adequate travel insurance (p. 20.) in case of theft.

Pickpockets and bag-snatching are a problem around popular tourist attractions in big cities, particularly Florence and Pisa. Beware groups of youngsters crowding around you. Mobiles and iPods are obvious targets.

In terms of road safety, **zebra crossings** don't mean what you think: wait until you know that drivers have seen you and slowed down before stepping into the road. Likewise, even in pedestrian zones (*zone pedonali*) watch for vehicles at all times.

On the **beach,** however shallow the water, don't let small children swim alone.

RESPONSIBLE TRAVEL

The concept of taking a 'green' or 'environmentally friendly' holiday isn't without controversy. However, there are things you can do to minimise the impact (and especially the carbon footprint) of your travels. These include switching off **air conditioning** wherever you go, including in your car, removing **chargers** from mobile phones, PSPs, laptops and anything else that draws from the mains once the gadget is fully charged, and switching idle appliances off, not to standby. Eat locally (it's better anyway) and shop in markets for **seasonal produce** rather than supermarket fruit and veg from the far side of the globe.

Most importantly, use **public transport** wherever possible. Many of Tuscany and Umbria's most attractive towns have good rail and/or long-distance bus links (detailed in the chapters that follow; see also p. 14); you can even reach the region by rail or bus from across Europe: see p. 14. For rural touring, rent bikes and go cycle-sightseeing, or enjoy the Tuscan hills from horseback. **Carbon offsetting** (again, not uncontroversial) can be arranged

TIP Happy Flying with Your Children

- Introduce first-time flyers to likely **scenarios** (check-in, security, the safety talk, a bumpy ride, noises) by playing 'let's go to the airport'.
- Read your toddler the 'Going on a Plane' chapter from *The Little Book of First Experiences* (Usborne, £5.99) before you go. (*Going on a Plane: Usborne First Experiences*, $4.99, in the US).
- Check the airline provides bolsters or **seats for under-2s.**
- Listen to the safety announcements. Read the safety card and clock the nearest exits, lifejackets and oxygen masks.
- Pack water, snacks and a few **toys** in your hand luggage.
- Make sure your child's seatbelt remains fastened: turbulence can occur at any time.
- Sit your child by the window or between two parents: it's harder for them to wander off.
- Read the handy tips at ***www.flyingwithkids.com*** and ***www.keepkidshealthy.com/parenting_tips/flying_with_kids.html*** before you go.

through global schemes such as **ClimateCare** (***www.climatecare.org***). **Responsible Travel** (***www.responsibletravel.com***), just one of a growing number of environmentally aware travel agents, offers a number of 'green holidays' in Tuscany and Umbria. Online green travel sections such as ***www.guardian.co.uk/travel/green*** and ***www.telegraph.co.uk/travel/hubs/greentravel*** are good places to keep up with the issues and get inspiration.

ESSENTIALS

Getting There

By Air For **Florence,** see Chapter 3; for **Pisa,** Chapter 5; for **Perugia,** Chapter 8.

By Car If you're packing the people-carrier to drive to Tuscany from the UK, two overnight stops en route make the journey comfortable. Florence is about 1,300km (800 miles) from Calais, Perugia about 1,550km (960 miles). The **ViaMichelin** website (***www.viamichelin.com***) is a great free European route planner that will also calculate your costs in petrol, tolls and so on. **Ibis** motels (***www.ibishotel.com***), Etap Hotels (***www.etaphotel.com***) or the **B&B** chain (***www.hotelbb.com***) are hard to beat for overnight family stops, in France especially. They're usually cheaper at weekends.

Most UK **car insurance** policies include 30–90 days abroad without the need to apply for a Green Card, but check with your insurer. And don't leave home without breakdown cover from the AA, RAC or a similar motoring organisation. Towing a car from Chianti to Cardiff can be *very* expensive. Make sure you pack your vehicle registration document **(Form V5)**, insurance policy and **driving licence** (both parts)—roadside *documenti* checks are common.

Budget for the **road tolls** in France; you'll save money if you go around them through Belgium and Germany, although the quality of roadside picnic areas is markedly poorer in the latter. In **Switzerland,** you need to make a one-off payment of SFr.40 (about 27.50€) at the border for a *vignetta* to use the motorway network; you'll be fined if caught without one.

If you enter Italy through the **Grand St. Bernard tunnel** (*www.letunnel.com*) south of Sion, your return ticket (33.10€) is valid for a month. Return tickets through the **Mont Blanc tunnel** (*www.tunnelmb.com*) from France are only valid for a week, so you'll need two singles (35.10€ each). The **Fréjus Tunnel** (*www.sftrf.fr*) linking Chambéry and Turin is the same: you'll need two singles at 35.10€. A final (free) scenic motorway route passes through the **St. Gotthard Tunnel** in Switzerland and crosses into Italy via Lugano and Como. There are mountain passes (Simplon, Petit St. Bernard, Grand St. Bernard), but these are both slower and closed from late autumn to spring due to snow.

Note that petrol is cheaper in **Luxembourg,** so with creative route-finding you can avoid tolls and refuel for less. Diesel is significantly cheaper in much of Europe (including Italy) than in the UK. At many garages in Italy, you'll get a discount if you fill up yourself (*fai da te*).

By Train If you're flexible on dates and times, you may be able to get from London to Florence, via Eurostar (2½ hr; *www.eurostar.com*) and a sleeper (12 hr) from Paris, for just over £200pp. This is with the lowest overnight class (6-berth sleeper) and a lot of luck on availability. **Artesia** (*www.artesia.eu*) operates the daily sleeper service from Paris Bercy to Florence Campo di Marte.

Rail agents in the UK worth contacting include **RailChoice** (☎ *0870 1657300. www.railchoice.co.uk*) and **Rail Europe** (☎ *08448 484064. www.raileurope.co.uk*). In the US, contact **Rail Europe** (☎ *800/622-8600. www.raileurope.com*), where you can also discuss rail pass options for your trip. **The Man in Seat Sixty-One** (*www.seat61.com*) is an absolutely invaluable bookmark for researching anything related to European rail travel, from timetables to eating options aboard specific trains.

By Bus If you're brave enough to attempt to reach Tuscany by coach from the UK, there's one weekly **Eurolines** (☎ *08705 808080. www.eurolines.co.uk*) departure to Florence from London's Victoria coach station. The journey takes 28 hours, with a 2-hour stopover in Paris and 30 minutes in Milan. Prices start at 79€. Eurolines also links several other European cities with Florence.

By Package Tour Find a rundown of **tour operators** with packages suited to families at www.donaldstratchan.com/familytuscany.

Getting Around

By Car Italians drive on the **right.** You'll need to develop a little patience with their on-road etiquette. *Autostrade* are motorways, denoted by green signs and a number prefaced with an A, including the Milan–Naples **A1** that bisects Tuscany. *Strade statali* are state roads and usually have two lanes. Their route numbers are prefaced with an **SS** or an **S.** Don't get hung up on the numbers, though: unlike *autostrade*, SS roads don't always have them on display; you'll just see blue signs listing destinations by name. If you happen to be on an **SP** (*strada provinciale*) road and cross a provincial border, the number changes anyway.

Unleaded petrol is *benzina senza piombo*; **diesel** is *gasolio*. Most filling stations are closed on Sunday, but some have a pump fitted with a machine that takes notes or cards. You pay by the km to use motorways, but prices are nowhere near those in France. **Autostrade per l'Italia's** website (***www.autostrade.it***) has a toll calculator, as well as providing weather forecasts and traffic updates. Milan to Florence, for example, is 18.10€, Verona to Siena 15.50€. Despite a plague of roadworks (*cantiere*), you'll usually make good time on the motorway—even the Florence ring-road (*tangenziale*) has improved recently, as carriageway widening works make progress. Journeys on minor roads can take an age, however.

INSIDER TIP

SOME DRIVING TIMES	
Florence to Siena	1 hour
Florence to Perugia	2¼ hours
Pisa to Florence	1 hour
Pisa to Grosseto	1¼ hours
Perugia to Orvieto	1½ hours
Perugia to Terni	1¼ hour

Driving Rules

Don't drink and drive: the legal blood alcohol limit in Italy is 0.5 mg. Besides the danger, **imprisonment** is a regular punishment. Seatbelts are compulsory. Under new EU law, children under 4 must have a suitable car seat or booster, while those between 4 and 12 can't travel in the front or back unless restrained (exactly how depends on the size of your child; see ***www.childcarseats.org.uk***).

Most road signs are similar enough to those in the rest of the world so work them out as you go. *Senso unico* means you're in a one-way street. A *zona pedonale* is a pedestrian zone. The **town centre** is indicated by a black-on-white circle with a dot in the middle (like a monochrome target).

Speed limits are as follows: motorway 130km/h; dual carriageway 110km/h; trunk road 90km/h (sometimes 70km/h); town 50km/h. In fog, the limit is 50km/h whatever the road.

There's clearly no crime in central Italy because everyone in a police uniform is standing on the side of a country road with a **speed gun:** you have been warned.

It's compulsory to carry a **warning triangle,** a **visibility vest for each passenger** and **spare headlight bulbs.** If you break down, you must put on the vest before getting out of the car and erect the triangle just up the road from where you stop. Check all this kit is in a rental car before you drive off. The use of mobile phones in cars is prohibited unless they're fitted with speaker devices or used with headphones.

If **fined** for a minor contravention, you pay on the spot (ask for a receipt).

Car Rental

If you're hiring a car, remember all parts of your driving licence—paper and card. You must have had a full licence for 2 years. Non-EU residents don't need an **International Driver's Licence** for car rental. When booking and picking up a hire car, you also need your **passport** and a **credit card** in the name of the main driver (a debit card *won't* do). Insurance on all vehicles is compulsory, but check the excess and what's not covered. You're sometimes better **booking everything in advance** from home, then you can offer a polite '*No, grazie*' to all the other stuff they'll inevitably try to flog you.

From the UK, **Holiday Autos** (*www.holidayautos.co.uk*) is reliable and competitive; the independent broker **AutoReservation** (📞 *0844 8266535. www.autoreservation.com*) offers sizeable discounts on rentals from the big players. From the US, try **Auto Europe** (📞 *888/223-5555. www.autoeurope.com*) or **Europe by Car** (📞 *800/223-1516. www.europebycar.com*). Metasearch sites such as **Kayak** (*www.kayak.com*) sometimes find very cheap prices by searching multiple websites from across the industry. **Insurance4carhire.com** (📞 *01883 724001*) is an annual policy to reimburse nasty excesses, starting at £49.

Parking

Find a *parcheggio* (car park) or park on the street; **white lines** indicate free public spaces, **blue lines** mean you have to pay (they're usually reinforced with a *sosta a pagamento* sign)—find a meter, punch in how long you want to park, pay and stick the ticket somewhere visible in your car. If you park in an area marked *parcheggio con disco orario*, look for the cardboard parking disc in your hire-car's glove compartment or buy one at a petrol station. Dial up the time of your arrival and display it on the dashboard. How long you're allowed will be marked clearly on the sign. **Never park in yellow spaces:** they're for residents or businesses.

By Train Italy's national train network is comfortable, regular and reliable, if often late. It's also **good value,** fast and easy to navigate. If you're intending to use the train, visit the **Trenitalia** website (***www.trenitalia.it***) before you leave home to check routes, timetables and fares.

There's little difference between first and second class, so don't waste your money. Outside rush hours, you're sure to get a seat, but on faster routes between cities you need to **book** to be sure of sitting together. If all you're doing is dotting about a region, you'll generally use **R** (*Regionale*) trains, which stop at all main stations. For longer journeys, aim for an **ES** (*Eurostar*) or **IC** (*Intercity*) train as these are faster (albeit more expensive).

When buying a ticket, *andata* means one-way, *andata e ritorno* return. Two singles cost the same as a return, so if you're not sure of your plans, buy a **single.** Not every train is the same price: for an ES or IC, ask for your ticket *con supplemento rapido* (with a fast supplement) to avoid on-board penalty charges; you'll also be allocated a seat. Most importantly, **stamp your ticket in the yellow box** on the platform (*convalidare*) before boarding; it's not unknown for tourists to get fined for unstamped tickets.

Again, **The Man in Seat Sixty-One** (***www.seat61.com***) dispenses invaluable advice.

By Bus Regional buses are called *pullman*, although *autobus*, the term for a city bus, is sometimes used. It's not easy getting hold of a timetable for local buses; it's often best to **download** them from the company websites (see below). News-stands or tobacconists (*tabacchi*) and local bars usually sell bus tickets; it's **more expensive** to buy them on the bus. Remember to stamp them using the yellow machine on board or you risk a fine.

The following bus companies contact details may be useful:

APM, Perugia. ☎ *075 506781.* ***www.apmperugia.it.***

ATL, Elba/Livorno. ☎ *0565 914392.* ***www.atl.livorno.it.***

ATAF, Florence. ☎ *800 424500.* ***www.ataf.net.***

CPT, Pisa. ☎ *050 505511.* ***www.cpt.pisa.it.***

LFI, Arezzo. ☎ *0575 39881.* ***www.lfi.it.***

RAMA, Grosseto. ☎ *0564 475111.* ***www.griforama.it.***

SITA, Florence. ☎ *055 214721.* ***www.sitabus.it.***

TRA.IN, Siena. ☎ *0577 204111.* ***www.trainspa.it.***

By Ferry For Livorno to **Capraia,** see p. 145. For Piombino to **Elba,** p. 151. For information on the ferry to **Isola Giglio,** see p. 161. If you're heading to Sardinia or Corsica by ferry, your first port of call should be the **Toremar** website, ***www.toremar.it.***

By Taxi The only city where you're likely to need a taxi while you're here is **Florence:** call ☎ *055 4242* or head to any of the city ranks (p. 43).

On Foot There's plenty of good **walking** all over Tuscany and Umbria, but not all of it is child-friendly; by the seventh Chianti winery, most toddlers are reaching their limit. You'll find gentle, family-friendly routes recommended in the main chapters.

By Bike Though renting a bike in central Florence amounts to madness, in some cities and towns two wheels are the best way to get you and the family round the sights. For **Lucca,** see p. 125; for Lago Trasimeno, p. 203; for cycling the Florence periphery, p. 66.

ACCOMMODATION

Hotels & B&Bs

If you plan to book a hotel yourself, spend a bit of time on **research** to make sure the area you choose has the right amenities and that the accommodation suits you and the children. Check its website and study the photos with your sceptical head on. If your Italian is up to it, call them yourself: you might get a deal. All the hotels listed by this guide are family-friendly—as is most of Italy.

Agency websites such as **Expedia** (***www.expedia.co.uk*** or ***www.expedia.com***), **Travelocity** (***www.travelocity.co.uk*** or ***www.travelocity.com***), **eBookers** (***www.ebookers.com***) and **Hotels.com**

TIP A Cheap Hotels Checklist

- Ask about **special rates** and other **discounts**: dial the hotel directly to ask the price of a room and push for a *sconto* (discount). Ask if children stay free in the room (and clarify at what age adult rates apply). If not, is there a family rate? Or a long-stay discount?
- Seek deals: see what price the hotel is offering and check if any **Internet sites** have it cheaper. Many hotels offer Internet-only discounts, or supply rooms to online agents such as ***www.lastminute.com*** or ***www.expedia.com*** at lower, 'wholesale' rates. Google can be your friend here.
- Avoid excess charges and **hidden costs:** when you book a room, ask whether the hotel charges for parking. When there, use your mobile or prepaid phone cards instead of dialling direct from rooms, and forget the minibar. Check the price of breakfast; if it's extortionate, scout out the nearest café. Finally, ask about additional charges (balcony, view, cot, air conditioning and so on)—it all adds up.
- Book an **apartment:** a kitchen allows you to shop and cook your own meals. This is a big money-saver, especially for long stays.
- **Avoid staying in Florence in high season:** make day trips in to see the sights.

(*www.hotels.com*) provide a fast, efficient booking service, with regular deals and offers. **Venere** (*www.venere.com*) is also good on Tuscany and Umbria.

The metasearch service at sites such as **TravelSupermarket** (*www.travelsupermarket.com*) and **Kayak** (*www.kayak.com*) allow real-time comparisons of room prices for hundreds of online resellers. Just plug in your dates and what level of luxury you're looking for and they fire back the best online rates. Deal sites such as **Travelzoo** (*www.travelzoo.com*), **Priceline** (*www.priceline.com*) and **Lastminute** (*www.lastminute.com*) are also worth bookmarking.

Although there are thousands of places to stay, major tourist spots get **very full** in July and (especially) **August** (except in Florence, which is relatively quiet in high summer), plus in the weeks around **Easter.** If you're going to splash out on a top-of-the-range place, take 2 minutes to check it hasn't been slated at **TripAdvisor** (*www.tripadvisor.com*). Always take a copy of your **reservation confirmation** with you: mistakes happen.

If your budget stretches to a bit of luxury, **The Hotel Guru** (*www.thehotelguru.com*) has recommendations for Florence, the Tuscan countryside, Tuscan towns and Umbria. Boutique website **Mr and Mrs Smith** (*www.mrandmrssmith.com*) also has a number of Tuscan offerings in the pricey bracket. Similarly style-conscious **i-escape** (*www.i-escape.com*) and **Travel Intelligence** (*www.travelintelligence.com*) have properties in Florence and rural Tuscany searchable by child-friendliness.

We've focused throughout the book on unique places to stay, but popular **chains** are a great alternative, especially for those on tight budgets or for short stops en route and in cities. Family-friendly **Ibis** (*www.ibishotel.com*), for instance, has two well-priced motels near Florence. One notch up, **Best Western** (*www.bestwestern.com*) runs hotels all over Italy. At **Novotel** (*www.novotel.com*), which has a hotel outside Florence, children stay free in parents' rooms and get a free breakfast, and there's all the baby kit you'll ever need.

There's a rundown of family **tour operators** serving the region at www.donaldstratchan.com/familytuscany.

INSIDER TIP

If you're staying in southern Tuscany, it's worth knowing that Article 151 of the law governing *alberghi* in the Province of Grosseto forbids you from putting anything in your **minibar** that wasn't there when you arrived. Honestly.

You might come across some new **vocabulary** on your hotel hunt. An *albergo* is the old name for hotel, sometimes translated as 'inn'. *Locanda* once meant an inn or carriage stop; it's now often used to refer to a place with charm or (delusions of) grandeur. A *pensione* is a guesthouse: these are often the cheapest and most cheerful, and are usually perfect for youngsters.

Hostels

Tuscany and Umbria have a number of cracking youth hotels (*ostelli*) with family rooms. These vary in size but all are economical and a great way to make friends (our favourite is in Lucca; p. 139). There's a list and booking service at the **Associazione Italiana Alberghi per la Gioventù** website, ***www.aighostels.com***. To obtain a Youth Hostel Association card, UK residents should visit ***www.yha.org.uk*** or call ✆ *0800 0191700* in the UK. In the US, join online at ***www.hiusa.com***. **Hostelworld** (***www.hostelworld.com***) and **Hostelbookers** (***www.hostelbookers.com***) are reliable hostel-booking services; both post user reviews and ratings on their websites.

Farm-Stay & Agritourism (*agriturismi*)

For a taste of rural Tuscany or Umbria, staying and eating in an *agriturismo* (converted farmhouse) can be a fantastic family experience. The official **Agriturism in Tuscany** website (***www.turismo.intoscana.it/agriturismo***) allows you to search for accommodation by province or town. Look out, too, for the *Agriturismo e vacanze in campagna* guide published annually by the Touring Club Italiano (20€); you'll find it in most good Italian bookshops. Check the **Agriturist** (***www.agriturist.it***) website for news, offers and itineraries in Italian. Also worth a look before you book are **Turismo Verde Toscana** (✆ *055 20022*. ***www.turismoverde.it***), and **Terranostra** (✆ *055 3245011*. ***www.terranostra.it***) and ***www.agriturismo.it***. General accommodation portal ***www.tuscanyholidayaccommodation.com*** also lists *agriturismi*.

Self-Catering

If you're in a large group, or fancy renting a villa, apartment or house independently, join the pan-European **Homelidays** (***www.homelidays.com***) network, whose versatile website allows you to search for properties by location, price range, facilities such as pools and air-con, accommodation type and size, and disabled access. You can even specify up to 50 required local amenities, such as golf, amusement parks or wine tours. It's free to join, and it currently lists more than 3,000 properties in Tuscany and Umbria.

Owners Direct (***www.ownersdirect.co.uk***), **HomeAway** (***www.homeaway.com*** or ***www.holiday-rentals.co.uk***) and **Holiday Lettings** (***www.holidaylettings.co.uk***) have similarly impressive ranges of holiday homes and villas. The **Slow Travel Network** (***www.slowtrav.com***) has exhaustive and informed reviews of properties and places in Tuscany. **HomeLink International** (***www.homelink.org***) is the established leader in the global house swap business.

The Best Holiday Reading

For You

The sheer number of Tuscany **travelogues** is overwhelming. Any bookshop worth its onions will have a half-dozen. Isabella Dusi's ***Vanilla Beans and Brodo*** (Simon & Schuster), set in Montalcino, stands out from a mawkish crowd. Iris Origo's gripping memoir, ***War in the Val d'Orcia: 1943–44*** (Allen & Busby), paints a grittier picture. You'll pick up plenty about Tuscany by packing Tim Parks' ***A Season with Verona*** (Vintage), even though it hardly mentions the place and is (or appears to be) mainly about football. Older teens used to adult themes will love it. Along the same lines, Luigi Barzini's ***The Italians*** (Penguin) remains a 40-year-old classic.

The *Silver Spoon* (Phaidon), more encyclopaedia than cookbook, has enough Tuscan recipes to keep you busy. James Lasdun's ***Walking and Eating in Tuscany and Umbria*** (Penguin) combines the two things Tuscans do best. Some of the walks are a bit long for young 'uns but you can easily shorten them. It's better on Tuscany than Umbria. There are also Sunflower walking guides to **Tuscany** and **Umbria and the Marches** (Sunflower Books) for more active families.

For wine lovers, Hugh Johnson's ***Tuscany and Its Wine*** (Mitchell Beazley) is worth the money, as is his ***World Atlas of Wine*** (Mitchell Beazley). Both are useful companions to Tuscan wine-tourism.

David D. Busch's ***Digital Travel Photography: Digital Field Guide*** (Wiley) is essential kit for keen snappers. Art-fiends should start with ***Renaissance Art: A Very Short Introduction*** (Oxford) before graduating to Giorgio Vasari's classic ***Lives of the Artists*** (Oxford), originally published in 1550. Mary McCarthy's

Plenty of **tour operators** have villas in their portfolio. See www.donaldstratchan.com/familytuscany.

Campsites & Holiday Parks

Happy campers will find lots of places to pitch up in Tuscany and Umbria; a number of sites also rent out camping gear for those who can't bring their own. Start with the **Federazione Italiana Campeggiatori** (☎ *055 882391. www.federcampeggio.it*). Other useful websites for comparing facilities are ***www.easycamping.it***, ***www.camping.it*** and ***www.campeggi.com***. If you're a serious camping family, or planning a longer tour of Tuscany and Umbria, buy a copy of the most recent annual **Alan Rogers' *The Best Campsites: Italy***. The

Stones of Florence (Mariner) is the best modern book written about the city's art, architecture and artists.

If it's fiction you're after, the tensions and pretensions of EM Forster's two Tuscan tales, ***A Room with a View*** and ***Where Angels Fear to Tread,*** are set in Florence and San Gimignano, respectively. Boccaccio's **The Decameron** (Oxford) is the Florentine classic, but pack your toothbrush—it's a long old journey. Ditto Dante's seminal **Divine Comedy**, in three volumes. Michele Guittari's hard-edged police thrillers, ***A Florentine Death*** and ***A Death in Tuscany*** (neither remotely suitable for children), take a more sinister look at central Italy.

For Children

Children of all ages should read (or be read) the classic Tuscan story ***Pinocchio*** by Carlo Lorenzini, especially if you're heading to Pinocchio Park (p. 129). Try to get the version before Disney got its hands on it. With really young ones, the film will do just fine.

Toddlers enjoy ***Vulca the Etruscan*** (OUP USA), a fun picture book about a boy, his dog and an Etruscan necropolis. It's out of print, but you should be able to pick up a cheap copy at Amazon's Marketplace. Older primary-age children into art and history will enjoy **Perugino's Path** by Nancy L Clouse, an illustrated book about the Umbrian painter.

For 'young adult' readers in the Harry Potter-ish age group, try the fantastical time-warping adventures of the Stravaganza series: Mary Hoffman's ***Stravaganza: City of Flowers*** (Bloomsbury) is set in an alternate Florence, ***Stravaganza: City of Stars*** in Siena. The second book in Stephanie Meyer's smash *Twilight* teen vampire trilogy, ***New Moon*** (Little, Brown), nears its denouement in (and below) Volterra.

companion website, ***www.alanrogers.com***, also takes bookings.

EATING OUT

The Italian day starts with *colazione* (breakfast). *Pranzo* (lunch) and *cena* (dinner) consist of *antipasti* (appetisers), a *primo* (first course) of pasta, soup or risotto, and a *secondo* (main course) of meat or fish, accompanied by a *contorno* (side dish) of veggies, finished off with *dolce* (dessert) or *formaggio* (cheese) and a *caffè* (coffee). But don't worry, you don't have to order the lot: a *primo* at lunch is usually enough; at dinner, an *antipasto* and *secondo* does the trick. For **Tuscan and Umbrian specialities,** see p. 73.

'I'll Have the White Ice Cream, Please'

If you think that white or yellow ice cream is just vanilla, think again: **Vaniglia** tastes strongly of vanilla but is only the start. **Crema** is creamy-white (sometimes egg-yolky) without the vanilla flavour, while **Crema Fiorentina** is yellow with a slight liquorice tang. **Fiordilatte** ('flower of milk') is bright white and milky. **Stracciatella** is (usually) *fior-dilatte* with veins or chunks of chocolate through it, whereas **Panna Cotta** ('cooked cream') is based on the sweet, rich Italian dessert, with a slightly toasted flavour. **Crema di Riso** is another bright-white concoction, not unlike cold rice pudding.

For our favourite ice-cream stops in Florence, see p. 74.

Don't get hung up on special menus for children: the 'kids' menu' is usually anything they want, including stuff not on offer to you. At the very least, staff will almost always cook a tomato or meat sauce with pasta. And there's always pizzerias: we've not listed too many in later sections, but as a general rule **walk two streets back** from the main piazza of any town and you're safe with a pizza anywhere.

INSIDER TIP

If you stand at a bar—*al banco*—you'll be charged the minimum for your drinks, ice cream and *panino*. If you sit down, you incur a cover charge and heftier prices for the same. Sit outside and you'll pay even more—there's an astronomical add-on for sitting on one of Tuscany's iconic piazzas.

A Wine Label

It would take a book at least the size of this one to explain the byzantine **Italian wine laws** and how they apply to Tuscany and Umbria. To keep things simple, here are some words to look out for:

Indicazione Geografica Tipica (IGT) A guarantee of grape variety and place of origin. Some of Tuscany's best wines are sold with IGT status.

Denominazione di Origine Controllata (DOC) The basic classification for a good wine, which has to conform to yield rules and quality checks.

Denominazione di Origine Controllata e Garantita (DOCG) Italy's best wines, which have to conform to the same checks as DOC wines and more.

Imbottigliato all origine A wine bottled where it was made—usually a good sign.

Riserva A special, aged selection.

Brunello di Montalcino Outstanding DOCG wine from the hills around Montalcino, made entirely from the Sangiovese grape. A good bottle will set you back around 40€. See p. 178.

Rosso di Montalcino What people on regular budgets buy if they want a Montalcino wine.

Vino Nobile di Montepulciano Quality DOCG wine from the hills around Montepulciano. See p. 172.

Chianti Classico A red from the (*classico*) Chianti zone: a staple Tuscan wine the world over. See p. 100.

Sagrantino di Montefalco Umbria's best DOCG wine—a velvety red that matches wild boar like a dream. See p. 230.

Vin Santo An almost yellow, sweet white wine, traditionally aged under the tiles of Renaissance *palazzi*.

'Super Tuscans' Words you won't see on a label, but if someone offers you a glass of **Sassicaia, Tignanello** or **Ornellaia,** say yes (as long as you're not paying).

THE 21ST-CENTURY TRAVELLER

Mobile Phones

GSM phones switch to an Italian network automatically on arrival, as long as they're set up for **international roaming.** Note, however, that roaming call charges are much higher than at home, and you pay to **receive calls,** sometimes even if they divert to voicemail. Receiving text messages is usually free, although you will pay much more than usual to reply. Smartphone users should ensure **data roaming** is switched off—a nasty bill may await your return otherwise.

For regular travellers to Italy, or for a long stay, it's almost certainly worthwhile purchasing an **Italian pay-as-you-go SIM.** The phone shop will need to photocopy your passport. The SIM should cost 5€–10€ and your

Know Your Apse from Your Nave

Apse The enclosed space behind the main altar

Campanile The bell-tower of a church

Cappella A chapel, a dedicated religious space created off the aisles or transepts of a church

Chiostro The cloisters—internal roofed walkways found in monasteries

Duomo Another word for *cattedrale*—the cathedral

Fresco A picture that was painted on wet plaster

Lunette The arched space between the walls and a vaulted ceiling

Nave The central aisle of a church leading from the main door to the altar

Sacristy The room where the priest's garments and sacred bits and pieces are (or were) kept

Transept The cross-arms of a church, running at 90° to the nave

Fast Facts: Tuscany, Umbria & Florence

Alcohol There is no enforced **minimum age** for drinking in Italy, although under-16s may not buy alcohol. There are no restrictions on where you can buy alcohol.

Babysitting See individual accommodation entries for places that offer babysitting services. Never be shy to ask about babysitting services (the Italian word is also *babysitting*!).

Banks Retail banks are open Monday to Friday 8:30am to 1:30pm and 2:30 to 4:30pm, or thereabouts. See the 'Fast Facts' section of individual chapters for convenient local branches.

Breastfeeding Breastfeeding in public is acceptable, but you may get stared at, especially if you're feeding an older infant. Brazen it out, or find an out-of-the-way spot. For handy spots in Florence, see p. 44.

Business Hours Regular hours are generally 9am to 12:30pm and 3:30 to 7:30pm.

Car Rental See 'Getting Around', p. 24.

Consulates The **British Consulate** is in Florence, at Lungarno Corsini 2 (*☎ 055 284133. **www.britishembassy.gov.uk***). It's open 9am to 1pm and 2 to 5pm Monday to Friday. **Irish** citizens should call their embassy in Rome (*☎ 06 6979121. **www.ambasciata-irlanda.it***). The **US consulate** is at Lungarno Vespucci 38, Florence (*☎ 055 266951. **florence.usconsulate.gov***).

Credit Cards For lost or stolen cards, make sure you have your emergency number handy (p. 14). Make a note of it and keep it separately. The main ones are: **American Express** (Italian *☎ 800 914912*); **Barclaycard** (UK *☎ +44 1604 230230*); **MasterCard** (Italian *☎ 800 870866*); **Visa** (Italian *☎ 800 819014*).

Currency See 'Money', p. 14.

Customs & Duty Free See 'Customs', p. 12.

Directory Enquiries For domestic calls, dial *☎ 12*. For international assistance, call *☎ 176*.

Electricity Italy uses 220V, 50Hz. Power sockets have two or three holes. Buy a two-pin **European adaptor** before you leave home.

Emergencies For **police,** call *☎ 113*. For the ***carabinieri,*** call *☎ 112*. For the **fire brigade,** call *☎ 115*. In a **medical** emergency, call *☎ 118*.

Hospitals For your nearest hospital, see the 'Fast Facts' section of individual chapters.

Internet & Wi-Fi See 'The 21st-Century Traveller', above.

Language English is spoken (or at least understood) in most places that tourists frequent. However, at least attempting to speak in Italian will be hugely appreciated by locals—even if you don't make too good a fist of it.

Legal Assistance The British Embassy website (***www.britain.it***)

has a list of lawyers; click 'Help for British Nationals' then 'If things go wrong'. There's also a detailed section on 'Lawyers and Notaries' under the 'US Citizen Services' tab at ***www.usembassy.it***. Your travel insurance company can also advise.

Mail It costs 0.65€ to send a postcard (or letter up to 20g/0.7oz) within Europe, 0.85€ to the US. Stamps can be bought in *tabacchi* and post offices. Postboxes are red and usually attached to walls.

Maps The plastic *Rough Guide Map: Tuscany 1:200,000* (£5.99/$9.99) has the distinct advantage of holding together when others are falling apart, and the distinct disadvantage of excluding Umbria. A decent driver's map of the whole area is Michelin's 1:400,000 *563: Toscana, Umbria*. For walkers, Kompass 1:50,000 maps have the detail you need.

Mobile Phones See 'The 21st-Century Traveller', above.

Newspapers & Magazines Florence's nominally national rag is *La Nazione*, read throughout Tuscany but rarely elsewhere. By the coast you're more likely to see *Il Tirreno*; in Umbria it's the *Corriere dell'Umbria*. The closest Italy has to national newspapers—*La Repubblica* (Roman, centre-left), *La Stampa* (Milanese, right-ish with a business bias) and *Corriere della Sera* (Milanese, centre-right)—are all widely available, as is the iconic pink sports paper, *La Gazzetta dello Sport*. *The Florentine* is Florence's free bi-weekly expat listings magazine; it's also online at ***www.theflorentine.net***.

Pets See 'Taking Pets', p. 13.

Pharmacies Look for the *farmacia* sign and the green cross. There is usually one chemist open late and on a Sunday in every town; there should be a note in the window of every *farmacia* stating which is open. It's also a good idea to take a first-aid course yourself; for a **CD-ROM** developed in collaboration with St John Ambulance in the UK and Australia, see ***www.firstaidforkids.com***. Also see 'Fast Facts' in the chapters that follow for addresses of convenient 24-hour pharmacies.

Police Dial *113*.

Smoking Italy banned smoking inside all bars, restaurants, public buildings and offices in 2005. Smoking on an outdoor terrace is still allowed.

Telephone Public telephones are plentiful. Some take credit cards and have instructions in English, but most use *schede telefoniche*, available from *tabacchi* and news-stands. To call home from Italy, first dial 00, then the country code (UK 44, US/Canada 1, Ireland 353); then the area code (dropping any initial 0); then the number. If you need operator assistance to make a call, dial *1720044* to reach BT in the UK or *1720353* for Ireland. See

also 'The 21st-Century Traveller', above.
Time Zone GMT/BST + 1hour; EST + 6 hours.
Tipping Check if service is included in the bill. Otherwise 5 to 10% is the norm but is by no means compulsory. Don't tip **bad service.**
Toilets & Baby Change There are few public toilets; you're best off making a small purchase at a bar or café and using theirs. Museums and galleries often have toilets but baby-changing facilities are trickier to find, if a little more prevalent than a few years ago. Large bars may only have a well-used fold-down changing table, so carry a changing mat with you for added hygiene.
Water Nobody in Italy drinks tap-water, though it's perfectly safe to do so. Still water is *acqua senza gaz* or *naturale*; sparkling is *acqua frizzante*.

Italian number will have lower call charges, including to home, and *much* lower **data (3G) charges** for smartphones. Make sure you've **unlocked** your handset before leaving (ask your network or local independent phone retailer).

The major Italian networks are all GSM: **TIM, Vodafone, 3** and **Wind.** If you're staying in a rural area, ask your host or hotelier which gets the best local reception, as Tuscany's hills cause havoc with networks. Consumer electronics giant **Euronics** (***www.euronics.it***) sells all the major networks; the website has a store finder. There are small phone retailers on almost every Italian high street.

Anyone staying in Wi-Fi-equipped accommodation can probably survive with **Skype** (***www.skype.com***) or **Truphone** (***www.truphone.com***) VoIP apps on a laptop, netbook or smartphone.

Internet & Wi-Fi

Internet cafés are relatively common in Tuscany and Umbria, but prices and the speed of service vary considerably. Under Italian **anti-terrorism laws,** every Internet café must photocopy the passport of non-Italian nationals and log their usage, so come prepared.

If you're bringing your own laptop, the number of places with **Wi-Fi** access is growing. Some **campsites** have hotspots; most hotels have it in the lobby at least. Prices are generally reasonable elsewhere. You might find downloading a global hotspot locator such as **JiWire** (***www.jiwire.com***) useful, or any local tourist office can point you in the right direction (some even let their own terminals). For a **3G dongle** (a *chiavetta*), ask in any mobile phone store or consumer electronics concession.

3 Florence

Firenze to an Italian, Florence ★★ to us, the great central Italian city on the Arno has drawn cultural pilgrims and Grand Tourists for centuries. The Tuscan capital that was once, briefly, also the Italian capital, could be the highlight of your family trip, too. Its canyon-like streets retain an occasionally severe, medieval character, and although parts radiate a staggering architectural beauty, there's one aspect that wows the hordes more than any other: art.

South of the Alps at least, Florence *was* the **Renaissance**, that blossoming of classical ideals, painting and sculpture in the 15th century that changed the Western world. The great Renaissance painters Botticelli and Michelangelo created some of their most inspired work here; Leonardo Da Vinci spent his formative years in the city. The Uffizi is Europe's greatest gallery, dripping with masterpieces.

But you need to do the city right to get the most from it as a family. Most importantly, you need to plan what you want to see in advance. The city is crammed with artwork, history and great buildings, so accept that you're not going to see everything. And visiting Florence isn't plain sailing: the streets teem with people, it's hard to get around with toddlers and it's more expensive than anywhere else in Tuscany. But don't be put off: missing Florence would be a big mistake. The *centro storico* is compact and pedestrianised in parts, and there are plenty of parks, offbeat museums, markets and scrumptious ice-cream opportunities to amuse even the youngest visitors. With a bit of forward-thinking, you can all enjoy Florence's cultural heavyweights without tears.

VISITOR INFORMATION

Information Centres

The main **tourist office** is at Via Cavour 1r, just north of the Duomo (✆ *055 290832. www.firenzeturismo.it*; 8:30am–6:30pm Mon–Sat, 8:30am–1:30pm Sun). Of the others scattered across the city, the most convenient is just off Piazza Santa Croce at Borgo Santa Croce 29r (✆ *055 2340444*; 9am–7pm Mon–Sat, 9am–2pm Sun). Opposite the **train station,** there's one at Piazza della Stazione 4 (✆ *055 212245*; 8:30am–7pm Mon–Sat, 8:30am–2pm Sun).

Of the numerous websites offering visitor information for Florence, try ***www.yourwaytoflorence.com***. Or pick up a copy of **The Florentine** (***www.theflorentine.net***), a bi-weekly English-language news and listings magazine.

Arriving

By Air Most European visitors fly to Pisa's **Galileo Galilei airport** (✆ ***050 849300. www.pisa-airport.com***), 95km (60 miles) west of the city and an hour away by train. **British Airways**

Children's Top Attractions in Florence

- Climb the **Duomo** for incomparable views over the city, p. 48.
- Jump the queue to see Botticelli, Michelangelo and Leonardo in the **Uffizi,** p. 52.
- Compare ***David*** in the Accademia with its two replicas, p. 58.
- Slurp the world's best **ice cream,** p. 74.
- Unleash budding scientists in the **Museo Galileo,** p. 54.
- Wander the city walls to **Piazzale Michelangelo,** p. 63.
- Discover the grottoes and gardens of the **Giardino di Boboli,** p. 62.
- Get medieval with the armour at **Museo Stibbert,** p. 60.
- Go back in time with a tour of the **Palazzo Vecchio** led by Cosimo de' Medici, p. 55.
- Explore the morning away at **San Miniato's evocative monumental cemetery,** p. 64.

(☎ *0844 4930787.* ***www.ba.com***) flies from London Heathrow; **Ryanair** (☎ *0871 2460000.* ***www.ryanair.com***) from Bournemouth, East Midlands, Edinburgh, Leeds Bradford, London Stansted, Prestwick and Liverpool in the UK, plus Dublin in Ireland, and **easyJet** (***www.easyjet.com***) from Bristol, Luton and London Gatwick. **Jet2** (☎ *0871 2261737.* ***www.jet2.com***) and **Thomson** (☎ *0871 2314787.* ***www.thomsonfly.com***) both operate summer services from Manchester.

Alitalia (☎ *08714 241424.* ***www.alitalia.com***) has domestic flights from Rome and **WindJet** (***www.volawindjet.it***) connects Pisa with Sicily.

Delta (***www.delta.com***) operates the only direct flight between Tuscany and North America, from New York's JFK Airport.

Shuttle buses operated by **Terravision** (☎ *06 32120011.* ***www.terravision.eu***) depart every hour to Florence's **Santa Maria Novella** station (70 min). It costs 10€ one-way (buy tickets from the booth in Arrivals). The train is a cheaper (5.70€) but slower option (70–100 min): there are six direct services between 6:40am and 10:20pm. Alternatively, trains connect the airport to Pisa Centrale (5 min) every 30 minutes for regular services to Florence (1 hr).

Florence Peretola (or 'Amerigo Vespucci') airport (☎ *055 3061300.* ***www.aeroporto.firenze.it***) is just 5km (3 miles) northwest of the city centre, **Meridiana** (☎ *0871 2229319.* ***www.meridiana.it***) operates regular flights to it from the UK (London Gatwick). City Jet has launched a new route from London City Airport to Florence,

View over Florence and the River Arno from high above Oltrarno

six-times-per-week. The **Vola in Bus** (800 424500. *www.ataf.net*) runs into the city every half-hour 6am to 11:30pm, 5:30am to 1pm in the other direction (5€; 30 min), terminating at the SITA bus station (p. 41) near Santa Maria Novella train station. Buy tickets on the bus or at machines in the terminal. Taxis should cost around 20€ and take 20 minutes.

By Car Florence has excellent road connections with the rest of Italy but arriving by car can be a headache. Traffic is intimidating, and parking is hard to find and mostly expensive. If you're hiring a car to tour Tuscany, start or end your holiday in Florence, and do the city itself without it. If driving from the UK, consider tackling the city via day trips from elsewhere.

It's best to arrange car rental before you arrive to get the best rates (p. 25), although most major rental companies have offices in Florence (see below).

If you do visit Florence by car, head for a car park and leave it there—driving around the city is pointless. Some hotels have garages or can at least point you in the direction of the nearest one: ask in advance. **Firenze Parcheggi** (*www.firenzeparcheggi.it*) runs 12 official city

TIP Free Parking!

If you don't have too much luggage, or a buggy, park for free at Piazzale Michelangelo (p. 63), just south of the Arno, then walk or take bus 12 or 13 into the centre. Watch out for scams: there are **no charges,** even if the friendly local guiding you into a space asks for some money.

The *piazzale* is easy to reach: from the A1 *autostrada*, take the **Firenze–Certosa** exit and head north along Via Senese (towards *centro*). The *piazzale* is signposted once you get into the city; if you go through the Porta Romana, you've missed the turning.

A Florence Timeline

59 B.C. Florence (Florentia) is founded by Julius Caesar, as a settlement for army veterans

552–1115 City ruled by the Goths, the Lombards and, finally, the Franks

1115 Florence granted independent status within the Holy Roman Empire

1348 Plague, the so-called 'Black Death', kills half the city's population

1406 Florence conquers Pisa

1469–92 Rule of Medici patriarch Lorenzo 'il Magnifico'—the Golden Age of Renaissance

1494 Extremist monk Fra' Girolamo Savonarola helps drive the Medici rulers from the city and takes control

1498 Savonarola burned at the stake for heresy; Florence becomes a republic until 1512, when the Medici return

1555–57 Florence takes control of Siena

1737 The last of the Medici dukes dies; Florence passes to the French House of Lorraine until 1859

1860 Florence joins the new state of Italy, becoming the capital 1865–70

1944 Retreating Germans spare just one of Florence's bridges, the Ponte Vecchio

1966 Great Arno Flood; the river rises up to 6m (19.5 ft) and destroys priceless treasures

1993 Car bomb damages the Uffizi and kills five

2009–10 Fiorentina football club makes a triumphant return to the Champions League after years in the doldrums

car parks: the most convenient are the 24-hour ones under Santa Maria Novella station (2€–3€/hr) and Parterre behind Piazza della Libertà north of the centre, at Via Madonna della Tosse 9 (1.50€/hr; 18€ for 24 hr). To find them approach Florence from the north and follow signs to the *centro*—you'll see parking signs as you approach the centre.

By Bus Long-distance **buses** to Florence are operated by various companies; most terminate around Santa Maria Novella station. The main **SITA** (*800 373760. www.sitabus.it*) terminal is on Via Santa Caterina da Siena, off Piazza della Stazione. SITA operates regular services from **Arezzo, Perugia,** and **Siena. TRA.IN** (*0577 204111.*

Learning as You Go

The mention of anything to do with school might elicit howls of protest from your youngsters, but almost everywhere you go in Florence can give your children an artistic leg-up.

Like most school programmes, the UK's **National Curriculum** has an **Art and Design** component, which suggests visiting galleries for all Key Stages: in Key Stage 1 (5–7 years) the emphasis is on getting children to focus on shapes, colour, form, line and texture; in Key Stage 2 (7–11 years) to build awareness of the role of art in different cultures and to compare ideas and approaches in others' art. In Key Stage 3 and beyond, these skills are further developed in more specialised units that include architecture and sculpture.

Note also that Florence's excellent **Museo Galileo** (p. 54) hosts regular school visits from around the world.

www.trainspa.it) services to **Siena** also depart from here. It's 7.10€ to Siena with either company (every 15–30 min; see ***www.sienamobilita.it***).

By Train Florence lies on the recently upgraded Turin–Naples high-speed rail line (☎ *892021.* ***www.trenitalia.it***) with fast services from **Bologna** (10€–24€), **Milan** (27.50€–52€), **Rome** (28€–44€) and **Venice** (22.50€–42€). Local trains connect with **Pisa** (5.70€) and **Arezzo** (5.70€–9.50€). For **Siena,** take the bus (see above). Trains arrive at **Santa Maria Novella,** the main station, a short walk west of the Duomo. The ticket office opens 5:45am to 10pm, and there are 24-hour machines inside the station.

Artesia (***www.artesia.eu***) runs a daily night-train service from Paris-Bercy to Florence Campo di Marte. Berths range from shared six-bed couchette compartments to private family sleepers. Adult tickets cost 117€ to 160€ each way (with significant discounts available for booking off-peak trains way in advance); for children aged 4 to 12 it's 55€ to 100€.

Getting Around

By Public Transport Most visitors tour Florence **on foot,** but although distances aren't great, the walking can be tiring for those with buggies or young children. **Local buses** are a useful alternative. Orange **ATAF** (☎ *800 424500.* ***www.ataf.net***) buses have plenty of space and buggy access. Buy tickets from automatic machines, shops and *tabacchi* all over the city, or the main ATAF info office just outside Santa Maria Novella (7:15am–7:45pm daily). Tickets are valid for unlimited travel within 90 minutes (1.20€). The **Ticket 4x90** provides four

90-minute tickets for 4.50€ and the electronic **Carta Agile** 10 trips for 10€. Always validate your ticket in the yellow machines on board—you'll be fined otherwise. You can buy tickets on the bus but there's **no change** and it's 2€ for a single. Several useful routes start outside Santa Maria Novella station: route **13** runs clockwise to Piazzale Michelangelo; **12** gets there by a less scenic route; while **7** takes you straight to Piazza San Marco and on to **Fiesole.**

The smaller electric ***bussini ecologici*** run through the centre and are handy if the children get tired: route **A** starts at the train station and runs past the Duomo and Piazza della Signoria before heading north of Santa Croce; while **D** runs from the train station to Ponte Vespucci and along the south bank of the Arno in a loop that includes Palazzo Pitti.

By Open-Top Bus One hassle-free and informative way to get around is by an open-top, commentated tourist bus operated by **City Sightseeing** (☎ *055 290451. www.firenze.city-sightseeing.it*). It runs two routes, both calling at Santa Maria Novella and more than 15 other stops around the *centro storico*. **Circuit A** (City) makes a loop from Santa Maria Novella station past Piazzale Michelangelo (1 hr total) while **B** (Fiesole) heads out to Fiesole (2 hr total). Tickets (22€, 11€ child 5–15, free under-5s, 66€ family) are valid for 48 hours on both routes. Bus stops are clearly marked on the street—start anywhere and jump on and off as you like. Buses run daily: in spring and summer every 30 minutes; every hour otherwise.

By Taxi Cabs are metered but relatively expensive for short journeys: it'll cost you 5€ to travel 100 metres (328 ft), but 10€ should cover the ride from the station to most hotels north of the river. In practice, it's tough to hail one in the street, so make for a central rank or call **Radio Taxi** on ☎ *055 4242*, ☎ *055 4798* or ☎ *055 4390*. Major ranks are found in Piazza Santa Croce, Piazza San Giovanni, Piazza della Repubblica, Piazza San Marco, Piazza Santa Trinita and Piazza Santa Maria Novella.

Planning Your Outings

The **River Arno** bisects Florence east to west, with most of the more famous sights lying to the north around the old centre (*centro storico*). The district south of the river, **Oltrarno,** has some sublime spots of its own, including the **Giardino di Boboli** and the classic view from **Piazzale Michelangelo.** The two banks are linked by eight bridges, most famously the **Ponte Vecchio** (p. 61).

At the heart of the *centro storico* lies **Piazza del Duomo,** home to the city's cathedral; a short walk south along Via dei Calzaiuoli is **Piazza della Signoria** and the **Galleria degli Uffizi** (p. 52). North of the Duomo lie the markets of **San Lorenzo,** with San Marco beyond attracting crowds to the **Accademia** to see Michelangelo's *David*, and to niche museums that appeal to children. Southeast of the Duomo is the district named after Florence's main Franciscan church, **Santa Croce.**

Baby-Changing & Breastfeeding

Changing nappies on the go in Florence can be a challenge as toilets are small. Italian mums bring their own changing mats. **Coin** department store at Via dei Calzaiuoli 56r (p. 68) has a baby room and toilet on the second floor; the **Prénatal** store at Via Brunelleschi 22r (p. 68) has a similar facility. You might have to pretend to buy something, but staff are generally sympathetic.

Florentine women tend not to breastfeed in public, but with a million foreigners in town, those who do so won't raise many eyebrows. The tourist office at Via Cavour is happy for mothers to feed inside; the baby rooms at the shops mentioned above are also good spots. Restaurants and cafés are usually happy to warm bottles (*riscaldare, per favore*).

Toilets

There are 11 public toilets in the centre, open every day (usually 0.50€). The most convenient are **behind the Bargello** at the top of Via Filippina; in the **tourist office** at Borgo Santa Croce 29r; in the **underpass** at Santa Maria Novella and inside the station itself; behind **Piazza Michelangelo** on Via Galileo; and at Via dell' Ariento 14, near the **Mercato Centrale.** The **OPA Visitor Centre,** at Piazza San Giovanni 7, has the centre's smartest public facilities (1€).

Safety

Florence is a **safe** city for families, although it attracts pickpockets and bag-snatchers, '*scippatori*', who tend to operate in large **crowds** of tourists. Don't flash expensive jewellery, cameras, watches and bags as you walk around, and wear money in a pouch or belt. Carry bags across your shoulders: it makes them harder to grab. If you're **parking** in the city, never leave anything of value inside. Avoid the area around the **train station** and especially **Parco delle Cascine** at night.

INSIDER TIP

For the latest travel and transport news in and around Florence, check ***www.muoversiafirenze.it*** (in Italian only).

Family-Friendly Events

Dating back to the First Crusade, the **Scoppio del Carro** (Explosion of the Cart) on Easter Sunday sees a cartload of fireworks pulled to the Duomo by six white oxen and ignited by a mechanical dove.

Fast Facts: Florence

Banks You'll find **ATMs** and *uffici di cambio* (exchange booths) throughout the centre, and major banks around **Piazza della Repubblica.** Opening hours are usually 8:30am to 1:30pm and 2:35 to 3:35pm Monday to Friday.

Car Rental **Avis,** Borgo Ognissanti 128r, ☎ *055 213629;* **Europcar,** Borgo Ognissanti 53r, ☎ *055 290438*; **Excelsior,** Via Lulli 76, ☎ *055 3215397;* **Hertz,** Via Maso Finiguerra 33r, ☎ *055 2398205;* **Thrifty,** Borgo Ognissanti 134r, ☎ *055 287161*. See also p. 25.

Consulates The **UK Consulate** is at Lungarno Corsini 2 (☎ *055 284133.* ***www.britain.it***). Citizens of **Ireland** should contact their embassy in Rome (☎ *06 6979121*). The **US Consulate General** (☎ *055 266951.* ***http://florence.usconsulate.gov***) is at Lungarno Vespucci 38.

Hospitals & Emergencies The main hospital in central Florence is **Ospedale Santa Maria Nuova** at Piazza Santa Maria Nuova 1 (☎ *055 27581*) with a 24-hour casualty/ER. The **Associazione Volontari Ospedalieri** (☎ *055 4250126*) provides 24-hour translators for medical emergencies. For English-speaking doctors, contact the 24-hour **Tourist Medical Service** on ☎ *055 475411.* (***www.medicalservice.firenze.it***). Their scheduled clinic is at Via Lorenzo il Magnifico 59 (11am–noon and 5–6pm Mon–Fri, 11am–noon Sat). Consultations cost at least 50€. For an **ambulance** or urgent first-aid, call ☎ *118.*

Internet & Wi-Fi There are Internet cafés and Wi-Fi providers scattered all over Florence; you must always show **photo ID** before accessing the Web. Franchise **Internet Train** (***www.internettrain.it***) has six outlets including those at Via Porta Rossa 38r (9:30am–midnight Mon–Sat, 10am–midnight Sun), Via de'Benci 36r (10am–midnight daily) and Borgo San Jacopo 30r (10:30am–11pm daily); under-26s get a discount.

Lost Property Property handed to the police or railway police gets taken to the city office at Via Circondaria 17b (☎ *055 3283942*); open 9am to noon Monday to Wednesday, and Friday and Saturday. Report **lost passports** or thefts at the Questura, Via Zara 2 (☎ *055 49771*), open 9:30am to 1pm Monday to Friday; translators are usually available. You'll have to fill in a form (*denuncia*) if you intend to claim.

Pharmacies You can find 24-hour outlets inside the **train station** (Farmacia Santa Maria Novella), at Piazza San Giovanni 20r, and at **Farmacia Molteni,** Via dei Calzaiuoli 7r. Pharmacies, scattered all over the centre, are usually open 8:30am to 1pm and 4 to 8pm Monday to Saturday.

Post Offices The main office is on Via Pellicceria, near Piazza della Repubblica (☎ *055 2736481*), open 8:15am to 7pm Monday to Friday, 8:15am to 1:30pm Saturday. You can buy stamps (*francobolli*) at tobacconist stores (*tabacchi*), identified outside by a white 'T' on a dark background, and inside the Uffizi.

CENTRAL FLORENCE

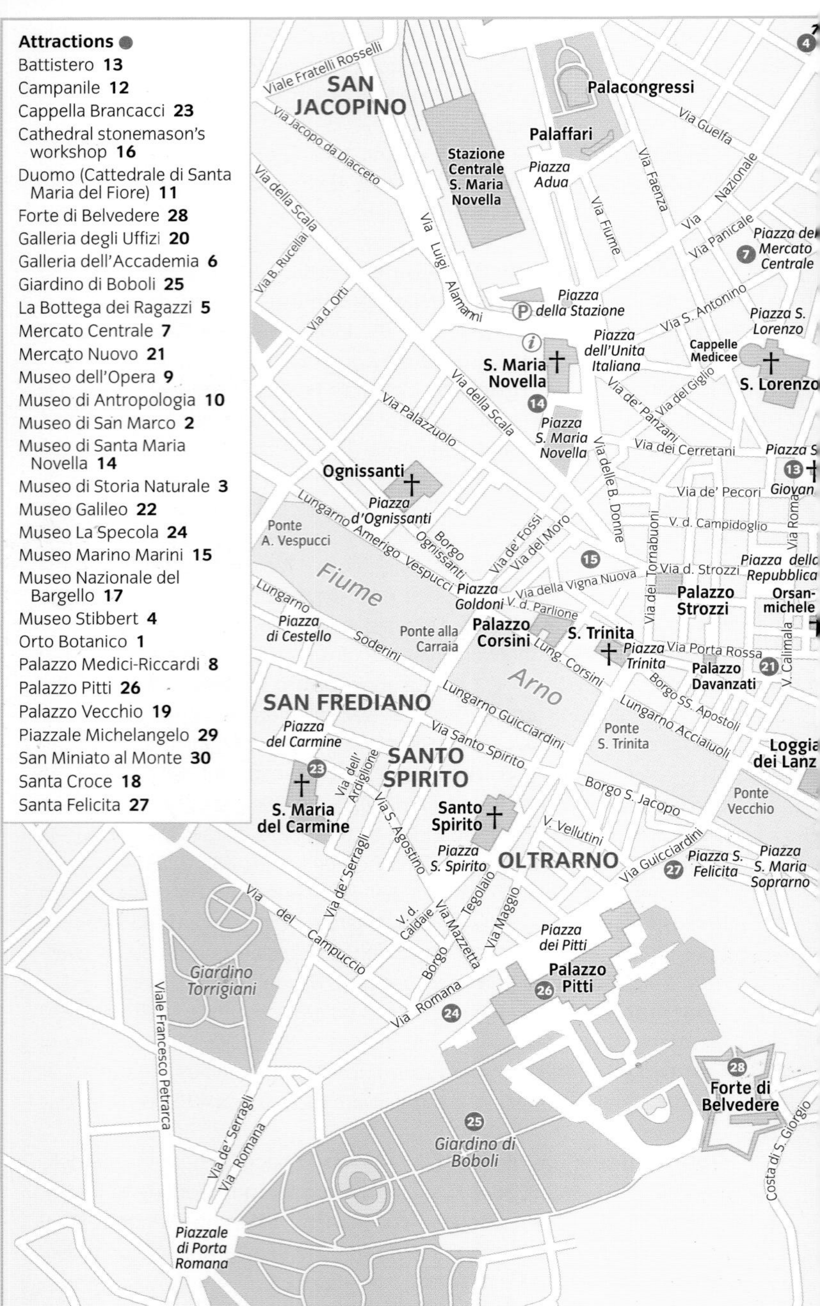

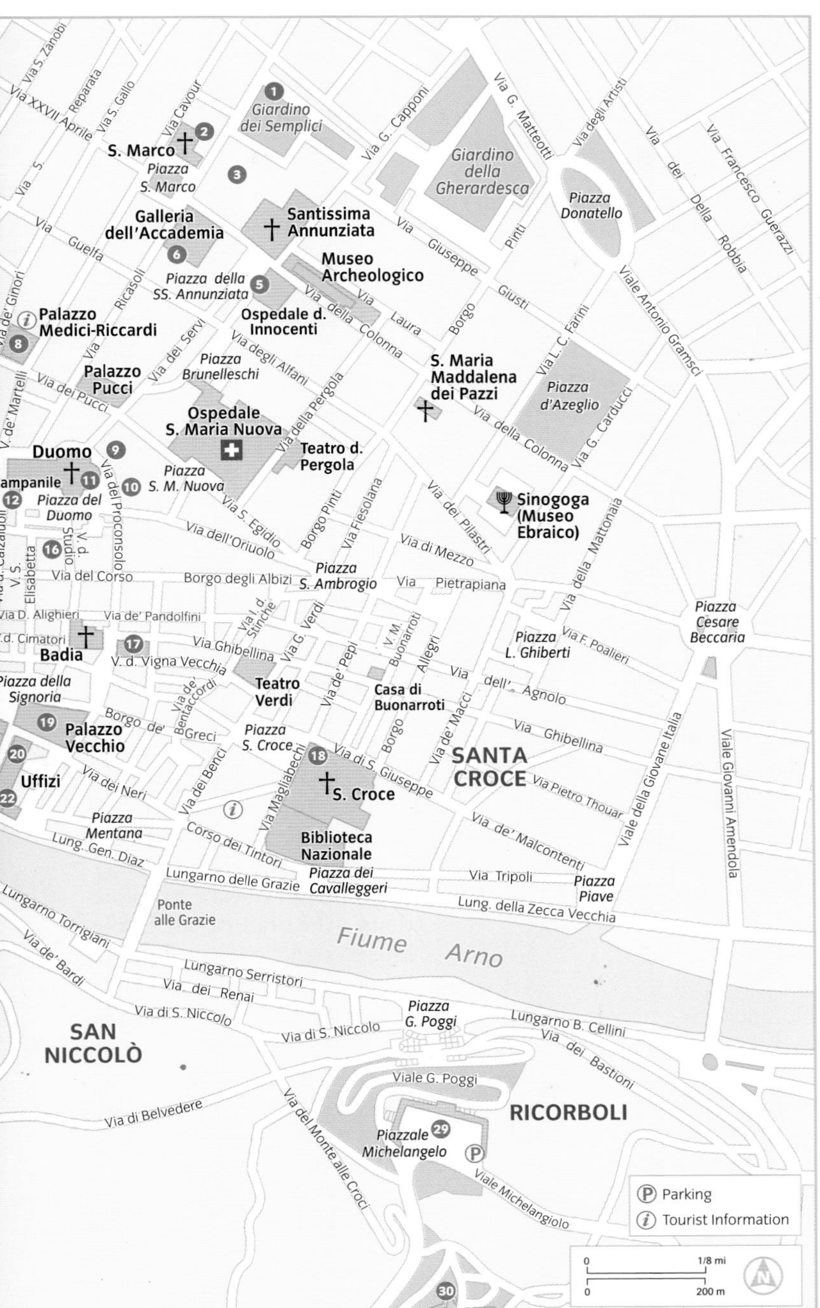
Giardino dei Semplici
S. Marco
Piazza S. Marco
Galleria dell'Accademia
Santissima Annunziata
Museo Archeologico
Piazza della SS. Annunziata
Ospedale d. Innocenti
Palazzo Medici-Riccardi
Palazzo Pucci
Piazza Brunelleschi
Ospedale S. Maria Nuova
Duomo
Campanile
Piazza del Duomo
Piazza S. M. Nuova
Teatro d. Pergola
S. Maria Maddalena dei Pazzi
Giardino della Gherardesca
Piazza Donatello
Piazza d'Azeglio
Sinogoga (Museo Ebraico)
Piazza S. Ambrogio
Piazza Cesare Beccaria
Piazza L. Ghiberti
Badia
Piazza della Signoria
Palazzo Vecchio
Uffizi
Teatro Verdi
Casa di Buonarroti
Piazza S. Croce
S. Croce
SANTA CROCE
Biblioteca Nazionale
Piazza Mentana
Piazza dei Cavalleggeri
Piazza Piave
Ponte alle Grazie
Fiume Arno
Piazza G. Poggi
SAN NICCOLÒ
RICORBOLI
Piazzale Michelangelo
Via XXVII Aprile
Via Cavour
Via G. Capponi
Via G. Matteotti
Via degli Artisti
Via Francesco Guerazzi
Via dei Della Robbia
Viale Antonio Gramsci
Via Guelfa
Via Ricasoli
Via dei Servi
Via della Colonna
Via Laura
Borgo Pinti
Via Giuseppe Giusti
Via L. C. Farini
Via G. Carducci
Via degli Alfani
Via della Pergola
Via dei Pucci
Via del Proconsolo
Via S. Egidio
Via dell'Oriuolo
Via dei Pilastri
Via di Mezzo
Via Fiesolana
Via della Mattonaia
Via del Corso
Borgo degli Albizi
Via Pietrapiana
Via D. Alighieri
Via de' Pandolfini
Via Ghibellina
Via G. Verdi
Via de' Pepi
Via dell'Agnolo
Via de' Macci
Borgo de' Greci
Via dei Benci
Via Magliabechi
Via di S. Giuseppe
Via Pietro Thouar
Via de' Malcontenti
Viale della Giovane Italia
Viale Giovanni Amendola
Via dei Neri
Corso dei Tintori
Lung. Gen. Diaz
Lungarno delle Grazie
Via Tripoli
Lung. della Zecca Vecchia
Lungarno Torrigiani
Via de' Bardi
Lungarno Serristori
Via dei Renai
Via di S. Niccolò
Lungarno B. Cellini
Via dei Bastioni
Viale G. Poggi
Via di Belvedere
Via del Monte alle Croci
Viale Michelangiolo
Parking
Tourist Information
0 1/8 mi
0 200 m

Held in the Parco delle Cascine on the first Sunday after Ascension Day (40 days after Easter), the **Festa del Grillo** ★ (Festival of the Cricket) sees hundreds of crickets sold in wooden cages; they are released en masse after a parade.

The **Festa di San Giovanni** (St. John's Day, 24th June) celebrates Florence's patron saint with a massive fireworks display at Piazzale Michelangelo and the first game of **Calcio Storico** ★★, medieval football. The *Calcio* is a chaotic three-match, week-long series held in Piazza Santa Croce and Piazza della Signoria, with teams representing the four ancient city districts. The winning team receives a calf to roast at a raucous street party.

The **Festa della Rificolona** ★ (Virgin's Birthday, 7th Sept) is marked by a colourful procession of children to Piazza Santissima Annunziata. Each carries a paper lantern with a candle inside, and the inevitable boisterous street parties follow.

WHAT TO SEE & DO

Florence has a history that goes back to the Romans, but most of what you see today is evidence of its **Golden Age** during the 1400s and 1500s: the late-medieval and Renaissance periods when its merchants and bankers, particularly the **Medici** family, made it one of Europe's largest and richest cities. Their cash, combined with a flowering of artistic genius, created an awesome legacy of painting, sculpture and architecture. In addition to the most famous sights, there's a huge amount that appeals to children too.

Piazza del Duomo

If you have only a short time in Florence, head straight for **Piazza del Duomo** ★★★, the spiritual heart of the city. This bustling square is dominated by an exotic cathedral topped with **Brunelleschi's** revolutionary dome. Aspiring builders can peek into the cathedral **stonemason's workshop,** just south of the piazza at Via dello Studio 23r.

Battistero AGE 5 & UP

Piazza San Giovanni. ☎ 055 2302885.

The Baptistery is the oldest building in Florence, with slightly mysterious origins in the Dark Ages. Its magical **bronze east doors** ★★, the 'Gates of Paradise', were cast by **Lorenzo Ghiberti** in the 15th century, but those on site are reproductions—the originals are in the **Museo dell'Opera,** at Piazza del Duomo 9. Inside, focus on the details of the stunning **mosaic ceiling** ★: the main vault depicts *Christ in Judgement*, flanked by images of Paradise and a particularly lurid vision of hell. The devil chomps away on a sinner, surrounded by demons and with serpents erupting from his horny head. Dante also appears: he's hooded in black, and being led through hell by Virgil, to the left of Lucifer.

Time** 30 min. **Open** 12:15–6:30pm Mon–Sat, 8:30am–1:30pm Sun. **Adm** 4€, free under-6s. **Amenities

INSIDER TIP

One way to really see Florentine art, especially in places like the Baptistery where mosaics are way above your head, is to bring **binoculars.** They make it easier to pick out the details that make the frescoes so absorbing: serpents, demons, angels and assorted products of the Renaissance imagination. To save your neck muscles, you could alternatively pack a small **mirror.**

Duomo (Cattedrale di Santa Maria del Fiore) ★★ AGE 6 & UP

*Piazza del Duomo. 055 2302885. **www.operaduomo.firenze.it**.*

With its mesmerising 19th-century marble exterior, the Duomo is the most imposing and most recognisable structure in Florence. Construction took most of the 14th century. By 1418 all was complete save the facade and a huge hole where the dome should be: in stepped Filippo Brunelleschi with the answer to an architectural riddle that had remained unsolved since Roman times. It was he who solved the engineering puzzle by designing and building the massive, double-skinned ochre dome between 1423 and 1436. He died in 1446, before the addition of the lantern in the 1460s.

Climbing Brunelleschi's dome ★★ is the highlight of Florence for many children, and is the only real way to appreciate how Brunelleschi's self-supporting dome-within-a-dome works. It pays to do this first thing (through a separate entrance on the north side of the cathedral); there are usually long **queues** unless you get there

TIP Beating the Queues

Children aren't patient, especially in the heat, so it's best to reserve popular gallery tickets in advance. All the State-owned **Firenze Musei** attractions sell pre-booked tickets. Queues at the **Galleria degli Uffizi** and **Galleria dell'Accademia** can be horrific, so we *strongly* advise you to use this service. Reserve your tickets at the office opposite the Uffizi entrance or (essential during busy periods) online in advance at ***www.firenzemusei.it***. There's a 4€ booking fee on top of the usual ticket prices, and unfortunately your purchase is non-refundable if your plans change due to illness or other unforeseen circumstances; you'll be given a time-slot and asked to collect your ticket before entry. This won't get you out of queuing altogether, but it will install you at the back of a much shorter one.

Admission to all State-owned museums is **free** for EU citizens under 18 and over 65 (show your passport). Many are closed on **Mondays** and none accept credit cards at the door. Last entry is usually 30 minutes before closing.

early. The views are magnificent and the clamber to the top lots of fun (warning: there are 463 steps). The first section ends at a narrow gallery that skirts the inside base of the dome, with a vertigo-inspiring drop down to the nave. You can eyeball Vasari's massive **fresco** of the *Last Judgement*; just try not to focus on the huge cracks in the ceiling. The final ascent is within the dome's shell, up to the white marble lantern for a rooftop panorama.

If there's a huge queue to get inside the cathedral itself, you can comfortably skip it, but there are a few interesting artworks inside. Top of the list is Michelino's *Dante Exploring the Divine Comedy*, with its mountain of purgatory on the left and a portrayal of the dome itself on the right. Red-robed Dante is painted in the middle, outside the city walls. Side-by-side portraits of famous Florentine *condottieri* (mercenary-generals) adorn the north wall, notably Paolo Uccello's 1436 **Giovanni Acuto** ★, a.k.a. John Hawkwood, of Essex, just outside London.

INSIDER TIP

An alternative **climb** provides a different city perspective and a close-up of Brunelleschi's dome. The **Campanile** ★, the cathedral's bell-tower, was started by Giotto in 1334 and finished by Andrea Pisano and Francesco Talenti several years later. The Campanile is slightly shorter, at 84.7m (278 ft), but with 414 steps to the viewing area (no lift) it's still quite a hike. It's open 8:30am to 6:50pm daily, and costs 6€ (under-6s free). When queues to climb the dome crawl around the block, there's often no one waiting here. For a still closer look, you can now take a guided **walk on the cathedral roof.** These run four times most days May to October. Book at the ticket office inside the Duomo; it costs 15€, which includes access to the cupola.

The Duomo, Campanile and Brunelleschi's awe-inspiring dome

Time *1½ hr.* ***Cathedral open*** *10am–5pm Mon–Wed and Fri, 10am–4pm Thurs; 10am–4:45pm Sat (to 3:30pm first Sat of month); 1:30pm–4:45pm Sun.* ***Adm*** *Free.* ***Dome open*** *8:30am–7pm Mon–Fri; 8:30am–5:40pm Sat (to 4pm first Sat of month).* ***Adm*** *8€.* ***Amenities***

Museo di Antropologia

AGE 8 & UP

Via del Proconsolo 12. 055 2743067. ***www.msn.unifi.it.***

This odd anthropology museum, a dusty collection of traditional garments and artefacts from tribal cultures hiding truly remarkable finds, is one of Florence's less-visited gems. The highlights are the grimly fascinating **Peruvian mummies** ★—petrified remains of Incas buried near Cuzco 500 years ago, which may not suitable for smaller children (the skulls, some still with scraps of hair, are a bit gruesome, and there are small babies wrapped in cloth and rope). Don't miss the pygmy bows and arrows in Sala 4, the Inuit jacket made from whale stomach and the multi-coloured feathers in the Amazon section.

Time *1½ hr.* ***Open*** *9am–1pm Mon–Tues, Thurs and Sun; 9am–5pm Sat.* ***Adm*** *6€, 3€ 6–21s, 10€ family.* ***Amenities***

Around Piazza della Signoria

The secular heart of the city, **Piazza della Signoria** ★★ is crammed with tourists and ringed by magnificent sculptures. At the heart of the piazza stands the austere **Palazzo Vecchio.** Look for the reproduction of Michelangelo's **David** (p. 55), Ammannati's 1575 **Fountain of Neptune** (Roman god of the sea) and Giambologna's supercilious equestrian statue of Medici duke **Cosimo I** (1587–94). The piazza's arcaded **Loggia dei Lanzi** ★★ is an open-air sculpture gallery whose steps are guarded by Marzocco mirror-images (the lion is the symbol of the city). Giambologna's marble 1584 *Rape of the Sabine Women* seems to mark the point when Florentine art abandoned drama in favour of melodrama. Cellini's iridescent bronze **Perseus** ★★ (1554), holding aloft Medusa's head, falls the other side of the good-taste line.

INSIDER TIP

If you're looking for a specific art picture of something you've seen on your visit, try the **newsstand** in the northwest corner of the piazza. The owner stocks 5,000 postcard images and will try to find what you're after.

FUN FACT **Size Matters**

When the Duomo was completed in the 1460s, it was the largest church in the world, holding the title until the completion of St. Peter's in Rome in 1626.

Neptune, Piazza della Signora

A few paces along Via Calimaruzza is the **Mercato Nuovo** (9am–7pm daily mid-Feb–mid-Nov; 9am–5pm Tues–Sat rest of year) with its souvenir shops and the bronze boar known as **Il Porcellino** ★. Children can clamber over it for a photo-op and, for luck, stroke its nose. If they can get a coin to fall from its mouth into a grille below its head, it's said that they're sure to return to Florence one day. Coins go to local children's homes.

Galleria degli Uffizi ★★★

AGE 7 & UP

*Piazzale degli Uffizi. 055 294883. **www.uffizi.firenze.it.***

The finest art museum in Italy, the **Uffizi** was built by Giorgio Vasari in 1560 as offices (*uffizi*) for his patron, Cosimo I de' Medici. The collection is mind-blowing, but there are few concessions for children. The usual advice for the time-pressed is to tour the first 15 to 20 rooms, dedicated to the Renaissance, but if you have youngsters and don't expect to come back, concentrate on the Uffizi's most famous works.

Room 2 charts where 'modern' art all began, in the 1200s. The monumental **Madonnas** ★★ of **Duccio, Cimabue** and **Giotto** steered painting away from Byzantine iconography and towards the portrayal of 'real' people and emotions. Room 3 is the most prominent reminder that Siena played a major role in Italian painting. Fourteenth-century works by the **Lorenzetti** brothers and **Simone Martini** (especially his **Annunciation** ★★) show exquisite craftsmanship.

The works of **Botticelli** are collected in Rooms 10 to 14, with **Primavera (Allegory of Spring)** ★★★ and **The Birth of Venus** ★★ his best known. Both were painted in the 1480s; they're striking and easy to appreciate. *Primavera* depicts Venus in the centre, surrounded by classical figures such as Flora

FUN FACT Big Whitey

The Neptune statue in Piazza della Signoria is known as il Biancone, 'Big Whitey'—an allusion to its white marble and large size. The statue has been vandalised six times, notably in 2005 when a hand was snapped off by drunken revellers.

TIP The Children's Museum

The **Museo dei Ragazzi** ★★ (☎ *055 2768224. **www.museiragazzifirenze.it***) organises workshops and events for children—mainly at its base, the **Palazzo Vecchio,** but sometimes at other museums. Most are in Italian, but you can find details of regular English-language tours by visiting the desk by the Palazzo Vecchio ticket booth (no need to pay to enter).

(goddess of spring). Botticelli may have used local beauty Simonetta Vespucci as his model for Flora, and again in *Birth of Venus*, where the goddess of love floats on a scallop shell.

Paintings by **Leonardo Da Vinci** are hung in Room 15. His **Annunciation** ★★ (1475) shows meticulous attention to detail and clever use of perspective (view it from the lower-right), and there's an unfinished **Adoration of the Magi** ★★.

Sadly, you can no longer actually walk through Room 18, the octagonal **Tribuna** ★, but you can view its newly restored glory. Room 21 showcases the different approach taken by Venetian artists, based round colour rather than geometry—notably in Bellini's **Sacred Allegory** ★, painted in the 1490s. The circular **Doni Tondo** ★ (1508) in Room 25 is one of **Michelangelo's** masterful combinations of paint and sculpture, depicting the Holy Family. Room 26 has a collection of **Raphael's** work, including **Pope Leo X with Cardinals Giulio de'Medici and Luigi de'Rossi** ★★. His depictions of this shifty-looking party are magical, as is his recently restored **Madonna of the Goldfinch** (1506) ★. Venetian master **Titian**'s sensual nude, **Venus of Urbino** ★★, the best-selling

Galleria degli Uffizi

postcard in the shop downstairs, is in Room 28.

There's *much* more, including Rembrandt's **Self Portrait as an Old Man** ★ in Room 44, a melancholy depiction of one of the world's greatest painters. **Caravaggio,** who dropped dead in the Tuscan Maremma (p. 161), is on the first floor, although he's outshone by Artemisia Gentileschi's (a rare female) grisly depiction of **Judith Slaying Holofernes** ★.

Time *At least 2 hr.* ***Open*** *8:15am–6:50pm Tues–Sun (until 10pm Tues July–Sept).* ***Adm*** *6.50€, 3.25€ 18–25s.* ***Amenities***

Museo Galileo ★★ AGE 5 & UP

Piazza dei Giudici 1. 055 265311. ***www.museogalileo.it.***

Florence's flagship **science museum** reopened in 2010 after a major revamp—and with a brand-new name to honour the importance of Pisa's great thinker and inventor (p. 119) in the history of European science. The museum's enlightening collection is a trove of fascinating instruments, giant spheres and telescopes—formerly the private collections of Florence's ruling Medici and Lorraine families—housed in an evocative setting straight out of Hogwarts. Helpful English-speaking custodians are on hand to offer explanations and demonstrate the more elaborate machines: children are encouraged to guess what will happen, then work out why. They'll be grimly intrigued by the middle finger of the great man himself, preserved in a glass jar in Room VII.

The museum runs an excellent programme of interactive weekend **educational activities** for children over 6 (in Italian), and 1½-hour family-friendly guided visits of the collection in English. Call *055 294883* or e-mail ***prenotazioni@operalaboratori.com*** to book (7€). Encourage science-minded youngsters to check the museum's **excellent website** ahead of your visit.

Time *1½ hr.* ***Open*** *9:30am–6pm Mon, Wed–Sun, 9:30am–1pm Tues.* ***Adm*** *8€, 5€ ages 7–18.* ***Amenities***

INSIDER TIP

Stately **Piazza della Repubblica,** a few blocks northwest of Piazza della Signoria, is known for its upmarket cafés (p. 69), and also has the old-fashioned Picci **merry-go-round** in one corner, open from 10am until well into the evening every day.

Museo Nazionale del Bargello ★ AGE 8 & UP

Via del Proconsolo 4. 055 2388606. ***www.firenzemusei.it/bargello.***

Fans of sculpture could hardly wish for more atmospheric surroundings in which to admire it than this former prison. Where once its outside was decorated with portraits of condemned men, now the rooms around its inner Gothic courtyard house marbles and bronzes by **Michelangelo, Lorenzo Ghiberti**

(1378–1455) and most notably **Donatello** (1386–1466).

Time** 1½ hr. **Open** 8:15am–5pm Tues–Sat, 1st, 3rd and 5th Mon of month, and 2nd, 4th Sun of month Apr–mid-July, 8:15am–1:50pm rest of year. **Adm** 4€, 2€ ages 18–25. **Amenities

Palazzo Vecchio ★★ AGE 8 & UP

*Piazza della Signoria. 055 2768325. **www.museicivicifiorentini.it/palazzovecchio.***

Dominating the piazza with Arnolfo di Cambio's crenellations and tower, Florence's old **city hall** is primarily an art museum, although part of it still houses the local government. It dates from 1299 and was extended by the ruling Medici family in the 1540s. The private Medici apartments inside can seem rather dry for children, but Giorgio Vasari's frescoes and the coffered ceiling in the **Salone dei Cinquecento** ★ will impress with their giant scale.

Ground-breaking **interactive family events** ★★ (arranged by 'The Children's Museum', p. 53) also make this one of the city's most rewarding attractions for youngsters. The English-language programme includes an interactive **fresco-painting**

The Big Three

Three of Italy's most celebrated Renaissance painters spent formative years in Florence. **Sandro Botticelli** (1444–1510) was the son of a Florentine tanner and spent most of his life in the city, where his enigmatic work ranged from early Renaissance studies to sombre, almost modern expressionism. His paintings exhibit a rare beauty—unlike Michelangelo, he could paint women, even if they all seem to resemble Cate Blanchett. He was a sensitive soul, a bit of an eccentric, and ended life as a pauper, virtually forgotten.

Leonardo Da Vinci (1452–1519), a great friend of Botticelli (although he disliked his work), was born in Vinci (p. 129), the illegitimate son of a peasant girl and a Florentine lawyer. He moved here at 12 and spent his early career in Florence before settling in Milan. Da Vinci was good-looking and self-confident, an intellectual force; his diagrams of machines and mechanical devices are as impressive as his paintings. He was also a bit of dandy.

Da Vinci detested the outstanding talent of the High Renaissance, **Michelangelo Buonarotti** (1475–1564), who was born in Caprese, south of the city, and grew up in Florence among impoverished gentry. He was too obsessed with God for science-minded Leo. At 26, Michelangelo was commissioned to create *David*. He moved to Rome in 1505, where he frescoed the Sistine Chapel, and he left Florence forever in the 1530s. Ruggedly handsome, he was an awkward man with a volatile temperament: his flat nose was broken in a fight on the steps of Santa Maria del Carmine (p. 61).

workshop (1½ hr, over-8s) and the **Fairytale of the Turtle and the Snail,** a 1-hour animated storytelling tour through the *palazzo* (the only event suited to 3–7-year-olds). Costumed guides lead groups on fantastic 1½-hour theatrical tours of the building on **A Guided Tour with Giorgio Vasari** and **An Invitation to Cosimo's Court.** For all tours, you need to **book in advance** (☎ *055 2768224* or e-mail ***info.museoragazzi@comune.fi.it***); tickets cost 8€, 5.50€ children, 22€ family. There's something in English every day.

Time *1½ hr.* ***Open*** *9am–6pm Tues–Sat, 9am–1pm Thurs.* ***Adm*** *6€, 2€ ages 3–17, 14€/16€ family (4/5 people).* ***Amenities***

Santa Croce ★ AGE 7 & UP

Piazza Santa Croce. ☎ *055 244619.* ***www.santacroceopera.it.***

Piazza Santa Croce is best known for its Gothic **church,** a stone edifice constructed for the Franciscans around 1294, with a soaring timbered ceiling and several **frescoes.** Giotto's damaged **Life of St. Francis** ★ is inside the Cappella Bardi, right of the altar; at the end of the same transept, his student Taddeo Gaddi steals the show with exquisite **Scenes from the Life of the Virgin** ★, painted between 1332 and 1338.

The **buried Renaissance celebrities** also hold an appeal for older children. **Michelangelo**'s body was brought here from Rome in 1574, 10 years after his death; his ludicrously ornate tomb was designed by Vasari. Next door is the neoclassical monument to **Dante,** who died in 1321 and is buried in Ravenna. Further up the aisle is the relatively simple white tomb of the writer **Machiavelli** (d. 1527), while **Galileo** is buried on the other side of the nave in another elaborate number topped with a statue of the great scientist (d. 1642); one hand holds a telescope while the other hovers over a globe. As you leave via the cloister, pause by Donatello's 1433 **Annunciation** ★ and Brunelleschi's idealised Renaissance **Cappella Pazzi** ★.

Time *1¼ hr.* ***Open*** *9:30am–5pm Mon–Sat, 1–5:30pm Sun.* ***Adm*** *5€, 3€ ages 11–17.* ***Amenities***

Around Santa Maria Novella

The area between Florence's main train station and the river is best known as a shopping mecca of largely upmarket stores. See p. 68.

Museo di Santa Maria Novella ★ AGE 6 & UP

Piazza Santa Maria Novella. ☎ *055 282187.* ***www.museicivicifiorentini.it/smn.***

One of the less-visited wonders of the city, this frescoed cloister and chapel was part of the Dominican convent of Santa Maria Novella. The **Chiostro Verde** ★ was partly frescoed by famously erratic Paolo Uccello (1397–1475), one of Florence's early pioneers of perspective painting. The extensive damage

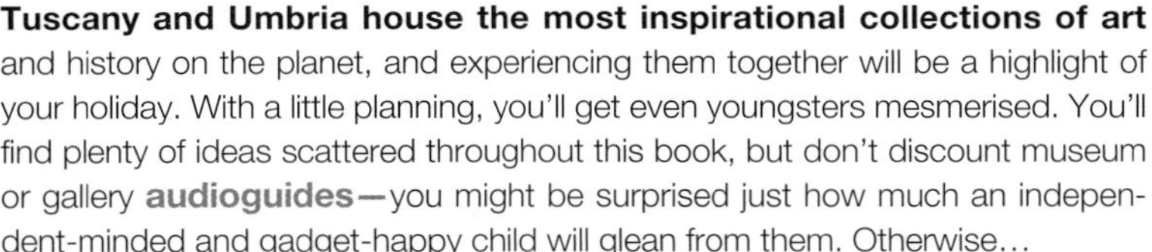

TIP Museums & Galleries with Children

Tuscany and Umbria house the most inspirational collections of art and history on the planet, and experiencing them together will be a highlight of your holiday. With a little planning, you'll get even youngsters mesmerised. You'll find plenty of ideas scattered throughout this book, but don't discount museum or gallery **audioguides**—you might be surprised just how much an independent-minded and gadget-happy child will glean from them. Otherwise…

Get arty Bring drawing materials—few museums will object to your youngster quietly scribbling—and set goals such as finding specific paintings or the work of the most famous painters (see 'The Big Three', p. 55).

Get cameras Cheap digital cameras (or the camera on your mobile phone) can be a great way to engage children. Check photography is allowed first, then get them to snap what they like best to reproduce back at home (or look over in the hotel that night). They could re-create statues or ancient pottery with modelling clay or Plasticine, if you've got room in the suitcase (the flat eight-colour packs of Plasticine are a good size for handbags).

Get creative with treasure trails With a bit of preparation (say, searching the museum's website ahead of a visit), you can knock up a list of 10 or more 'best things to see' to create your own treasure trail, and get each child to tick them off. Multi-coloured clipboards are a good idea. If you don't have time for that, visit the gift shop first, buy postcards and use those instead. You can also get children to keep a record of how many times characters (Mary, David) or scenes (Assumption, Last Supper) appear, and chat about how they differ. Some museums have their own pre-prepared children's trails (*percorsi per bambini*): make the welcome desk your first stop.

Be focused With young children make sure you limit your time in galleries to small doses, focusing on something your child finds appealing: period dresses or dolls; paintings of animals, battles or ships; or even ancient weapons and tools.

---

to his work is the result of the **Great Arno Flood** of 1966—lines still visible on the pillars show just how high the water reached here. The restored **Cappellone degli Spagnoli** ★ was decorated in the 1360s by Andrea di Bonaiuto, whose paintings illustrate complex Biblical arguments, with Dominican saints such as St. Peter Martyr, St. Thomas Aquinas and St. Dominic himself winning the day, of course.

Time *40 min.* ***Open*** *9am–5pm Mon, Tues and Thurs–Sat.* ***Adm*** *2.70€, 1€ ages 4–17.* ***Amenities***

Museo Marino Marini ★

FIND AGE 3 & UP

Piazza San Pancrazio. 055 219432. ***www.museomarinomarini.it****.*

This innovative gallery displays more than 180 works by Marino Marini (1901–80), the Pistoiese sculptor whose recurring themes of horse and rider dominate

Get arty—children can create their own masterpieces

the collection. It's the space, as much as his bronzes, that appeals to children—the restored church has a warren of castle-like walkways and passages, all great fun to explore, and a basement walk-in space devoted to hands-on art **activities for children** ★.

Time *At least 1 hr.* ***Open*** *10am–5pm Mon and Wed–Sat exc. Aug.* ***Adm*** *4€.* ***Amenities***

San Marco & Around

As you walk towards San Marco along Via Cavour, Benozzo Gozzoli's 1459 painted chapel inside the **Palazzo Medici-Riccardi** (*055 2760340.* ***www.palazzomedici.it***. 9am–7pm Thurs–Tues; 7€, 4€ ages 6–12), at no. 3, has an innovation designed to appeal to technophile teens—inside 'Lorenzo's Workshop' are two giant screens showing the fresco cycle, and if you stand on the hotspot in front of them, you can scroll forward and back, or single out areas of the images to hear detailed commentary—all with a wave of your finger. It's one giant **virtual video game** where you direct the *Procession of the Magi*! As well as Gozzoli's fresco, parts of the rest of the building are open to visitors, including architect Michelozzo's sublime courtyard and the Medici state rooms upstairs.

Galleria dell'Accademia ★

AGE 7 & UP

Via Ricasoli 60. 055 2388612. ***www.firenzemusei.it/accademia.***

Each year, many thousands of people visit the Accademia to see just one thing: Michelangelo's 1504 **David** ★★★. The sculptural detail is truly sublime, right down to the veins on David's hands, and make this worth every euro (see 'David, Goliath & Michelangelo', below). More than 4m (13 ft) tall, it took 4 days, ropes, winches, 40 men and a wooden cage to move from the artist's studio into Piazza della

Signoria, where it stood for centuries. Locals immediately dubbed it *Il Gigante* (the giant). When it was transported to the Accademia, special tracks were laid so the statue could be moved by rail truck.

Older children will appreciate the spectacle and reverence accorded the statue. The gallery also contains the **Four Slaves** ★ (or '*Prisoners*'), unfinished expressive figures by Michelangelo, still bearing the rough chisel marks of the master, as well as a collection of pre-Renaissance panels from the 1200s and 1300s. We *strongly* recommend you book tickets in advance (p. 49).

Time** 1 hr. **Open** 8:15am–6:20pm Tues–Sun. **Adm** 6.50€, 3.25€ ages 18–25. **Amenities

Museo di San Marco ★★

AGE 3 & UP

Piazza San Marco. 055 2388608. www.firenzemusei.it/sanmarco.

Housed in the former Dominican convent of San Marco, next to the church, this museum is packed with exquisite art by **Fra' Angelico** (1395–1455), Florence's master of the rich decorative style known as 'international Gothic'. His **Annunciation** ★ on the first-floor wall is what most come to see, but even better are his **Deposition** ★★ and **San Marco Altarpiece** ★★ in the old hospice, on the right by the entrance. Quite novel for youngsters are the 44 frescoed **friars' cells** ★ upstairs. Squeeze inside to view the simple wall-paintings, and imagine months spent in silent contemplation.

David, Goliath & Michelangelo

David's clash with Goliath is one of the most memorable tales in the Old Testament: humble David slew the Philistine champion, a feared warrior and giant, with a single stone from his sling, and went on to replace Saul as king of a united Israel.

Jump forward 2,000 years to 15th-century Florence where David was regarded as a symbol of the city's independent Republican status: little Florence standing proud against the tyrannical bullies of the Papacy and the Holy Roman Empire. Florentine nobles took to commissioning sculptures of their hero: Donatello's bronze *David*, made for Cosimo de' Medici in 1430, was one of the first to evoke the humanist Renaissance style. It's in the **Bargello** (p. 54) along with Andrea Verrocchio's *David* (1476). In 1501 Michelangelo was commissioned to create yet another *David*—unveiled in Piazza della Signoria in 1504. It was moved to the Accademia in 1873.

Don't miss the two **replicas,** one in Piazza della Signoria, the other in Piazzale Michelangelo. Ask the children if they can spot any differences.

Zealous friar Savonarola, who ruled Florence between 1494 and 1498, had a cell here. At the other end are large VIP cells once occupied by the convent's founder, Cosimo de' Medici. Those laden with a **buggy** will find this one of Florence's most pleasant art spots to visit.

Time *1¾ hr.* ***Open*** *8:15am–1:20pm Tues–Fri, 8:15am–6:20pm Sat, 8:15am–1:20pm 1st, 3rd and 5th Mon of month, 8:15am–6:20pm 2nd and 4th Sun of month.* ***Adm*** *4€, 2€ ages 18–25.* ***Amenities***

Museo di Storia Naturale AGE 5 & UP

Via La Pira 4. 055 2346760. ***www.msn.unifi.it.***

Florence's natural history museum is an umbrella organisation for a series of five collections, mostly excellent for children: the **anthropology** (p. 51) and **zoology** (p. 63) collections are elsewhere, but nip into the University of Florence and you'll find two absorbing sections: the **Museo di Mineralogia e Litologia** ★ and the **Museo di Geologia e Paleontologia.**

The **Mineralogia** is a treasure trove for aspiring gemmologists. Raw lumps of hundreds of minerals, and a great display of fluorescence, are followed by a short section showing what minerals look like in their finished state—based on the Medici collection of snuff-boxes, cups and vases. There are a couple of displays little ones are encouraged to touch. The **Geologia** is perfect for children who love fossils, with one of the world's largest collections—including a handful of dinosaur and mammoth skeletons.

Pop into the **Orto Botanico,** around the corner at Via Micheli 3, if you fancy a break in the sun.

Time *About 40 min. each.* ***Open*** *9am–1pm Mon–Tues, Thurs–Sun; 9am–5pm Sat.* ***Adm*** *4€, 2€ ages 6–14, 10€ family.* ***Amenities***

Museo Stibbert ★★ AGE 5 & UP

Via Stibbert 26. 055 486049. ***www.museostibbert.it.*** *Bus: 4.*

This unusual museum is a trek north of the centre, but if any of your children are into castles, knights or Harry Potter, they'll love it. Set in an opulent villa once owned by half-Italian, half-Scot Frederick Stibbert (1838–1906), its rooms are a blend of exotic castle decor and ornate Baroque. Stibbert's eccentric collection of **weaponry** stands out: lances, swords, pikes and muskets, as well as numerous suits of European, Japanese, Middle Eastern and Arabic armour. You have to tour as part of a (fairly relaxed) **escorted group** (maximum 20 people) leaving every 30 minutes and taking about an hour; you get several minutes in each room to wander around alone. There's plenty of space inside but some steps, so it's tricky with a **buggy.**

Time *1 hr.* ***Open*** *10am–2pm Mon–Wed, 10am–6pm Fri–Sun.* ***Adm*** *6€, 4€ ages 3–12.* ***Amenities***

Oltrarno

Oltrarno, the only part of the ancient city south of the **Arno,** is

FUN FACT » Shhhhh!

The enclosed corridor that runs along the top of the Ponte Vecchio is part of the **Corridoio Vasariano,** a private elevated passageway linking the Palazzo Vecchio to the Palazzo Pitti and now hung with the world's best collection of artists' self-portraits. Medici Duke Cosimo I found the idea of mixing with the *hoi polloi* on the way to work rather distressing, and so commissioned Vasari to design his secret VIP route in 1565. It's often possible to **walk** the corridor, although closures for restoration work are common—check ahead by emailing ***firenzemusei@operalaboratori.com***.

best approached by walking across the **Ponte Vecchio** ★. This bridge, a Florentine icon and firm family favourite (a bridge *with shops on it!*), is a medieval legacy groaning with crowds enjoying the views and the gold stores. The current bridge, built in 1345, was the only city bridge spared destruction by the retreating German Army in 1944.

Cappella Brancacci ★★

AGE 12 & UP

Santa Maria del Carmine, Piazza del Carmine. ☎ *055 2768224.* ***www.museicivicifiorentini.it/brancacci.***

The images painted here between 1424 and 1428 stand on the cusp of a new artistic age that we now call the **Renaissance.** Compare the two representations of Adam and Eve up high at the entrance to the chapel. The one on the right, painted by **Masolino,** is a beautifully realised but template image of the couple—do they *really* look tempted? **Masaccio's** depiction of the **Expulsion from Eden** ★★★, meanwhile, is raw with realism and despair; anyone familiar with Edvard Munch's *The Scream* will recognise Eve's expression. Masaccio was the most studied (and copied) artist between Giotto and Michelangelo; had he not died aged just 27, his name would be much more familiar.

Ponte Vecchio, Florence's most ancient bridge

Most of the chapel interior was frescoed by Masolino and Masaccio with *Scenes from the Life of St. Peter*, but it was completed by **Filippino Lippi.** See if you can tell who did what —or grab one of the handy cheat cards (available in English). If you're passing by early during busy months, we recommend you **book** your timed entrance slot for later in the day (you get 15 minutes in the chapel itself, plus a short video and unlimited time to wander the cloister).

Time** 30 min. **Open** 10am–4:30pm Mon, Wed–Sat, 1–4:30pm Sun. **Adm** 4€, 1.50€ ages 4–17. **Amenities

Giardino di Boboli ★★

ALL AGES

Behind Palazzo Pitti. ☎ 055 2388786. www.firenzemusei.it/boboli.

The **Boboli Garden,** laid out in the 16th century behind the Palazzo Pitti, is a great place for children to let off steam. Picnics are discouraged but it's easy to find a secluded spot to munch in peace. There's plenty to see and explore, with grottoes, elaborate water features and statues all over the place. The Mannerist **Grotta Grande** ★ is crammed with almost surreal statuary, including replicas of Michelangelo's *Four Slaves* (originals are in the Accademia, p. 58); it opens on the hour for 15 minutes. The nearby **Fontana di Bacco** features a fat dwarf sitting on a giant turtle; he was modelled on Morgante, a jester at the Medici court. Other

Boboli's Isolotto

highlights include the **Isolotto,** a dreamy island in a pond full of huge goldfish with Giambologna's *L'Oceano* composition at its centre.

A couple of **short, sharp gradients** and pebbled walkways make the Boboli tricky for buggy-pushers.

Time** 1½ hr. **Open** 8:15am–4:30pm daily Nov–Feb, 8:15am–5:30pm Mar, 8:15am–6:30pm Apr, May, Sept and Oct, 8:15am–7:30pm June–Aug, closed 1st and last Mon of month. **Adm** 6€, 3€ ages 18–25 (includes Galleria del Costume, Museo delle Porcellane, Museo degli Argenti). **Amenities

INSIDER TIP

On the same ticket as the Boboli, the Pitti's **Galleria del Costume** ★ exhibits a selection of dresses and robes from the 1700s onwards, while the **Museo degli Argenti** houses silverware and decorative items.

Museo La Specola ★ AGE 8 & UP

*Via Romana 17. ☎ 055 2288251. **www.msn.unifi.it**.*

Parts of this zoology section of Florence's **Museo di Storia Naturale** (p. 60) specialise in morbid fascination, so are **unsuitable for younger children.** Highlights include the 'Room of the Skeletons', a collection of dinosaurs and extinct stuffed animals: the Tasmanian tiger (thylacine), great auk and passenger pigeon. The 600 models of skinned, dissected human arms, legs, cadavers and organs in the **Cere Anatomiche,** once used to train surgeons are, alas, extremely lifelike. The final room is particularly **grisly:** three lurid tableaux created by Gaetano Zumbo for Cosimo III (1670–1723) depicting Florence during the Plague, complete with rats, rotting flesh and heaps of the dead. To top it off, there's a showpiece dissected wax head in the centre of the room. Nice.

Time** 45 min. **Open** 9am–4pm Tues–Sat, 9am–6pm Sun. **Adm** 6€, 3€ ages 6–14, 10€ family. **Amenities

Palazzo Pitti AGE 8 & UP

*Piazza Pitti. ☎ 055 2388614. **www.palazzopitti.it**. Bus: D.*

Built in the 15th century for the Pitti family, the largest palace in Florence was acquired by the Medici family in 1549 and today houses several museums and the **Giardino di Boboli** (p. 62). The most prestigious section, the **Galleria Palatina** ★, is dedicated to the lavish and very personal art collection of the Medici family, displayed in their former apartments. It's a huge and haphazard gathering that appeals to fans of High Renaissance and Baroque painting in particular: Raphael, Titian, Bronzino, Giorgione, Perugino, Rubens and many, many more are all represented. Look out too for insanely intricate intarsia tables in the Florentine style known as *pietre dure*.

Time** 2 hr. **Open** Tues–Sun 8:15am–3:30pm Jan, Feb, Nov and Dec, 8:15am–5:30pm Mar, 8:15am–6:30pm Apr, May, Sept and Oct, 8:15am–7:30pm June–Aug. **Adm** 8.50€, 4.25€ ages 18–25. **Amenities

> **INSIDER TIP**
>
> If you want to tour the Palazzo Pitti, Giardino di Boboli and the other, more specialised museums in the complex, buy the **Cumulativo di Palazzo Pitti** ticket for 11.50€, valid for 3 days.

Piazzale Michelangelo ALL AGES

You know those classic rooftop-and-dome **views** ★★★ of Florence you see *everywhere*? They're snapped from this piazza-cum-car-park on the southern edge of Oltrarno, lined with touristy stalls and a couple of cafés. It's also the home of another huge copy of Michelangelo's *David* (p. 59), looking out across the city to his original home outside the Palazzo Vecchio. The best way to reach the square is to walk up from the river or along the city walls (see below), although bus 13 and City Sightseeing bus A also stop here.

***Time** 30 min.*

Fine Art & Florentine History on a Budget

Florence's many churches are as full of precious paintings as its famous museums. Most are still free to enter, so you can take a crash-course in A-grade art without spending a euro.

Symbolically equidistant from the civic and spiritual hearts of the city, **Orsanmichele,** on Via Arte della Lana, has been a place of importance to Florentines since it was built as a grain store in 1337. The frescoed Gothic vaults and tabernacle are the work of Andrea Orcagna (around 1359), built to honour the *Madonna delle Grazie* panel, to which miraculous cures during the Black Death of 1348 were attributed.

The cavernous Gothic interior of **Santa Trinita** ★, at the bottom of Via de' Tornabuoni, was once home to two of the Uffizi's prize pieces, Gentile da Fabriano's *Adoration of the Magi* and Cimabue's *Santa Trinita Maestà*. Two precious chapels remain: Lorenzo Monaco painted the *Annunciation* and frescoes in the last chapel on the right as you enter, in 1424; sharp eyes examining Domenico Ghirlandaio's 1480s' *Life of St. Francis* will spot Piazza della Signoria looking (broadly) similar to today, though shorn of its statuary. Lorenzo Ghiberti, Michelozzo, Luca della Robbia and Sangallo all worked in Santa Trinita, too.

San Miniato al Monte ★★

ALL AGES

Viale Galileo. 📞 055 2342731. Bus: 12, 13.

A trip to this 11th-century church high above Oltrarno reminds you that, even in Renaissance-obsessed Florence, there remained an appetite for the *truly* ancient. The basilica is built in the **Pisan-Romanesque** style and sports an atmospheric interior decorated with frescoes by Taddeo Gaddi and Spinello Aretino, both 14th-century followers of Giotto.

But more intriguing for children is San Miniato's **monumental cemetery** around the back—one enormous 'city of the dead' whose streets are lined with tombs and mausoleums, elaborate pastiches of every genre of Florentine architecture (with a noticeable preference for the Gothic and the Romanesque). It's a peaceful spot soundtracked by birdsong and the occasional tolling of church bells.

Time** 1¼ hr. **Open** 8am–6pm Mon–Sat, 8am–1pm Sun. **Adm** Free. **Amenities 🛍

INSIDER TIP

San Miniato's Benedictines celebrate mass with **Gregorian chant** at 5:30pm daily.

Indoor Activities

Our favourite spot for a family time-out in Florence is the children's section on the second

Nearby **Ognissanti's** gilded Baroque interior also contains frescoes by Ghirlandaio: his *St. Jerome* faces Botticelli's *St. Augustine* across the nave; both were painted in 1480. Ognissanti was the Vespucci church, and Ghirlandaio's *Madonna della Misericordia* here (second chapel on the right) shows the Virgin Mary protecting the family, including Lisabetta, mother of explorer Amerigo, after whom America was named.

The Chiostro dei Voti at **Santissima Annunziata** ★, in the piazza of the same name, is the place to come to get acquainted with the post-Renaissance painting school known as **'Florentine Mannerism'**. All the giants of the genre frescoed panels here: Andrea del Sarto (1486–1530), Rosso Fiorentino (1494–1540) and Pontormo (1494–1557). Pontormo's masterpiece, however, is at **Santa Felicita,** just across the Ponte Vecchio. This ancient and much remodelled church (Vasari's Corridor, see p. 61, passes across the facade) is notable for the Brunelleschi-built **Cappela Capponi** that houses Pontormo's extraordinary **Deposition** ★ (1528).

Most churches open daily; some are closed on Sundays and all take a long pause for lunch, and ask that you don't make tourist visits during services.

floor of the **Biblioteca delle Oblate** (☎ *055 2616512.* ***www.bibliotecadelleoblate.it***. 9am–11pm Tues–Sat, 2–6:45pm Mon), at Via dell'Oriuolo 26. As well as books (some in English), there are always drawing materials left out and plenty of space to kick-back in a beanbag. The cafeteria on the loggia-cum-terrace serves the usual snacks plus pasta dishes and other simple lunches for 6€ to 7€—and there's a baby-change facility.

The most convenient ***ludoteca*** (play-centre) for visitors is **La Bottega dei Ragazzi** ★ at Via de Fibbai 2 (☎ *055 2478386.* ***www.labottegageiragazzi.it***. 9am–1pm and 4–7pm Mon–Sat), by Piazza Santissima Annunziata. It's free; just drop in and make use of the space and toys. On Saturdays, the Bottega stages 1½ hour creative activities for children aged 3 to 11, including art, history and music (you don't have to stay with them). Call in advance to book: once a month they're in English, costing 10€ per child.

Spectator Sports

Italy's *Serie A* is one of the most exciting **football** (soccer) leagues in the world. The Florence team is **Fiorentina,** known as *I Viola* for their violet-coloured shirts. They usually play alternate Sundays during the season at the Stadio Comunale Artemio

Franchi, near Campo di Marte. To get there from Santa Maria Novella, take a train (5 min) to Campo di Marte or bus **52** or **54** on matchdays (25 min).

Italians do take their children to games, but although Fiorentina has a decent safety record, it's rare to see under-8s. Check with the tourist office about the visiting teams, as some games (such as those against **Juventus**) can be feisty. There's plenty more Fiorentina information on the official club website, ***www.violachannel.tv***.

Chiosco degli Sportivi (*055 292363.* 10am–7:30pm Tues–Sat, 10am–12:30pm Sun during season) at Via degli Anselmi 1, a booth in an alley off Piazza della Repubblica, sells match tickets. Ask for a *tribuna tranquilla* if you're attending with children and want to avoid the noisy *curva* and its fanatical devotees. Tickets cost upwards of 30€. There's not much food at the ground, so bring snacks. For merchandise, see ***www.fiorentinastore.com*** or head to **Ale' Viola** at Via del Corso 69r, where small Fiorentina shirts cost upwards of 10€.

For Active Families

Cycling

Although there's little joy in pedalling round its crowded *centro storico*, Florence is developing an ambitious network of **peripheral cycle routes** that offer a break from indoor sightseeing for active families; route maps are available at tourist offices (p. 38), or download one from ***www.muoversiafirenze.it/materiali/piste_ciclabile.pdf***. Among the best is the **Ciclopista dell'Arno,** running 12km (7 miles) along the banks of the river.

There are four **Punti Biciclette** (bike points) around the city, where you can hire bikes (adult-sized only) for 8€/day or 1.50€/hour. You must leave a photocopy of your passport and return cycles before closing time. The most convenient is in front of the train station at Piazza della Stazione (*055 6505295*; 7:30am–7pm Mon–Sat, plus 9am–7pm Sun in summer).

For trips into Chianti, **Florence by Bike,** Via San Zanobi 120r (*055 488992.* ***www.florencebybike.it***), arranges cycle tours in English or rentals only from 3€/hour to 14.50€/day. Their website suggests some ride maps. **I Bike Italy** (*055 0123994.* ***www.ibikeitaly.com***) also runs a day-long excursion into the Chianti hills. Children need to be about 12+ to complete a Chianti ride.

> **INSIDER TIP**
>
> Note that wearing a **cycle helmet** is obligatory in Italy, although plenty of locals don't bother.

A Walk along the Walls

If your children still have energy after a trip to the Boboli (p. 62), up the dose of fresh air by walking along the southern edge of the old walls to Piazzale

TIP The Red & the Black

Somewhat eccentrically, Florence's central streets have two separate sequences of numbers for buildings: red (suffixed 'r') and black (no suffix). Work out which sequence you want and ignore all other numbers.

Michelangelo (p. 63). This is a quiet part of the city with fine views and lanes lined with olive trees. From the back of the Boboli, signs lead around the solid-looking **Forte di Belvedere** (a star-shaped fortress dating from 1590) and along the narrow lane on the other side: here signs point down the hill to **Giardino Bardini,** but turn right instead to Porta San Giorgio, the old gate.

From the gate follow the road downhill to the left (Via Belvedere), along the base of the impressive walls. It's not busy, but watch out for the occasional speeding Fiat. At the bottom of the hill (Porta San Miniato) turn right until you come to the steps on the left (Via San Salvatore al Monte)—it's a short but steep climb up here past the **rose garden** (open May–July) to the *piazzale*, where **Ristorante Michelangelo** is a convenient ice cream and coffee stop.

The Parco delle Cascine

The largest park in Florence, **Parco delle Cascine** along the northern bank of the river Arno west of the centre, is a good place to picnic, play on **swings and slides,** or take a dip in the open-air **swimming pool,** Le Pavoniere, Viale della Catena 2 (*055 333979*). The park is safe and popular with local families during the day, but don't linger after **dark.**

Trip Out of Town

The ancient Etruscan settlement of **Fiesole** ★ offers a welcome change of pace from Florence itself and an escape from the high-season crowds. The village, 300m (nearly 1,000ft) up in the hills north of the city, offers scintillating **views** ★ back over the entire city from beside the Convento di San Francesco, cooling breezes, plus two minor museums and an open-air archaeological zone (see ***www.fiesolemusei.it*** for details). Fiesole's **tourist office** (*055 5961323;* 9:30am–6:30pm Mon–Fri, 10am–6pm Sat, 10am–1pm and 2–6pm Sun Apr–Oct; slightly shorter hours outside tourist season) is at Via Portigiani 3, next to the archaeological area. Bus **7** from Santa Maria Novella station whisks you to Fiesole (20 min)—with older children, you can comfortably walk all or part of the route back downhill.

Shopping

Some parts of the centre can be great for retail therapy. **San Lorenzo market,** in the streets

TIP Outlets in Style

Serious shoppers can take things up a notch at one of Tuscany's luxury designer outlet malls. Best of the bunch is **The Mall** (***www.themall.it***. 10am–7pm daily exc. public hols), a half-hour southeast of the city in Leccio Reggello. Units include Bottega Veneta, Stella McCartney, Gucci, Armani, Dior and about 20 others, and there are steep discounts off last season's threads for women, men and children.

With 1 day's notice, you can pre-book a shuttle bus to collect you from any Florence hotel (☎ *055 8657775* or email ***info@themall.it***; 25€ pp, 15€ ages 4–12, free under-4s), or take the train from Santa Maria Novella to Rignano sull'Arno then a short cab ride.

around the church of the same name, is the place for touristy trinkets, cheap leather and souvenir T-shirts for youngsters. The **Mercato Centrale** ★, on Via dell'Ariento, is a wonderland of Tuscan food—salami, cheeses, agricultural produce, wine, and much more (p. 73).

For *haute couture*, head to **Via de' Tornabuoni:** Prada, Emilio Pucci, Salvatore Ferragamo and others are all there. **Via della Vigna Nuova** also packs a high-style punch.

The **Cascine market** in the Parco delle Cascine every Tuesday morning has stalls selling good-value clothes and shoes. Mother-and-baby chain **Prénatal** (***www.prenatal.com***) has its best central store at Via Brunelleschi 22.

Alice's Masks ★

Via Faenza 72r. ☎ *055 287370.* ***www.alicemasks.com***.

Established by master craftsman Agostino Dessi and his daughter Alice, this wonderful little shop is crammed with handmade papier-mâché masks in Venetian *Carnevale* and *Commedia dell'arte* styles.

Open *9am–1pm and 3:30–7:30pm Mon–Sat.* ***Credit*** *AE, MC, V.*

Città del Sole

Via dei Cimatori 21r. ☎ *055 2776372.* ***www.cittadelsole.it***.

This old-fashioned chain toy store sells wooden puzzles, board games, puppets, science kits and (crucially) bubbles (*bolle*)!

Open *10am–7:30pm Mon–Sat.* ***Credit*** *AE, MC, V.*

Coin

Via dei Calzaiuoli 56r. ☎ *055 280531.* ***www.coin.it***.

The city's top department store has a strong children's section and a baby room.

Open *10am–8pm Mon–Sat, 10:30am–8pm Sun.* ***Credit*** *AE, MC, V.*

Ferrari ★

Via degli Strozzi 4R. ☎ *055 2399125.* ***www.ferrari.com***.

This is a must-stop for speed freaks for the sheer wow factor of the racing cars on display and the novelty value of the merchandise, which includes everything from Ferrari buggies and clothing to children's stuff ranging from ride-on cars to teddy bears, toys and games.

Open *10am–8pm Mon–Sat, 10:30am–8pm Sun.* ***Credit*** *AE, MC, V.*

Le 18 Lune FIND

Via Romana 18r. 055 5120306.

Trinkets, craft cards, necklaces, leather-bound diaries and other lovely things for girls, most at pocket-money prices.

Open *10am–2pm and 3:30–7:30pm Mon–Fri, 10am–6:30pm Sat.*

Paperback Exchange

Via delle Oche 4r. 055 293460. ***www.papex.it.***

English-language books aren't cheap in Florence, but if you're in need, Papex has the best range of fiction and non-fiction in town—including for children.

Open *9am–7:30pm Mon–Fri, 10am–7:30pm Sat.* ***Credit*** *AE, MC, V.*

Scuola del Cuoio ★

Piazza Santa Croce 16. 055 244534. ***www.leatherschool.com.***

Florence's training school for leather artisans operates this shop and open workshop behind Santa Croce church. It's not cheap, but everything from belts and bags to coats and accessories is handmade on the premises. There are small items such as bracelets and change-purses for less than 10€.

Open *9:30am–6pm Mon–Sat, 10am–6pm Sun (closed Sun Nov–Mar).* ***Credit*** *AE, MC, V.*

FAMILY-FRIENDLY DINING

Florentine cuisine is among the simplest and tastiest in Italy, although tourism has made bargains in the *centro storico* elusive. Most restaurants open solely for lunch and dinner, which means **eating late:** we've noted some exceptions below. Snack places are generally open all afternoon.

Snacks, Cafés & Food-on-the-Go

Florence is packed with cafés and snack bars, ranging from the elegant and expensive to cheap-and-simple pizza-slice parlours. Top of the heap are the posh cafés that ring **Piazza della Repubblica,** the ancient heart of the city. They are expensive but worth at least one trip for the experience: **Gilli** ★ is the oldest, established in 1733 with an opulent interior and terrace, best visited for its sublime (but pricey) hot chocolate in five flavours. Slightly less pretentious, **Giubbe Rosse** across the piazza at no. 14r has tables outside and a similar café-society atmosphere; ditto **Rivoire** in Piazza della Signoria.

For an earthier snack experience, make for **Pugi** ★, famed for its *schiacciata alla Fiorentina*, sweetish olive oil flatbread loaded with toppings. The branch at Piazza San Marco 9b is open 7:45am to 8pm Monday to Friday, 7:45am to 2:15pm Saturday; you take a ticket and

FLORENCE ACCOMMODATION & DINING

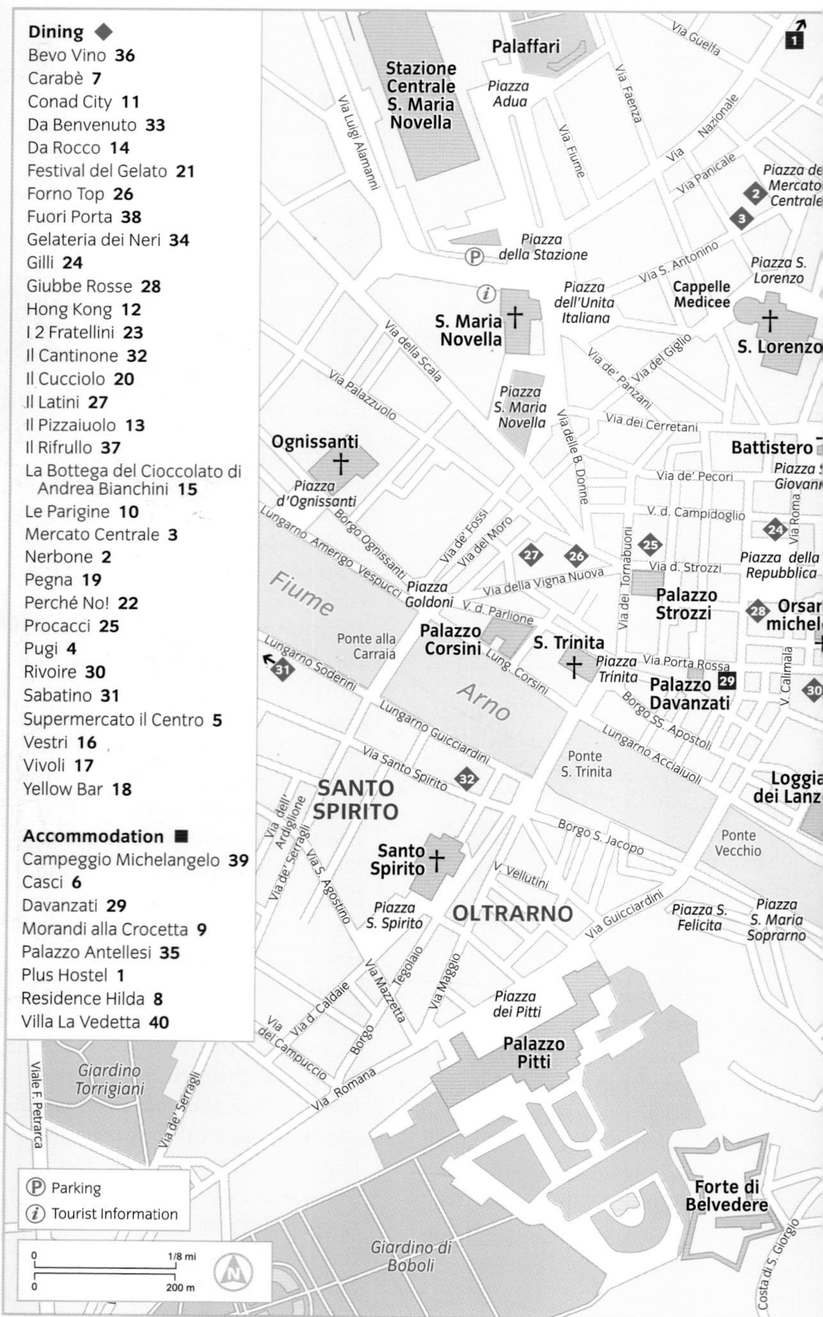

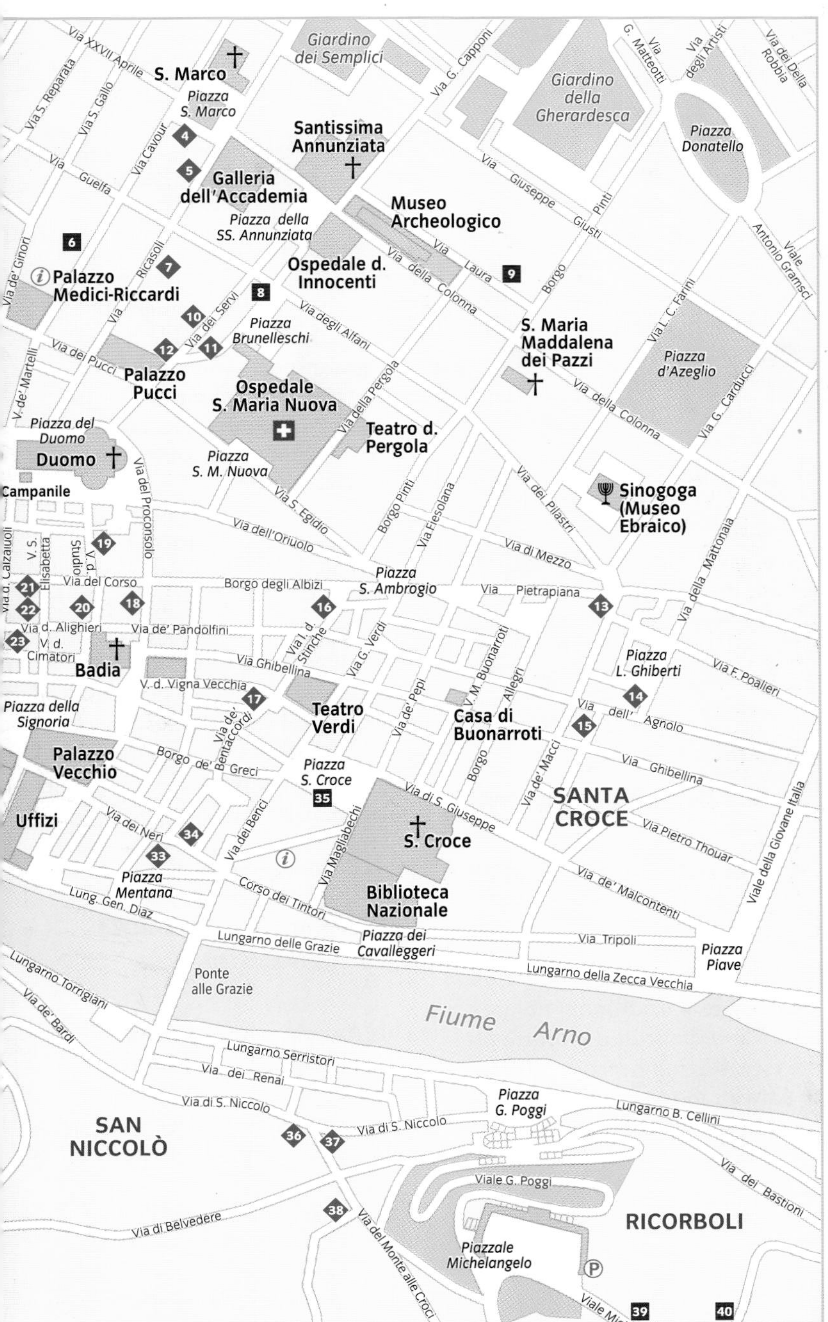
S. Marco
Piazza S. Marco
Giardino dei Semplici
Santissima Annunziata
Galleria dell'Accademia
Piazza della SS. Annunziata
Museo Archeologico
Ospedale d. Innocenti
Giardino della Gherardesca
Piazza Donatello
Palazzo Medici-Riccardi
Piazza Brunelleschi
Palazzo Pucci
Ospedale S. Maria Nuova
Piazza S. M. Nuova
Teatro d. Pergola
S. Maria Maddalena dei Pazzi
Piazza d'Azeglio
Sinogoga (Museo Ebraico)
Piazza del Duomo
Duomo
Campanile
Piazza S. Ambrogio
Piazza L. Ghiberti
Badia
Piazza della Signoria
Palazzo Vecchio
Uffizi
Teatro Verdi
Casa di Buonarroti
Piazza S. Croce
S. Croce
SANTA CROCE
Biblioteca Nazionale
Piazza Mentana
Piazza dei Cavalleggeri
Piazza Piave
Ponte alle Grazie
Fiume Arno
Piazza G. Poggi
SAN NICCOLÒ
RICORBOLI
Piazzale Michelangelo
Via XXVII Aprile
Via S. Reparata
Via S. Gallo
Via Cavour
Via Guelfa
Via G. Capponi
Via Giuseppe Giusti
Borgo Pinti
Via G. Matteotti
Via degli Artisti
Via dei Della Robbia
Viale Antonio Gramsci
Via L. C. Farini
Via G. Carducci
Via della Colonna
Via Laura
Via Ricasoli
Via dei Servi
Via degli Alfani
Via de' Ginori
Via dei Pucci
V. de' Martelli
Via della Pergola
Via del Proconsolo
Via S. Egidio
Via dell'Oriuolo
Borgo Pinti
Via Fiesolana
Via dei Pilastri
Via di Mezzo
Via della Mattonaia
Via d. Calzaiuoli
V. S. Elisabetta
V. d. Studio
Via del Corso
Borgo degli Albizi
Via Pietrapiana
Via d. Alighieri
Via de' Pandolfini
V. d. Cimatori
Via Ghibellina
Via I. d. Stinche
Via G. Verdi
Via M. Buonarroti
Via F. Poalieri
V. d. Vigna Vecchia
Via de' Bentaccordi
Via de' Pepi
Via dell' Agnolo
Borgo Allegri
Borgo de' Greci
Via de' Macci
Via di S. Giuseppe
Via dei Neri
Via dei Benci
Via Magliabechi
Via Pietro Thouar
Viale della Giovane Italia
Via de' Malcontenti
Corso dei Tintori
Lung. Gen. Diaz
Lungarno delle Grazie
Via Tripoli
Lungarno della Zecca Vecchia
Lungarno Torrigiani
Via de' Bardi
Lungarno Serristori
Via dei Renai
Via di S. Niccolo
Lungarno B. Cellini
Via dei Bastioni
Viale G. Poggi
Via di Belvedere
Via del Monte alle Croci
Viale Mic
4
5
6
7
8
9
10
11
12
13
14
15
16
17
18
19
20
21
22
23
33
34
35
36
37
38
39
40

wait for your number to be called. **Forno Top** at Via della Spada 23r (7:30am–1:30pm and 5–7:30pm Mon–Sat) is another no-nonsense bakery serving *schiacciata*, as well as *focaccia* and pizza.

For any of 30 filled sandwich rolls washed down with a 'shot' of Chianti, all for less than 4€, join the lunchtime queue at **I 2 Fratellini** ★ (***www.iduefratellini.com***. 9am–8pm Mon–Sat), at Via dei Cimatori 38r. **Procacci** ★ at Via de' Tornabuoni 64r (10:30am–8pm Mon–Sat exc. Aug) is best known for its drool-worthy *tartufati*, truffle-butter rolls. Children also love **Il Cucciolo**, at Via del Corso 25r (closed Sun), for the *bomboloni*: plain, cream or choc-filled doughnuts made upstairs and tossed down a tube, still piping hot.

Restaurants

Near the Duomo & Piazza della Signoria

Da Benvenuto ★ VALUE TUSCAN

Via de' Neri 47/Via Della Mosca 16r. ☎ 055 214833.

This no-frills trattoria is the closest thing to a **traditional neighbourhood diner** in the centre of the city, serving hearty portions of Tuscan food in cosy surroundings. The best pasta dishes are old favourites ravioli and gnocchi, but the *simpatico* staff are used to serving children and happily whip up plain spaghetti with tomato sauce on demand. To branch out into more traditional Tuscan cooking, there's a good 12.50€ set menu.

***Open** 12:30–3pm and 7–10:30pm Mon, Tues and Thurs–Sat. **Main Courses** 6€–12€.*

Hong Kong CHINESE

*Via dei Servi 35r. ☎ 055 2398235. **www.ristorantehongkong.com**.*

It might seem like sacrilege, but Florence is a good place for those looking for a change of cuisine: the aroma inside Hong Kong transports you away from those trattoria staples the moment you enter. The nominally **Cantonese kitchen** knocks out favourites from all over China, with a slight but discernible Italian bias (be sure to specify it's noodles you want, not pasta). The excellent food includes succulent spring rolls, steamed dumplings and a vast range of noodle or rice dishes. The sizzling plates of beef with pepper are a good choice, and you can't go wrong with the pork.

***Open** Noon–2:30pm and 7:30pm–midnight daily. **Main courses** 6€–12€. **Credit** AE, MC, V.*

Yellow Bar VALUE PIZZA/PASTA

Via del Proconsolo 39r. ☎ 055 211766.

This American-style restaurant is a great option for children for two reasons: its tasty hamburgers and pizzas provide a break from the predominantly Italian restaurants in town, and it's **open all day.** It also knocks out a decent selection of pastas, such as homemade spaghetti with prawns. The diner-like

TIP Pack a Picnic Treat

The indoor Mercato Centrale ★ is chock-full of Tuscan specialities, multi-coloured pastas, bread, cheese and meats downstairs, with fruit and vegetables upstairs, as well as nuts, wine, ready-made sandwiches and food stalls; it's open 7am to 2pm Monday to Saturday plus 4 to 8pm on winter Saturdays. **Pegna** (***www.pegna.it***. 9:30am–5:30pm Mon–Sat) at Via dello Studio 8 is an all-purpose picnic-packing shop, selling cold cuts, cheeses, jarred sweets, wine, truffled everything, and more (but no bread), in the shadow of Brunelleschi's dome.

For the basics, including cold drinks on the move, there are several **supermarkets** close to the *centro storico*: **Supermercato il Centro** (***www.ilcentro.biz***) has 10 branches, including Via Ricasoli 109r opposite the Accademia, Via Donizetti 64, and Via dei Ginori 41r (all 8am–8pm Mon–Sat, 10am–7pm Sun). **Conad City** has a branch at Via dei Servi 56r, open 8:30am–8pm Mon–Sat.

The most exotic **chocolatier** in Florence is **La Bottega del Cioccolato di Andrea Bianchini** ★ at Via de'Macci 50 (10am–noon and 4–7:30pm Tues–Sat), with a small but exquisite range of handmade chocolates. For everything cocoa, including superb **hot chocolate** closer to the centre, try **Vestri,** Borgo degli Albizi 11r.

---

hall has comfy seating and wooden tables.

***Open** 12:30pm–2am Wed–Mon. **Main courses** 6.50€–18€. **Credit** AE, MC, V.*

Near Santa Maria Novella

Il Latini ★★ TUSCAN

*Via dei Palchetti 6r. ☏ 055 210916. **www.illatini.com.***

Opened in 1950, this is one of the most popular tourist haunts in Florence but is an essential experience nevertheless. Children love the **cellar-like surroundings,** the hams hanging from the ceiling and the bustling atmosphere. Diners are often thrust together on communal tables where large portions of Tuscan favourites are delivered with gusto. The menu is short and focused, with a handful of main dishes, few costing more than 15€—a *primo* is 5€ to 9€. It's all good, but the ravioli always wins rave reviews and the *bistecca* is a safe bet for main.

***Open** 12:30–2pm and 7:30–10:30pm Tues–Sun; closed 2 weeks in Aug. **Main courses** 14€–22€. **Credit** AE, MC, V.*

Nerbone ★ FLORENTINE LUNCH

Mercato Centrale (Via dell'Ariento entrance, stand 292). ☏ 055 219949.

One of several no-nonsense snack bars inside the Mercato Centrale (p. 73), this stall established in 1872 serves the best **bagnato** (boiled-beef sandwich with gravy) in town. It makes a tasty, convenient lunch stop for families but is a little adventurous at the same time. If the *bagnato* looks fatty,

Ice Cream Heaven

Italy gave the world pasta, pizza and the cappuccino, but *gelato,* created in the 16th century, has proved its most addictive export as far as *bambini* are concerned. As a general rule, signs proclaiming *produzione propria* (homemade) are an indication of quality. Cones range from a standard 1.80€ to 8€ for *un gigante*.

Carabè ★ Via Ricasoli 60r. The most celebrated **Sicilian** ice cream in the city. ***Open*** 10am–midnight daily mid-May–Sept, 10am–8pm Tues–Sun Oct and Nov, mid-Feb–mid-May.

Festival del Gelato ★★ Via del Corso 75r. Almost as good as Vivoli (below), with more choice (70+ extraordinary flavours) and a better location between the Duomo and the Uffizi. ***Open*** 11am–1am daily summer, Tues–Sun winter.

Ice Cream Heaven—Festival del Gelato

Gelateria dei Neri ★★ Via dei Neri 20–22r. Vivoli gets more acclaim, but just as many locals think this is the best in town. Ricotta and fig *gelato* is our favourite here. ***Open*** 11am–midnight daily.

Le Parigine ★★ Via dei Servi 41r. ***www.gelaterieartigianali.com***. A shop committed to quality local and organic ingredients where possible, offering fewer, but more interesting, flavours, such as pine nut, *After Eight* or chocolate orange. ***Open*** 11am–11pm daily (to 8pm out of high season).

Perché No! ★ Via dei Tavolini 19r. ***www.percheno.firenze.it***. A shop knocking out great flavours since the 1930s: try the rum-laced tiramisù or *cioccolato bianco* (white chocolate). ***Open*** 11am–midnight Wed–Mon, closed Nov.

Vivoli ★★ Via Isola delle Stinche 7r. ***www.vivoli.it***. Often claimed to be the best ice-cream place in Italy—and one confident enough about its wares to ban cones. Make a pilgrimage at least once to say you've been. ***Open*** 9am–9pm Tues–Sun, until midnight Apr–Oct.

there are plenty of other good-value pasta and sandwich options on offer, from 6.50€. Just five tables stand opposite the stall, so get here before the rush (12:30pm) to sit down.

Open *7am–2pm Mon–Sat, closed 3 weeks in Aug.* ***Main courses*** *3€–7€.*

Near Santa Croce

Da Rocco ★ VALUE FLORENTINE LUNCH

Mercato di Sant'Ambrogio.

This tiny trattoria, one of the **best bargains** in the city, is a trek from the centre, tucked away in the heart of Mercato di Sant'Ambrogio, an indoor food hall east of Santa Croce. It's a great place to introduce the children to a proper local eating experience, with simple food they're bound to enjoy. Behind the take-away counter is an enclosed seating area with booths big enough for four. Staff are friendly but rushed off their feet, so don't expect any special attention—luckily, the menu is in English too. Hearty dishes of lasagne, various pastas or roast meat straight from the market rarely cost more than 5€. Get here before 1pm if you want a table.

***Open** Noon–2:30pm Mon–Sat. **Main courses** 3.50€–4.50€. **Credit** MC, V.*

Il Pizzaiuolo ★ GOURMET PIZZA

Via de' Macci 113r. ☎ 055 241171.

For a special pizza night, this is the place—the only **Neapolitan pizzeria** in the old city. Legend has it that pizza was created in Naples in the 18th century: the Margherita topped with basil, mozzarella and tomatoes is named after the Savoy queen, who visited the city in 1869 (to remind her of the new *tricolore* Italian flag). Honouring this tradition, pizzas here are the real deal. A Margherita is 5.50€, but there are another 20 mouthwatering options. Reservations are essential for dinner.

***Open** 12:30–2:30pm and 7:30pm–midnight Mon–Sat; closed Aug. **Main courses** 6€–14€.*

Oltrarno

Il Cantinone ★ VALUE FLORENTINE LUNCH

Via Santo Spirito 6r. ☎ 055 218898.

This old cellar *osteria* is popular with students and tourists, partly for its *crostoni*—thick slabs of bread smothered with ham, tomatoes, sausage and cheese. The long tables mean plenty of space for families. Food is simple, cheap and unbelievably tasty: most lunch platters will set you back no more than 6€ to 7€ and are more than enough for small children—split them in half for toddlers. Cantinone also serves more substantial meals.

***Open** 12:30–2:30pm and 7:30–10:30pm Tues–Sun. **Main courses** 6€–12€. **Credit** AE, MC, V.*

Sabatino ★★ VALUE FLORENTINE

Via Pisana 2r. ☎ 055 225955.

It feels way off the tourist trail—and indeed it is—but a mere 10-minute walk from the Cappella Brancacci and you're in a **Florentine world before the advent of mass tourism.** Sabatino is the kind of place where local families and work colleagues meet to eat good food in simple surroundings, for a modest outlay. Dishes are straightforward and Florentine: *tortellini in brodo* (in broth), a

TIP The Best Wine Bars in Town

If you're looking to socialise and sip some local *vino rosso*, head for the buzzy Porta San Miniato corner of Oltrarno. A cluster of excellent wine bars here also serve food—some substantial Tuscan dishes as well as *antipasti* platters to share. Our favourite well-stocked *cantinas* are **Bevo Vino** ★ (*055 2001709*), Via San Niccolò 59r; **Il Rifrullo** (*055 2342621*), Via San Niccolò 57r; and **Fuori Porta** ★ (*055 2342483*), Via Monte alle Croci 10. For those with babysitters, it goes on here 'til late.

selection of pasta dishes for less than 4€, daily-changing roast meats such as stuffed chicken, guinea fowl or veal. Whitewashed walls hung with farming implements remind you that it's all about the produce.

***Open** Noon–2:30pm and 7:15–10pm Mon–Fri. **Main courses** 3.70€–5.20€. **Credit** AE, MC, V.*

FAMILY-FRIENDLY ACCOMMODATION

Staying in Florence is **expensive** and, although there are some good-value, family-friendly hotels around the city, an **apartment rental** has major advantages, even for a very short visit: you'll get a proper kitchen, more space (usually with a separate room for the children), more freedom to work to your own timetable, and cheaper rates for longer stays. We've picked out a couple of our favourite apartment units below; reputable local rental agencies include **Florence and Abroad** (*www.florenceandabroad.com*), **Windows on Italy** (*www.windowsonitaly.com*), **Rentxpress** (*www.rentxpress.com*) and **Cross-Pollinate** (*www.cross-pollinate.com*). Wherever you choose, **book well ahead** for high-season arrivals: May, September and especially June are very busy.

APARTMENTS

Palazzo Antellesi ★★

Piazza Santa Croce 21. 055 244456. www.florencerentals.net.

These traditionally decorated apartments in a 16th-century frescoed *palazzo* are perfect for families of all sizes: the largest sleeps seven to eight, the smallest three to four. All have fully equipped kitchens. The **Donatello** suite, ideal for large groups, is arranged around an inner courtyard on the second floor; you also get a small terrace and spacious dining room with a table for 12, three bedrooms and three bathrooms. Two-bedroom **Belvedere** also has a sun terrace. All feature tall windows and tasteful furniture in period style: frescoed ceilings, wooden beams and antique chairs, plus plenty of potted plants.

Apartments** 13 (sleep 3–8). **Rates** 1740€–5000€/wk. **Amenities** **In apartment

Residence Hilda ★★

*Via dei Servi 40. ☎ 055 288021. **www.residencehilda.it**.*

What these elegant apartments lack in period charm they make up for it with space and crisp, **modern** facilities—and the fact that they're available by the night. All have large living areas with a double or twin sofa-bed, big bathrooms, well-equipped kitchens, and a double bedroom; suites are big enough to set up home in. The airy, **cool design** includes stripped and polished wood floors, cream walls and sliding divider doors. The location, between the Duomo and Santissima Annunziata, is ideal.

Apartments** 12. **Rates** Doubles 150€–280€, family suites 250€–350€/ night. Cots and highchairs free. Extra bed 30€, under-12s 20€. **Credit** AE, MC, V. **Amenities** **In apartment

CAMPSITES & HOSTELS

Campeggio Michelangelo ★

*Viale Michelangelo 80. ☎ 055 6811977. **www.ecvacanze.it**.*

Basing yourself in Oltrarno at the city's favourite **campsite** is still a popular option, with good reason: Michelangelo is pleasantly surrounded by gardens and olive trees, a short bus ride (12 or 13) from the centre, and views are stupendous. Unsurprisingly, it's packed in high season. Renting the comfortable two- or three-person tents, with firm camp-beds with sheets and pillows, is naturally more expensive than pitching your own or parking a camper. There's also a **playground;** the restaurant 50m (164 ft) down the road (offering a 10% discount with a camp pass) has a tennis court and football field.

Open camping** Sleeps 1,000. **Rates** Adults 9.30€–10.90€, children 2–12 4.60€–5.60€, pitch 11.40€–13.40€, car 5.70€, tent hire (2 people) 36€, (3 people) 46.50€. **Credit** MC, V. **Amenities

Plus Hostel

*Via Santa Caterina D'Alessandria 15. ☎ 055 4628934. **www.plusflorence.com**.*

Though lacking a little in character, the rooms at this lively, modern 'flashpacking' hostel are ample in size and clean, and come with hotel accoutrements (towels, linen). Triples have a three-berth bunk (double down, single up) with plenty of floor-space for a cot (bring your own). The phenomenal **services** beat those offered at most hotels in town—a pool, a Turkish bath, a mini-spa and beauty salon, and free Wi-Fi throughout. Front-facing rooms have more traffic noise.

Rooms** 110. **Rates** Double 29.50€–65€, triple 25€–84€. Breakfast 5€. **Credit** MC, V. **Amenities** **In room

HOTELS/BED & BREAKFASTS

Casci VALUE

*Via Cavour 13. ☎ 055 211686. **www.hotelcasci.com**.*

This maze-like 15th-century *palazzo* hotel is **great value,** especially outside high season. It was owned by the composer Rossini in the 19th century, and rich frescoes are visible on the ceilings. Its spacious triples and quads are mostly very quiet; all rooms are clean and simply decorated with tiled floors and comfy beds. Best for families are **28** and **29,** with a two-room, suite-style configuration. In low season, the hotel sometimes supplies one free museum ticket per guest for stays of three nights or more.

Rooms *26.* ***Rates*** *Double 80€–150€, triple 100€–190€, quad 120€–230€.* ***Credit*** *AE, MC, V.* ***Amenities*** ***In room***

Davanzati ★★ VALUE

Via Porta Rossa 5. 055 286666. ***www.hoteldavanzati.it.***

A dizzying array of recently renovated rooms, each high spec, plus a great location and unbeatable value for money make this our favourite family hotel in the *centro storico*. All rooms come with LCD TV, PlayStation and a **Wi-Fi-enabled laptop** as standard. No two units in the sympathetically converted *palazzo* are the same; just tell staff your party details and they'll advise on the most suitable. Our favourite is room **100,** in light wood with cream fabrics and multiple split-levels plus a private parents' bedroom.

Rooms *21.* ***Rates*** *Double 120€–188€, quad 150€–312€. Cots free.* ***Credit*** *AE, MC, V.* ***Amenities*** ***In room***

Morandi alla Crocetta ★

Via Laura 50. 055 2344747. ***www.hotelmorandi.it.***

The characterful rooms in this former convent are tastefully furnished in a blend of antique and modern influences—Persian rugs, religious relics, eccentric floor-plans, alcoves and wooden beams add to an **authentically historic** feel. Larger rooms are perfect for a family of four (with space for a cot in addition); aim for one that has a **patio,** with table, chairs and plants to add a homey feel. The hotel welcomes young children and will even supply books and furry toys on arrival if requested in advance.

Rooms *10.* ***Rates*** *Double 110€–220€, triple 130€–295€, quad 150€–370€. Cot 20€.* ***Credit*** *AE, MC, V.* ***Amenities*** ***In room***

Villa La Vedetta ★★

Viale Michelangiolo 78. 055 681631. ***www.villalavedettahotel.com.***

The city's best **boutique hotel** for families occupies two regal neo-Renaissance villas high above Oltrarno. Family suites are split-level with one or two marble bathrooms, decked out in cool creams and greys with dashes of exuberant colour. Best is **Bellavista**—when you see the view over Florence's rooftops, you'll see how it got its name. Public spaces, including the 'Winter Garden' breakfast room and panoramic pool, are equally chic. Book early for the best deal.

Rooms *18.* ***Rates*** *Doubles 189€–1100€, suites 499€–2000€. Cots free.* ***Credit*** *AE, MC, V.* ***Amenities*** ***In room***

4 Siena & the Central Hill-Towns

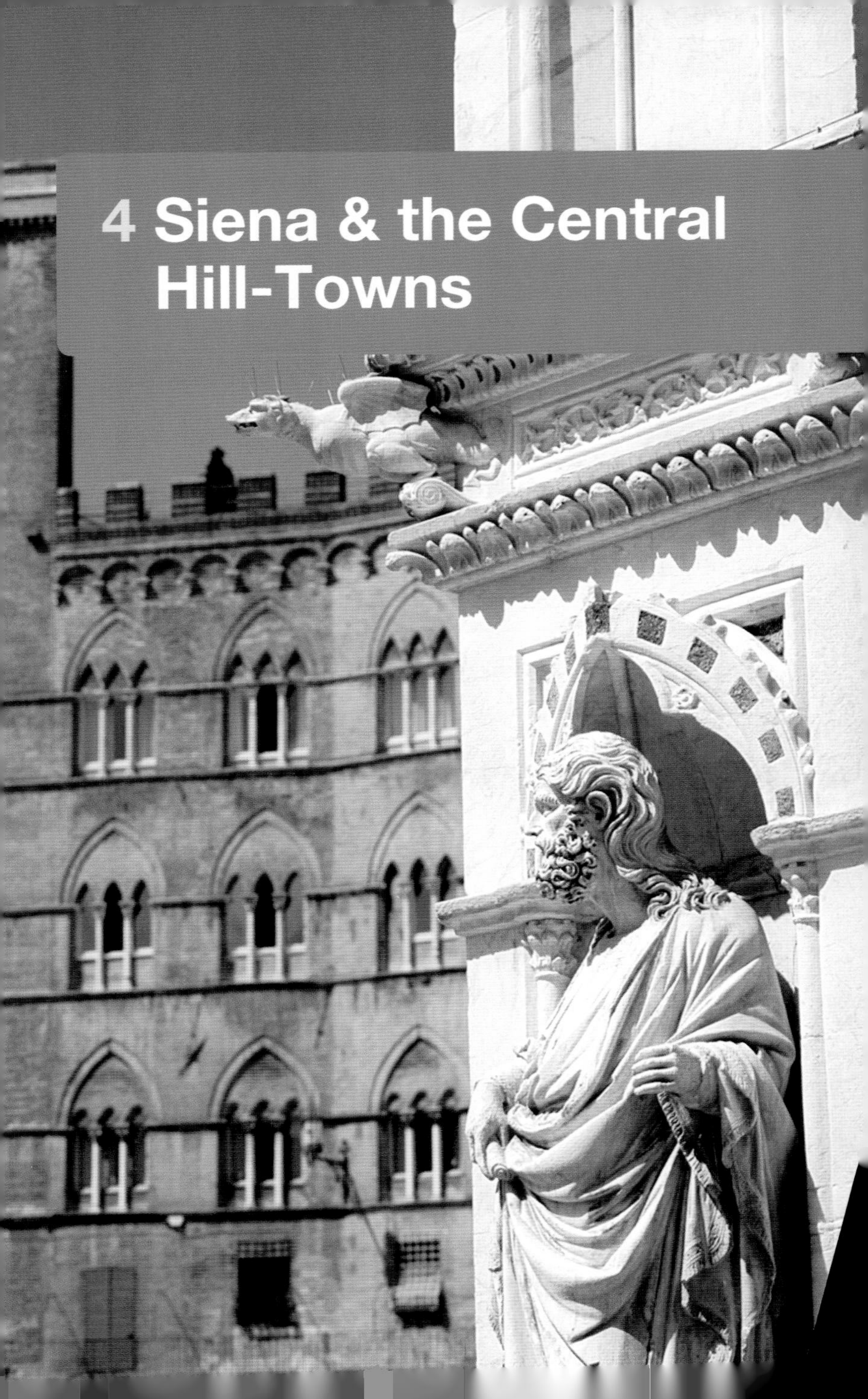

Central Tuscany is the bit that looks as it's meant to—the Tuscany of a thousand postcards and kitchen wall-calendars. Ridiculously corrugated hills roll and roll and roll their way to a misty horizon; to add to the savage beauty, up pops a medieval walled town with foundations laid before Christ, rearing up above orderly vine-clad fields. You can hardly believe it's real, but from the wine hills of Chianti to the cypress-studded horizons of the Val d'Elsa and the secluded corners of the Crete Senesi, it truly does look like that.

Right at the core of central Tuscany is rose-coloured **Siena.** No Tuscan tour is complete without at least a day trip or two into this ancient city with its fan-shaped piazza and uniquely preserved Gothic architecture. The astounding art is only one part of what makes your visit a special experience.

Spiky, medieval **San Gimignano** and Etruscan **Volterra** complete the classic trio of atmospheric hill-towns. Throw in laid-back **Arezzo,** with one of the great treasures of Western art, and you have the keystones of a classic Tuscan itinerary. Villas dot the hillsides and there's plenty here for children if you know where to look: historic towns to explore, amazing works of art to discover and wild, idyllic countryside to roam.

SIENA

One of Europe's finest medieval cities, **Siena** ★★★ occupies a series of steep ridges south of Florence. Like its former political rival, Siena has a rich artistic legacy dating to the pre-Renaissance period, and is a magical place for children to visit. It's easiest to see on foot because it's laid-back and elegant, and appears to absorb peak-season crowds a little better than its neighbour to the north.

Founded by Roman Emperor Augustus as **Saena Julia** around A.D. 30, Siena became one of the richest Italian republics in the early Middle Ages, thanks primarily to successful banking families and a booming wool industry. The **Black Death** of 1348 dealt a massive blow, reducing the population by two-thirds and ushering in a period of decline. In 1555 Siena was finally seized by **Florence** and almost all development ceased, helping to explain why the city appears frozen in time.

Visitor Information

Information Centres

The main **tourist office** is at Piazza del Campo 56 (☎ *0577 280551. www.terresiena.it*; 9am–7pm daily). Another indispensable **website** tailor-made for family visits to the city and surrounding countryside is *www.terresienabambini.it*.

Arriving

By Car Driving to Siena is straightforward, especially from

CENTRAL TUSCANY

Florence—a 1-hour cruise up the *SI-FI raccordo* (not actually a motorway). The problem is **parking**: try to get in before 10am (take the **Siena Ovest** exit) and aim for **Parking Fortezza** or **Stadio** (follow the little football sign); both are by the *stadio* and cost 1.60€/hr. **Don't** head for 'Parking piazza il Campo'—it isn't in the Campo at all but a 20-minute uphill walk away.

INSIDER TIP

If you know Siena already, there *is* free parking (for now), against the north-western walls of the Fortezza and along the adjacent road. Funnily enough, it isn't signposted, so get in early and navigate by the sun (it worked for Columbus).

By Bus Forget the awkward train link: the easiest way to reach Siena on public transport is by **bus**. From Florence, **SITA** (*800 373760. **www.sitabus.it***) and **TRA.IN** (*0577 204246. **www.trainspa.it***) use the terminal at Via Santa Caterina da Siena 17r, near Santa Maria Novella station. Take the **Rapido:** it has hourly services (fewer on Sundays) and it's fast (about 1¼ hr). Tickets are 7.10€ in advance. In Siena, buses terminate at **Piazza Antonio Gramsci,** a short walk from the Campo; the ticket office is below street level.

Children's Top Attractions of Central Tuscany

- Scaling Siena's **Torre del Mangia,** p. 88, then rewarding yourself with Tuscany's **tastiest *gelato*,** p. 94.
- Discovering room after room inside Siena's converted hospital museum, **Santa Maria della Scala,** p. 87.
- Snapping classic Tuscan views in **Le Crete,** p. 91.
- Exploring **San Gimignano's historic centre** at dusk, p. 90.
- Eating ice cream with the **Gelato World Champions,** p. 94.
- Standing humbled before Piero della Francesca's **Legend of the True Cross,** p. 105.
- Dressing up medieval-style at **Volterra A.D. 1398,** p. 98.
- Munching on a Mac like they've never tasted before, in Panzano's **MacDario,** p. 101.
- Surfing the Web poolside at **Podere Marcampo,** outside Volterra, p. 111.

Getting Around

Siena is best explored **on foot:** the *centro storico* is pedestrianised and compact—buses are mostly banned. Don't plan to do too much: there's **barely a flat street,** so little legs (and buggy-pushers) will tire. The small orange ***pollicini*** buses can be useful for longer trips: tickets cost 1€, are valid up to 1 hour, and can be purchased from the bus station or any *tabacchi*.

Family-Friendly Events

Every year, on 2nd July and again on 16th August, Siena's Piazza del Campo is host to Italy's most spectacular and exciting festival, the **Palio delle Contrade** ★★★. This chaotic and sometimes aggressive **bareback horse-race** around the Campo involves 10 of Siena's 17 *contrade* (districts). Equally captivating is the pre-race flag-waving ceremony and parade. Frenzied celebrations greet the winning rider, and the day is rounded off with communal feasts in each district.

Taking small children to the Palio can be **difficult.** Crowds are overwhelming (50,000+), you'll end up standing for hours in the sun, and it's a nightmare getting to a toilet. If you don't mind paying 150€ to 300€ *each*, reserve seats in the temporary stands; do this months, or preferably a year, in advance via local travel agent **Il Palio Viaggi,** Piazza La Lizza 12 (📞 *0577 280828*. ***www.paliovaggi.it***).

To experience the event for free, aim for the **trial races** ★, also held in the Campo (starting 29th June and 13th Aug). It's still busy but it's bearable, at least for the morning sessions.

FUN FACT Find the Fountain

Siena is divided into 17 *contrade* (districts), each with its own flag, council, church, insignia, patron saint and museum. They also each have a **fountain,** once crucial to their water supply (e.g., Fontebranda belongs to Oca; see p. 89). A fun family activity is to try to find them—getting all 17 would be quite an achievement.

Trial races are not as fast and furious as the real thing but are just as **photogenic** and fun to watch; there are usually six: mornings (9am) and late evenings (7:45pm June, 7:15pm Aug).

Fonte Gaia

What to See & Do

The ideal place to start a tour of Siena is **Piazza del Campo** ★, the fan-shaped heart of the city, ringed with cafés and shops, and home to a 19th-century reproduction of the **Fonte Gaia,** an ornate fountain sculpted in 1419 by Jacopo della Quercia.

Fast Facts: Siena & Central Tuscany

Banks In Siena, you'll find banks with ATMs galore along **Banchi di Sopra.** In Arezzo, make for **Corso Italia.**

Hospitals & Emergencies The main hospital is **Le Scotte** (☎ *0577 585111*), near Siena's train station on Viale Mario Bracci. In a medical emergency, dial ☎ *118*.

Pharmacies **Antica Farmacia Parenti,** Banchi di Sopra 43, Siena (☎ *0577 283269*), has English-speaking staff and posts out-of-hours pharmacy rosters in the window.

Post Offices The most convenient of Siena's several offices is at Via di Città 142 (☎ *0577 46471*). In Arezzo, make for Via Guido Monaco 34 (☎ *0575 332504*).

Toilets Public loos are scarce; there are facilities in Siena near the Campo at Via di Beccheria 3 (just off Via di Città) and on the far side of Piazza del Mercato. You'll also find some on the northern side of San Domenico and at the Casa di Santa Caterina below. All require a 0.50€ coin.

SIENA

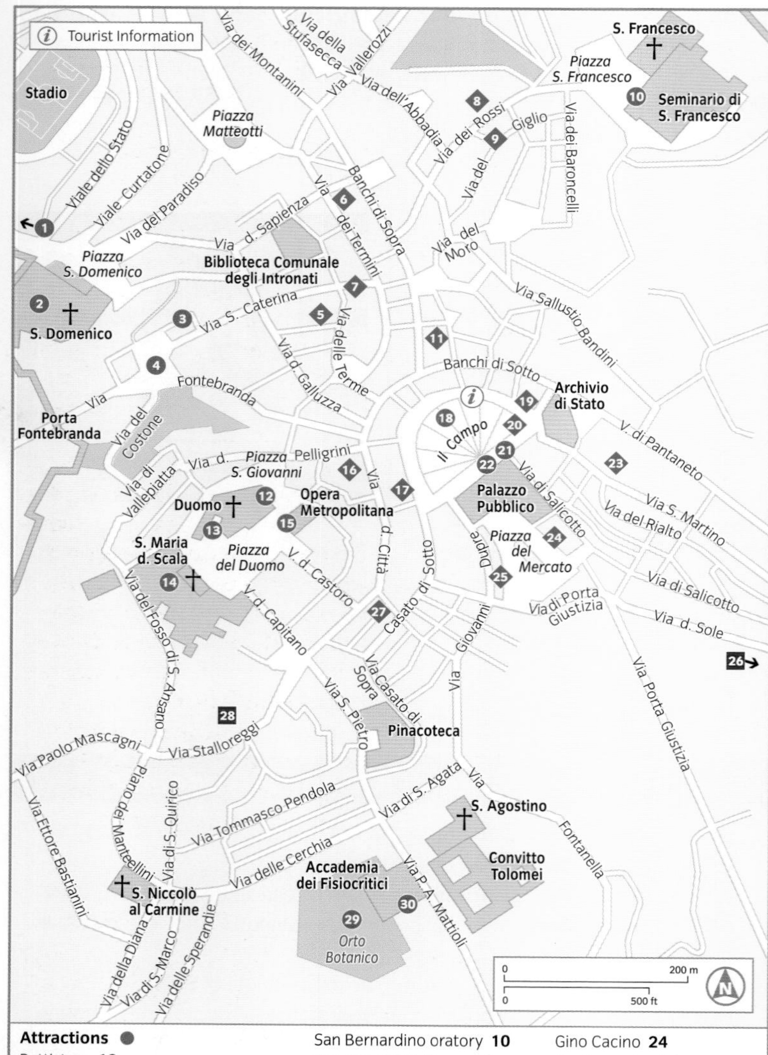

Attractions ●

Battistero **12**
Casa di Santa Caterina **3**
Duomo **13**
Fonte Gaia **18**
Fontebranda **4**
La Lizza & the Fortezza di Santa Barbara **1**
Museo dell'Opera **15**
Museo di Storia Naturale (Accademia Fisiocritici) **30**
Orto Botanico **29**
Palazzo Pubblico/Museo Civico **22**
San Bernardino oratory **10**
San Domenico **2**
Santa Maria della Scala **14**
Torre del Mangia **21**

Dining ◆

Antica Drogheria Manganelli **17**
Antica Trattoria Papei **25**
Brivido **16**
Caribia **19**
Forno dei Galli **7**
Gallo Nero **23**
Gino Cacino **24**
Key Largo Bar **20**
Kopa Kabana **9**
La Fontana della Frutta **5**
L'Osteria **8**
Nannini **11**
Pizza al Taglio **6**
Pizzicheria de Miccoli **27**

Accommodation ■

Duomo **28**
Santa Caterina **26**

Duomo ★ AGE 5 & UP

*Piazza del Duomo. ☎ 0577 283048. **www.operaduomo.siena.it**.*

Siena's opulent stripy **cathedral** was built between 1136 and 1382 on the site of an earlier structure. Its most striking exterior feature is the zebra-like black-and-white marble, but the interior is equally ostentatious and fun to explore, with a marble intarsia **floor** ★★ laid by Siena's finest Renaissance artists (usually covered, except Aug–late Oct), a star-painted ceiling and striped pillars. Its major-league artwork is the magnificent 13th-century stone **pulpit** ★ by Nicola Pisano, jammed with carved figures from the Bible: check out the lurid scenes of the *Last Judgement*, with sinners squirming in hell.

Pinturicchio's frescoed **Piccolomini Library** ★, showing scenes from the life of Pope Pius II in technicolour, will interest anyone who's already been to **Pienza** (p. 175).

Time *45 min.* ***Open*** *10:30am–7:30pm Mon–Sat, 1:30–7:30pm Sun Mar–Aug, rest of year 10:30am–6:30pm Mon–Sat, 1:30–6:30pm Sun.* ***Adm*** *3€ (inc. Piccolomini Library), free under-12s.* ***Amenities***

La Lizza & the Fortezza di Santa Barbara ALL AGES

Fortezza Medicea.

A 10-minute walk northwest of the Campo, **La Lizza** is a gravelled public garden laid out in 1779, home to the city's largest **market**—not to be missed for local delicacies—on Wednesdays. To amuse the children there are a fountain and pond with goldfish, ducks and turtles, a slide, and most days a carousel; in winter you can **ice-skate** ★ with your Tuscan neighbours.

The gardens run up to the walls of the **Fortezza di Santa Barbara,** established by Charles V and rebuilt by Cosimo I in 1560. Today it's an exhibition and concert space, but little visitors can let off steam on the expansive ramparts and

The striking interior of Siena's Duomo

bastions—a touch scruffy these days, but quiet and traffic-free.

Inside the fort, you'll find the **Enoteca Italiana** (*0577 228843. **www.enoteca-italiana.it***. Noon–8pm Mon, noon–1am Tues–Sat), which sells more than 1,600 Italian wines. There are usually 10 to 15 bottles on the tasting table, costing 3€ to 7€ a glass.

Time** 1 hr. **Open** 24 hr. **Adm** Free. **Amenities

Museo Civico ★★★ AGE 7 & UP

Palazzo Pubblico. 0577 292368.

The austere Gothic **Palazzo Pubblico** was home to Siena's city government for centuries, but most of it now houses the Civic Museum, principally a collection of fine medieval art. Two top-class rooms stand out for children: the **Sala del Mappamondo** ★★ showcases **Simone Martini's** *Maestà*, a stunning 1315 depiction of Mary holding Jesus as a child. On the opposite wall is (though this is disputed) Martini's fresco of *Guidoriccio da Fogliano*, whose Sienese army is about to besiege a city. More sublime frescoes cover the **Sala della Pace** ★★★ next door: **Ambrogio Lorenzetti's** astounding *Allegories of Good and Bad Government*, commissioned in 1338. One fresco depicts an idealised version of life in 14th-century Siena; a happy tableau of shops, builders, hawkers, dancers, school rooms and people working the fields beyond the city walls. There's plenty here to keep youngsters riveted: point out the 'dancing maidens', who were probably young men—it would have been shocking to paint women frolicking in public at the time. Within a decade, *Bad Government* pretty much came to pass, as the Black Death killed 70,000 including Siena's leading artist; Tuscany's supreme work of civic art is a fitting memorial.

As you leave through the **Anticamera del Concistoro**, children who've already seen San Gimignano's **Collegiata** (p. 94) should spot *St. Sebastian* right away. The adjacent **Concistoro** ★ features more notable secular frescoes, of a later vintage. Siena's great Renaissance painter Domenico Beccafumi frescoed the ceiling on the theme of civic virtues in 1529–35.

Time** 1½ hr. **Open** 10am–7pm daily 16 Mar–Oct, 10am–6pm rest of year. **Adm** 7.50€, 12€ with Torre del Mangia, free under-11s. **Amenities

Museo di Storia Naturale (Accademia Fisiocritici) FIND AGE 7 & UP

*Piazzetta Silvio Gigli 2 (at Sant'Agostino). 0577 47002. **www.accademiafisiocritici.it**.*

This free **natural history museum** inside a 12th-century monastery is well off the tourist trail; you may have to ring the bell to get in and might have the place to yourself. On the ground floor, hundreds of fossils arranged in antiquated wooden cabinets around a courtyard include a vast collection of seashells, bones and rocks. There's also the Serini Collection of

terracotta mushrooms. But the real highlight sits in the middle of the courtyard: the **skeleton of a fin whale ★**, the second-largest animal on Earth after the blue whale. Upstairs, corridors are lined with stuffed mammals, birds, snakes, fish, insects and skeletons, including a small giraffe. The 'monstrosities' case with its twin-headed lambs and other freaks of nature may be too much for young children.

Time *45 min.* ***Open*** *9am–1pm and 3–6pm Mon–Wed and Fri, 9am–1pm Thurs.* ***Adm*** *Free.*

Orto Botanico ALL AGES

Via Pier Andrea Mattioli 4. ☎ 0577 232874.

Downhill from the Museo di Storia Naturale, Siena's **botanical garden** is a welcome patch of green where children can join in playing with local youngsters. The gardens contain a well-stocked herbarium and special plants such as the 'living stones' with two wide leaves that look like rocks. The garden is also said to have a **ghost:** local hero Giomo, who died in battle in 1207. Those with buggies or wheelchairs beware: there are steep access steps and the garden itself is terraced. There are **swings and a slide** just uphill outside Sant'Agostino.

Time *45 min.* ***Open*** *8am–5pm Mon–Fri, 8am–noon Sat.* ***Adm*** *Free.*

Santa Maria della Scala ★★ ALL AGES

Piazza del Duomo 2. ☎ 0577 224811. ***www.santamariadellascala.com.***

There are several important galleries in Siena but this **former hospital** is the best option with children. One of the earliest hospitals in Europe, it was founded in the 11th century and took care of the sick as well as helping the poor, pilgrims and *gettatelli* ('throw-away' orphans) abandoned by unmarried mothers.

The hospital closed in 1995; today its halls and chapels are being transformed into exhibition spaces. Inexplicably, it's often **quieter** than more-established sights in town, and its deserted basements have room for children to run around in (literally).

Just beyond the main entrance, the **Pellegrinaio ★★** (Pilgrim's Hall) is covered with cheery frescoes dating from 1440, by Vecchietta among others. They record **everyday hospital life** in the Middle Ages: compare the simple clothes of the poor with the robes of the rich, and spot carpenters, workers, bricklayers, doctors and those lucky orphans. But where's the anaesthetic?

Don't neglect the rest of the building; seek out the atmospheric **Oratorio di Santa Caterina ★**, Matteo di Giovanni's surreal, brutal 1482 ***Massacre of the Innocents*** **★** hanging outside the **Cappella della Madonna,** and the recently restored **Sagrestia ★**. Siena's **Museo d'Arte per Bambini** (or **Bambimus;** ***www.comune.siena.it/bambimus***) occupies the Sala San Leopoldo on the ground floor with its special selection of

TIP Pick Up a Pass

If you intend to visit several major sights in Siena, pick up a *biglietto* *cumulativo*: the **Opera della Metropolitana** pass (10€ from Museo dell'Opera; valid for 3 days, with no rule to say you can't share your pass with others), covers the **Duomo, Battistero** (with its multi-tiered **baptismal font ★** embellished by Ghiberti, Donatello and Jacopo della Quercia), **Museo dell'Opera** (for the definitive *Maestà* by **Duccio di Buoninsegna ★★**), **Crypt** and **San Bernardino oratory.** It also allows you to scale the **Facciatone ★** from inside the Museo, to enjoy dizzying views down into the Campo and over the countryside for miles around. A week's pass covering the main religious sites as well as the Museo Civico and Santa Maria della Scala (the '**S.I.A.**') costs 14€ to 17€ depending on the season.

---

paintings and sculptures set at child-friendly heights, plus objects to handle and activities.

The other highlight is in the hospital's bowels: the **Museo Archeologico ★★** follows a labyrinth of tunnels, catacombs and creaking walkways, dimly lit and lined with display cases. The spooky setting is the star, making the artefacts—mostly Etruscan ceramics and bits and pieces from the Bronze Age, and local Roman ruins, including a collection of funerary urns and a tomb—seem more interesting.

Time *2 hr.* ***Open*** *10:30am–6:30pm daily.* ***Adm*** *6€, 3.50€ students, free under-11s.* ***Amenities***

INSIDER TIP

Santa Maria della Scala's bookshop has an excellent selection of **children's reading materials.** To help make the city fun for young ones, invest in **Siena: Playing with Art** (6€), which takes them on a voyage of discovery round the medieval city's art and history.

Torre del Mangia ★★

AGE 7 & UP

Palazzo Pubblico. 0577 292368.

Almost every child who sets eyes on the 102-m (335-ft) **bell-tower** of the medieval Palazzo Pubblico, dominating Piazza del Campo, wants to climb it. Make it your **first stop** of the day to get in before the tour groups arrive (only 25 people are allowed up at a time). The tower was built between 1325 and 1348 and is accessed by a separate entrance opposite the Museo Civico. The climb is an energetic yomp up 388 narrow steps, rewarded by a panorama of the city rooftops, piazzas and the countryside for miles around. With luck or planning, you can be there when they ring the bells (three times a day), but be warned that it's a temporarily deafening experience. The climb isn't suitable for anyone with asthma, claustrophobia or a cardiac condition.

Time *1 hr.* ***Open*** *10am–6:15pm daily mid-Mar–Oct, 10am–3:15pm rest of year.* ***Adm*** *7€, 12€ with Museo Civico, free under-6s.*

St. Catherine (1347–80)

Not just patron saint of Siena but also of Italy, Europe, nurses, firemen and sick people, Catherine Benincasa grew up in Siena. She had visions of God as a child and became a Dominican nun aged 8 but is best known today for the **letters** she wrote to the Pope and other Italian leaders appealing for nationwide peace.

San Domenico in Piazza San Domenico (9am–6:30pm daily) is a cavernous church enlivened by the **Capella di Santa Caterina,** which houses Catherine's venerated head, preserved in a glass case (her thumb is sealed in another cabinet by the chapel door). Also seek out works by Sienese Renaissance painters Matteo di Giovanni (c. 1430–95) and Francesco di Giorgio Martini (1439–1502). The **Casa di Santa Caterina,** Costa di Sant'Antonio (*0577 44177*; 9am–6pm daily), once Catherine's home, has been preserved as a religious sanctuary; her former kitchen is now an oratory with a spectacular 16th-century majolica-tiled floor. Entry to both is free.

Walk downhill from the Casa to the **Fontebranda** to find the cross marking the spot where Catherine fell (the story goes she was pushed by the Devil). The fountain, dating from 1246 and the best preserved of Siena's medieval water sources, is now home to some happy fish.

Trenonatura ALL AGES

Ferrovia Val d'Orcia, Piazza Rosselli 5. 0577 207413. ***www.ferrovieturistiche.it.***

This tourist train running on lines closed to scheduled services offers an enjoyable jaunt through the scenic, undulating countryside to discover more remote corners of southern Tuscany. The train, normally a 1950s' diesel and more rarely a steam train, makes a 140-km (87-mile) loop from Siena's main station in Piazza Stazione to **Asciano** (p. 91), wine-producing country in Monte Antico and up the wild Val d'Orcia three times a day; you can get off and explore if you catch the first train in the morning.

Time *At least half a day.* ***Runs*** *Sun Apr–Sept but not every week—check in advance.* ***Adm*** *18€ from Siena, 12€ from Asciano, with one child under 10 travelling free with each paying adult; steam trains 29€.*

Shopping for a Picnic

Siena is packed with delicious delis and **food shops**—great places to find a gift or furnish the ingredients for a lavish picnic in the hills. **Pizzicheria de Miccoli** ★ at Via di Città 95 is the most famous; the air inside is rich with the smell of expensive cured hams, salami and pecorino cheese. **Antica Drogheria Manganelli** at Via di Città 71–73 comes a close second in prestige: its aged wood cabinets are stacked with posh olive oils,

Panforte

Siena is famous for its *panforte,* a sweet, dense cake sold in shops all over town, including along **Banchi di Sopra,** where you can buy it fresh by the *etto* (100g/3½ oz). Made from candied fruit and nuts, glued together with honey, it resembles a gloopy fruit cake. Although popular across Italy, the first *panforte* was created in Siena in the Middle Ages: each shop has its own recipe, with the most popular varieties being sweet **Panforte Margherita** and bitter **Panforte Nero.** Try a slice from several shops to compare recipes, if you dare. **Drogheria Manganelli** (p. 89) and **Bini** (Via Stalloreggi 91–93) are great places to start.

truffle-infused polenta and the like. But our favourite stop is altogether more down to earth: **Gino Cacino** ★ (☎ *0577 223076. **www.ginocacinosiena.it***) at Piazza Mercato 31 will load you a sandwich with pecorino aged in olive oil, Tuscan salami, anchovies or anything else you fancy from his top-quality produce counter. Perch at any of three tables or take it away with you. A filling roll and a drink should cost only about 4€—bargain!

La Fontana della Frutta, Via delle Terme 67, is a reliable, central grocer also offering tasty precooked pasta dishes. The biggest **supermarket** in the centre is **Conad City** in the Galleria Metropolitana off Piazza Matteotti (9am–8pm Mon–Sat, 9am–1pm and 6–8pm Sun).

INSIDER TIP

Siena is an expensive place to shop for most things but does have an ancient artisan reputation. Avoid the touristy streets and make for **Via Stalloreggi**—fittingly, the very lane that housed the workshop of painter Duccio di Buoninsegna 700 years ago. At no. 79, **Ceramiche Bonci** (☎ *0577 280335*) is one of few remaining places where ceramics are locally painted by hand, on the wheel. Almost opposite, at no. 70, **Sator Print** ★ (☎ *0577 247478. **www.satorprint.com***) sells hand-decorated prints and original art and calligraphy based on historic Sienese designs. Neither is cheap, but you'll find an affordable, authentic gift or souvenir with little trouble. Watching the artisans at work is encouraged—and a privilege.

SAN GIMIGNANO

There ought to be a prize for the first guidebook writer not to mention 'medieval Manhattan' in an introduction to **San Gimignano** ★★. (We've just blown it.) The similarities are remarkable—and not just the obvious towers (or 'skyscrapers'). In high season San Gimignano can seem

Le Crete

The scarred clay hills east of Siena, Le Crete Senesi, are rightly famous for their spectacular Tuscan **views** ★★★. For the best panoramas, drive or cycle the children and the camera along the **SS438** Asciano–Siena road; wind up at **Monte Oliveto Maggiore** (p. 177) or pass a couple of hours in Asciano. The latter's **Museo Corboli** (*0577 719524.* 10:30am–1pm and 3–6:30pm Tues–Sun Apr–Oct, rest of year shorter hours Fri–Sun, adm 4€, 3€ ages 6–12), inside a 13th-century *palazzo* at Corso Matteotti 122, houses an impressive collection of Sienese art, Etruscan artefacts and restored civic frescoes, notably an allegory of the seasons on the ceiling of Sala 13.

Pizza 'n'pasta in the garden at **La Mencia** (Corso Matteotti 85. *0577 718227.* ***www.lamencia.it***) is the cream on top. Heading out of Asciano, the road to **San Giovanni d'Asso** is another panoramic corker.

more like a **medieval theme park** than a real town, brimming with visitors crowding its perfect piazzas and ancient cobbled streets. But try to get here early or stay late and you'll soon understand why we love the secretive ambience of the place—the **medieval centre at dusk** ★★★ is one of Tuscany's special places.

The town got its name from Gimignano, a bishop of Modena, and in its heyday was a major stop on the pilgrim road to Rome, which gave it great wealth—mostly in merchant hands (there were no noble families here). As in Siena, the **Black Death** of 1348 called time on the good years, and the town slept for 600 years until mass tourism discovered its beauty and its **towers.** At one time, the latter numbered at least 72—symbols of medieval clan power, not to mention handy spots from which to pour pitch when things got nasty. Now just one tower is accessible of the 14 to survive.

Visitor Information

Information Centres

The **tourist office** is at Piazza del Duomo 1 (*0577 940008.* ***www.sangimignano.com.*** Daily 9am–1pm and 3–7pm Mar–Oct, 2–6pm Nov–Feb); staff will recommend combined tickets for a multi-museum hop. Both of the main piazzas (della Cisterna and del Duomo) have **ATMs.**

Arriving

San Gimignano is easiest reached by car: from Florence, get off the *raccordo* (main road) at *Poggibonsi*

SAN GIMIGNANO

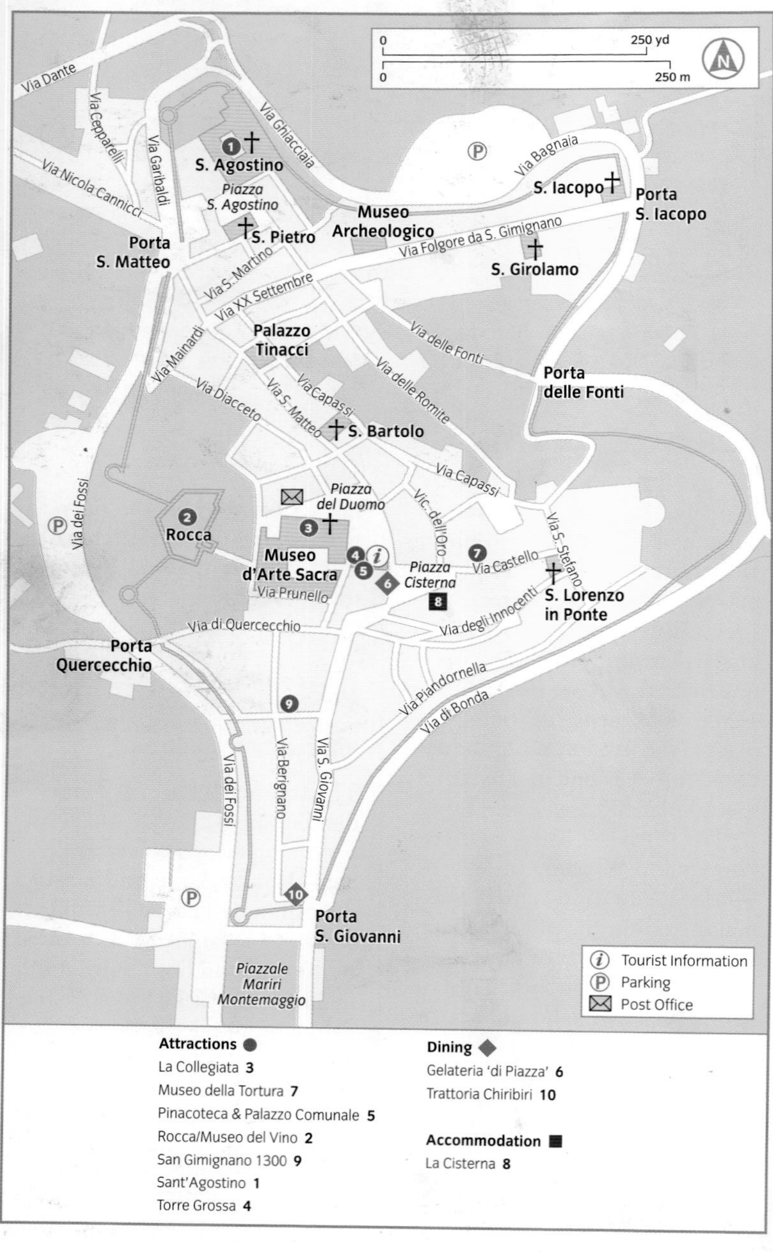

The 'skyscrapers' of San Gimignano

nord and follow signs; from Siena take the *Colle Val d'Elsa sud* exit.

The centre of town is pedestrianised. All park-and-ride car parks are well signed on the approaches. Car park **P1** is the farthest from the centre but also the cheapest (1€/hr; 1€ in total 8pm–8am). It's a steep climb from there, so drop the children at the gate first or take the park-and-ride bus together. Stamp your car-park ticket by the cashier's office to pay your return bus ticket, too (1€). If you're only stopping for a couple of hours, **P2** (2–3€/hr) is the closest and most convenient.

INSIDER TIP

Keep your parking ticket handy: it's worth a 1€ **discount** off the 7.50€ *biglietto cumulativo* for all the civic museums.

Family-Friendly Events

The third Saturday and Sunday in June sees the usual medieval shenanigans at the **Fiera delle Messi,** a *faux* knightly tournament. San Gimignano celebrates its **patron saint** on 31st January, when just about everything closes.

What to See & Do

First orientate yourselves. **Piazza della Cisterna** ★ (named after the well) and adjacent **Piazza del Duomo** are the heart of town. All streets lead to and from here.

You don't need a guidebook to tell you that the climb up the **Torre Grossa** (☎ *0577 990312*), the highest of San Gimignano's towers, on Piazza del Duomo, is going to end with a stunning **view** ★★ over the Val d'Elsa and beyond. Look hard enough and you may spot some poolside family accommodation or plot a family walk through the vines—there's plenty out there, and the tourist office can suggest specific routes. Admission is 5€, 4€ for children aged 6 to 18; the same ticket is valid for some hardcore art at the **Pinacoteca** and **Palazzo Comunale.** All are open 9:30am to 7pm daily March to October and 10am to 5:30pm November to February.

If you're clever, you can get almost the same view for **free** by making the 5-minute climb uphill from Piazza del Duomo to the ruined **Rocca.** Walk to your left when you get to the fort and look down (there's also a view your little ones will appreciate: a park with **swings** and a **slide**).

There are plenty of shops along **Via San Giovanni,** but you're mostly being scalped, of course. **Via San Matteo ★**, north of the main piazzas, is *slightly* quieter and less touristy. Little **Via San Martino ★**, by the Porta San Matteo, is good for authentic artisan shops.

Judging by the queues they don't need the plug, but the **Gelateria 'di Piazza' ★★** at Piazza della Cisterna 4 (*0577 942244*) has been Gelato World Champion several times. For a local flavour, try its **Crema di Santa Fina,** with saffron. While in town, also try Tuscany's only white DOCG wine (p. 32): **Vernaccia di San Gimignano** is available to taste by the glass (3€–5€) at the slightly misnamed **Museo del Vino** (*0577 941267*), in the Rocca.

La Collegiata ★★ AGE 5 & UP

Piazza del Duomo. 0577 940316.

This externally plain collegiate church is covered in **fresco** on almost every bit of its internal wall space.

It helps to know the **stories** behind religious art. On the far main wall from the entrance are 14th-century scenes from the **Life of Christ** (authorship is disputed); no prizes for naming the only guy at the *Last Supper* without his halo. Looking right up the nave, the figure absorbing all the arrows is Benozzo Gozzoli's 1465 **St. Sebastian.** Miraculously he survived, but only to be later bludgeoned to death on the orders of Roman emperor Diocletian (in a cruel twist, he's

TIP Have San Gimignano to Yourself

To get the full SG experience, stay over: it's at night and in the early morning that the town shows its best. Hotel **La Cisterna** (*0577 940328.* ***www.hotelcisterna.it***) within the medieval walls is a friendly place with character. Doubles are 80€ to 136€, with an extra bed 25€ to 30€, depending on season and room grade (some have a bath). Our favourite berth is room 59, with stupendous views from its panoramic terrace. Ask staff about bringing your car into town to unload.

TIP More Frescoes for Free

The door to the right of the tourist office in Piazza del Duomo leads into a courtyard of the Palazzo Comunale. As you emerge into the courtyard, turn right for some free 14th-century treats: Taddeo di Bartolo's *Madonna and Child* flanked by two works on the theme of justice by Sodoma, who painted the abbey at **Monte Oliveto Maggiore** (p. 177). The best-preserved fresco is on the right, a near-monochrome **St. Ivo.** All just painted on a wall.

now the patron saint of archers). Above St. Sebastian is a gruesome **Last Judgement ★** by Taddeo di Bartolo (1410), with androgynous human figures suffering all manner of ills at the hands of little devils.

The best frescoes in the church are Domenico Ghirlandaio's in the **Cappella di Santa Fina ★★** opposite the entrance, painted in 1475. They portray Fina, a local girl who fell mortally ill aged 10 and lay on a plank of wood for 5 years to repent her sins—which notably included having once accepted an orange from a boy. The scene on the right shows St. Gregory foretelling Fina's death; on the left, mourners grieve, and you can see the towers of San Gimignano in the background.

Time** 1 hr. **Open** 10am–6:40pm Mon–Fri, 10am–5:10pm Sat, 12:30–5:10pm Sun Apr–Oct; rest of year (exc. 2nd half Nov, 2nd half Jan, 12th Mar and 1st Sun in Aug) 9:30am–4:40pm Mon–Sat, 12:30pm–4:40pm Sun. **Adm** 3.50€, 1.50€ children 6–18. **Amenities

Museo della Tortura AGE 12 & UP

Via del Castello 1–3 (on Piazza della Cisterna). 0577 942243.

Let's get this straight: there's some upsetting stuff in here, so **don't bring young or easily scared children.** The **Torture Museum** showcases some astoundingly creative methods of inflicting pain spanning the history of torture from the Spanish Inquisition to the guillotine and beyond. Most pieces in the nine rooms, subterranean 'prison' and recently added garden are originals: the 'Iron Maiden of Nuremberg', 'Heretic's Fork' and 'Scavenger's Daughter' are all far worse than they sound. Vivid descriptions in clinical English complete the grisly experience. Make sure you get the right torture museum; this is the original and best.

***Time** 1 hr. **Open** 10am–6:30pm daily Apr–Oct; 10am–5:30pm Nov–Mar. **Adm** 8€, 5.50€ anyone in full-time education.*

San Gimignano 1300 ★

ALL AGES

*Via Berignano 23. 0577 941078. **www.sangimignano1300.com.***

It took a team of five skilled craftsmen (two named Michelangelo and Raffaello—honestly) 3 years and a tonne of clay to build the 800 structures that make up this 1:100 scale reproduction of the town around 1300 (with all 72 towers intact). Serious historical and archive research from the universities at Pisa and Florence contributed to what is an accurate re-creation of the medieval walled town you're standing in right now. There's a didactic edge, of course, but it's fun and fascinating too.

Time** 30 min. **Open** 8am–11pm daily in summer, rest of year 8am–8pm. **Adm** 5€, 3€ under-12s. **Amenities

Sant'Agostino ★ AGE 5 & UP

Piazza Sant'Agostino. No phone.

Frescoes galore decorate the walls of this simple basilica. Florentine **Benozzo Gozzoli** was originally commissioned to paint *Saint Sebastian* on the left wall of the nave (1464), in thanks for delivering the town from plague, and the patrons liked his work so much, he was given the job of the *Life of Saint Augustine* in the apse chapel (0.50€ for lights).

***Time** 20 min. **Open** 7am–noon and 3–7pm daily Apr–Oct, exc. Mon mid-Nov–mid-Dec and Mar. **Adm** Free.*

VOLTERRA

You can't miss **Volterra** ★★—the ochre grimace it points at the world from way above the pastures of the Valdera is visible for miles in every direction. This **Etruscan** walled city grew wealthy from what's below your feet: alum for dyes and alabaster, a marble-like stone traditionally worked by Volterran craftsmen.

Comparisons with San Gimignano are inevitable, but Volterra is less pickled in its medieval state than its neighbour, with more locals and fewer tourists doing the rounds (despite being the setting for the bestselling teen novel *Twilight: New Moon*). Perhaps unfairly, but mercifully for visitors, Volterra is permanently stuck at number two on the Tuscany day-trip chart.

Visitor Information

Information Centres

Staff at the excellent **tourist office** (☎ *0588 87257. **www. volterratur.it.*** 10am–1pm and 2–6pm daily, from 9am in summer) at Piazza dei Priori 19–20 can't do enough to help you, and if you hire an **audioguide** (5€), they throw in a free one for children to play with. There's an **ATM** opposite.

Arriving

Volterra is only feasibly accessible with children by **car.** It's on the **SS68,** 41km (25 miles) east of Cecina. If you see a space in the **Vallebuona** car park (follow *teatro romano*; not Sat 6am–3pm), grab it. Otherwise, drop the family (the climb into town is long and steep) at adjacent Porta Fiorentina and head for car park 3, **Docciola,** also free and usually with spaces, even in peak season.

VOLTERRA

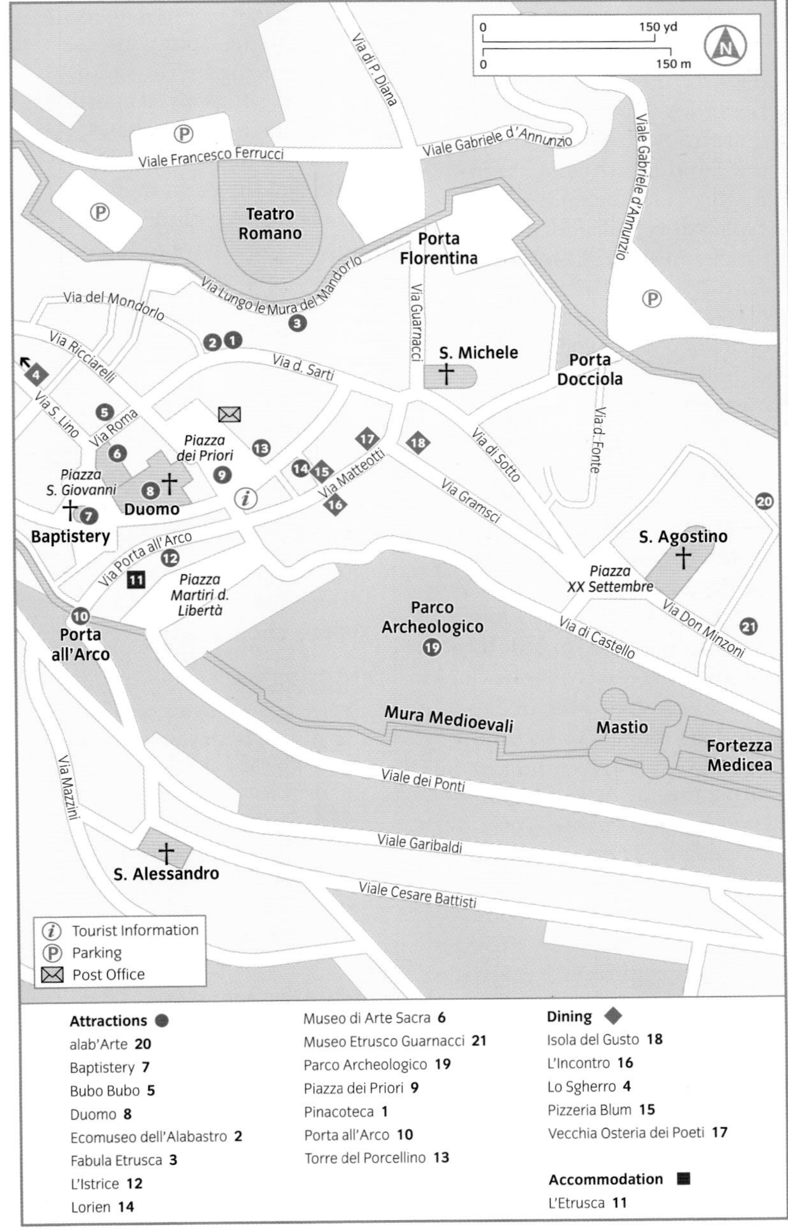

Attractions

alab'Arte **20**
Baptistery **7**
Bubo Bubo **5**
Duomo **8**
Ecomuseo dell'Alabastro **2**
Fabula Etrusca **3**
L'Istrice **12**
Lorien **14**
Museo di Arte Sacra **6**
Museo Etrusco Guarnacci **21**
Parco Archeologico **19**
Piazza dei Priori **9**
Pinacoteca **1**
Porta all'Arco **10**
Torre del Porcellino **13**

Dining

Isola del Gusto **18**
L'Incontro **16**
Lo Sgherro **4**
Pizzeria Blum **15**
Vecchia Osteria dei Poeti **17**

Accommodation

L'Etrusca **11**

Family-Friendly Events

Volterra's famous *festa* is the **Astiludio,** a re-enactment of 15th-century flag-throwing on the first Sunday of September. Better for young children is **Volterra AD1398 ★**, on the third and fourth Sundays in August. The theme is self-explanatory; the added bonus is that youngsters get to don 14th-century dress (10€ max. charge), play-work as wool merchants or craftsmen and maybe speak a bit of Italian with the others. See ***www.volterra1398.it***.

What to See & Do

Very much the centre of town since the Middle Ages is **Piazza dei Priori ★**, with its **Palazzo** that was the model for Florence's **Palazzo Vecchio** (p. 55). If the tower in the eastern corner looks a bit squat after those of San Gimignano, take solace in the fact that Volterra's is festooned with a unique little pig (*porcellino*), hence its name: **Torre del Porcellino.** The modest-looking **Duomo** round the back of the piazza is notable for its painted wooden **Deposition ★** carved in 1226, a magnificent Renaissance ceiling and some horrendous 19th-century marble work. The serene octagonal **Baptistery** opposite has a marble font by Andrea Sansovino (1467–1529). Finish your historical highlights tour at the **Porta all'Arco,** all that remains of the original 7½km (4½ miles) of sandstone Etruscan wall.

The ideal family **picnic** spot is the **Parco Archeologico** (free adm; 8:30am–8pm daily summer, 8:30am–5pm winter). Despite being on the site of an Etruscan acropolis, it sports some not-so-ancient **swings** and a **slide.** Whichever way you approach the park, there's a short but steep climb up flagstones: you'll have to lug buggy and passenger(s).

For offbeat toys and children's books you won't see elsewhere, try **Lorien's** two shops, opposite a superb **bakery,** at Vicolo delle Prigioni 1–5. The *biscotto* ice cream at **L'Incontro ★** (Via Matteotti 18, ☎ *0588 80500*) is a wonder, perhaps just edging out the ice cream at **Isola del Gusto** at Via Gramsci 3. The former also does a mean line in **artisan chocolate.**

INSIDER TIP

You'll find Volterra's best **eating** on p. 100, but if you're only looking for a slice on the move, **Pizzeria Blum** at Corso Matteotti 47 (☎ *0588 86931*) is our favourite, offering a slice and a bottle of water for around 2.50€. You can tuck in at their tables for no extra charge.

alab'Arte AGE 7 & UP

Via Orti S. Agostino 28. ☎ *0588 87968.* ***www.alabarte.com.***

Volterra's essential purchase is **alabaster,** ghostly white calcium sulphate mined from local hills and worked by the town's artisans for millennia. You can buy alabaster of varying quality all over town, or bring children to

TIP Volterra: It's Crafty

Volterra's reputation for workmanship extends beyond its numerous alabaster outlets. **Fabula Etrusca** (☎ *0588 87401*. ***www.fabulaetrusca.it***) at Via Lungo le Mura del Mandorlo 10 sells exquisite (and expensive) hand-crafted jewellery, much made according to Etruscan-influenced designs.

Prints and lithographs created from hand-engraved zinc plates are another speciality. Our two favourite workshops, where everything is created by hand on-site, are **L'Istrice** ★ (☎ *0588 85422*. ***www.laboistrice.it***) at Via Porta all'Arco 23 and **Bubo Bubo** ★ (☎ *0588 80307*) at Via Roma 24. Prints are priced from a few euros upwards.

this last **open sculptural workshop** in town, where you'll see alabaster in various stages of workmanship and buy finished pieces if any statues catch your eye. Or call ahead for your very own mini-tour.

If you go alabaster-crazy, there's also a museum: the **Ecomuseo dell'Alabastro,** in Piazzetta Minucci (11am–5pm daily 16th Mar–Oct, rest of year Sat and Sun 9am–1:30pm; adm 3€, 2€ children 6–18).

Time *20 min.* ***Open*** *9:30am–12:30pm and 3–7pm Mon–Sat.* ***Credit*** *MC, V.*

Museo Etrusco Guarnacci & Pinacoteca ★ AGE 8 & UP

Museo: *Via Don Minzoni 15.* ☎ *0588 86347.* ***Pinacoteca:*** *Via dei Sarti 1.* ☎ *0588 87580.*

The three cultural musts of Volterra can be seen on a single ticket. Skip the **Museo di Arte Sacra** if you're with children, but do head for the **Museo Etrusco Guarnacci,** for one of Italy's most important Etruscan collections. Downstairs are hundreds of haphazardly displayed funerary urns; the action peaks upstairs with the intricate *Urna degli Sposi* (married couple's urn), the *Ombra della Sera*, a surprisingly touching elongated bronze of (maybe) a fertility god, and best of all (in Room 16), a series of carved reliefs showing scenes from the *Odyssey*. The vivid depiction of **Odysseus** ★ enticed by the Sirens is easy to spot.

Across town, in the Palazzo Minucci-Solaini, Volterra's **Pinacoteca** has several outstanding pieces of religious art. If time's tight, focus on the first floor: the gap between Taddeo di Bartolo's **Enthroned Madonna** ★ polyptych and Rosso Fiorentino's Mannerist **Deposition** ★★★ was about a century. The comparison is stark: the first is a religious icon of exquisite beauty, the second an expressive work of modern art. That, in a nutshell, was the Renaissance.

Time *About 1 hr each.* ***Open*** *9am–6:45pm daily mid-Mar–Oct, 8:30am–1:30pm rest of year.* ***Adm*** *9€, 5€ children 6–18, 18€ family, audioguide 3€.* ***Amenities*** 🛍

The Very Best of Chianti

Although ideally sited for day trips into Florence, Siena and the hidden corners of the Val d'Elsa, Chianti itself can be a tricky sell for children, especially young ones. One spin through these famous hills to admire the idyllic **vistas** ★★ might be enough for them. The **SS222,** the *Chiantigiana*, between Castellina in Chianti and Greve, is the classic drive, through a landscape smothered in vineyards and olive groves, punctuated by woodland and peppered with *case coloniche*—stone farmsteads with trademark square dovecotes protruding from the roofs.

Greve itself is very much a wine town, the place **Chianti Classico** ★ red wine, and the Gallo Nero rooster that has become its symbol, call home. The handsome triangular piazza is lined with *enoteche* and good eateries, including **Nerbone** (✆ *055 853308.* ***www.nerbonedigreve.com***. Closed Tues), at no. 22, a sister to the one in Florence's Mercato Centrale (p. 68). Specialities such as tongue, *lampredotto* (cow's stomach) and *trippa* (tripe) are joined on its menu by more standard pasta dishes. Mains cost 10€ to 13€.

Our favourite place to taste wine in town is the **Enoteca del Chianti Classico** ★ (✆ *055 853297.* ***www.chianticlassico.it***) at Piazza Santa Croce 8, a dusty, labyrinthine wine shop with a massive selection, fair prices and usually a few bottles open on the tasting table. At **Le Cantine di Greve in Chianti** (Piazza delle Cantine 2. ✆ *055 8546404.* ***www.lecantine.it***) you buy a prepaid card and wander the vast cellar sampling any of 140 wines at prices ranging from 0.80€ to 6€ a dose—pressure-free and lots of fun. Both are open daily and will ship your purchases home.

To get a feel for where the produce of Chianti is made, it's hard to beat a winery visit. **Vignamaggio** ★★ (***www.vignamaggio.it.***10:30am–6:30pm daily), on the road from Greve to Lamole, has perhaps the best perch of any in Chianti, overlooking a landscape straight from a Renaissance painting. Book a guided tour to see the best of the house, formal gardens and winery, or just turn up to taste (free) at their 'wine bar'. The estate's **Riserva** ★★, aged in oak and made in only the best years, is dark, concentrated and outstanding—it costs 26€ or thereabouts for one special bottle. But Vignamaggio also makes a fine **Classico** (c. 12€) and an everyday drinking wine. If you fall in love with the place (who wouldn't?), well-equipped, traditionally furnished apartments can be rented (2 nights min). The peaceful complex has two pools, a playground, a woodland walking trail, and a small spa. Rates are 150€ to 275€/night to stay in the manor in which Leonardo's subject for his *Mona Lisa* was born and raised.

Bucolic countryside lies between Greve and Panzano, home of **MacDario** ★★ (☎ *055 852020.* ***www.dariocecchini.com.*** Lunch only Mon–Sat; no reservations, credit cards accepted), at Via XX Luglio 11, offering fast food, Tuscan-style—Mac-starved children can feast on a breadcrumbed beefburger, oven-cooked 'chips', sides of pickles and shredded red onion and two great relishes. The atmosphere is convivial and fun, with long, shared tables, but the quality of the food (set menus: 10€ and 20€) is as serious as at Dario Cecchini's noted (m)eateries, **Solociccia** and **Officina della Bistecca.** The top-notch butcher's shop downstairs, where the Cecchini success story began, is well worth a browse if you're self-catering.

A few kilometres further brings you into the Sienese Chianti and its principal town **Castellina** ★. This is a delightful (pedestrianised) place to wander around; children enjoy the subterranean **Via delle Volte** ★, a passageway below the old town walls, and the short '*Dietro le Mura*' walk just outside them. The gallery of **Andrea Rontini** (☎ *0577 742016.* ***www.andrearontini.it***) at Via delle Volte 36 is the place to pick up a photographic souvenir of the Tuscan countryside. Castellina's gelateria, **L'Antica Delizia** ★ (☎ *0577 741337.* ***www.anticadelizia.it***. Closed Tues), at Via Fiorentina 4 right by the main road, is the best within a day's cycle in any direction.

Yet another pretty drive follows the **SS429** meandering east through woodland and rolling vineyards from Castellina, ending up close to **Cavriglia Nature Park** (☎ *055 967544.* ***www.parcocavriglia.com***. Daily 8am–dusk. Adm free). Here you'll find indigenous animals, a picnic area and a child-friendly restaurant and *tavola calda*. Note that the park is just west of Massa Sabbioni, *not* near Cavriglia.

When you've ticked that little lot off your to-do list, spend the rest of your time hiding out in a villa or farmhouse, walking, relaxing by the pool and soaking up landscapes that have inspired writers and painters for centuries. Many tour operators (p. 24) have a particularly strong offering in Chianti. Chianti's most useful **tourist offices** are in Greve (Via delle Capanne 11, at Piazza Matteotti. ☎ *055 8546287*) and Castellina (Via Ferruccio 40. ☎ *0577 741392*). Both are open daily most of the year but do close for part of the winter.

TIP Staying Inside the Walls

Although nowhere near as crowded as San Gimignano, Volterra is also at its best without the day-trippers. Our family accommodation choice inside the walls is **L'Etrusca** (📞 *0588 84073. **www.volterraetrusca.com***), at Via Porta all'Arco 37–41, a climbing, winding street seemingly plucked straight from the Middle Ages. Apartments are basic but spacious, well equipped, and bang in the centre of town, with free Wi-Fi; unlike almost everywhere else in Tuscany, they can be booked by the night (100€–110€) all year. Stock up on local goodies and cook for yourselves—you'll feel like an Italian.

Parco Preistorico FIND

AGE 2 & UP

*Via dei Cappuccini, Peccioli. 📞 0587 636030. **www.parcopreistorico.it**. Signposted (badly) 1km (0.6 miles) north of Peccioli (22km/14 miles north of Volterra).*

You can enjoy this family theme park on two levels—parents appreciate the kitsch sight of an oversized plastic stegosaurus basking in a Tuscan wood, while for the children, there's, well, all those **dinosaurs**—including a 12-m (39-ft) hunk of brachiosaurus with his head above the pines. It's a lot of nonsense, but youngsters love it—it's outside, shaded and they can let off steam. The spectacle of a crimson **volcano** erupting plastic balls may stay with you for some time.

If you're touring in a **camper,** you can overnight at the park (with electricity and showers) for free.

Time** 1 hr. **Open** 9am–dusk daily. **Adm** 4€. **Amenities

The triceratops is just one of the residents of the Parco Preistorico

AREZZO

The *città* of painter Piero Della Francesca, art historian Giorgio Vasari, a lopsided piazza, and an unnatural number of dogs, **Arezzo ★** is a little different from central Tuscany's other hill-towns. It profits more from making exquisite gold jewellery and selling antiques than from catering to the tourist euro. There are some scruffy suburbs to overlook (blame World War II), but the **medieval heart** is a gem—it's positively tranquil compared to San Gimignano and Siena, and even spending 5 minutes with *The Legend of the True Cross* would justify jetting in from Honolulu.

Visitor Information

Information Centres

Arezzo's **tourist office** (✆ *0575 377678*. ***www.apt.arezzo.it***. 10am–7pm daily mid-Mar–mid-Nov, rest of year 10am–6pm Mon–Sat and first Sun of month) is at Piazza della Repubblica 82, outside the train station.

Arriving

By Car Driving to Arezzo is easy and quick. It's right by the **A1**, and all **car parks** are signed as you approach the walls; the handiest is **Pietri** (free). A system of escalators (*scala mobile*) takes you uphill to the **Duomo.** If you're arriving after 10am, you may have better luck at **Eden** (1.30€/hr).

By Train Arezzo is on the main Florence–Rome line and is served by a regular train (✆ *892021*. ***www.trenitalia.it***) service. A **Florence** train can take anything from ½ hour to 1½ hours, and costs from 5.70€. There's also a regular direct service from **Perugia** (1¼ hr, 5.30€).

By Bus From **Siena,** take the TRA.IN bus (✆ *0577 204111*. ***www.trainspa.it***); line 138 takes about 1½ hr.

Family-Friendly Events

Arezzo is home to one of Tuscany's iconic festivals: the **Giostra del Saracino ★**, a medieval jousting contest between the city's four *quartieri*. Expect extravagant fancy dress and Tuscan melodrama as they compete for the **Golden Lance.** The festival takes place twice a year: on the second-last Saturday in June and the first Sunday in September. Phone the office (✆ *0575 377462*) or e-mail the society (***giostradelsaracino@comune.arezzo.it***) from March onwards to book your ticket.

Less famous but just as likely to amuse little ones is the **Carnevale Aretino Orciolaia ★** (✆ *0575 28353*. ***www.carnevalearetino.it***), with colourful floats, little trains and giant inflatables. It takes place Sundays late Jan–mid-Feb.

The first Sunday of every month and the Saturday before heralds a world-renowned **antiques fair** in Piazza Grande.

AREZZO

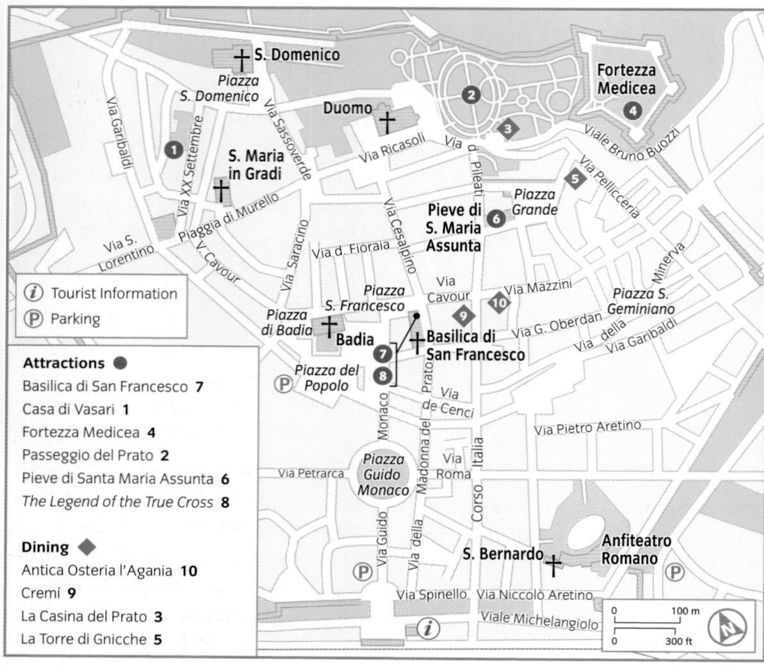

What to See & Do

The half-ruined, 16th-century **Fortezza Medicea** is the highlight of Arrezo for many children—the 360° **views** ★ from its ramparts stretch all the way to Florence and the arc of the Apennines. The fort, which has been undergoing restoration work, is usually open dawn–til dusk daily. The way in is through a tunnel from an adjacent park, the **Passeggio del Prato**—a quiet spot for a family picnic or kicking a ball about, with **swings** and a **slide,** and **La Casina del Prato,** a snack bar with a terrace.

On your way downhill from the castle, don't miss crazy-sloping **Piazza Grande** ★—its southern corner began sinking in about 1200 and has been unstoppable since.

Next find **Corso Italia,** home of Arezzo's *passeggiata*, all the best shops and **ATMs** galore. At the top of the Corso, view the **Pieve di Santa Maria Assunta** (*✆ 0575 361319*) from the outside: every column decorating this **Romanesque** church has a unique design and the bell-tower has 40 windows. **Busatti** ★ (*✆ 0575 355295*. ***www.busatti.com***), at number 48, has an unmatched range of fine linens that can be hand-made to order for children or the home, shippable anywhere.

The sloping Piazza Grande, Arezzo

The ice cream at **Cremí** (Corso Italia 100) is a treat.

Casa di Vasari ALL AGES

Via XX Settembre 55. 0575 409040.

Much more fun than an art museum is this smallish house partly built, decorated and inhabited by architect, art historian, courtier and all-round Renaissance man Giorgio Vasari. His charming frescoed 'Fireplace Room' gives a real insight into the Renaissance mind's obsession with an idealised classical world.

***Time** 30 min. **Open** 8:30am–7:30pm Mon, Wed–Sat, 8:30am–1:30pm Sun (ring bell if door closed). **Adm** 2€, children free.*

The Legend of the True Cross ★★★ AGE 7 & UP

*Piazza San Francesco. 0575 20630. **www.pierodellafrancesca.it**. Credit card bookings 0575 352727 or **https://ticketing.ribesinformatica.it/arezzo**.*

Within the Cappella Bacci of the **Basilica di San Francesco** is the reason everyone comes to Arezzo: **Piero della Francesca's** *The Legend of the True Cross*. It's a giant of Western art: a piece of work whose size, grace and technical artistry is almost shocking. It took the artist 250 days between 1452 and 1466 to paint it, and latterly it took more than 15 years to restore. Della Francesca's ability to suck all the movement from a moment, leaving frozen, timeless perfection, has never been bettered.

The 10 slightly battered panels tell the story of the wood used to build Christ's cross, based on Jacopo da Varagine's **'Golden Legend'**. The wood is traced from the **Death of Adam** to Heraclitus returning the True Cross to Jerusalem in the 7th century (the two scenes face each other in opposite lunettes). Two panels stand out: the **Meeting of Solomon and the Queen of Sheba** ★★ is majestic; while the haunted gaze of the servant in **Constantine's Dream** ★★★,

FUN FACT Acqua Aretina?

Get your children drinking Arezzo's water. There's obviously something in it—for a small place, Arezzo's list of notable sons is long, including the philosopher **Petrarch** (1304–74), art historian **Vasari** (1511–74) and **Guido d'Arezzo** (c. 992–1033), who invented the music score.

Art Matters

Tuscany's rich cultural and artistic heritage is part of the region's *spirito*—part of what it means to be Tuscan, even in the 21st century. But the importance of art and architecture goes even further: it changed the course of modern warfare, saving lives in the process. In August 1944, the retreating Nazi army destroyed every bridge in Florence, except the **Ponte Vecchio** (p. 61). Partisans defending Volterra the same year risked their lives to brick up the hill-town's greatest Etruscan artefact, the **Porta all'Arco** (p. 98), in case it was targeted by a German assault. More remarkable still is the story of **Sansepolcro.** The British officer commanding the heights over the town in 1944 remembered he'd once read an essay by Aldous Huxley—'The Greatest Picture'—that accorded that status to Piero della Francesca's *Resurrection of Christ*, still in the town gallery. He ordered the shelling to cease lest a masterpiece be lost.

Art, architecture, history, landscape and life: in Tuscany, these can never be separated.

on the lower right of the stained-glass window, follows you around the chapel—you can see him (or is that the other way round?) from the entrance.

Booking in advance is **essential.** Each visit to the chapel lasts a maximum of 30 minutes (you're free to roam the rest of the church at your leisure). Turn up at least 15 minutes before your booked slot to claim your ticket.

If you develop a thing for Piero, you can follow his art trail to the nearby towns of **Sansepolcro** and **Monterchi.**

TIP The Back Road

If you're seeking a scenic route from Arezzo to Florence, head north into the little visited **Casentino.** This wild forested upland is the source of Tuscany's great river, the Arno, and an area long popular with religious orders for its remoteness and silence. The Apennine sanctuary of **La Verna,** on the spot where St. Francis (p. 206) is said to have received the stigmata, lies on the fringe of the protected **Parco Naturale delle Foreste Casentinesi** (***www.parcoforestecasentinesi.it***).

The driving detour is simple to navigate: take the **SS71** north from Arezzo, then turn left onto the **SS70** just after Bibbiena and follow this road all the way to Pontassieve, just east of Florence. **Poppi,** with its medieval streets and 13th-century **Castello dei Conti Guidi** (***www.buonconte.com***), is the best spot to break your journey (but avoid the 'zoo'). The whole detour, at an easy pace, takes about 2 hours plus stops.

TIP Parents' Tuscany, Too

If you're lucky enough to have friends, grandparents or a nanny in tow, Tuscany has countless magical corners awaiting your **escape** without the children. For romance, dreamy landscapes and a weekend by yourselves under the Tuscan sun, try any of these:

- Book 2 nights at the luxury **Villa La Vedetta** (p. 78) to tour the paintings and sculptures in Florence's unparalleled museums.
- Dine by candlelight on classic Tuscan food at Montefollonico's **Botte Piena** (p. 188) or share a Fiorentina at **Acquacheta** in Montepulciano (p. 187).
- Contact Montepulciano's **Consorzio** (p. 175) to arrange a wine-tasting itinerary in the surrounding countryside's finest Vino Nobile *cantinas*.
- Book a table at Montalcino's **Re di Macchia** (p. 189) and a night at the **Porta Castellana** B&B (p. 191) and wake up to breakfast on the terrace as the mists rise from the Val d'Orcia below.
- Escape to Asciano for wonderful walks and bike rides in the clay hills of **Le Crete** (p. 91) and fine Renaissance frescoes at the abbey of **Monte Oliveto Maggiore** (p. 177).
- Pamper yourselves silly at the award-winning **Terme di Saturnia Spa and Golf Resort** (p. 191).

Time** 40 min. **Open** 9am–7pm Mon–Sat, 10am–7pm Sun Apr–Oct; rest of year 1 hr earlier. **Adm** 6€, 4€ 18–25s, 2€ under-18s. **Amenities

INSIDER TIP

To warm children up for the *Legend of the True Cross*, see ***www.pierodellafrancesca.it*** for some **educational games** (in English) inspired by Piero's masterpiece.

FAMILY-FRIENDLY DINING

Eating On the Go in Siena

Historic bakery **Forno dei Galli,** Via dei Termini 45 (*0577 289073;* 9am–7pm daily), sells a great variety of breads, including *schiacciata* (flatbread), plus slices of pizza to take away. It often runs specials such as *panino kids* for 1€. Not far away at Via delle Terme 94–96, the decent **Pizza al Taglio** sells well-loaded slices for 3€. Upmarket **Nannini ★** (Via Banchi di Sopra 22–24. *0577 41591*), the most lauded café in town, is worth popping into to check out the spectacular range of cakes (including *ricciarelli*—almond cookies). **Key Largo Bar,** just off Piazza del Campo on Via Rinaldini, is great fun if you can squeeze onto the narrow **balcony** upstairs—perch on small benches overlooking the Campo and munch on cakes or *panini* (2€).

Making the call as to who sells the best *gelato* in Siena isn't easy, but backstreet **Kopa Kabana ★★** (Via dei Rossi

52–54 and Via San Pietro 20. *0577 223744*) has the edge with its daily-changing range of mind-blowing flavours. Almost as good are **Brivido ★**, at Via dei Pellegrini 1, and **Caribia ★**, next door to Key Largo.

INSIDER TIP

While the touristy cafés on Siena's Piazza del Campo are overpriced, you can't beat the location **at night ★**. Save money by eating a large lunch elsewhere and grabbing a table on the piazza for evening snacks and drinks.

Restaurants

Antica Osteria l'Agania ★

ARETINE

*Via Mazzini 10, Arezzo. 0575 295381. **www.agania.com**.*

This informal little *cantina* up a sidestreet near Arrezo's Piazza Grande, specialising in Aretine cooking, has been serving up *ribollita* (vegetable soup-cum-stew), *fegatelli* (liver) *all'Aretino* and *bistecca alla Fiorentina* to a mixed local and tourist crowd since 1905—and judging by the stickers on the door, it's been in every restaurant guide going since about 1906. Children enjoy creating their own **pasta'n'sauce combo** from a choice of six of each, including plain tomato and buttery sage sauces. Parents might enjoy the house Chianti at 4€ a bottle.

Open *noon–2pm and 7–10pm Tues–Sun.* ***Main courses*** *6€–14€.* ***Credit*** *AE, MC, V.* ***Amenities***

INSIDER TIP

At nearby **La Torre di Gnicche ★**, Piaggia San Martino 8 (*0575 352035. **www.latorredignicche.it***), you'll find a firm commitment to local produce and a more limited, but high-quality, menu. Its outdoor tables fit four at a squeeze.

Antica Trattoria Papei ★

SIENESE

Piazza del Mercato 6, Siena. 0577 280894. Behind Palazzo Pubblico.

This popular restaurant is becoming a favourite with day-trippers but is still the best place to introduce the children to traditional Sienese cuisine. It's good value, with plenty of large tables inside (tables outside are smaller, but it's hardly a picturesque location anyway—the piazza comes with added car park).The menu caters to all tastes: youngsters can have the pasta basics, superb *gnocchi* or a plain veal cutlet. For the more adventurous, specialities are *pappardelle* in wild boar *ragù* or duck stewed with tomatoes. Round it off with *cantuccini* biscuits and you'll find that the *vin santo* is plonked down on the table.

Open *noon–3pm and 7–10:30pm Tues–Sun.* ***Main courses*** *7€–15€.* ***Credit*** *AE, MC, V.* ***Amenities***

Gallo Nero ★ MEDIEVAL THEMED

*Via del Porrione 65–67, Siena. 0577 284356. **www.gallonero.it**.*

This is the most entertaining restaurant in Siena, at least if any of your children are into **knights,** castles or anything medieval. It's not just the frescoed vault and waiters in medieval garb, but the food too: ordering from the *Medioevale* menu is all part of the fun. You'll find faithfully recreated dishes from the Middle Ages, mostly elaborate concoctions taken from cookbooks of the time. Try guinea fowl roasted in *vinsanto* or *fagioli del purgatorio con cotiche* (white beans with pork rind).

Open** noon–3pm and 7–11pm daily. **Main courses** 9€–18€. **Credit** AE, MC, V. **Amenities

La Mencia, Asciano, see p. 91.

Lo Sgherro ★ VALUE TUSCAN

Borgo San Giusto 74 (a 10-min downhill stroll from Porta San Francesco), Volterra. 0588 86473.

There's no ceremony at this neighbourhood trattoria—just solid regional cooking at prices that have gone out of fashion. Tuscan pasta staples are all present—hare and boar, plus the usual tomato or meat *ragù*—joined in the evening by pizzas. A long list of tasty *secondi* might include rabbit cooked in Vernaccia wine or salt cod *alla livornese*. The dining room could use a lick of paint, and if you know Tuscan food there are few surprises here, but you won't find a more authentic eating experience this close to the lair of the Volturi.

***Open** noon–2pm and 7–10pm Tues–Sun. **Main courses** 5€–11€. **Credit** MC, V.*

L'Osteria ★★ TUSCAN GRILL

Via dei Rossi 79–81, Siena. 0577 287592.

The mission at this boisterous grill in the heart of Siena's Bruco *contrada* is simple: to turn out simple, tasty cooking, using **local ingredients** where possible. The grill's the star, with flavour packed into seared beef, boar, lamb or (our favourite) succulent pork from the Cinta Senese breed of pig. Pair any of the above with a simple side of *patate fritte* or chickpeas with olive oil and you have yourself a Tuscan taste sensation. **Book ahead** to secure a spot on one of just four street-front tables. In fact, book ahead anyway; it's always busy.

***Open** 12:30–2:30pm and 7:30–10:30pm daily. **Main courses** 7.50€–20€. **Credit** AE, MC, V.*

MacDario, Panzano in Chianti, see p. 101.

Nerbone, Greve in Chianti, see p. 100.

Pizzeria Blum, Volterra, see p. 98.

Trattoria Chiribiri ★

VALUE CLASSIC ITALIAN

Piazzetta della Madonna 1, San Gimignano. 0577 941948.

This eight-table trattoria in a tiny vaulted cellar at the southern tip of walled San Gimignano has virtually none of the attributes required for family dining: it's cramped, has no highchairs, doesn't take credit cards, and the food is Italian trattoria classics. But we always eat together here: the welcome mat is out whatever your age, and the food—beef in Chianti, wild boar stew, *ossobuco*, ravioli with pumpkin, plus straight lasagne and spaghetti with meat sauce (in half-portions if you ask)—is **brilliantly executed** considering the tight squeeze. An oasis of value in the heart of rip-off city.

***Open** 11am–11pm daily. **Main courses** 6€–12€.*

Vecchia Osteria dei Poeti ★ TUSCAN

Via Matteotti 54, Volterra. ☎ 0588 86029.

Don't be fooled by the location on Volterra's tourist drag: this is a **seriously good** traditional eatery. The vaulted dining room serves up the staples you'd expect, including *pappardelle* with hare, *gnocchi* with truffles and local peasant soup, *zuppa Volterrana* (mixed seasonal veg and beans poured over bread). For something with a flourish, try the rabbit with aromatic herbs or sliced Chianina beef with pecorino cheese and toasted walnuts. There's the usual simple pasta options for the children, too, and note that it's open earlier than the norm for lunch and dinner.

***Open** 11:30am–3pm and 6:30–10pm Fri–Wed. **Main courses** 9€–22€. **Credit** AE, MC, V.*

FAMILY-FRIENDLY ACCOMMODATION

For more ideas on finding accommodation in central Tuscany, see p. 27.

APARTMENTS, VILLAS & FARM-STAYS

Agriturismo Al Gelso Bianco ★★

*Via Sant'Appiano 47, Barberino Val d'Elsa. ☎ 055 8075658. **www.algelsobianco.it**. Signposted off road from Barberino to Sant'Appiano after 2km (just over a mile).*

Perched on a ridge above the vines and olive groves between Chianti and San Gimignano (20 min), these seven renovated **apartments** are designed to very high standards and with families in mind, so there are almost guaranteed to be potential playmates for your children. Units are spacious; mostly terracotta-tiled, and individually decorated with a modern edge, they come with full kitchens. For the best view, ask for **'Ginestra'**: its roof terrace looks out at San Gimignano's towers. **'Gelsomino'**, the latest addition, packs a chic, monochrome punch.

June to September only **week-long bookings** are taken. Recent additions to the ever-changing array of on-site services are cooking courses and wine tastings.

Apartments** 7. **Rates** 1-bed 760€–1080€/wk, 2-bed 1120€–1850€/wk. Cots free. Closed mid-Jan–Feb. **Credit** MC, V. **Amenities** **In apartment

Agriturismo I Lauri ★★ FIND

*Loc. Pancole, San Gimignano. ☎ 0577 955081. **www.santopietro.it**.*

These four converted farm buildings are spread across a

240-hectare (593-acre) estate producing olive oil and wines, including San Gim's famous white Vernaccia. The apartments within them are traditionally but individually embellished with rustic wooden antique furniture; there's a bathroom for every bedroom, and each unit has its own outside space. **Views** from the vast garden are really something, and **Coiano,** a two-bedroom, private villa set slightly apart, boasts a panoramic side-wall almost entirely made of glass, with unforgettable views across the hills to Certaldo and beyond.

Apartments *17.* ***Rates*** *1-bed 550€–920€/wk, 2-bed 750€–1290€/wk, Coiano 1020€–1840€/wk. Cot 20€/wk.* ***Credit*** *MC, V.* ***Amenities*** ***In apartment***

L'Etrusca, Volterra, see p. 102.

Linearis ★ FIND

Strada di Linari S. Stefano 1–3, Barberino Val d'Elsa. 055 8078856. ***www.linearis.it.***

This small complex centred around a converted 17th-century farmhouse and stables feels stranded amid classic Tuscan countryside while being less than 5 minutes from the SI–FI *raccordo* (p. 80). Apartments come in all shapes and sizes; all are simply decorated with traditional Tuscan furniture, cream walls and cool terracotta floors. Only week-long bookings are taken during high season.

Apartments *8.* ***Rates*** *1-bed 457€–800€/wk, 2-bed 550€–1043€/wk.* ***Credit*** *MC, V.* ***Amenities*** ***In apartment***

Podere Marcampo ★★ FIND

0588 85393. ***www.agriturismo-marcampo.com.*** *1km (0.6 miles) northwest of Volterra.*

This recently restored brick and stone *agriturismo* commands unique 360° views of Volterra, Le Balze and the rolling Valdicecina. Despite a 5-year conversion, the place has retained its traditional farmhouse feel, with terracotta floors and dark-wood fittings keeping the large, fully equipped apartments firmly rooted in their Tuscan heritage.

The free Wi-Fi works all over the property, whether you're relaxing by the sizeable pool or taking part in a cookery course, although it may not stretch as far as the mushroom forages that happen in season. It's weekly bookings only all summer but they come with a 12% discount on nightly rates.

Units *6 (3 apartments, 3 rooms).* ***Rates*** *Double (sleeps 3) 90€, 1-bed (sleeps 4) 125€, 2-bed (sleeps 6) 160€. Breakfast 10€ (free with room bookings). Extra bed 25€/night.* ***Credit*** *AE, MC, V.* ***Amenities*** ***In room***

Villa Agostoli ★

Strada degli Agostoli 99, Siena. 0577 44392. ***www.villaagostoli.it.*** *5km (3 miles) west of Siena.*

This complex of mini-villas amid olive groves and vineyards a 10-minute drive from the centre of Siena offers space and **freedom** for families with a car. Each villa has a kitchen, spacious bathrooms and plenty of amenities, and there's room for four or five people, plus a terrace

TIP Alternatives In & Around Siena

Hotels in Siena book up fast, especially in summer, and the choice is limited in the *centro storico* if you're looking for large rooms, good prices and facilities for children. One option is **apartment rental;** the official Terre di Siena office will help you arrange this if you e-mail them with your requirements at: ***booking@vacanzesenesi.it***.

Many families visit the city on a day trip; if you have a car, accommodation possibilities widen considerably. See ***www.agrituristsiena.com*** for a list of local *agriturismi*. We've selected the best for review here, but there are literally hundreds more in the hills of central Tuscany.

The best local **campsite** is the revamped **Campeggio Siena Colleverde** (*0577 280044.* ***www.campingcolleverde.com***. Mid-Mar–mid-Nov), 2km (just over a mile) north of the city, with a shop, bar and outdoor pool. Pitches start at 5.70€; 4-bed mobile homes cost 105€ per night.

---

equipped for eating alfresco. The gardens are perfect for picnics and playing, and the pool is a real winner with children.

Small villas *10.* ***Rates*** *2-bed 490€–1370€/wk, 3-bed 860€–1650€/wk.* ***Credit*** *Deposit only (AE, MC, V).* ***Amenities*** ***In room***

HOTELS/BED & BREAKFASTS

Duomo ★

Via Stalloreggi 38, Siena. 0577 289088. ***www.hotelduomo.it***.

If you're keen to stay in the medieval centre of Siena, this converted 12th-century *palazzo* has one of the best locations in town, a short walk from the Duomo. There's some choice among reasonably priced triples and quads, but the best family room by far is no. 54, with a suite-style extra room and a stunning panorama over to the cathedral and beyond. All rooms are bright, modern and functional, despite the archaic exterior, though bathrooms are a little cramped.

Rooms *23.* ***Rates*** *Double 105€–150€, triple 140€–200€, quad 175€–250€.* ***Credit*** *AE, MC, V.* ***Amenities*** ***In room***

La Cisterna, San Gimignano, see p. 94.

Santa Caterina

Via Enea Silvio Piccolomini 7, Siena. 0577 221105. ***www.hscsiena.it***. *Bus: A, N, 2.*

Set in a roadside 18th-century villa just outside the Porta Romana, this friendly Sienese hotel has four cosy rooms for families. In low season, children under 18 stay free, so you pay double rates for a triple. The compact, split-level rooms themselves are tastefully decked out with antique wooden furniture and tiled floors, and there's a terraced garden where you can breakfast in the summer. This is an excellent touring stopover.

Rooms *22.* ***Rates*** *Double 85€–195€, triple 98€–255€. Cots 15€.* ***Credit*** *AE, MC, V.* ***Amenities*** ***In room***

5 Pisa, Lucca & Northern Tuscany

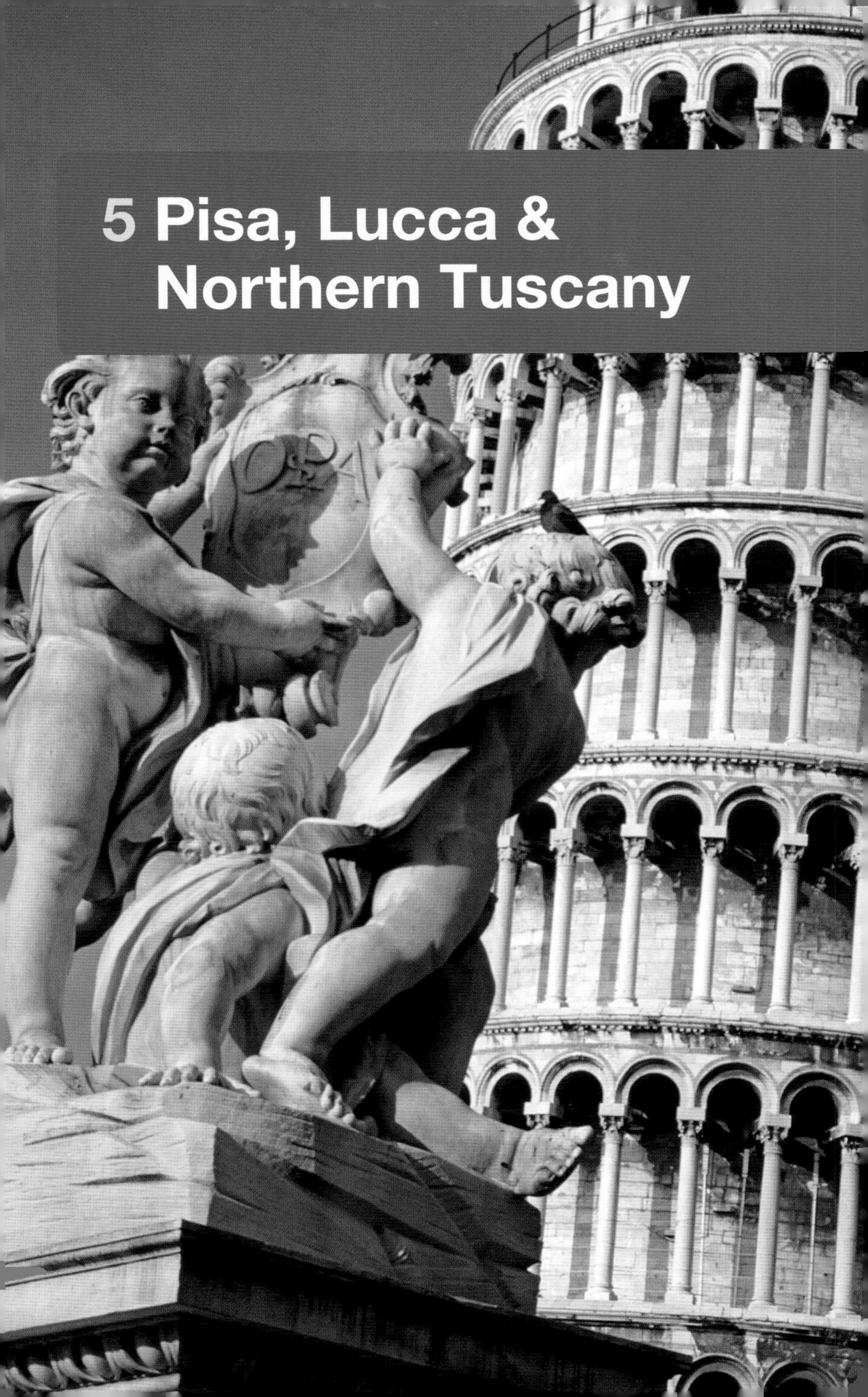

NORTHERN TUSCANY

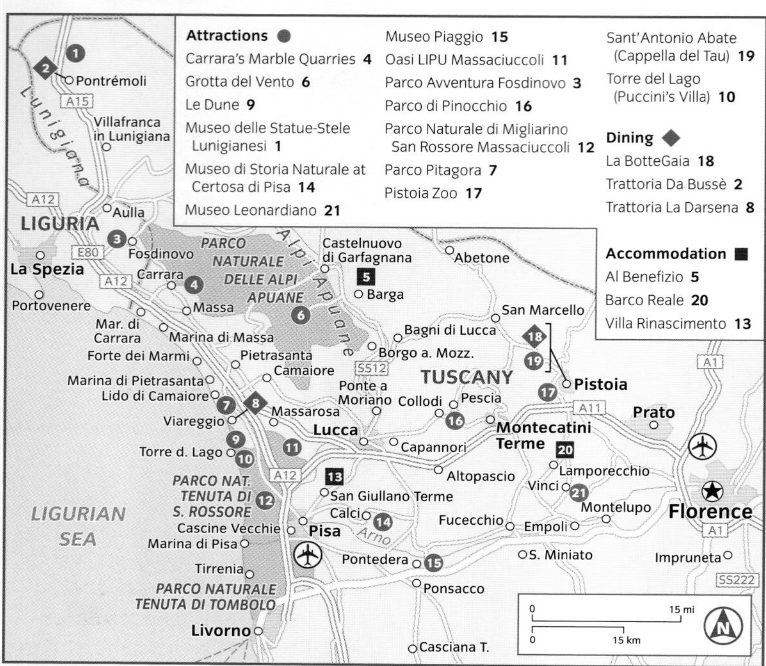

A visit to the Tuscan north doesn't stop at Pisa, despite the presence of an iconic tower looming over it. The city's **Campo dei Miracoli** is Italy's most dramatic piazza, for sure, but close by, Roman galleys unearthed from the silt of the Arno make for a fascinating visit. And nearby Lucca's elevation from hidden gem to major tourist stopover has been rapid: its medieval ramparts, some of the best preserved in Tuscany, provide the unique track for one of Tuscany's very best bike rides. Undervisited **Pistoia** has a quiet charm and one of our favourite Gothic sculptures, and there are still peaceful corners and truly great art everywhere.

The great outdoors also pulls visitors northwards. The busy beaches of the **Versilian coast** are wide, shallow and perfect for families; wealthy Florentines flock here in August to see and be seen. The mountainous **Garfagnana** and the **Apuane Alps** are paradises for walkers and cavers, dotted with charming villages and small towns in which to hide away. And you can still find a part of Tuscany that most won't even have heard of, let alone visited: rugged, forested and castle-dotted **Lunigiana,** ripe for exploring by car and ideal for a holiday away from the crowds.

For children, the north of Tuscany means great sandy stretches of beach to run around on, miles of virgin countryside to hike, and still more astounding architecture and art.

Children's Top Attractions of Northern Tuscany

- Scaling Pisa's **wonky tower,** below.
- Hanging out in the **Field of Miracles,** p. 117.
- Discovering **Roman ships** buried in the mud, p. 118.
- Circling **Lucca's walls** on bikes or rollerblades, p. 123.
- Dangling from zip-slides and crossing Tibetan bridges in the **Lunigiana,** p. 134.
- Tucking into Tuscany's tastiest **pesto,** p. 138.
- Having family fun at Viareggio's **Carnevale,** p. 131.
- Tracking wolves and lynx at Pistoia's **Moonlight Zoo,** p. 130.

PISA

Tuscany was the epicentre of the **Renaissance** and is home to the world's most inspiring art collections, but the one sight certain to drive children wild with excitement has its roots way before all that: the **Leaning Tower of Pisa.** It's a mesmerising piece of botched engineering, and one that the children will want to climb right away.

Pisa was a busy trading port during the Roman era (when the sea came farther inland) and by the early Middle Ages was one of Italy's most powerful maritime republics, controlling an empire that included Corsica, Sardinia and the Balearics. After its mighty navy was destroyed in battle with Genoa in 1284 and when the river Arno began to silt up, the city never recovered its fortunes. Today it's a sophisticated and bustling city with a cobbled *centro storico* scattered with typically Italian bars and cafés and a respected university founded in 1343, one of Europe's oldest.

Visitor Information

Information Centres

The most convenient **tourist office** for the Leaning Tower is in Piazza Arcivescovado (✆ *050 560464;* 9am–6pm daily), inside the **Museo dell'Opera del Duomo.** You'll find fewer tourists at the office near the **station,** at Piazza Vittorio Emanuele II 16 (✆ *050 42291;* 9am–7pm Mon–Fri and 9am–1:30pm Sat). The **airport** also has a Pisa tourist desk (✆ *050 502518;* 11am–11pm daily).

The official city and province **websites** are fairly informative: ***www.comune.pisa.it/turismo*** and ***www.pisaunicaterra.it***; ***www.pisaonline.it*** is another to bookmark.

Arriving

By Air For flights to Galileo Galilei airport, see p. 38. To get into the city, take the **LAM Rossa** (red) bus—4 to 7 an hour connect the airport, train station and Campo dei Miracoli in around 20 minutes (1€).

Trains connect the airport to Pisa Centrale every 30 minutes (5 min; 1.10€). **Taxis** to the centre (10–15 min) cost about 8€. There is ample **parking** at the airport (2€/hr).

By Car Pisa is easy to get to by car, with the **A11** connecting it to Florence (1 hr) and the **A12** passing just to the west. Use free 'park and rides' on the edge of town or drive farther in and pay. The best free spot is **Park Pietrasantina,** just north of the action, connected to the main sights by the LAM Rossa bus and the **Navetta Torre** (1€; pay on board). The closest to the Tower is **Parcheggio Torre Pendente** (1.75€/hr 6:30am–11:30pm; 0.85€/hr 11:30pm–6:30am) at Via Cammeo 51 near Porta Nuova, just west of Campo dei Miracoli. At the time of writing, a new car park was being built under **Piazza Vittorio Emanuele II**—it should be open by the time you read this. Away from peak tourist season, there are enough street spaces for you to be able to head for the Leaning Tower (you can see it for miles) and find something in the surrounds (1.25€/hr).

By Train Pisa Centrale, the main train station, is connected by fast services with Rome, Genoa, Milan, Turin, Naples and Livorno. Local trains shuttle from **Lucca** (25 min; 2.40€) and **Florence** (1¼ hr; 5.70€) throughout the day. From Lucca, get off at **San Rossore** if you're heading to the Leaning Tower.

Getting Around

Pisa's handsome centre is small enough to explore on foot, but there is a comprehensive local bus network run by **CPT** (☎ *050 505511*. *www.cpt.pisa.it*) if anyone gets tired. Tickets are 0.90€ for a single journey within an hour (1.50€ bought on the bus). Children less than 1m (3.3 ft) in height travel free with an adult.

As in Florence, an enjoyable and hassle-free alternative is the tourist bus, **City Sightseeing** (☎ *328 8090205*. *www.pisa.city-sightseeing.it*). **Line A** (hourly) starts just east of the Leaning Tower at Piazza Arcivescovado and makes a loop around the city; **Line B** starts in the same place and makes three runs a day to Parco San Rossore outside Pisa. Tickets (15€, 7€ for 5–15s) are valid for

TIP

Campo dei Miracoli: Joint Admissions

Admission charges to the sights around Campo dei Miracoli (except the Leaning Tower) are tied together, although you can visit the **Duomo** on a single ticket (2€). The full art-and-architecture package, the **Baptistery, Campo Santo, Museo dell' Opera del Duomo** (for Pisano sculptures and more), **Museo delle Sinopie** (fresco sketches) and Duomo, costs 10€; to visit two of these is 6€. Seeing any individually (apart from the cathedral) is 5€. See ***www.opapisa.it*** for more details.

PISA

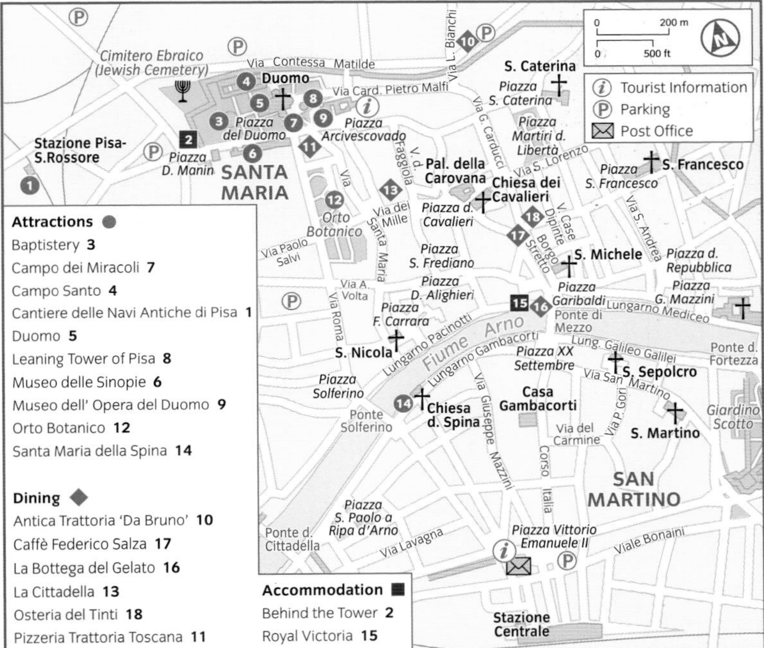

24 hours and can be used on both lines, starting anywhere. Buses operate daily April to October.

Family-Friendly Events

Pisa's best festivals both happen in June. The **Festa di San Ranieri** ★★ (16th–17th June) honours the patron saint of Pisa, a local boy who died in 1160 and was buried inside the Duomo. The celebrations begin with the *luminara*, when 70,000 candles on white wooden frames light up the Arno. The following afternoon four teams compete in a regatta, dressed in medieval garb.

The **Gioco del Ponte** ★ (last Sun in June) is great fun to watch, kicking off with a procession along the river Arno, followed by a sort of 'push-of-war' across Ponte di Mezzo. Two teams compete to see who can shove a cart to the opposite end of the bridge first.

What to See & Do

Pisa's celebrated cluster of dramatic religious sites squat around the lawns of the **Campo dei Miracoli** ★★★ ('Field of Miracles'), 1km (less than a mile) northwest of the centre and the river Arno, and a long walk from the train station (take the LAM Rossa bus). Here you'll find the medieval Duomo, the long loggias of the Campo Santo, the

Fast Facts: Pisa & the North

Banks **Unicredit** (*050 590111*) is at Piazza Garibaldi 1, Pisa.

Hospitals & Emergencies **Ospedale Santa Chiara** at Via Roma 67, Pisa (*050 992111*), has English-speaking doctors. In a medical emergency, call *118*.

Internet & Wi-Fi **Koine Internet** at Via dei Mille 3, Pisa, is open 10am to 10pm Monday to Friday, 2 to 10pm Saturday and Sunday (3.50€/hr, 10€/5 hr). Staff will also print out documents.

Pharmacies **Farmacia Comunale No. 5,** a short walk west of Campo dei Miracoli at Via Cammeo 6a, Pisa, is open 24 hours.

Post Offices Pisa's main office is at Piazza Vittorio Emanuele II 7–9 (*050 519514*). Lucca's most central office is at Via Vallisneri 2 (*0583 433555*).

Toilets Pisa's most convenient public toilets are on Campo dei Miracoli, near the **Campo Santo** (0.50€).

richly sculpted Baptistery and, yes, the Leaning Tower itself. The Campo, or Piazza del Duomo as it's known locally, crawls with tourists in high season (although apart from one small area, parking yourself on the grass is frowned upon). All sights are free for children under 10, except the tower, which you must be 8+ to climb.

Cantiere delle Navi Antiche di Pisa ★★ FIND AGE 7 & UP

*Via Bianchi Bandinelli (behind San Rossore station). 055 5276633. **www.cantierenavipisa.it.***

Pisa's best-kept secret is a number of ancient Roman galleys discovered on the edge of reclaimed marshland that once served as the **city's harbour,** where the Auser and Arno rivers emptied into the sea. At the time of writing it was uncertain when the museum will re-open, but here at the yards you get to see the boats being painstakingly excavated and restored, which is actually more interesting for children. Join a **tour** (1¼ hr); guides usually speak English.

Sometime between the 3rd century B.C. and 5th century A.D., a series of catastrophic floods sunk at least 33 boats and preserved them in the mud. Since 1998, when a construction team stumbled on the first wreck, 30 have been recovered. The first part of the tour gives a bird's-eye view of the main dig site (sadly, you can't go down) where the shapes of wrecks are clearly visible. Beyond here lie labs where the restoration process is underway: wooden hulls are encased in fibre-glass 'cages' and treated with chemicals for several years before going on display. There's also an exhibition of items retrieved from the wrecks, coins, and amphorae in pristine condition—with Roman fish paste still in them. Yeugh.

Time** 1¼ hr. **Tours** 10am, 11am, noon, 3pm, 4pm Fri–Sat; by advance booking at other times. **Adm** 8€, free under-10s. **Amenities

Duomo ★ AGE 5 & UP

*Piazza del Duomo. 050 560547. **www.opapisa.it**.*

Pisa's magnificent **cathedral,** banded in different hues of marble and decorated with tiers of arches and columns, is an exuberant archetype of Pisan–Romanesque architecture. Built between 1063 and the end of the 12th century, it has a facade heavily influenced by contact with the Arab world through trade. Within the arcaded marble interior, Giovanni Pisano's magnificent carved **pulpit** ★ (1302–10) in the nave is covered in relief panels of scenes from the New Testament. Try to identify the Nativity, Adoration of the Magi, Crucifixion and Last Judgement.

Time** 30 min. **Open** 10am–8pm daily Apr–Sept, 10am–7pm Oct, 10am–12:45pm and 2–5pm Nov–Feb, 10am–6pm Mar. **Adm** 2€ (free Nov–Feb and Sun morning), free under-10s. **Amenities

Leaning Tower of Pisa ★★★

AGE 8 & UP (TO CLIMB)

*Piazza del Duomo 17. 050 560547. Advance tickets **www.boxoffice.opapisa.it/**.*

If there's one sight guaranteed to impress children, it's the lopsided **bell-tower** of the Duomo, the *Torre Pendente*. Construction started in 1173 and continued (minus two long interruptions) for about 200 years. The lean wasn't intentional; it started during the early phases of construction (see 'Why Doesn't It Fall Down?', p. 120).

The only way to climb the arcaded tower is to **book a visit** in the office on the north side of the piazza—or for peak season, online well in advance. You should be punctual for your slot, and children aged 8–18 need to be accompanied by an adult (8–12s must hold your hand at all times). Leave bags at the cloakroom next to the ticket office behind the Duomo opposite the Tower. The climb is surprisingly steep, with 293 steps to a height of around 55m (180 ft)

The First Scientist

Galileo Galilei (1564–1642), born in Pisa, is regarded as the founder of modern physics. In 1590 he's reputed to have climbed the Leaning Tower and dropped two wooden balls, of differing sizes, from the top. When they hit the ground at the same time, he had proved that **gravity** exerts the same force on objects no matter what they weigh. It makes a good story… but experts now think that it probably never happened.

The **Duomo** has its own Galileo legend: he supposedly discovered the laws of **pendulum** motion (a pendulum's swings always take the same amount of time) by watching the bronze chandelier now known as the 'Lamp of Galileo'.

Why Doesn't It Fall Down?

So, why doesn't it?

Until the end of the 20th century the Leaning Tower *was* falling down—just very, very **slowly.** Indeed, if construction had been faster, it would have collapsed years ago. By 1990 the tower was leaning an extra 1.2mm per year and was closed to the public. An ambitious project to stabilise it involved removing soil from the base and adding lead counterweights; now it leans about 4.1m (13½ ft) off-centre and is much safer.

How did it get like that?

The most widely held theory is that the ground underneath is too unstable and sandy to hold the weight of all that marble. Check out the magnificent **Baptistery** opposite: it's got a distinct lurch of its own.

Who built it?

This is a bit of a mystery. Giorgio Vasari, who wrote *Lives of the Artists* in 1550, claimed the original architect was local boy **Bonanno Pisano,** though recent studies have revealed an obscure architect, **Biduino,** as a more likely candidate. Giovanni di Simone worked on it in the 13th century, and Tommaso Pisano finished it off in 1360. The actual work was done by hundreds of builders, masons and craftsmen.

What's it for?

It's the bell-tower (*campanile*) of the Duomo, housing seven **giant bells.**

How big is it?

The tower is 58.36m (191½ ft) high from its foundations and 55.86m (183 ft) from the ground on the lowest side, 56.7m (186 ft) on the highest side. It weighs 14,453 tonnes.

up, but it's great fun—you really notice the lean and are rewarded with fantastic views over Pisa.

***Time** 30 min. **Open** 8:30am–8pm daily Apr–Sept, 9am–7pm Oct, 9:30am–5:30pm Nov, Feb–Mar; 10am–4:30pm daily Dec and Jan. **Adm** 15€ (17€ online).*

INSIDER TIP

Don't buy so much as a *caffè* around the Campo dei Miracoli without checking the price first. It's not unusual to be charged **triple** what you're expecting.

Museo di Storia Naturale at Certosa di Pisa AGE 7 & UP

*Via Roma 79, Calci. 050 2212970. **www.msn.unipi.it**. 6km (4 miles) east of Pisa; follow signs for 'Certosa di Calci'.*

Tucked away inside the largest Carthusian monastery in Italy, the University of Pisa's **natural history museum** will divert older children for an hour or two—the presentation is a little didactic for younger ones. There's a huge collection of stuffed carnivores and reptiles, plus a tropical aquarium.

The highlights, though, are the multimedia re-creations of landscapes from the age of dinosaurs, all reconstructed from local fossil records. A realistic **giant mako shark** might scare little ones.

Visits to the lavishly Baroque **monastery** itself are by guided tour (1 hr; usually in Italian; hourly from 8:30am–6:30pm Tues–Sat; last visit on Sun goes at 12:30pm. Adm 4€, under-18s free). Most interesting are the cells where the monks passed their years in silence.

Time *2 hr.* ***Open*** *9am–5pm Mon–Fri, 9am–6pm Sat, 10am–7pm Sun Apr–June; 9am–2pm Mon–Fri, 9am–6pm Sat, 10am–7pm Sun July, Aug and Oct–Mar; 9am–1:30pm and 2:30–5:30pm Mon–Fri, 9am–6pm Sat, 10am–7pm Sun Sept.* ***Adm*** *7€, 3.50€ ages 6–18.* ***Amenities***

Museo Piaggio ★ FIND

AGE 10 & UP

Viale Rinaldo Piaggio 7, Pontedera. 0587 27171. ***www.museopiaggio.it****. Signposted 14km (8½ miles) southeast of Pisa off SS67.*

Parco Naturale di Migliarino San Rossore Massaciuccoli

On Sundays between May and September (10am and 1pm; return boats leave at 3:30pm), you can take an open-top **boat ride** along the River Arno to admire Pisa from a new angle and give your feet a break. **Il Navicello** (*050 530101*. ***www.ilnavicello.it***) runs trips into the **Parco Naturale di Migliarino San Rossore Massaciuccoli** and back. Tickets (sold on board) are 8€, 7€ ages 3 to 10. You can catch the boat at San Paolo, not far from **Santa Maria della Spina** church.

To properly explore the Parco Naturale (***www.parcosanrossore.it***), which has fantastic wildlife and **birdwatching** trails, pre-book a guided tour on foot, bike or **horseback** ★. These depart from the visitor centre in Cascine Vecchie, 4½ km (3 miles) west of central Pisa. Guided cycle tours lasting 2½ hours cost 12.50€, 10.50€ for children 12 and under; on horseback a 1½-hour guided outing is 19.50€; a 2-hour guided walk costs 10€. Email ***visitesr@tin.it*** or call *050 530101* to book (*338 3662431* for horse-riding).

There are also around 10km (6 miles) of flat cycle and walking trails open to free public wandering, but access to Gombo beach (where drowned Romantic poet Shelley's body washed up in 1822) is only possible on a guided visit. The park is open (and offers bike-hire) on weekends and national holidays all year.

Another fine family walk along this stretch of unspoilt coast follows the mouth of the River Serchio and brings you to a good beach (avoid it on summer weekends). Leave the SS1 just south of the '*Pisa nord*' *autostrada* junction and follow signs for Marina di Vecchiano; stop at the car park as the road turns 90° right and follow the path past simple moorings where Pisans have come to fish and relax for decades.

TIP Glorious *Gelato*

La Cittadella at Via dei Mille 18 (7am–7:30pm daily) is an excellent place to grab a *gelato* or coffee between Campo dei Miracoli and the city centre. At the bottom of Pisa's main shopping street, at Piazza Garibaldi 11, **La Bottega del Gelato** ★ (*050 575467.* 11am–midnight daily) serves the best in town.

Though Piaggio have made trains, planes and automobiles, they're known worldwide for one thing: the **Vespa.** It's no surprise, then, that their **company museum** is largely given over to celebrating 60-plus years of Italy's iconic scooter—this is the only place in the world where fashion-conscious mums, dads and teens get to admire models from the 1940s and 1950s all together, including the 1943 'Paperino' ('Donald Duck'), a prototype for the original 1946 Vespa. As well as the bikes, there are old adverts, concept prototypes, and early designs and photos, plus a multimedia presentation on the development process from idea to production line—great for budding designers. Otherwise, there are **'do not touch'** signs everywhere, so this isn't a place to bring agile young sprites.

Time *45 min.* ***Open*** *10am–6pm Tues–Sat.* ***Adm*** *Free.* ***Amenities***

Orto Botanico ALL AGES

Via Luca Ghini 5. 050 560045.

Lose the crowds and take a breather after the chaos of the Campo at this quiet slice of green just south of the Leaning Tower. Established in 1544 and moved to here in 1595, it's the **oldest botanical garden** in Europe and contains ponds, shady palm trees, greenhouses and herb gardens, plus plenty of space to run around (although not on the grass!). The eccentric

TIP Shopping Pisa

For shops with a proper local flavour, handsome, arcaded Borgo Stretto in the old centre is a great spot for window-browsing, with fair prices if you're tempted to buy something. **Hobby Centro** at no. 57 (*050 580888*) has a large selection of toys, while baby chain **Prénatal** has a branch at no. 14 (*050 579618*). For a treat, pop into **Caffè Federico Salza** ★, a 19th-century café with pastries and sumptuous hot chocolate. But do note that much of Borgo Stretto is closed Sundays, Monday mornings and most of August.

The **touristy stalls** around the Campo dei Miracoli seem a bit tacky but your children might love a Leaning Tower T-shirt, mug or pen, all less than 15€. And you should at least buy a model of the tower: a small one will only set you back about 1€.

TIP Packing a Pisan Picnic

Your main stop should be Pisa's weekday market, crammed into the twin squares of Piazza San Omobono and Piazza delle Vettovaglie. There, seasonal produce stalls are supplemented by shops selling fresh and cooked meat, fish and tasty deli products.

The cheapest place to stock up on everything else is **PAM** supermarket; the branch at Viale delle Cascine 1 (8am–7:30pm daily) is near San Rossore station, a short walk from Campo dei Miracoli; the one at Via Pascoli 8 (7:30am–8:30pm Mon–Sat, 9am–1pm Sun) is in the centre.

original botanical institute with its shell-embellished facade is a sight to be seen.

Time *45 min.* ***Open*** *8:30am–5:30pm Mon–Fri, 8:30am–1pm Sat.* ***Adm*** *2.50€, 1.50€ ages 6–12, 6€ family ticket.* ***Amenities***

LUCCA

These days **Lucca** ★ has just about ditched its 'undiscovered' label: this cobbled provincial capital, wrapped in a perfect set of walls, is now firmly on the Tuscan town trail. But it's still one of Italy's most delightful towns, with a flamboyant cathedral, lovely squares and numerous charming, Liberty-style shopfronts. There's plenty here to keep families occupied for a day or two.

Visitor Information

Information Centres

The main **tourist office** (*0583 919931. www.luccaturismo.it.* 9am–8pm daily Apr–Oct, rest of year 9am–12:30pm and 3–6:30pm Mon–Sat) is at Piazza Santa Maria 35. There are smaller offices inside the Palazzo Ducale (*0583 91994*), in Piazzale Verdi (*0583 583150. www.luccaitinera.it*) and in Piazza Curtatone (*0583 495730*).

Arriving

Lucca is easiest to reach by **train** (*892021. www.trenitalia.it*). There are regular links with **Florence** (1½ hr, 5.10€), **Pisa** (30 min, 2.40€) and **Pistoia** (50 min, 3.60€). The station is in Piazza Ricasoli, just south of the walls.

Getting here by **car** is simple enough: Lucca is bang on the **A11**, 72km (45 miles) west of Florence. The town is busy and **parking** can be tricky. Your only options for free are outside the walls: north of town there's the vaguely signposted **Palasport.** Just inside the eastern walls, it's 1€/hr to park underground at **Mazzini;** turn right as you come through Porta Elisa. From there it's a 10-minute walk to the action.

LUCCA

Family-Friendly Events

Children might enjoy some of the modern acts at Lucca's **Summer Festival:** the programme is regularly updated at ***www.summer-festival.com***. Recent headliners have included Joss Stone, Paolo Nutini and Alicia Keys. For lovers of the the music of Lucca's favourite son, composer Giacomo Puccini (1858–1924), **Puccini e la sua Lucca** (***www.puccinielasualucca.com***) hosts 1-hour recitals and concerts every evening, all year, in the Basilica di San Giovanni. Tickets cost 17€, 12€ under-23s.

A vast **antiques market** is held in Piazza San Martino on the third Sunday of each month (and previous Saturday), spreading into the streets around the cathedral. Further one-off events are usually advertised in widely available English-language monthly **Grapevine.**

What to See & Do

In theory, Lucca is a **pedestrian** *città*, but that's 'pedestrian' in the Italian sense of allowing cars and buses to drive everywhere. It's a town of secret alleys, misshapen piazzas and hidden courtyards, tricky to get oriented in; find **Via Fillungo** ★, the medieval mall, and take it from there. You'll eventually come across **Piazza Anfiteatro,** where the

TIP Shopping Lucca

The glorious Liberty-style shopfronts of Via Fillungo are the place to join the locals on their evening *passeggiata*, but prices for shoppers can be steep. **Via Buia** and **Via Santa Lucia** are also crammed with independent shops selling everything from spices to jewellery.

For a local tipple, including **Montecarlo DOC,** and a massive range of Tuscan labels at all prices ensconced in a wine-filled warren, **Enoteca Vanni** ★ (*0583 491902. www.enotecavanni.com*) at Piazza San Salvatore 7 is the best bottle-shop in town.

Pasticceria Taddeucci at Piazza San Michele 34 (*0583 494933. www.taddeucci.com*) is the home of the **Buccellato** ★, a dense, sweet bread flavoured with fennel seeds and raisins—a delicious snack as you roam.

---

outline of a Roman amphitheatre has been preserved; the gates into this piazza are the very ones gladiators walked through. The phenomenal facade you'll bump into in Piazza San Michele is **San Michele in Foro** ★; the inside's a let-down, but the exterior is a masterpiece of elaborate **Pisan-Romanesque styling.**

Biking the Walls ★★ AGE 2 & UP

Blame Marie-Louise Bourbon—it was she who turned Lucca's defensive ramparts into shady boulevards of plane, chestnut and ilex. Built between 1500 and 1645, the 11 bastions, six gates and 4km (2½ miles) of flat wall are ideal for **cycling** and **sightseeing.** Start in Piazza Santa Maria, where you can hire bikes next to the tourist office at **Cicli Bizzarri** (*0583 496031*. 8:30am–1pm and 2:30–7:30pm Mon–Sat, plus Sun Mar–Sept). Bikes cost 2.50€/hr (plenty of time for one circuit); tandems, *cammellini* (little bikes hooked to the back of yours) or trailers for tots are all 5.50€.

On summer afternoons and weekends, the ramparts are

Explore Lucca by bike

crowded with families, joggers, cyclists and people having picnics or lazing on the grass. Head clockwise, with the town on your right, and you'll soon see a couple of oak trees growing from the roof of the **Torre Guinigi,** which are best viewed from right above the playground by Porta Elisa (head to Via Sant'Andrea to climb the tower for a closer look). About a minute farther along, there's another slide, with shade. On the right is the **Orto Botanico,** complete with Tuscan plants and lily pads. The elevated ramparts provide an alternative view of the cathedral (see below) and square **campanile;** the red-brick tower visible just after is the **Torre delle Ore,** Lucca's 13th-century clock tower. Still farther, the gate standing next to another playground is the medieval **Porta San Gervasio.**

Just before you get back to Piazza Santa Maria, look down into the manicured Baroque gardens of the **Palazzo Pfanner.** The church of **San Frediano** stands behind with a fine 13th-century **mosaic** ★ shimmering on its facade.

Some warnings: there's plenty of room on the ramparts but **no fence** on the inner edge of the walls, so cycle that side of young ones if they're pedalling themselves; there are occasional fatal accidents. And those little taps you keep seeing are **drinking water,** so use them—it gets very hot and sunny up here in summer.

Time *1 hr.*

INSIDER TIP

A cool way for older children to 'do' the walls is on **rollerblades.** Alas, no one in Lucca rents them out yet, so bring your own or buy them in child sizes at **TuttoSport** (*0583 91600*) at Via Mordini 25.

Cattedrale di San Martino ★

AGE 10 & UP

Piazza San Martino. 0583 490530.

You could stand for hours staring at the facade of Lucca's largely Pisan–Romanesque cathedral and still spot new details in its magnificent Gothic carved masonry. Inside, a towering ceiling and constant twilight conceal some rather forbidding Baroque art. Within a chapel by Matteo Civitali (1436–1502) that looks like Brighton Pavilion, the ***Volto Santo*** is a poignant image of Jesus on the cross, reputedly carved by Nicodemus at the time

Cattedrale di San Martino, Lucca

of the Crucifixion. Carbon-dating has placed the cross firmly in the 13th century, but it's processed through the town by candlelight every 13th September in the **Luminara di Santa Croce ★**. More interesting is the **Tomb of Ilaria del Carretto ★** in the Sacristy (2€); Jacopo della Quercia's masterpiece depicts Ilaria, wife of Paolo Guinigi, 15th-century ruler of Lucca, who died in childbirth. The dog at her feet symbolises fidelity.

Time** 45 min. **Open** 9:30am–5:45pm Mon–Fri, until 6:45pm Sat; 9:30–10:45am and noon–6pm Sun. **Adm** Free. **Amenities

Museo Nazionale del Fumetto (Comic Museum) ★ AGE 7 & UP

*Piazza San Romano. 0583 56326. **www.museonazionaledelfumetto.it**.*

Don't be fooled by appearances: this isn't *just* the pretty, medieval convent of San Romano. In 2004 part of the building and courtyard were converted into a multimedia shrine to the comic. Its occasionally grown-up collection features Italian cult classics mixed with familiar international names, including original 1940s' *Topolino* (Mickey Mouse) comics, 1960s' *Batmans* and 1980s' *Supermans*. The best part is the **Viaggio nel '900** ('Voyage to the 1900s'), where you can wander among lifesize models of Clark Kent's phonebox and Mickey's kitchen. Children of all ages are also free to scrawl in themed creative spaces such as Disney's *Art Attack* room and a *Casa di Pooh*.

Under-12s must be accompanied at all times. There is English signage and leaflets, but unless you read Italian, a handful of the exhibits will be a little remote.

Time** 1 hr. **Open** 10am–6pm Tues–Sun. **Adm** 4€, 3€ ages 4–10. **Amenities

PISTOIA & ITS PROVINCE

Many visitors to Tuscany neglect **Pistoia ★** in favour of its more famous neighbours, but take the trouble to spend some time in this vibrant little town—you won't regret it.

Situated at the base of the Apennines, the city has long shed its medieval reputation for mindless violence to become northern Tuscany's **market garden.** It's famous today for its plant nurseries; the surrounding plains are lined with orderly rows of trees and shrubs in back-to-back *vivaii*. Many of the cypresses that stud the fields and decorate postcards of rural Tuscany began their life right here.

Visitor Information

Information Centres

The friendly city **tourist office** (*0573 21622. **www.pistoia.turismo.toscana.it***. 9am–1pm and 3–6pm daily) is at Piazza del Duomo 4. Head for the tallest tower you can see to find it (Pistoia's a maze, so you'll need a map). Staff will also advise on visiting the rest of the province.

Arriving

If you're based in Florence, three **trains** (📞 *892021. www.trenitalia.it*) an hour leave Santa Maria Novella for Pistoia, taking 40 minutes and costing 3€. For those arriving by car, the parking signposted by the *stadio* (Oplà) and at Cellini is free and not too far from the centre on foot.

What to See & Do

Pistoia's medieval, walled *centro storico* is almost intact and incorporates some wonderful buildings and great art, so repays an extended stroll. Start your tour in **Piazza del Duomo** ★, a fine civic square and a match for anything in more fashionable Lucca. It's dominated by the zebra-hooped **Baptistery** and Romanesque **Cattedrale di San Zeno** (📞 *0573 25095*). The interior has a towering nave and is rich in adornment; the half-ruined **crypt** is fun to explore (8:30am–12:30pm and 3:30–7pm daily, plus some lunchtimes in summer. Adm free).

Walk 5 minutes north of the piazza to see the **Ospedale del Ceppo,** or rather the glazed terracotta frieze on its facade: carved by Giovanni della Robbia in the early 1500s, it features a motley collection of Pistoiese pilgrims and sick patients. The building is still a hospital. Nearby, silent, unassuming **Sant'Andrea** ★ (8:30am–12:30pm and 3–6pm daily) is the unlikely yet somehow apt home for Tuscany's greatest carved **pulpit** ★★. Completed in 1301 by Giovanni Pisano, it features five panels dealing with different Biblical episodes—among them a torrid *Massacre of the Innocents* and a graphic *Last Judgement.*

INSIDER TIP

On Saturday mornings Pistoia's ancient piazzas burst with market stalls, and you'll usually find great-value **children's shoes** in Piazza dello Spirito Santo.

Sant'Antonio Abate (Cappella del Tau) ★ AGE 5 & UP

Corso Silvano Fredi 70. 📞 *0573 32204.*

This plain stone cube on a main road houses Pistoia's lesser-known **art treasure:** the interior surface of the chapel was frescoed by **Niccolò di Tommaso** and **Antonio Vite** in (probably) the 1370s. Parts of the walls are badly mutilated, but the ceiling is almost complete. The frescoes relate Biblical stories, starting from the back-right corner as you walk in (facing you is **Paradise**). The ceiling and top level illustrate stories from the **Old Testament;** the middle level narrates the **New Testament.** Large bronzes by Pistoia native Marino Marini (1901–80) now share the space.

Aross the road, **Magico Chiosco** knocks up cheap, tasty *panini* (from 2€).

Time *30 min.* ***Open*** *8:30am–1:30pm Mon–Sat.* ***Adm*** *Free.*

Ospedale del Ceppo, Pistoia

What to See & Do Elsewhere in the Province

You'll need a car to make tracks to some of the further-flung corners of Pistoia's scenic province. For **car-hire** advice, see p. 25.

Museo Leonardiano ★

AGE 12 & UP

Vinci. ☎ *0571 933251.* ***www.museoleonardiano.it.*** *24km (15 miles) south of Pistoia.*

Yes, *that* Vinci (which is actually just outside Pistoia's province, but let's not quibble). Such has been the success of Tuscany's original **Leonardo da Vinci** museum that it exists in a state of constant renewal: first the **Castello dei Conti Guidi**'s two floors of marvellous machines were joined by another at **Palazzina Uzielli,** then the original Castello space got an overhaul in 2010. Although the new rooms have some multimedia additions, including PC terminals showing the machines in 3D, the drill's the same: accurate, well-explained models of the weird, wonderful and downright genius inventions from the Renaissance master's *Codex Atlanticus*. Highlights include the massive crane, the famous flying (actually, flapping) machine and some cool stuff on **optics.**

Alas, the presentation is a bit dry for young ones. In fact, the physics is so complex that this is really not for young children at all. That said, it's worth the drive for mechanically minded older children and adults—the trip south from Pistoia through the olive terraces is a corker, and there's a brilliant **campsite** nearby (p. 139). Plus, overcrowding has eased since the Dan Brown-induced Leo craze a few years ago.

Avoid the rest of Vinci, however.

Time *1½ hr.* ***Open*** *9:30am–6:15pm daily Mar–Oct, 9:30am–5:15pm Nov–Feb.* ***Adm*** *6€, 4.50€ ages 14–18 and adults accompanying under-18s, 3€ ages 6–14.* ***Amenities***

Parco di Pinocchio ★ AGE 2–7

Collodi. ☎ *0572 429342.* ***www.pinocchio.it/park.htm.*** *Signposted off SS435 15km (9 miles) east of Lucca; BluBus 109 from Pescia station.*

More 'themed park' than theme park, this little world of Carlo Lorenzini's creation, Pinocchio, lies midway between Lucca and

Public Scribbles

Young Italians, especially those living south of the Apennines, are very attached to their indelible markers, but the resulting **graffiti** is rarely original. An amorous 'so-and-so *ti amo*'; *forza!* the local team; occasionally, the mayor is a *fascista* or *comunista*. Saying something rude about the neighbours is delivered with untranslatable relish—one reason not to teach the children *too much* Italian vocabulary, perhaps.

The Sienese have centuries of issues with the Florentines; *Lucchese* look down their noses at the Pisans. But they're all agreed, Romans are... We're too polite to write exactly what. *Campanilismo*—literally, loyalty to one's bell-tower—is alive and well in teen Tuscany.

Pistoia. Negotiate some tricky first impressions (**overpriced,** needs a lick of paint) and you will start to enjoy yourself. The main 'Paese dei Balocchi' ('Land of Toys') beyond the giant mosaic is a fantastical maze of steps, ramps and bronze statues of characters from Lorenzini's tale, skilfully designed to keep tots wondering what's round the next corner, with the giant whale at the story's climax revealed gradually through a bamboo forest.

As well as the maze, there's the **Painting Corner** (10am–12:30pm and 3–6:30pm), three live **shows** a day (Italian only), carousels (1€) and Pinocchio-themed face-painting (weekends only). The park could use a spruce-up, but the old-fashioned style is perfect for imaginative youngsters.

Time** 3 hr. **Open** 8:30am–dusk daily. **Adm** 11€ ,8€ ages 3–14. **Combined ticket** 18€/14€ with Villa Garzoni Gardens and Butterfly House (☎ 0572 429590). **Amenities

INSIDER TIP

If the children don't know **Carlo Lorenzini's** surreal story, make your first stop the **mechanical theatre,** where an English hand-out and original 1920s' marionettes will bring them up to speed.

Pistoia Zoo AGE 2 & UP

*Via di Pieve a Celle 160a. ☎ 0573 911219. **www.zoodipistoia.it**. 2km (just over 1 mile) west of 'Pistoia Ovest' exit from ring road.*

Packed with Italian families at weekends, the **Giardino Zoologico di Pistoia** is by far the best in Tuscany, with 600 animals, including big cats and lots of snakes, to keep little ones transfixed. Every weekend sees a free all-day *Incontri Bestiali* programme when children (and parents) can touch and learn about tortoises, harmless snakes, goats and the like. Other structured children's programmes ('*per piccoli visitatori*') highlight the zoo's commitment to conservation. But better still is the **Moonlight Zoo** ★ (10pm Wed–Sun Apr–Nov), offering 1½-hour guided visits that take in animals that don't do much during daylight, allowing you to see wolves, owls and lynx at their most active. **Call** the zoo at least 5 days in advance to book; if you don't speak Italian, ask when the Moonlight guide who speaks English will next be running a tour.

Time *3 hr.* ***Open*** *9:30am–5pm Mon–Fri, 9:30am–7pm Sat and Sun.* ***Adm*** *12.50€, 9.50€ ages 3–9.* ***Children's programmes*** *18.50€ inc. entry (ages 5–11).* ***Moonlight Zoo*** *18.50€/14.50€ (55.50€ family) inc. entry.* ***Amenities***

VIAREGGIO

A popular seaside resort since the 19th century, Viareggio is the principal town of **Versilia,** Tuscany's Riviera. It has retained an air of faded gentility, with grandiose Belle Epoque buildings lining its long seafront. In summer, it heaves with holidaymakers (mostly from Florence) and in many ways it's the quintessential Italian beach destination. It'll be bucket-and-spade heaven for your children.

Visitor Information

Information Centres

The main **tourist office** (✆ *0584 962223.* ***www.aptversilia.it***. 9am–2pm and 3–7pm Mon–Sat, 9am–12:30pm and 3–6pm Sun) is tucked away in a courtyard at Viale Carducci 10. There's an **ATM** next door. The train station also has a small tourist office, in Piazza Dante (✆ *0584 48881.* ***stazione.vg@aptversilia.it***. Mon–Sat mornings).

Arriving

Viareggio is at the junction of the **A12** and **A11,** 22km (13½ miles) from both Pisa and Lucca. If you drive, there are plenty of central spaces and **car parks,** but arrive late on a summer weekend and you may have trouble getting on the seafront. Parking generally costs about 1€ per hour.

By **train** (✆ *892021.* ***www.trenitalia.it***), there are easy, regular links with **Lucca** (20 min, 2.40€), **Pisa** (20 min, 2.40€) and **Florence** (1½ hr, 6.60€)—if you're based in any of those, don't come by car in summer.

INSIDER TIP
Most hotels in Viareggio are overpriced, so do as many Tuscans do and make it a **day-trip** destination.

Family-Friendly Events

Since 1873, Viareggio has hosted Italy's second-biggest **Carnevale** ★ after that of Venice. The seaside comes alive with floats, masked dances and noise, but the party atmosphere has a child-friendly flavour. Events take place throughout **February,** with the main parades on Sundays and Shrove Tuesday. Tickets for these cost 15€, 10€ for 11- to 13-year-olds; under-10s go free. Call ✆ *0584 47077* or e-mail ***biglietteria@ilcarnevale.com*** to book a seat in the stands (15€ extra); otherwise, pay on the day and wander at will. Book Carnival accommodation well in advance. See ***www.viareggio.ilcarnevale.com*** for more.

For the **Puccini Festival,** see below.

What to See & Do

Viareggio's **promenade,** lined with cafés and (pricey) shops, is a pleasant spot to stroll with a buggy—or on rollerblades. A statue of **Burlamacco,** official mascot of the Carnival since 1930, guards the sands opposite Piazza Mazzini. The town's famous promenade 'sight', the Art Nouveau **Gran Caffè Margherita,** is a puffed-up architectural oddity, but the interior is worth a peek (half of it is now a bookshop).

The marine-themed displays at the **Museo della Marineria** (*0584 391004;* Fri–Sun 6–11pm in summer, 4–7pm in winter. Adm 2.50€, free under-14s) across the canal at Via Peschiera 9 kill half an hour. While you're there, see the **day's catch** traded at what is still a working **fishing port.**

Statue of Burlamacco, symbol of Carnevale

But the real draw is Viareggio's **beach** ★: wide and flat, it has a shallow shelf that means little ones can paddle safely. Various private **bathing companies** (*stablimenti balneari*) guard their own stretches. In return for a fee (about 7€pp/day, or roughly 20€ for a family), you get a patch of groomed sand, facilities to change and shower, and a parasol and sunlounger; some (bizarrely) even have swimming pools. Prices fluctuate by day and season; you'll get the best deal if you're here for a week and book with one company for the duration. We like the vaguely *aloha* style of **Tre Stelle** at Viale Margherita 64/1 (*0584 44370*), but there's plenty to choose from.

There's also a public beach, **Le Dune** ★, 1½km (nearly a mile) south of town along Viale Europa. If you're out this way, there's also a playground with **swings** and **slides** at the corner of Viale Kennedy and Viale dei Tigli, and plenty of shady strolling or **cycling** under the *pineta*.

Oasi LIPU Massaciuccoli

ALL AGES

Via del Porto 6, Massaciuccoli. 0584 975567. ***www.oasilipumassaciuccoli.org****. 6km (4 miles) south of Massarosa, direction Pisa/Lucca.*

Puccini's Lake

Separated from Viareggio by a glorious avenue of lime trees, Torre del Lago is forever bound to the composer of *Tosca*, *Madam Butterfly* and *La Bohème,* Giacomo Puccini (1858–1924), although a 40-minute tour of the lakefront **villa** (☎ *0584 341445.* ***www.giacomopuccini.it;*** timed visits 9 times daily 10am–5:40pm exc. Mon and all Nov; adm 7€) where he lived and composed is a must-do for diehard fans only.

A few companies run 1-hour boat-trips on reed-fringed **Lago di Massaciuccoli,** a WWF reserve—part of the **Parco Naturale di Migliarino San Rossore Massaciuccoli** (p. 121)—where you can spot rare marsh birds and enjoy the silence. Buy tickets (6€, children 3€) on board. The lake also provides the backdrop for the the summer **Puccini Festival** (☎ *0584 359322.* ***www.puccinifestival.it***. Seasonal **ticket office** at Viale Puccini 257/a; tickets 35€ to 125€). The rest of the year, fans can enjoy daily Puccini concerts in Lucca: see p. 124.

Young ornithologists should visit Lago di Massaciuccoli

If you can't make it down to the nature reserves of the Maremma (p. 161), this is the best spot in northern Tuscany for a young **ornithologist:** raised walkways above the reed-beds link bird-watching hides on the fringes of Lago di Massaciuccoli (p. 121) opposite Torre del Lago. Residents such as the marsh harrier and several species of wader punctuate the silence with their song. Check the website or call ahead for events. **Guided boat tours** of the lake and its inhabitants (8€, 5€ children) leave from the jetty on summer Sundays after lunch.

Time *At least 1 hr.* ***Open*** *Daily exc. Tues Nov–Feb.* ***Adm*** *Free.* ***Amenities***

Parco Pitagora FIND AGE 1–11

Via Aurelia, Lido di Camaiore. ☎ *0584 611008.* ***www.parcopitagora.com****. Off SS1 1½ km (less than 1 mile) north of Viareggio, junction Via Pitágora.*

Ask staff at the tourist office to show you this park on the map: it's dastardly to find but worth it with young children, despite being slightly scruffy—there are carousels, a mini-train, **bouncy castles,** trampolines, bumper hovercraft, tyre swings, slides... Older children can play basketball or video games, and there's plenty of shade. Entry is free, you pay for rides with **tokens** (sold 10am–12:30pm, 3:30–7:30pm and 9–11:30pm: 1€ each or 20€ for 40).

FUN FACT **Ghostly Sighting** 

When the Garfagnana's main dam enclosing Lago di Vagli empties every 10 years for cleaning, a former iron-working village reappears. **Fabbriche di Careggine**'s rebirth from 70m (230 ft) of water is expected again in 2014.

Time *At least 1 hr.* ***Open*** *10am–midnight daily June–Aug, 10am–7pm Sept–May.* ***Adm*** *Free.* ***Amenities*** 

TUSCANY'S FAR NORTH

To the hills! Tuscany's northwest corner is defined by the impassable Apennines, which shadow the **Garfagnana** and the **Lunigiana** ★. Just north of the Apuane Alps, the Garfagnana is a treasure box of wild crags, seemingly endless chestnut forest and miles of rock formations above and below ground. Its trough was cut by the River Serchio, which threads along the core; the only busy bit of the valley follows the SS445 along its banks. Escape from there and you're in an emerald-green heaven for walkers, climbers and potholers.

The Lunigiana, named after its port, is west of Garfagnana and even **emptier.** Aside from the **marble quarries** at Carrara on its edge, its insular, Ligurian terrain is rarely visited by anyone, Italian or British. So you'll have isolated villages, rugged vistas, twisting mountain roads and terraced olive groves all to yourself.

Visitor Information

Adventurous outdoors families seeking to make the most of what's on, in and under the Garfagnana will need expert guidance: contact the tourist office in **Barga** (Via di Mezzo 47. ☎ *0584 724743.* ***urp@comunedibarga.it***) and consult ***www.luccatourist.it***. Also look out for Vittorio Verole-Bozzello's *Discover Garfagnana* (15€), with 38 hiking itineraries.

For the Lunigiana, the most useful tourist offices are in **Carrara** (Viale XX Settembre. (☎ *0585 844136*. Mornings daily) and in **Aulla** (Piazza Gandhi. (☎ *0187 409474*. Fri–Sun). The tourist office publishes an irregularly updated but excellent and free guide to the best of the area, *Qualità Lunigiana*. See also ***www.aptmassacarrara.it***.

INSIDER TIP

The most spectacular way into the Lunigiana by car is the **SS446** from Carrara to Fosdinovo. This road follows a ridge that fringes the Apuane Alps, offering unbelievable **views** ★★ of the Apennines and back towards the Versilia coast and the city of La Spezia. From Carrara follow signs for **Castelpoggio** or **Campocecina.**

What to See & Do

Carrara's Marble Quarries

ALL AGES

☎ 0585 844136. Colonnata, Fantiscritti and Torano are north of Carrara; follow signs from town.

David woz here: the piece of rock that became Michelangelo's **David** (p. 59) started life in the marble quarries just outside Carrara. The world-famous mines at **Colonnata, Fantiscritti** and **Torano** are all still operational, and you can tour these three major quarries by car, along a well-signed trail. Carrara's tourist office advise that you don't attempt the drive up to Torano, but you can get close enough to appreciate the scale and smell the dust.

If you want to see inside a working *galleria* (Apr–Oct), contact **MarmoTour** (☎ *339 7657470.* ***www.marmotour.com***. 7€, 3€ children).

Time *1½ hr.* ***Open*** *Always.* ***Adm*** *Free.* ***Amenities***

Grotta del Vento ★ AGE 4 & UP

Vergemoli. ☎ 0583 722024. ***www.grottadelvento.com****. Gallicano turn-off from SS445, 16km (10 miles) southwest of Barga.*

Dip your toes into the underground Garfagnana at the **Wind Cave,** a massive complex of formations, waterfalls and bottomless pits cut from the karst, and an ideal place to bring physical geography alive. Trips through the cave are guided only (the knowledgeable guides speak English), and follow three itineraries: the obvious choice with young children is the first but even that has **300 steps.** The white and gold tongues of **calcite** in the living cave are things of surreal beauty: they are hard as marble, look like sponge and forever change, with stalactites, stalagmites, 'cave pearls' and spaghetti rock formations shifting and growing. Come when it's raining and you're accompanied by the din of rushing water.

Bring **warm clothing:** it's always 11°C (52°F) inside the cave. Come early during peak season or at weekends, and note that baby backpacks and buggies are not allowed; front-loading baby slings are fine. Drive up the ramp when you see the *Grotta del Vento* sign: you don't need to pay to park outside.

Time *At least 1½ hr.* ***Open*** *10am–6pm daily Mon–Sat Nov–Mar; (itinerary 1 leaves on the hour except 1pm itinerary 2 leaves 11am, 3pm, 4pm and 5pm; itinerary 3 leaves 10am and 2pm).* ***Adm Itinerary 1*** *9€, 7€ under-11s;* ***itinerary 2*** *14€/11€;* ***itinerary 3*** *20€/16€.* ***Amenities***

Museo delle Statue-Stele Lunigianesi ★ AGE 7 & UP

Castello del Piagnaro, Pontrémoli. ☎ 0187 831439. ***www.statuestele.org****.*

This little museum in a 16th-century castle above **Pontremoli** ★ hosts one of Tuscany's **weirdest** collections: Iron Age stone figures (*stele*) that have been found in Europe from Galicia to the Crimea but rarely so precisely carved or in such concentration as around the Lunigiana. That so many have been decapitated is a sure sign the Catholic Church got here before the archaeologists.

For more itineraries around Pontrémoli, Tuscany's northernmost town, the old pilgrim road, the **Via Francigena,** or the Lunigiana, contact the provincial tourist office: **Massa-Carrara** (*0585 240063.* ***www.aptmassacarrara.it***).

Time *1 hr.* ***Open*** *9am–12:30pm and 3–6pm daily May–Sept; 9am–12:30pm and 2:30–5:30pm Tues–Sun Oct–Apr.* ***Adm*** *4€, 2€ ages 6–16.* ***Amenities***

Parco Avventura Fosdinovo ★ FIND ALL AGES

320 9060749. ***www.parcoavventurafosdinovo.com.*** *500m (1,640 ft) north of Fosdinovo, direction Fivizzano.*

Get harnessed up for **extreme** fun at this adventure park on the edge of the Apuane Alps. Hidden in a pine wood off the road is a bunch of **treetop fun:** zip-slides, Tibetan bridges, cargo nets and the like. There are six levels, starting with a *percorso* for 4-year-olds, but the focus is on **teens** and young adults. Despite the madcap atmosphere, safety is taken very seriously. This is recommended for all but the most confirmed vertigo-sufferer—bored teens most of all. Prices are a little steep, and Sundays get busy.

Time *2½ hr.* ***Open*** *10am–7pm daily mid-June–mid-Sept; 11am–5pm Sat and Sun Apr–mid-June; 1–5pm Sat, 11am–5pm Sun mid-Sept–Oct.* ***Adm*** *20€, 15€ under-18s, 8€ children's courses only; 3 hr maximum stay.* ***Amenities***

FAMILY-FRIENDLY DINING

Antica Trattoria 'Da Bruno' ★ PISAN

Via Luigi Bianchi 12, Pisa. 050 560818. ***www.anticatrattoriadabruno.it.***

Pisan specialities abound at this rustic trattoria, with a definite focus on seafood—a reminder of the city's maritime past. This is the best place near the Tower to introduce your children to **authentic Pisan food,** and though it's not cheap, there is a 25€ menu that perfectly represents the cooking. For a more genuine experience, aim for dinner rather than lunch—evenings are mellower, local affairs, and as a family you'll get special attention. Favourites include sea-bass ravioli, grilled swordfish and stockfish *alla Pisana*, and there are also roast meats such as beef and lamb or *zuppa Pisana* (a soaked-bread and veggie broth).

Open *7–10:30pm Mon, 1–3:30pm and 7–10:30pm Wed–Sun.* ***Main courses*** *12€–20€.* ***Credit*** *AE, MC, V.*

Da Leo ★ VALUE TUSCAN

Via Tegrimi 1, Lucca. 0583 492236. ***www.trattoriadaleo.it.***

This rollocking good family-run trattoria is justifiably popular, so book ahead at weekends and all summer to claim a table inside the lively dining room or out on a typically atmospheric, cobbled Lucca street. The handwritten menu has something for everyone, from a raft of simple but tasty pasta dishes and grilled meats with roast potatoes to Lucchese specialities such as *zuppa di farro* (a broth plumped up with the traditional local pulse, spelt wheat). In what has become an expensive town in recent years, Da Leo offers fantastic value for food prepared with the freshest ingredients and served with a smile.

Open *12:30–2:30pm and 7:30–10pm Mon–Sat; 7:30–10pm Sun lunch.* ***Main courses*** *6€–11.50€. No credit cards.* ***Amenities***

La BotteGaia ★ VALUE

REFINED TUSCAN

Via del Lastrone 17, Pistoia. 0573 365602. ***www.labottegaia.it.***

Tables inside and out fill fast at this bustling, *cantina*-style eatery near Pistoia's produce market. Tuscan *osteria* classics are elevated just a notch: the *ragù* is made only from the Cinta Senese breed of pig, veal is milk-fed and slow-cooked for succulence. The short menu also makes clever use of seasonal produce (asparagus and artichokes in spring, *porcini* mushrooms in autumn). However, although the food is serious, the welcome for children is as effusive as at any family trattoria.

The same owners have an excellent *enoteca* and food shop round the corner at Via di Stracceria 4: **I Sapori della BotteGaia.**

Open *12:30–3pm and 6:30–11pm Tues–Sat; 6:30–11pm Sun.* ***Main courses*** *8€–14€.* ***Credit*** *AE, MC, V.*

Osteria del Tinti TUSCAN/ITALIAN

Vicolo del Tinti 26, Pisa. 050 580240.

This cosy local restaurant knocks out high-quality food down a sidestreet off Pisa's Borgo Stretto. The atmospheric cellar-like rooms hold lots of appeal for curious youngsters, though there aren't many tables that seat more than four. The pasta is excellent: the *testaroli* (a pancake-like pasta), with olive oil and pecorino and the seasonal pasta specials are always worth the visit. Relatively simple dishes such as grilled tuna and *zuppa Toscana* should satisfy most, while the more adventurous can opt for wild boar (*cinghiale*) or cuttlefish with beet.

Open *Noon–2:30pm and 7–10:30pm Thurs–Tues.* ***Main courses*** *9€–18€.* ***Credit*** *MC, V.*

Pizzeria Trattoria Toscana

PIZZA & PASTA

Via Santa Maria 163, Pisa. 050 561876.

Although this cheerful restaurant is aimed squarely at **tourists** piling into Pisa's Campo dei Miracoli, it's a convenient and easy option for those with children in tow, and **open all day.** The English-speaking staff can conjure up basic pasta dishes for finicky eaters and fall over themselves to accommodate baby requests.

Food is adequate rather than exceptional, but you can't go wrong with the pizzas—good value (4€–9€) with a large choice of toppings. However, a 15% service charge will appear on your bill—such are the economics of life by the Campo.

Open *8am–11pm Thurs–Tues.* ***Main courses*** *4€–14€.* ***Credit*** *AE, MC, V.*

Trattoria Da Bussè ★★★

VALUE LUNIGIANESE

Piazza del Duomo 31, Pontrémoli. 0187 831371.

Hidden away in Pontrémoli's warren of ancient streets, Da Bussè is *the* place in northern Tuscany for astoundingly good-value **home cooking.** It's not just the food either: you really do feel as if you're lunching in someone's country kitchen. Specials are traditional and local, with a whiff of Liguria about them: *testaroli*, rabbit stew, salami and veal. If the **pesto's** on, as it often is at lunchtime, you'll be treated to the best in Tuscany. There's a *gelateria* on the piazza to round off a perfect lunch.

***Open** 12:30–2:30pm Mon–Thurs, 12:30–2:30pm and 7:45–9:30pm Sat and Sun. **Main courses** 7€–10€.*

Trattoria La Darsena SEAFOOD

*Via Virgilio 150 (at junction of Via Euro Menini), Viareggio. 0584 398249. **www.trattorialadarsena.it**.*

There are plenty of places to eat decent **seafood** in Viareggio but few you won't leave feeling a bit scalped. La Darsena's location away from the seafront ensures a more discerning clientele, better cooking and (slightly) better prices. The atmosphere is discerning without being stuffy, and families are welcome. Classics such as *spaghetti alle vongole*, lobster and mixed fried fish are joined by the catch of the day, cooked however you fancy.

***Open** Noon–2:30pm and 7:45–10:30pm Mon–Sat. **Main courses** 11€–24€. **Credit** AE, MC, V.*

FAMILY-FRIENDLY ACCOMMODATION

APARTMENTS, VILLAS & FARM-STAYS

Al Benefizio ★ FIND

*Località Ronchi 4, Barga, 0583 722 201. **www.albenefizio.it**.*

Offering dreamy picture-postcard views over neighbouring Barga from its lovely pool, this welcoming *agriturismo* produces acacia and chestnut honey and extra-virgin olive oil—the owner Francesca will show you and your children how, and offers tastings. Handily, the three apartments in the converted stable building are available from one night and up. One sleeps three; it can be used as an overflow for either of the others, which both sleep up to four, plus a baby or toddler in a cot, and have a covered terrace. Guests are free to pick products from the vegetable and herb gardens and the fruit trees, but watch your toddlers—the ground falls away steeply on this hilltop site.

Apartments** 3. **Rates** Double 45€–60€, apartment for 4 65€–110€. Cot free. **No credit cards. Amenities** **In apartment

Behind the Tower ★ VALUE

*Porta Nuova, Pisa. **www.behindthetower.com**.*

This simple **rental apartment** gives families of up to five the freedom of having a fully equipped kitchen and a lot more space than a hotel room—but

TIP Apartment Rental

For longer stays in and around Lucca and the Tuscan north, an apartment or *agriturismo* offers better value and more space than night-by-night hotel rooms. Reliable local rental agency and association websites include ***www.ingarfagnana.com***, ***www.abitarelucca.com*** and ***www.alfastudio.com***. Lucca's tourist office also lists farm-stay and alpine holiday homes across the province: see ***www.luccaturismo.it***.

it's a **major deal,** so book early. Bright and modern, it has one double or twin bedroom and a living room with a sofa-bed for two, plus the option of a third bed (free) for the bedroom. The spotless bathroom (shower only) is compact but big enough. Owners Marcel and Gloria will pick you up from the airport for free and provide all the local information you need.

Apartment *1.* ***Rates*** *3 nights 280€, 4–6 nights 80€/night, 500€/wk.* ***Credit*** *AE, MC, V, online deposit only.* ***Amenities*** ***In apartment***

CAMPSITES & HOSTELS

Barco Reale ★

Via Nardini 11, San Baronto. 0573 88332. ***www.barcoreale.it.*** *On SP9 between Pistoia and Empoli.*

This campsite might just have the best **views** in northern Tuscany: from its ridge on Monte Albano you look down on Pistoia and Prato to the north and all the way to Livorno and the Ligurian Sea to the west. The **mobile homes** are plain, adequately sized and well equipped (you need to bring your own towels); the Ginestra type and Barco wooden bungalows have air conditioning. The site itself is a child's paradise, with a kids' club in July and August, and activities all summer plus plenty of shade and the benefit of the *montagna*'s breeze when the day heats up. It's always booked up for late June to mid-August, so advance reservations (Sat–Sat only) are **essential.**

Pitches *230, + 26 mobile homes (closed Oct–Mar).* ***Camping*** *Adults 7.20€–10.60€, children 4€–6.70€, pitch 10.20€–15.60€.* ***Mobile homes*** *family of 4 41€–128€/night. Cots free.* ***Credit*** *MC, V.* ***Amenities*** ***In mobile homes***

Ostello San Frediano ★★ VALUE

Via della Cavallerizza 12, Lucca. 0583 469957. ***www.ostellolucca.it.***

The best value within Lucca's walls, the eight split-level family rooms in this handsome hostel have private bathrooms and clean, simple decor, and are reasonably spacious. Public areas are cool and quiet, even quite grand. You need to book well ahead: this sort of price for a central room sleeping four, with on-site parking thrown in, is a serious deal. With babies/toddlers you'll also need to bring your own cot.

Rooms *28.* ***Rates*** *Double 58€, triple 78€, quad 100€. Breakfast 3€.* ***Credit*** *MC, V.* ***Amenities***

HOTELS/BED & BREAKFASTS

La Luna

Corte Compagni 12, Lucca. 0583 493634. ***www.hotellaluna.com****.*

Affordable family hotels this close to Lucca's Via Fillungo are scarce; this is the best. Rooms are plain and bathrooms could do with an update, but they're plenty big enough for a family—and downstairs there's always a smile, plus a TV room and **Internet** to keep older children in touch with their world. Note that of the two spacious family suites (connecting rooms sharing a bathroom), only room 122 has a bathtub.

Rooms *29.* ***Rates*** *Double 110€–140€, triple 120€–170€, quad 130€–180€, family suite 190€–250€. Cot 15€ per night.* ***Credit*** *AE, MC, V.* ***Amenities*** ***In room***

Royal Victoria ★

Lungarno Pacinotti 12, Pisa. 050 940111. ***www.royalvictoria.it****.*

Pisa's first hotel, opened in 1839 and still owned by the Piegaja family, is the most welcoming for families. Set in a haphazard but somehow romantic series of medieval houses and towers by the river, it has various spacious configurations for families, including a riverfront junior suite for four that offers the best price/quality ratio. The 'family room' (two interconnecting rooms sleeping up to five) lacks the atmosphere of other options. All the doubles are fairly roomy; those facing the river have the best views.

Rooms *48.* ***Rates*** *Double 120€–150€, junior suite 152€–190€, family room 160€–200€. Cots free.* ***Credit*** *AE, MC, V.* ***Amenities*** ***In room***

Villa Rinascimento ★

Santa Maria del Giudice. 0583 378292. ***www.villarinascimento.it****. Off SS12 8km (5 miles) south of Lucca.*

You'd be hard pushed to find a better **base** for exploring northern Tuscany than this 15th-century villa among the olive groves of Monte Pisano, 15–20 minutes from Lucca or Pisa. Large grounds, the architectural flourish of a first-floor *loggia* and scrambled eggs for breakfast combine to complete a tempting package. The individually decorated rooms have plenty of space, with terracotta floors and exposed beams creating almost a country-manor feel. Of the 14 lower-priced (but newer, slightly smaller and less characterful) rooms in the annex, those with odd numbers have a better view and a sun terrace. Smaller families can be housed in a large double, with an extra bed.

Rooms *31.* ***Rates*** *Double 130€–155€, double in annex 95€–105€. Cots free. Extra bed 16.50€–33€.* ***Closed*** *Mid-Jan–Mar.* ***Credit*** *MC, V.* ***Amenities*** ***In room***

6 The Tuscan Coast: Livorno to Lazio via Elba

THE TUSCAN COAST

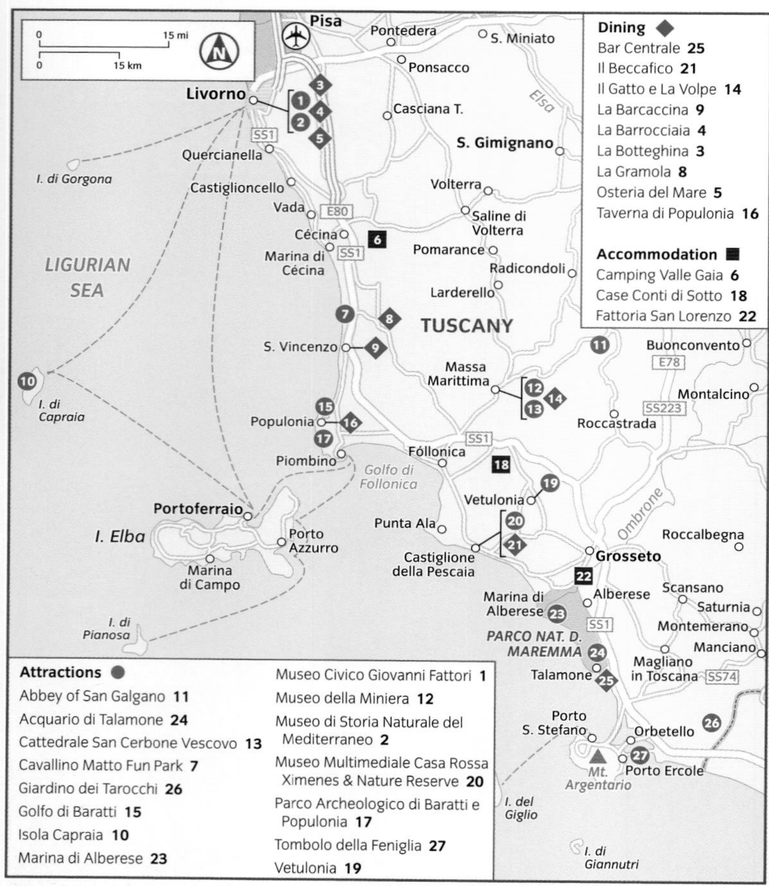

Tuscany has a shore spanning three seas, and though it's hardly known abroad for its beaches, Italians populate the sandy strands of Mediterranean, Tyrrhenian and Ligurian coastlines every summer. Many stretches get packed to the gunnels, and not all are idyllic, but there are patches your children will love—if you know where to look. Plus you'll benefit from the fashionable bars, cafés and restaurants that follow whenever Italians hit the sand. The beaches of the island of **Elba** are among Europe's best, and though they're packed in high summer, in May or September you could be in the Seychelles.

Tuscany's coast is also great for grabbing some nature. The **birdlife** in the marshes and foothills of the Maremma, as well as Orbetello's salty seawater lagoon, make binoculars an essential luggage item. The culture-deprived can bail out at inland **Massa Marittima,** where fine art and architecture sit happily alongside a chance for the children to go underground in a mine. We haven't even got started on the coast's hiking, museums or sublime seafood restaurants—you'll just have to read on.

LIVORNO

Hundreds of people disembark from cruise ships in **Livorno** harbour every day but sadly only a handful ever make it into the city. It was badly damaged during World War II bombing raids and many of its graceful buildings were replaced with some fairly hideous architecture. However, Livorno has a fascinating history as a 'Free Port', and there are plenty of things to do as a family—such as exploring the canals of Venezia Nuova free from worry about paying tourist prices, because you're the only ones in town.

Tuscany doesn't come any more 'authentic' than Livorno, and the city's **seafood cuisine** is famed throughout Italy, especially *cacciucco*, a fishy soup-stew.

Visitor Information

Information Centres

The most useful of Livorno's three **tourist offices** is the booth currently in the middle of Piazza del Municipio (✆ *0586 204611;* Apr and May Mon–Sat 9am–5pm, Sun 9am–1pm; June–Sept 9am–6pm daily; rest of year 9:30am–12:30pm and 2–5pm Mon–Sat); by the time you read this, it might have moved to the port.

Arriving

Easy to find, Livorno is 20 minutes south of Pisa along the **A12** or **SS1.** Driving in the centre is a

Children's Top Attractions of Tuscany's Coast

- Hiking in the **Parco Regionale della Maremma,** p. 158.
- Poking around in **rockpools** at Sant'Andrea, p. 153.
- Finding your own patch of soft sand at **Fetovaia,** p. 153, or the **Tombolo della Feniglia,** p. 161.
- Gawping at the **Mediterranean panoramas** from Monte Capanne, p. 152.
- Discovering the world underneath **Massa Marittima,** p. 154.
- Catching some **calcio** at family-friendly football club AS Livorno, p. 19.
- Tucking into Tuscany's best **seafood** in Livorno, p. 164.
- **Birdwatching** through a webcam at Diaccia Botrona, p. 157.

casino (a 'mad-house'); **park** for free at the station (well signposted) and take a **bus** (10 min; 1€) from **Piazza Dante.** If you insist on driving in, there are usually spaces at **Piazza Unità d'Italia** (1€–2€/hr), by the port. Good luck!

For **trains** (☎ *892021. www.trenitalia.it*) linking the city with the **Costa degli Etruschi,** see p. 147. There's also a regular link with **Pisa** (15 min; 1.90€), and **Florence** (1½ hr; 6.70€).

Family-Friendly Event

Livorno's best event for the whole family is the **Effeto Venezia** in early August, when the city's canal quarter springs to life with impromptu markets, street performers and the like.

What to See & Do

Build your day around a meal at one of Livorno's outstanding, great-value **seafood restaurants ★★** (p. 164). A tour of the major sights won't take long—it isn't that kind of city. The best part for a charming mooch and a coffee is the ambitiously named **Venezia Nuova** (New Venice) quarter, between the **Fortezza Nuova** and **Fortezza Vecchia.** The forts are a bit shabby and the quarter's 18th-century merchants' palaces are visibly crumbling, but the colonial streets and canals, especially along **Via Borra** as far as the little church of **Santa Caterina da Siena** (*www.chiesadisantacaterina.it*), have atmosphere and an untainted local flavour. To circumnavigate the old walls via the waterways, take a multilingual **boat trip** (☎ *348 7382094*; 10€, 8€ ages 6–12) from the tourist office in Piazza del Municipio, running daily in summer.

Livorno's major work of public art, the statue of Ferdinand I in Piazza Micheli, is far better known for the Mannerist **Quattro Mori** (Four Moors) at his feet. They were cast by **Pietro Tacca** in 1626. South of the centre, the best seafront

Fast Facts: Livorno & the Tuscan Coast

Banks There's a **Monte dei Paschi di Siena** at Via Cairoli 41, Livorno (☎ *0586 842255*), and countless others around the city centre.

Hospitals & Emergencies **Ospedale Livorno** is at Viale Alfieri 48 (☎ *0586 223111*). **Ospedale di Portoferraio** is at Località San Rocco (☎ *0565 926111*). In a medical emergency, dial ☎ *118.*

Pharmacies **Farmacia Comunale 8** at Piazza Grande 39, Livorno (☎ *0586 894490*) is open 24 hours.

Post Offices Livorno's central post office is at Via Cairoli 12 (☎ *0586 276473*). On Elba, make for Via Manganaro 7, Portoferraio (☎ *0565 934731*).

FUN FACT Brits Were Here

Almost everywhere you look in Livorno throws up some British history. The poet **Shelley** sailed to his death from Livorno, while the port itself was designed by an Englishman: 'Roberto' Dudley's plaque is on the wall behind the Quattro Mori in Piazza Micheli. The city's much-rebuilt **Cattedrale di San Francesco** was designed by British architect Inigo Jones in the 17th century, and Piazza Grande, where it stands, served as the model for Jones's Covent Garden, in London. The city's first major railway was even designed by an Englishman, Robert Stephenson (son of George, of *Rocket* fame).

promenading and panoramas are to be found at the spectacular chequer-board seafront balcony known as the **Terrazza Mascagni** ★. There are alfresco cafés and usually also a carousel.

If you're packing a picnic, call in at Livorno's stacked 19th-century **food market,** the 'Vettovaglie', on Via Buontalenti. Family-oriented chain shops line the handsome arcaded streets of **Via Grande:** Oviesse, Prénatal, Geox and the like.

Isola Capraia AGE 10 & UP

Ferry from Livorno.

When you get that I-want-to-be-alone-on-a-Tuscan-island feeling, **Capraia's** the one to head for. This scrub-covered slab of desolate beauty with its one road is the quietest accessible island in the Tuscan archipelago, with deserted hiking trails, hidden coves and azure views galore, although no decent beach. If your luck's in, you might spot the rare **Audouin's gull.**

Getting here is a journey you'll only want to make with older children: it takes 2½ hours (12.50€ each way). There's usually just one ferry a day; occasionally in high season you can get the 8:30am from Livorno and return on the 6pm, but make sure you book. Check timetables with **Toremar** (*📞 892123. **www.toremar.it***). **Agenzia Viaggi e Turismo Parco** (*📞 0586 905071. **www.isoladicapraia.it***) can arrange family packages, including **diving** ★.

***Time** At least 1 day.*

INSIDER TIP

For detailed advice, contact the island's **tourist office** (*📞 0586 905138. **www.prolococapraiaisola.it***).

Museo Civico Giovanni Fattori ★ AGE 10 & UP

Via San Jacopo in Aquaviva 65. 📞 0586 808001. Bus 1,8.

Livorno's arty highlight inside the extraordinary rococo-meets-colonial **Villa Mimbelli** south of the centre exhibits the work of the local **Macchiaioli School:** kind-of Impressionists without the water lilies. Monet it ain't, certainly. Among three levels of pleasant but unremarkable work, the highlights are jammed on the top floor. If you've been to the

Serie A (or maybe B) away from the Limelight

They might not be a household name, but AS Livorno ★ (gli *amaranto*, 'the purples') are riding the crest of a wave, historically speaking. In 2004 the team returned to Italy's elite Serie A after a 55-year wait, and then promptly qualified for the UEFA Cup in 2006. They've bounced between A and B since. Tickets, which go on sale about 7 to 10 days before games, cost 16€ to 50€, with the uncovered Gradinata (our recommended perch) costing 25€ to 30€. Children under 8 only pay 1€; under-14s get 7€ to 8€ off the full price. Although the Curva Nord has no reputation for trouble, it is loud and occasionally angry: young children probably shouldn't be there.

The tatty Stadio Armando Picchi is in Piazzale Montello, not far from the Museo Fattori. You'll find somewhere to **park** nearby, or take **bus 1** from the station or **bus 5** from Piazza Grande. Buy match tickets from the **Punta Amaranto** at the main stadium entrance (on match-days the ticket office moves to outside the Palazzetto dello Sport). You need to show photo ID. See the club website (***www.livornocalcio.it***) for a fixture list.

Maremma, Giovanni Fattori's 1893 painting of bearded *butteri* (cowboys, see p. 159) will be of interest. Our other favourite is Lodovico Tommasi's rather lovely, autumnal **La Caduta delle Foglie.** It all marks a perhaps welcome change of gear from wall-to-wall religious art.

Another bonus is the setting: inside there's a lush, shaded civic park with **swings** and a **slide.**

Time *1½ hr.* ***Open*** *10am–1pm and 4–7pm Tues–Sun.* ***Adm*** *4€, 2.50€ ages 7–18.* ***Amenities*** ♿

Museo di Storia Naturale del Mediterraneo FIND AGE 8 & UP

Via Roma 234. ☎ 0586 266711. www.provincia.livorno.it. Bus: 5, 8n/r to Piazza Matteotti.

The complexity of entrance pricing options to the **Museum of Mediterranean Natural History** is Byzantine: the areas most suited to non-Italian-speakers are the **Orto Botanico** and **Sala del Mare.** The second of these is the highlight, especially the **giant skeleton of a fin whale ★**, named 'Annie', which washed up on Livorno's beach in 1990. Children can touch the massive jaw and ribs and try to work out just *how* far it is to the tip of the tail. At the far end of the small **Orto Botanico,** in the Zona Umida, there's a pond with turtles and a kitchen garden with medicinal plants.

There's plenty more with a didactic bias in the museum—geology, palaeontology, even a Planetarium—but you or the children need to speak Italian to get much out of it.

Time *1¼ hr.* ***Open*** *9am–1pm Wed and Fri, 9am–1pm and 3–7pm Tues,*

Thurs and Sat; 3–7pm Sun. **Adm** *4€, 2€ ages 7–12 Mare or Orto; 6€, children 3€ Mare/Orto/Sala Invertebrati; 10€, children 5€ everything; 20€ family everything.* **Amenities** ♿

THE ETRUSCAN COAST

Just south of Livorno, the **Maremma Pisana** begins. Or, at least, it did until some sharp marketeer decided to rebrand it the **Costa degli Etruschi,** the 'Etruscan Coast'. Once a sparsely inhabited malarial swamp, it now hosts most of the Tuscan mainland's summer seaside action. Guidebooks are often snotty about it, with good reason—some stretches exhibit the dark side of the Italian seaside experience, all concrete, campsites and crowds. It is possible to avoid the worst excesses and find some decent spots, but if you like a beach all to yourself, this is the wrong place.

Visitor Information

Information Centres

HQ for Costa degli Etruschi tourism is in **Livorno** (*0586 204611. www.costadeglietruschi.it*), upstairs at Piazza Cavour 6.

Most resorts have well-signposted seasonal offices, occasionally more than one, but only a handful are open all year. They include those in **Castiglioncello,** at Via Aurelia 632 (*0586 754890. apt7castiglioncello@costadeglietruschi.it*); in **Marina di Cecina,** at Piazza S. Andrea 6 (*0586 620678. apt7cecina@costadeglietruschi.it*); and in **San Vincenzo,** at Via della Torre (*0565 701533. apt7sanvincenzo@costadeglietruschi.it*).

There are a couple of **websites** worth consulting before you go: the useful official portal *www.costadeglietruschi.it* and the unofficial *www.costaetrusca.com*.

Arriving

The coast is easiest by car—it follows the **SS1** south from Livorno to Piombino—but is also straightforward by **train** (*892021. www.trenitalia.it*) except on Sundays. Every half-hour or so a *Regionale* service connects Livorno with **Cecina** (25 min; 3.10€) and **San Vincenzo** (5 min; 4.20€). A regular-ish stopper also calls at **Castiglioncello** (18 min; 2.40€) and **Bolgheri** (37 min; 3.70€).

What to See & Do

Beaches

You need to pick your spots. The **Bay of Quercetano** has the views, especially at **sunset** ★, but its beaches are narrow and rocky. Castiglioncello's **Chamaeleon Ice** ★, however, is one very tasty *gelato* stop (at Via Aurelia 660, in the centre).

There's a decent, though busy, stretch of white sand around **Vada:** park just south or 1½ km (less than a mile) north of the main piazza on either side of the road and cut through the scrub.

San Vincenzo was the scene of the Florentine army's rout of

Pisa in 1505, remembered by Vasari's frescoes in the **Palazzo Vecchio** (p. 55). Its beach is flat and fluffy, but the concrete wall rather spoils the view.

Your best bet along this coast is the **Golfo di Baratti** ★. Park on the left of the road (7.70€/5 hr in summer only); if you reach the archaeological park (see below), you've gone too far. Views of the promontory of **Populonia** are super; the sand improves the farther east you walk.

Other Sights along the Coast

Besides the sea, there are one or two things to amuse. Marina di Cecina has a small **Museo Archeologico** (*0586 680145.* ***www.comune.cecina.li.it/museo.archeologico/index.html****.* 6–10pm Tues–Sun June–Aug, 3:30–7pm Sat and Sun Feb–May and Sept–Nov), in well–signposted colonial Villa Guerrazzi north of town. The small but well-displayed collection focuses on the many local Etruscan finds, including cinerary urns and intricate, small bronzes. Entry is 4€ adults, 2.50€ for 6 to 18s. A family ticket costs 8€; another 4€ gets you all into Cecina's Roman Archaeological Park, too.

Cavallino Matto Fun Park

AGE 3–8

Via Pò 1, Marina di Castagneto. 0565 745720. ***www.cavallinomatto.it****. 1km (less than 1 mile) from SS1 Donoratico exit.*

Tuscany's **not-quite-a-theme-park** does roughly what it says on the tin: highlights include mini roller-coasters, mazes, inflatables, a pirate ship, daily shows and now the 50-m (164-ft) **Shocking Tower.** It's not Disney, but under-10s usually love it. You, on the other hand, may end up grumbling about the price as you seek shade under the pines. Check the website for discounted ticket offers.

Time *3 hr.* ***Open*** *10am–6pm daily mid-May–mid-Sept, 10–7pm Aug; 10am–6pm Sat and Sun mid-Sept–Oct and Apr–mid-May.* ***Adm*** *20€, 16€ ages 3–10, free under 90cm (3 ft) height.* ***Amenities***

Parco Archeologico di Baratti e Populonia ★ AGE 5 & UP

0565 226445. ***www.parchivaldicornia.it****. Signposted from SS1.*

The Etruscan Coast's major Etruscan site got a **revamp** in 2007. The original two areas covering 80 hectares (198 acres) were joined by an Etruscan–Roman **Acropolis** and Roman road at the top of Populonia's promontory. The more recent finds confirmed that Populonia's status as a major iron and metal-working centre didn't end with the Etruscans.

Scientifically the most interesting area remains **San Cerbone,** the only Etruscan necropolis ever found by the sea. It's the easiest to explore with youngsters: relatively intact circular tombs litter a field right by the visitor centre. With older children, a 2-hr round-trip on foot to **Le Grotte,** where a series of tombs are hewn from solid rock, is well worth

Liquid Riches

The coastal Maremma is the source of some fine Tuscan nectar. The hills around the village of **Castagneto Carducci,** inland from San Vincenzo, are said to produce Italy's best **olive oil.** There isn't much to do in the pretty town itself, bar wandering the steep cobbled streets and slurping ice cream (our favourite stop is **Casalini,** at Via Vittorio Emanuele II 48). Reserve a terrace table at **La Gramola** on Via Marconi 18 (*0565 763646.* ***www.lagramola.it***. Closed Wed) for Tuscan staples, proper pizza from a wood oven, erratic service and fine **views** ★ of the Etruscan Coast below. Mains cost 6€ to 11€.

Wine devotees might prefer a stop at **Bolgheri,** home of legendary 'Super Tuscan' red wines Sassicaia and Ornellaia. The pleasant medieval village centre has plenty of *enoteche* offering tastings.

it—not just for the views. English signage everywhere makes it all easy to follow and understand. The site runs children's activities from Easter to October.

Time *At least 2 hr.* ***Open*** *9:30am–7:30pm daily July and Aug; 10am–sunset daily Mar–June, Sept and Oct; 10am–4pm Sat and Sun Nov–Feb.* ***Adm*** *one site 9€, 6€ children 6–14; 2 sites 13€, 9€ children; 3 sites 15€, 11€ children; family (5 people) 2 sites 33€, 3 sites 39€.* ***Amenities***

INSIDER TIP

There's little left of the adjacent medieval hamlet at **Populonia Alta** with its *turismo* and *tipico* shops but its **Castello** (***www.castellodipopulonia.it***. Daily 10am–6pm. 2€, 1€ ages 6–12) has the best **panorama** ★ up the Etruscan Coast. It's right by the Acropolis area. The **Taverna di Populonia,** on the only real street, serves Tuscan pasta staples, at reasonable prices, in a pretty, shaded garden.

ELBA

As places to be exiled go, Napoleon struck seriously lucky with **Elba** ★★. If the mainland's beaches are a touch underwhelming, you can't say the same about those on Italy's third-largest island, where every bend in the road reveals an expanse of rock, sea or sand more picturesque than the last. However, it's a little busier these days than it was in the 19th century: almost **2 million visitors** come every year to have their fill of azure water. Families should follow some simple rules—most importantly, **don't come between late July and the end of August.** Everything's full, prices are astronomical, resorts are noisy and roads are clogged. May, when the greens and browns of the island's scrubby interior are interlaced with perfumed yellow, red and violet blooms, is great. In September, the water is warmer and the

ELBA

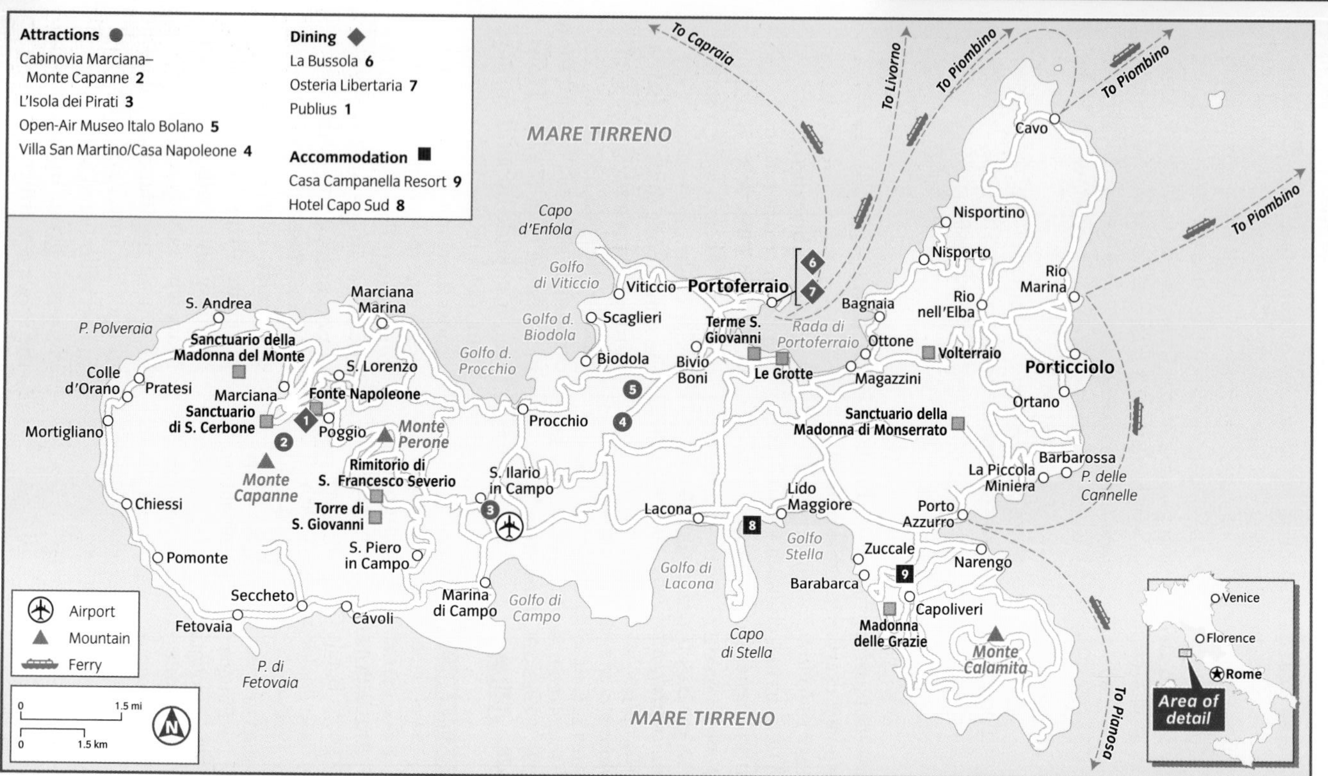

Attractions
Cabinovia Marciana–Monte Capanne 2
L'Isola dei Pirati 3
Open-Air Museo Italo Bolano 5
Villa San Martino/Casa Napoleone 4
Dining
La Bussola 6
Osteria Libertaria 7
Publius 1
Accommodation
Casa Campanella Resort 9
Hotel Capo Sud 8
MARE TIRRENO
To Capraia
To Livorno
To Piombino
To Piombino
To Piombino
To Pianosa
Cavo
Nisportino
Nisporto
Rio Marina
Rio nell'Elba
Porticciolo
Ortano
Volterraio
Bagnaia
Ottone
Magazzini
Rada di Portoferraio
Portoferraio
Terme S. Giovanni
Le Grotte
Viticcio
Capo d'Enfola
Golfo di Viticcio
Scaglieri
Golfo d. Biodola
Biodola
Bivio Boni
Golfo d. Procchio
Procchio
Sanctuario della Madonna di Monserrato
Barbarossa
P. delle Cannelle
La Piccola Miniera
Porto Azzurro
Lido Maggiore
Lacona
Golfo Stella
Golfo di Lacona
Capo di Stella
Zuccale
Barabarca
Narengo
Capoliveri
Madonna delle Grazie
Monte Calamita
MARE TIRRENO
Marciana Marina
S. Andrea
P. Polveraia
Sanctuario della Madonna del Monte
S. Lorenzo
Colle d'Orano
Pratesi
Marciana
Fonte Napoleone
Sanctuario di S. Cerbone
Poggio
Monte Perone
Mortigliano
Monte Capanne
Rimitorio di S. Francesco Severio
S. Ilario in Campo
Torre di S. Giovanni
Chiessi
S. Piero in Campo
Pomonte
Marina di Campo
Golfo di Campo
Secchetto
Cávoli
Fetovaia
P. di Fetovaia
Airport
Mountain
Ferry
0
1.5 mi
0
1.5 km
N
Venice
Florence
Rome
Area of detail

island quieter than in peak season. When budgeting, think twice about bringing your car on the **ferry** for just a day trip: it's expensive, and Marina di Campo beach is easy to reach by bus.

Visitor Information

Information Centres

The only **tourist office** open all year is in Portoferraio (☎ *0565 914671*. *www.aptelba.it*. 8am–7pm Mon–Sat, 8am–1pm Sun; sometimes closed afternoons out of season), opposite the quay as you sail in, on the corner of Calata Italia and Viale Elba. They are the best people to ask for advice about **diving ★**, **trekking ★**, cycling, paragliding, climbing and all kinds of outdoor activities around the island. Another useful trip-planning resource is *www.elba.org*.

Arriving

By Ferry Two ferry companies link Piombino and **Portoferraio** on Elba: **Toremar** (☎ *892123*. *www.toremar.it*) and **Moby** (☎ *199 303040*. *www.moby.it*). Frequencies (at least half-hourly in summer) and prices vary by season, becoming hideously expensive on August weekends. The crossing takes an hour. Toremar also runs a hovercraft (*aliscafo*) service for passengers only (four daily, 40 min). Except from late July through August, you should be able to roll up and sail without booking.

If you want to leave your car at Piombino, the **long-stay car park** signposted by the docks costs 8€ to 12€ per day. There's also an **ATM,** a pizzeria and an Autogrill inside the port.

By Air Plans are in place to expand the service offered by **ElbaFly** (☎ *0565 977900*. *www.elbafly.it*), to include regular, affordable air links with Pisa and Florence airports. Check the website for the latest and ask your accommodation provider on Elba for help securing the best fare.

Portoferraio Harbour, Elba

TIP A Glass of Elba

Uncharacteristically for Tuscany, the island's best wine is white: Elba Bianco DOC. Follow it down with anything pulled out of the sea and you're more than halfway to the perfect lunch. Pick up a good bottle to take home from the fine selection at **Enoteca della Fortezza** (*335 8393722*) on Via Scoscesa, a ramp alongside the Fortezza Medicea in Portoferraio.

Getting Around

Unless you have a car, Elba's more remote areas and less-visited beaches are hard to reach. However, **Procchio** (20 min) and **Marina di Campo** (½ hr) are served hourly-ish until dusk by **ATL buses** (*0565 914392. www.atl.livorno.it*). You want route 116 from opposite the Toremar dock in Portoferraio; there's a ticket office adjacent, at Viale Elba 22. Some buses continue to **Fetovaia** (45 min). The service on route 117 to **Capoliveri** (½ hr) runs a little less frequently.

What to See & Do

If you're not coming for the outdoors in some form or another, there's little point coming at all. Still, the island isn't without cultural and historical interest. The main harbour and capital of **Portoferraio** was a major iron-ore centre for centuries, hence the name and the forts you'll spot from the ferry—defence always follows the money, after all. The **Fortezza Medicea** (*0565 944024;* 9am–8pm daily mid-June–mid-Sept, 10am–1pm and 3:30–7:10pm Easter–mid-June and mid-Sept–Oct), built in the 16th century for Cosimo I, has a dominant view over the harbour from its ramparts. Admission is 3€ (children 2€); you enter on Via Guerrazzi.

If you're on the way to San Martino, Procchio or farther west, plan half an hour at the free **Open-Air Museo Italo Bolano** (*0565 914570. www.italobonano.com*. Mon–Sat 10:30am–1pm and 4–6pm June–Sept), signposted by the side of the road in San Martino where eerie but fun ceramic sculpture adorns a shady garden.

The tourist office in Portoferraio has a continually updated list of **play parks** (*parco giochi*) on the island; the go-kart track near Campo nell'Elba (*www.isoladeipirati.it*) is perennially popular.

Cabinovia Marciana–Monte Capanne ★★ AGE 3 & UP

0565 901020. By road outside Marciana.

There's no doubt that you'll get the best **views** ★★★ of Elba 1,019m (3,343 ft) up Monte Capanne—the 20-minute ride in open cages to the highest point on the island is your only **essential stop** here other than the beach. The 360° views take in the arc of the Tuscan coast from Livorno to Monte Argentario.

Elba's Beaches

Despite it having 147km (91 miles) of coastline, you're not going to 'discover' any beaches on Elba: every patch of sand is **busy** in summer, so unless you come way out of season, you're unlikely to find a deserted spot. There's a very good reason for this: Elba's beaches are **among Italy's best.**

Most often recommended to families are the 1.7km (1 mile) of sand at **Marina di Campo** ★ and its northern counterpart at **Procchio** ★. Both are wide with shallow shelves, and fairly easy to park near for free; you're never far from a pizza or *gelato* on either. The *Spiaggia Grande* at **Lacona** is also wide and flat, with soft sand. West of Procchio, there's pay parking around the stunning cove at **Sant'Andrea** ★★, with its small white beach with coarse sand and shallow rock-pools at the eastern end.

Well signposted south of Capoliveri, the small sand-and-pebble coves at **Innamorata** ★ and **Morcone** are oriented perfectly to catch the sunset. You'll find a parking spot at either if you hunt around a bit. Further north, follow the signs from the main road for **Zuccale** ★ and **Barabarca** ★; park (for a small daily charge) at the end of the road (Zuccale to the right, Barabarca the left). You walk down a path to both, so **don't bring buggies.**

The **natural beauty** quotient jumps a notch higher on the island's southwest. The coves at **Fetovaia** ★★ and **Cavoli** ★★ are idyllic—white sand and transparent, turquoise sea—but have the inevitable summer crowds. Fetovaia has more shade and the sand is less grainy, but Cavoli's crescent just edges the beauty contest. There's pay parking around both.

Cavoli Beach, Elba

There are **disabled beach facilities** at Marina di Campo (☎ *0565 976966*), Procchio (☎ *0565 907366*), Lacona (☎ *0565 964364*), Fetovaia (☎ *0565 988037*) and Cavoli (☎ *0565 987288*).

For an extended stay, with lashings of beach, read up on the 153 described in the book ***Elba: All Its Beaches*** (aka '*Tutte le Spiagge*'), available at Piombino port and bookshops on Elba (try **Il Libraio** at Via Veneto 10, on Portoferraio's harbour, which also stocks a small selection of books in English).

Seawards, the Mediterranean panorama spans the Tuscan archipelago and out to Corsica.

There's no room for **buggies,** so you'll need a back or front pouch to take a baby up. It's possible to **hike** down (1½–2 hr) but not with under-8s; wear proper boots. And lastly, hold on to your hats—ours are still up there somewhere.

Time *1¾ hr.* ***Open*** *10am–12:20pm and 2:20–5pm daily.* ***Adm*** *10€ single, 17€ return, 7€ ages 4–10.* ***Amenities***

Villa San Martino/Casa Napoleone AGE 6 & UP

Località San Martino. ☎ 0565 914688. Signposted off Portoferraio–Procchio Road.

A glade populated with twittering birdlife is the setting for the **neoclassical mansion** occupied by French emperor **Napoleon** in 1814–15, during his exile on Elba. Only one floor is open to the public, but it's enough to give an insight into the life and mind of the French general.

With children, a good game is to spot how many times his various imperial insignias (the eagle, the imperial bee, the Legion of Honour Star, among others) appear as design elements throughout. Also point out to them that from the mansion's cleverly located spot, Napoleon could remain secluded while simultaneously seeing every single ship entering and leaving Portoferraio's harbour—you'd be forgiven for imagining the pocket-sized Frenchman had some kind of complex.

Time *1 hr.* ***Open*** *9am–7pm Tues–Sat, 9am–1pm Sun.* ***Adm*** *3€, 1.50€ children.* ***Amenities***

MASSA MARITTIMA

Gripping the side of a hill 350m (1,148 ft) up in the Colline Metallifere (Metaliferrous Hills) is the misnamed 'maritime' capital of the Alta Maremma, **Massa Marittima** ★. This charming mining town was hit hard by plague in 1348 and took 600 years to bounce back. It's now an **overlooked diamond:** an empty hill-town of shuttered buildings, steep, narrow lanes and a fine, cobbled piazza, well off the usual trail. The only sounds you'll hear during the lunchtime *riposo* out of season are the occasional marital dispute from a first-floor window. Bliss.

Visitor Information

Information Centres

The mega-helpful **tourist office** (☎ *0566 902756*; 9:30am–1pm and 4–7pm Wed–Mon May–Sept, 9:30am–1pm and 3–6pm Mon–Sat Oct–Apr) is at Via Todini 3–5, down the side of the Palazzo Podestà. The handiest **ATM** is the Banca Toscana in Piazza Garibaldi. There are **swings** and a **slide** on Via Valle Aspra by Piazza XXIV Maggio.

Arriving

Getting to Massa Marittima by car is a doddle: the town is on the **SS439,** 13km (8 miles) inland from the main coastal highway (SS1). There's a **car park** (1€/hr) on Piazza Mazzini, just before Massa's pedestrian zone if you're approaching from the coast.

The only feasible public transport option is the approximately hourly **RAMA bus** (*0564 475111. www.griforama.it*) from Follonica.

Family-Friendly Events

Massa's main annual event is the **Toscana Foto Festival** ★ (*0566 901526*) during the first half of July, with exhibitions around town and workshops.

The town's *terzieri* battle it out in the **Balestro del Girifalco,** on the Sunday after 20th May and the second Sunday in August. Expect crossbows and flag-juggling. Music fans should make plans to be here during the first week in August for **Lirica in Piazza** ★ (*0566 902010. www.liricainpiazza.it*), a short open-air opera festival featuring works by the likes of Puccini and Donizetti. Tickets cost 10€ to 44€.

What to See & Do

Città Nuova

The direct route to the 'New Town' up Via Monconi is the quickest, but beware: it's short, sharp and nigh on impossible with a buggy. At the top you'll bump into the 40-m (131-ft) **Torre del Candeliere** (*0566 902289. www.massamarittimamusei.it*), part of Massa's 13th-century Sienese-built defences. The castle keep and fine views over the chequerboard plains below are accessible Tuesday to Sunday 10am to 1pm and 3 to 6pm April to October (some weekends there's no lunch break), 11am to 1pm and 2:30 to 4:30pm November to March. Admission is 2.50€, 1.50€ for children 6 to 14.

The artistic focus of Massa's upper tier is the **Museo di Arte Sacra** (*0566 901954. www.massamarittimamusei.it*. Tues–Sun 10am–1pm and 3–6pm Apr–Oct, rest of year 11am–1pm and 3–5pm). Entry is 5€, children 3€. Highlights are an iconic **Maestà** ★ by Sienese Ambrogio Lorenzetti (1285–1348) and a stained glass *Crucifixion* by his brother Pietro (1280–1348).

Museo della Miniera ★ AGE 6 & UP

Via Corridoni. 0566 902289. www.massamarittimamusei.it/anticaminiera. Follow yellow signs; 700m (2,296 ft) uphill from Piazza Garibaldi.

Did you know that **mules** were more economical mine workers than machines until the 1950s? Or that Massa's miners kept their lunch in metal tins so foot-long rats couldn't chew through them? Don your hard hats for this look at a miner's life in the Colline Metallifere and you'll soon know it all. The 700-m (2,296-ft) long authentic **replica**

The Other Sword in the Stone

Halfway between Siena and Massa Marittima is the roofless Gothic ruin of the 13th-century Cistercian **Abbey of San Galgano** (8am–11pm daily; free). This mighty structure sits alone in its windy field in the middle of nowhere—and as long as your visit doesn't correspond with the arrival of a tour bus, is very atmospheric.

There are several legends regarding Saint Galgano himself. One has noble young **Galgano Guidotti,** dedicated to worldly pleasures, out riding when the Archangel Michael appeared with flaming sword. Galgano fell to the earth, took his own sword from his belt and threw it against a nearby rock. It was swallowed, remaining stuck like a cross. You can see 'the sword' driven into its rock up the hill at the circular **Cappella di Montesiepi (**usually open). A side-chapel has faded frescoes by Ambrogio Lorenzetti.

of a working 1940s' mine, complete with echoes and eccentric machinery, is a sure winner for children. It's all on the flat, so little walkers should be fine as long as you wrap them up warm—the mine is 12°C (53°F) all year.

Time *45 min.* ***Guided tours*** *approx. hourly 10am–noon and 3–5:45pm Tues–Sun Apr–Oct, rest of year 10am–noon and 3–4:30pm.* ***Adm*** *5€, 3€ ages 6–15.*

Città Vecchia

The lower town, the **Città Vecchia,** is dominated by **Piazza Garibaldi ★**. As well as the Duomo (see below), it's where you'll find Massa's best ice-cream stop: **Bar Gelateria Centrale ★** at Corso Libertà 13. The rest of the 'old' town, as far as Piazza Cavour and lots of side lanes, is ideal mooching territory. **Il Salumeria ★**, at Vicolo Butigni 10, is the place to stock up for a picnic, on everything from wild boar salami and pecorino cheese to local wines.

Cattedrale San Cerbone Vescovo ★ AGE 3 & UP

Piazza Garibaldi. No phone.

Massa's **Duomo** is a fine Romanesque pile that shows architectural influences from Pisa (arcades, lozenges) and Siena, which called the shots round here for most of the 1300s. It's dedicated to Massa's patron, San Cerbone; Bishop of Populonia between 570 and 575, he made his name taking a flock of geese to see the Pope. Check out his stone geese on the portal above the main door. The interior makes liberal use of worked travertine and has a **Madonna delle Grazie ★** by (maybe) Duccio in a transept chapel.

Time *30 min.* ***Open*** *8am–noon and 3–6pm daily (exc. during services).* ***Adm*** *Free.*

CASTIGLIONE DELLA PESCAIA

Just south of Follonica is the charming bucket-and-spade town of **Castiglione della Pescaia,** stuck on the side of a rocky outcrop of Monte Petriccio. Despite its nightmare one-way system and parking hell, it's well worth the detour, for its seafood restaurants (p. 164) and wetlands.

Visitor Information

The town overlooks the marshy mouth of the Bruna river, 23km (14 miles) west of provincial capital **Grosseto.** The **tourist office** (*0564 933678. www.lamaremma.info.* Closed Sun afternoon Nov–Mar) is at Piazza Garibaldi 6, opposite the marina and right next to a small **car park** and **pirate-themed playground.**

What to See & Do

The major draw here is the seaside: there's a south-facing **beach** right by the coast road serviced by several bathing companies (*stablimenti*). If you have time and a car, however, there's better sand farther south at **Marina di Alberese** (p. 160). Castiglione's **Borgo Medioevale** (old town) makes a fine if tortuously steep walk, and it's mostly deserted—the action migrated downhill to the sea long ago.

Museo Multimediale Casa Rossa Ximenes & Nature Reserve ★ GREEN AGE 5 & UP

Località Casa Rossa. 347 2290051. www.diacciabotrona.it. 0.5km (third of mile) east of centre; turn after Ponte Giorgini.

This museum and marsh is one of Europe's most important **wetlands** reserves and a perfect place to bring a young birdwatcher. The 'multimedia' museum inside the 18th-century Casa Rossa hosts live feeds from three **webcams** scattered about the marsh, which you can pan and zoom to get close to the birdlife without disturbing them. There's also an interactive guide to the marsh's inhabitants (in Italian only) and their calls (in Bird only).

The 18th-century Casa Rossa Ximenes

Depending on the season, residents include the marsh harrier and flamingo.

Out on the marsh itself, a haphazard network of rough paths (unsuited to buggies) meanders through the stillness of 2,300 hectares (5,683 acres) of empty Diaccia Botrona. It's ideal for birdwatching. There's also a 2-hour guided boat trip along the canal system, with views back to Castiglione.

Time *At least 1 hr.* ***Open*** *4–10pm Tues–Sun June–Aug, 2:30–7:30pm Wed–Sun Sept–May. Boat trips 6pm Tues–Sun June–Aug, by arrangement only Sept–May (min. 4 people).* ***Adm*** *Museum and marsh only 3.50€, free under-12s; with boat trip 12€, 5€ ages 2–12.* ***Amenities***

Vetulonia ALL AGES

21km (12 miles) northeast of Castglione della Pescaia.

These days an unassuming little place with a scenic approach road, Vetulonia has an esteemed ancient history uncovered by much archaeological study. Local finds from the Etruscan era in particular are well displayed in the **Museo Civico Archaeologico,** Piazza Vetluna 1 (*0564 948058*), but to get a proper feel for the past, head out into the digs themselves—less than 1.7km (1 mile) from town, towards Grosseto, are the *scavi di città* (free adm), dating to the first three centuries B.C. when the Romans were in charge. The custodian can supply a detailed map and English-language guide to the preserved Etruscan tombs of **Diavolino** and **Pietrera** down the road.

Time *2 hr.* ***Museum open*** *10am–2pm and 4–8pm Tues–Sun June–Sept, 10am–4pm Oct–Feb, 10am–6pm Mar–May.* ***Adm*** *4.50€, 2.50€ children.* ***Amenities***

PARCO REGIONALE DELLA MAREMMA

The outstanding **Parco Regionale della Maremma** ★★, with its unspoiled *macchia* coastline, miles of parasol pines and deserted beaches, is the Number 1 reason to base yourselves in southwestern Tuscany. The coastal hills of **Monti dell'Uccellina** forming the park's core got their name from the area's teeming birdlife (an *uccello* is a bird), so pack binoculars. Residents include goshawks, tawny owls and jays. The park is spectacular in autumn, when thousands of wild ducks, geese and herons invade on their way south to the sun. The highest peak in the park is **Poggio Lecci** at just 415m (1,361 ft), so much of the 100 square kilometres (38 square miles) of park is accessible to older primary-school-age children, and various sections of it to anyone out of a buggy.

Visitor Information

The park's main **visitor centre** (*0564 407098*; 8:30am–8pm mid-June–mid-Sept, 8:30am–1:30pm mid-Sept–mid-June) is at Via Bersagliere 7–9 in Alberese—you can't miss it. There are no roads inside the park: the **car park** charges 6€ a day in high season only. There's an **ATM** at the visitor centre. The park's website is ***www.parco-maremma.it***.

Entrance to the park's main **trails** is 9€, 5.50€ for children 6–14. The **Forestal and Faunal trails** (shorter and flatter for youngsters, and with **disabled access**) are 6€, children 4€. From mid-June to mid-September, entrance to the best park trails is by **guided group visits** only (8:30am, 9:30am, 4pm and 4:30pm), because of brushfire risk. On Fridays, the 4:30pm trek is guided in **English.**

Canoeing ★ trips (2 hr) along the nearby Ombrone river are organised by **SILVA** (✆ *0564 385534*. ***www.silvacoop.com***). **Bike hire** is also available locally for around 3€/hr or 8€/day.

INSIDER TIP

There are **no services** in the park. Pack a picnic, sunblock, basic first-aid kit and change of clothes, and make sure **footwear** is sturdy trainers with a good tread *at least*. You'll also struggle for phone reception.

What to See & Do

Several marked trails head out from **Pratini,** where the shuttle bus from the visitor centre drops you, in the heart of the park. The deeper in you get, the more olive groves give way to **Mediterranean woodland** of cork, ilex and ash. Suddenly you're alone in a wilderness of butterflies, bird calls and (if you're very lucky) wild boar.

Our favourite trail for families is the **A2,** *Due Torri*, which takes in a couple of Medici-built **watchtowers.** Many were repeatedly sacked by Barbary pirates in the 1500s and have lain abandoned since. The **view** ★★★ from the first of the two towers is up there with the best in Tuscany. At less than 6km (4 miles), the hike is manageable, though steep in parts. Leave at least 2½ hours.

Trails **A1, A3** and **A4** are equally rewarding but longer (A3 is also a little gentler). With older children, you'll want to tackle them too.

A popular alternative route heads from Pratini straight for the park's **beach** ★★, Cala di

Italian Cowboys

Real cowboys, the butteri, have herded longhorn cattle and horses on the marshes of the Maremma and Lazio for centuries. They still do, but now they also organise 1½-hour **equestrian shows** for tourists (20€, free for 4–12s, weekly in summer) and treks for experienced riders. Half-day trips start at 50€, up to week-long Tuscan horseback tours at 1,740€. For both, contact **Equinus** (✆ *0564 24988*. ***www.cavallomaremmano.it***).

Forno. The flatter **Forestal and Faunal** trails, **A5** and **A6** ★, depart from close to the visitor centre.

Night treks in the Parco are available all year for groups of 8 to12 (15€pp, ***info@parco-maremma.it***), if you book ahead.

Acquario di Talamone

FIND AGE 3 & UP

Via Nizza 12, Talamone. 0564 887173. 150m (492 ft) uphill from marina.

This slightly ramshackle little aquarium houses fish and crustaceans found in the Orbetello lagoon. The lagoon's waters vary from very salty to almost fresh, and the tanks here reflect those changing environments. Marine sound-effects set the mood, and English signage helps you around. The aquarium also serves as a hospital for **sea turtles** caught in fishermen's nets, and staff will happily show you the recuperating patients.

Time *40 min.* ***Open*** *10am–noon and 3–5pm Tues–Sun (Sat and Sun only out of season).* ***Adm*** *3€, 2€ children 6–14; combined ticket with Parco Regionale della Maremma (routes T1, T2, T3) 7€, children 5€.* ***Amenities***

INSIDER TIP

If you're hungry after the aquarium... the spaghetti *alla pescatora* (with seafood) in the non-descript **Bar Centrale** (Via Aurelia Vecchia 20. *0564 884914*), in Fonteblanda between the SS1 and Talamone, is extraordinary.

Marina di Alberese ★ ALL AGES

Follow signs; 8km (5 miles) from Alberese.

Along with the **Tombolo della Feniglia** (p. 161), this is the best Tuscan **beach** south of Elba, with serene pine-backed sands and gentle dunes blessed with fine views of **Isola Giglio** in the haze. It can get **busy** on summer weekends, but if you come out of season you might have no more than a fox for company. Look out for Maremman long-horn cattle by the road.

Time *At least 1 hr.* ***Open*** *8am–dusk daily.* ***Adm*** *Free.* ***Amenities***

MONTE ARGENTARIO

This scrubby rock protruding from the Tyrrhenian Sea got itself a grand name: **Monte Argentario** ★, 'the silver mountain'. Once an island, it is now connected to the mainland by a forested isthmus guarded by **Orbetello.** The town's lagoon is a vital wetland **nature reserve**—another great place along this coast to **birdwatch** ★.

Visitor Information

Information Centres

The peninsula's helpful **tourist office** (*0564 814208*; 9am–1pm and 4–8pm daily Apr–Sept; rest of year 9am–1pm and 3–7pm Mon–Sat, 9am–12:30pm Sun) provides trail maps and advice

TIP On to Lazio

If you're carrying on towards Rome, make a detour to the **Giardino dei Tarocchi** ★ (☎ *0564 895122. www.nikidesaintphalle.com*. 2.30–7.30pm daily April–mid-Oct), an outdoor wonderland of Gaudì-esque sculptures and paths, created on a tarot theme by artist Niki de Saint Phalle. It's signposted just outside Pescia Fiorentina. At 10.50€ adults, 6€ children (under-7s free), it's a bit pricey but great fun.

on **hiking** ★ around Monte Argentario or driving the scenic **Via Panoramica** ★. It's just on your left as you drop down the hill into Porto Santo Stefano, at Piazzale Sant'Andrea 1.

There's more information at the town hall's website, ***www.comunemonteargentario.it***.

Family-Friendly Event

The peninsula's big event is the **Palio Marinaro del Argentario:** on 15th August, five-strong teams from Porto Santo Stefano's four *rioni* (quarters) don medieval dress and race heavy rowing boats in the bay. Madness, in every sense.

What to See & Do

Monte Argentario itself is populated by two fishing villages turned resorts, fashionable among Florentine and Roman weekenders: **Porto Santo Stefano** and **Porto Ercole.** They're pleasant out of season but packed to the rafters in summer. Both ports have **ATMs** right on the harbour fronts. You'll need them—either resort can eat into a carefully planned budget. Porto Ercole was where artist and errant genius **Caravaggio** dropped dead of fever in 1610—right by a great **beach** (see below).

Porto Santo Stefano has clear water and a pleasant promenade—plus a summer traffic problem. This is the jumping-off point for ferries to **Isola Giglio,** run by **Toremar** (☎ *081 0178* or ☎ *0564 812920. **www.toremar.it***) and **Maregiglio** (☎ *0564 812920. **www.maregiglio.it***). Singles cost 10€, 5.50€ children; there are 2 or 3 daily crossings in winter, up to seven or more in high season, taking 1 hour. The town also has a small **Acquario** (☎ *0564 815933. **www.acquarioargentario.org***. All day mid-June–mid-Sept, rest of year afternoons only; entrance 4.50€, €1 4–12s).

Tombolo della Feniglia ★

ALL AGES

Off SP2 3½ km (2 miles) from Orbetello, direction Porto Ercole.

The long, flat expanse of sand stretching almost all the way from Monte Argentario to the mainland is an ideal, shallow-shelved **family beach.** It's serviced (in season) by **Mamma Licia Bar** (☎ *0564 834187*), **Il Tridente** (☎ *0564 834141*) and others, close to the parking, but farther along

Tombolo della Feniglia, Monte Argentario

you're on your own. When the sun gets too much, there's shade under the **parasol pines**—and more solitude the farther you walk towards the mainland.

Time *At least 1 hr.* ***Open*** *always.* ***Adm*** *Free.* ***Amenities***

FAMILY-FRIENDLY DINING

Bar Centrale, Fonteblanda, see p. 160.

Il Beccafico ★ MAREMMAN/SEAFOOD

Via Montebello 7, Castiglione della Pescaia. 333 8287021.

At first sight this place looks a little grown-up, and the soft music seems a bit intimate for a family lunch. But the **exuberant service** soon puts you at ease and staff at this cellar-style dining room on the way up to Castiglione's Borgo Medioevale will happily make up pasta with tomato or meat sauce or cook an escalope to your children's taste. For adults, the menu changes monthly; rotating daily specials might include *tagliolini* with octopus, tagliatelle with venison, or salt cod *alla Livornese*, all cooked to a high standard.

Open *12:30–2pm and 7:30–10pm Thurs–Tues (call ahead for low-season lunchtime closures).* ***Main courses*** *12€–28€.* ***Credit*** *MC, V.*

Il Gatto e La Volpe

CLASSIC MAREMMAN

Vicolo Ciambellano 12, Massa Marittima. 0566 903575. ***www.ristoroilgattoelavolpe.it****.*

This antique-feeling cellar restaurant with its less formal terrace is down an atmospheric lane in Massa's *centro storico*. The short menu goes right for what the Alta Maremma does best: tasty vegetarian 'peasant' soups such as *acquacotta* and *ribollita* and meat or game stews. Classic wild boar with olives often features, as does *peposo* (peppery beef stew). Unusually for Tuscany, staff will do a half-portion of anything for children—and there's always a bowl of simple pasta and sauce if you ask, served with a smile.

Open** Noon–2:30pm and 7–10pm Tues–Sun. **Main courses** 9€–16€. **Credit** AE, MC, V. **Amenities

INSIDER TIP

Neighbour (at no. 4) **La Tana del Brillo Parlane ★★** (*0566 901274.* Closed Wed) has a well-earned, loftier 'Slow-Food' reputation, but its tiny dining room and outdoor tables for two aren't very family friendly. However, if you can arrange a babysitter (and reserve well ahead), this is Massa's best food experience.

La Barcaccina ★★ SEAFOOD

*Via Tridentina 1, San Vincenzo. 0565 701911. **www.barcaccina.it**. At southern end, next to Parco Comunale.*

There are a million places to eat seafood along the Etruscan Coast but this one on San Vincenzo's beach is a **bit special.** Fish is fresh from the morning market and the menu changes accordingly, but always features mixed fish grills and plenty of shellfish. Despite the serious attitude to food, the atmosphere is **informal:** youngsters can run amok on the beach while you wait to eat; you can also dress up or down as you please. For children, they'll grill a white fish and serve it with **proper chips.** Book ahead in summer.

Open** 12:30–2:30pm and 7:30–9:30pm Thurs–Tues exc. Nov–Easter. **Main courses** 10€–24€. **Credit** AE, MC, V. **Amenities

La Gramola, Castagneto Carducci, see p. 149.

Publius ★ ELBAN/TUSCAN

*Piazza del Castagneto 11, Poggio Marciana, Elba. 0565 99208. **www.ristorantepublius.it**.*

One of the best views on Elba is complemented by competent cooking at this much-recommended hill-top eatery. The interesting mix of rustic Tuscan food (boar or duck *ragù*, for example) and fish plucked straight from the sea 350m (1,148 ft) below, then prepared with finesse, might include an oven-baked millefeuille of *rombo* (turbot) or black tagliolini *al branzino* (with sea bass). Publius also specialises in gluten-free dishes. Book ahead in summer.

Open** Noon–2pm and 7–10pm daily, Mar–Nov only. **Main courses** 12€–22€. **Credit** MC, V. **Amenities

Taverna di Populonia, Populonia Alta, see p. 149.

FAMILY-FRIENDLY ACCOMMODATION

For more accommodation ideas, see p. 27.

APARTMENTS, VILLAS & FARM-STAYS

Casa Campanella Resort ★★ GREEN FIND

*Località Piano di Mola, Capoliveri, Elba. 0565 915740.**www.casacampanella.it**. Right turn at Zuccale junction 500m (1,640 ft) before Capoliveri.*

Families make up about 90% of the clientele at this boutique

Seafood Cities: Livorno & Portoferraio

You'll find the freshest, tastiest seafood right along Tuscany's coast, but in the port city of **Livorno,** on the mainland, and in Elba's main town, **Portoferraio,** it counts as the major attraction.

Memorable meals at a great price are standard in Livorno but nowhere more than at **La Botteghina ★★**, almost opposite the Mediterranean Natural History Museum (p. 146). There's no menu to speak of—just a daily rotating list of tasty *antipasti*, *primi* and *secondi*, bound to include some featuring cuttlefish, fresh anchovies, *baccalà alla Livornese* (salt cod stewed with tomatoes), or even Livorno's signature dish, *cacciucco* (similar to Marseille's fishy *bouillabaisse*). A set meal should cost around 15€, including wine and coffee. For tots, chefs will cook up spaghetti with a tomato sauce or an escalope to their taste.

The **Osteria del Mare ★★** is more of a tablecloth and napkin place, but don't let that put you off: its small, wood-panelled dining room hung with local memorabilia is the setting for fine cooking complemented by attentive service, usually including classic coastal *primi* such as spaghetti *alle vongole* (with clams) and *riso nero* (cuttlefish ink-blackened risotto). Other mains are very much catch-dependent (there's nothing from the freezer here)—if you're lucky the giant house *fritto misto* will include baby squid and fresh anchovies. Mains range from 7€ to 15€.

The music may be a bit funkier at **La Barrocciaia ★**, but this small central trattoria is steeped in the food traditions of its port city. Out front it's a *paninoteca* selling rustic sandwiches. In the back, a few informal tables serve up keenly priced Livornese classics.

Don't pass through **Elba's capital** without trying at least one of two outstanding seafood restaurants. It doesn't matter where you

apartment complex in the southeastern corner of Elba. Units in the converted 19th-century villa come in three grades but all are simply decorated, with two spacious and cool rooms plus modern kitchenettes and large bathrooms. Superior and Deluxe apartments add yet more space, designer bathroom suites, bedroom LCD TVs and Wi-Fi, to an already high spec.

Apartments are bookable by the night outside high summer, when it's weekly bookings only. Ask them to include your travel to the island (they secure better rates, or sometimes free ferry crossings). The complex also makes extensive use of green and sustainable products, including energy.

Apartments** 15. **Rates** Classic 60€–240€/night. **Credit** AE, MC, V. **Amenities *In room*

sit in tiny, family-run **Osteria Libertaria ★★**, you'll be dining to the pleasing din of **sizzling fish.** The usual suspects—including fried or grilled whatever-looked-good-at-this-morning's-market—are joined by Elban specialities: maybe *riso nero* or salt cod *all'Elbana* (with black olives and pine nuts). There's always a token grilled meat; for children, they'll cook a simple pasta sauce or plain grill a white fish, and they also do chips (*patate fritte*). **Arrive early** to grab one of two prime quayside tables; there's more terrace seating out back. Main courses cost 9.50€ to 14€.

The seafood is equally sublime across town at **La Bussola ★★**, with dining inside and on a terrace abutting Le Ghiaie beach. It's an informal place with gregarious hosts, but don't think the cooking is anything but serious: signature *antipasto* steamed salt-cod on a bed of pureed chickpeas with fried, shredded leeks, invented here, is a stupendous mix of flavours and textures. Elsewhere on the varied menu are super-fresh shellfish-plus-pasta combinations, and meat or vegetarian dishes if you prefer. There's also a proper pizza oven. Mains range 10€ to 23€; pizzas are less.

Livorno **Osteria del Mare,** Borgo Cappuccini 12 (☎ *0586 881027*); closed Thurs. **La Botteghina,** Via Roma 159 (☎ *0586 805110*); closed Sun. **La Barrocciaia,** Piazza Cavallotti 13 (☎ *0586 882637*); closed Mon and Sun lunch. Cash only, except at Osteria del Mare (where reservations are advisable).

Portoferraio **Osteria Libertaria,** Calata Matteotti 12 (☎ *0565 91478*). **La Bussola,** Via Cairoli 2 (☎ *0565 917726*). Both open lunch and dinner daily from Easter until end of Sept. Out of season it's weekends only or closed; call ahead. Both take credit cards. Reservations essential in peak season.

Case Conti di Sotto FIND

☎ 335 6648171. ***www.casacontidisotto.it.*** *1km (less than 1 mile) outside Gavorrano.*

These small, stone-built, **rustic apartments** on a former farm complex are ideal for a family holiday in the coastal Maremma. Family units are mid-sized and basic but adequate, with occasional flourishes such as four-posters; bathrooms and kitchens could do with a modernising touch. But the charm and seclusion remain undented—and a little altitude and plenty of trees keep the place slightly **cooler** than the searing seaside a short drive away. Our favourite family units are **Ginestra** and **Rosmarino.**

Apartments *7.* ***Rates*** *364€–812€/wk. No credit cards.* ***Amenities*** ***In apartment***

Fattoria San Lorenzo ★★

Via Antica Aurelia 50, Grosseto. ☎ 0564 21562. ***www.fattoriasanlorenzo.it****. 3km (2 miles) southwest of Grosseto direction Trappola.*

These tastefully restored **farm buildings** in the flat countryside between Grosseto and the sea suit young families, who make up most of their clientele. The three sites (on both sides of the road) are ideal for the Parco Naturale della Maremma (p. 158) and Monte Argentario, trips down to the local beach, or simply utter relaxation down on the *fattoria*. Most of the well-equipped **mini-houses** are on two floors with bedrooms up and down, a lounge and kitchenette, plus a shower room and a bathroom. If you intend using the in-house restaurant, go for adjacent **Tenuta Livia** rather than **Le Capanne** or **Il Pozzino.**

In high season, it's week-long bookings (Sat–Sat) only; in spring or autumn, you can book for 3–4 days.

Apartments *30 (on 3 sites, open Easter–Nov).* ***Rates*** *1-bed 534€–1815€/wk, 2-bed 653€–1860€wk. Cot 26€/wk. Final cleaning (compulsory) 75€–85€.* ***Credit*** *AE, MC, V.* ***Amenities*** ***In room***

CAMPSITES

Camping Valle Gaia

☎ 0586 681236. ***www.vallegaia.it****. SS1 exit Cecina centro; follow signs to Casale M.*

This friendly little **campsite,** ideally located away from the coast, is perfect for mixing the beach and the medieval sights of central Tuscany. From its pine-shaded patch just outside Casale Marittimo, Marina di Bibbona is 15 minutes, while Volterra is 40 minutes in the opposite direction. There are the usual campsite services; the on-site **pizzeria** (which also does take-away) deserves a medal.

Pitches *150 (open Apr–Oct).* ***Rates*** *Adults 4€–8.50€, children 2–10 3€–6€, pitch 7€–14.90€. No credit cards.* ***Amenities***

HOTELS/BED & BREAKFASTS

Hotel Capo Sud ★ FIND

Lacona (above Margidore beach), Elba. ☎ 0565 964021. ***www.hotelcaposud.it.***

Set in a quiet corner of Elba, east of Lacona, the Capo Sud with its **clifftop views** and friendly staff makes a lasting first impression. Rooms are set in small blocks wedged into a slope down to Margidore's dark beach: **Il Sole** and **La Luna** offer the best combination of seclusion and private beach access but accommodate double-plus-cot combos only. The best 'proper' triples are in **Il Pino; L'Aleatico** offers the facility to make adjoining doubles into a mini-apartment. Rooms are cool and spacious, if a bit bland. Each has its own outside space: invest a little extra to make it a **sea view.**

Rooms *40 (open late Apr–Sept).* ***Rates*** *Double 72€–182€ (garden view), 92€–202€ (sea view). Cot 15€. Extra bed 28€–70€. Breakfast included.* ***Credit*** *MC, V.* ***Amenities*** ***In room***

7 The Val d'Orcia,
Valdichiana & Pitigliano
PIENZA

SOUTHERN TUSCANY

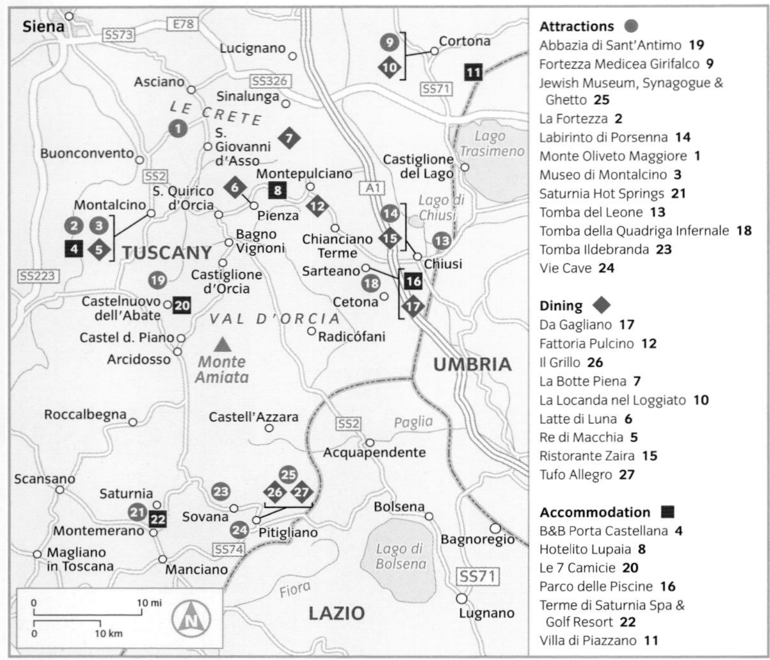

Southern Tuscany has a reputation among those in the know. This spectacular manicured land of bleak farms, bright greens and limestone ridges seems lifted straight from the background of a Renaissance painting. It's dotted with grown-up attractions: cue sage nods in the illustrious *cantinas* of Montalcino and Montepulciano, furrowed brows in arty Cortona and among the architecture buffs admiring Pienza's *palazzi*, and hushed tones in the abbeys of Monte Oliveto Maggiore and Sant'Antimo. Italy's Etruscan heartland is frequented by holidaymakers who are *very serious indeed*. Or at least, that's the stereotype. But don't you dare give up on it.

Montalcino's best spot for tasting its iconic wine, Brunello di Montalcino, is inside a cool castle, while Pienza's little balcony has a view of the Val d'Orcia that'll knock children dead—if the one over the Valdichiana from Cortona's keep hasn't wowed them already. You'll find local shops selling quality pecorino (sheep's milk cheese), extra-virgin olive oils and fine wines round almost every corner in the area's hill-towns, and gourmet Chiusi has enough beneath its streets to keep imaginative little minds ticking over.

We haven't even mentioned Pitigliano yet—an untouristy little town anchoring a network of ancient subterranean walkways, wide open and free, with only your puff and a 9pm bedtime to limit you. Who said the Etruscans were boring?

Just don't forget the car-sickness pills: there's plenty of twisty-turny driving, too.

CORTONA

Despite its dramatic Valdichiana lookout, ancient **Cortona** ★ has a slightly stern look from a distance. Once you're inside the massive stone walls, however, its charm is revealed: a warren of paved streets and limestone *palazzi*, busy with swifts, swallows and stone staircases that disappear into blind alleys. Though the unwitting star of a publishing phenomenon, Frances Mayes' *Under the Tuscan Sun* (1998), it remains a rustic hill-town with a real life beyond its artistic heritage. Both Luca Signorelli (1445–1523) and Sassetta (1392–1451) were Cortonese.

Visitor Information

Information Centres

The **tourist office** (☎ *0575 630352*. *infocortona@apt.arezzo.it*. Easter–Sept 9am–1pm and 3–6pm Mon–Sat, 9am–1pm Sun; rest of year 9am–1pm and 3–6pm Mon–Fri, Sat 9am–1pm, Sun closed) is at Via Nazionale 42. Be warned that mobile phone reception in Cortona is hopeless.

Arriving

Cortona is easily reached by **car,** 24km (39 miles) south of Arezzo off the SS71 and less than 1 hour from Perugia and Lago Trasimeno's resorts. **Parking** is another matter: when the road divides just below Cortona, turn right and park for free in the lot on your right. From there, an escalator flies you up the worst of the hill.

Hourly-or-so **LFI buses** (☎ *0575 39881*. *www.lfi.it*) from Arezzo (3.70€, 50 min) terminate in Piazzale Garibaldi, by the gate.

What to See & Do

Cortona is simply a great place to hang out. With young children, though, we strongly advise you to limit your wanderings to the bottom 'storey', running northwest from Piazzale Garibaldi to Piazza del Duomo and taking in the best two museums—the rest is major-league steep.

The illustrious **Museo dell'Accademia Etrusca e della Città** (☎ *0575 637235*. *www.cortonamaec.org*. 10am–7pm daily Apr–Oct, rest of year Tues–Sun 10am–5pm), or MAEC, is justly lauded for its well-signed multimedia trip into Cortona's Etruscan and Roman past. The sudden first-floor leap from Late Antiquity to local 1920s' Futurist **Gino Severini** marks the start of a chaotic but diverting procession through medieval Sienese altarpieces, Florentine heraldry

Children's Top Attractions of Southern Tuscany

- Catching a first glimpse of Pitigliano seemingly growing from **living rock,** p. 184.
- Exploring the town's Jewish heritage and **ghetto,** p. 185.
- Basking in the warm **spa waters** at Saturnia, p. 186.
- Hiking the Etruscan **Vie Cave,** p. 187.
- Scaling **Cortona** to the Fortezza Girifalco, p. 169.
- Braving the **labyrinth** under Chiusi, p. 182.
- Discovering ancient **wall art** in the Tomba della Quadriga Infernale, p. 183.
- Tucking into **Tuscany's best steak** at Acquacheta, p. 187.

and Egyptian mummies. Admission is a steep 8€, 4€ for children 6 to 12.

Among some modest panels in the **Museo Diocesano** (☎ *0575 62830*), opposite the Duomo, are a pair of corkers: Fra' Angelico's **Annunciation** ★ rightly gets the plaudits, but Luca Signorelli's **Lamentation over the Dead Christ** ★★ is an outstanding example of his work, loaded with despair and surreal background detail. Hours are the same as MAEC; admission is 5€, 3€ for children 6 to 14. Joint tickets to both are 10€, 6€ for children.

The ice creams at **Gelateria Snoopy** (10am–11pm daily), opposite MAEC at Piazza Signorelli 29, couldn't possibly live up to the hype but it's still the best place in town. The steps under the 13th-century **Palazzo Comunale** ★, round the corner in Piazza della Repubblica and right opposite some fine piazza cafés, are the ideal slurping spot.

Before you move on, check out the beautifully hand-painted ceramics at **L'Antico Cocciaio** ★,

Fast Facts: Southern Tuscany

Banks Monte dei Paschi di Siena (☎ *0575 630284*) is at Via Nazionale 42, Cortona, by the tourist office. Banca Etruria (☎ *0578 757134*) is at Via Voltaia nel Corso 31, Montepulciano.

Hospitals & Emergencies Ospedale Valdichiana (☎ *0578 713111*) is at Via Provinciale 5 in Gracciano. In a medical emergency, call ☎ *118*.

Internet & Wi-Fi Montepulciano's **tourist office** (p. 172) has an Internet point (3.50€/hr).

Post Offices Cortona's post office is at Via Benedetti 2 (☎ *0575 601511*), Montepulciano's is at Via delle Erbe 12 (☎ *0578 757635*).

FUN FACT On the Level

So rare are lanes without a slope in Cortona that its main street, Via Nazionale, has earned the nickname **'flat street'**.

Via Benedetti 24 (*0575 605294. **www.lanticococciaio.com***. 9am–7pm daily). It also runs pottery classes.

Fortezza Medicea Girifalco

★★ AGE 10 & UP

0575 637235.

Cortona's major highlight is all uphill. If your children are old enough to tackle steep climbs, the best route follows the wall from Piazza Garibaldi along Via Santa Margherita, the **Via Crucis** ★. It's a torturous, stepped ascent enlivened by 15 mosaics depicting the **Stations of the Cross** by Cortonese Futurist Gino Severini.

By the second time Christ falls, you'll feel like doing the same. This route is **impossible** with a buggy; don't attempt it with under-10s or if you have asthma or a heart condition. And pause for a restorative drink at the bar by **Santuario Santa Margherita.**

Built in 1556 by a relative of Pope Pius IV, the four surviving bastions of the **Fortezza** have unmatched **views** ★★★ as far as Castiglione del Lago, Arezzo and the colossal Monte Amiata.

Time** 1½ hr. **Open** 10:30am–1:30pm and 2:30–6pm daily. **Adm** 3€, 1.50€ children 6–12. **Amenities P

The Etruscans in 162 Words

Greek historian Herodotus reckoned that the Etruscans came from Turkey, but the more usual explanation is that they were simply the people who lived around here, who gave their name to 'Tuscany'. There are signs of Etruscan civilisation in the area from about 800 B.C.: farmers, seafarers and miners, they had complex government structures, language and artistic forms.

Fast forward to A.D. 100 and they've disappeared, assimilated by the rise of Rome. Their most important 12 cities, the **Dodecapoli**, included *Velzna* (now Orvieto), *Arretium* (Arezzo), *Clevsin* (Chiusi) and *Curtun* (Cortona). Though each was largely autonomous, at their peak they controlled the territory between the Tiber and the Arno, with lands as far north as the Po and south to Salerno.

To swot up before your trip, see ***http://en.wikipedia.org/wiki/Etruscans***. Should the Etruscan bug catch, the best places to head are the **Tomba della Quadriga Infernale** in Sarteano (p. 183) and the museums in **Orvieto** (p. 226), **Volterra** (p. 99) and **Cortona** (p. 169).

MONTEPULCIANO

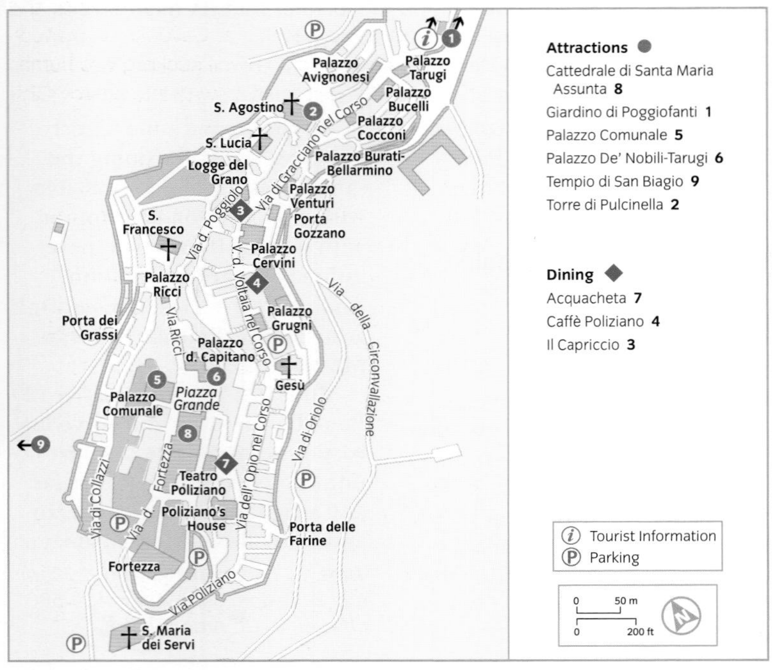

MONTEPULCIANO

Best known for its aristocratic wine, Vino Nobile, **Montepulciano** ★ is perched 664m (2,178 ft) up a volcanic ridge above the Valdichiana. This is the southern Tuscan hill-town par excellence, with emphasis on the *hill* bit. Little legs and buggy-pushers will struggle: it's **seriously steep.** The narrow streets are lined with Renaissance architecture and shops offering wine tastings and *tipico* produce. Eagle-eyed fans of the *Twilight* saga will also spot that you've just walked on to the *New Moon* set: though Stephenie Meyer set her tale in Volterra, the film was shot here.

Visitor Information

Information Centres

The **tourist office** (☎ *0578 757341*. ***www.prolocomontepulciano.it***. 9am–12:30pm and 3–8pm daily Apr–Sept, rest of year Mon–Sat 9am–12:30pm and 3–6pm) is at Piazza Don Minzoni 1, outside Porta al Prato, with a Banca Etruria ATM opposite.

Arriving

By Car Montepulciano is 72km (45 miles) southeast of Siena, on the SS146. **Parking** can be tricky: follow signs for *centro storico/corso* as you enter town and drive past

FUN FACT Whose Side Are You On, Anyway?

It's easy to spot a hill-town's traditional protector and friend: the *marzocco* (heraldic lion) seen in Montepulciano's Piazza Savonarola, symbolises **Florence,** while **Siena** is represented by a she-wolf suckling two human children (Romulus and Remus)—you can't miss it as you walk into nearby **Chiusi**'s Piazza Duomo.

the tourist office down the narrow hill: you can park there for free. **Pay parking** is right above, under the Porta al Prato (1.20€/hr), but you'll need luck to bag a space. Opposite, the **Giardino di Poggiofanti** has **swings** and a **slide.** An alternative entry point is **car park 8** (also free): take the uphill left fork *immediately after* the Pienza/Chianciano junction. The route up from the car park alights at the **Fortezza** (private), adjacent to which there's a shady public garden with more **swings** and a **slide.** You're far closer to Piazza Grande this way, but the climb is murder with a buggy or little legs.

By Bus Between four and eight daily **TRA.IN buses** (☎ *0577 204246*. ***www.trainspa.it***) link **Siena** and Montepulciano, via Pienza, in 1½ hour.

If you have young children, avoid the uphill trek to Piazza Grande: orange hopper buses ***(pollicini)*** make the journey every 15 to 20 minutes. Buy **tickets** from the tourist office (1€), good for an hour of travel.

Family-Friendly Festivals

Montepulciano's major *festa* is the **Bravio delle Botti** ★. On the penultimate Sunday in August, teams from the town's *contrade* race to push a wine barrel the length of the main street, the Corso, in medieval costume. The YouTube videos don't do it justice.

The view from Montepulciano, across vineyards and the Tempio di San Biagio

Montepulciano's Corso

What to See & Do

Winding streets lined with Renaissance *palazzi* lend Montepulciano a sophisticated ambience. Antonio da Sangallo (the Elder) and Michelozzo were kept busy for years applying the architectural theories dreamt up by Pope Pius II and Rossellino in Pienza 50 years earlier (see below). They lined the Corso with fine examples, but the highlight is Sangallo's **Palazzo De' Nobili-Tarugi,** in Piazza Grande.

For youngsters, a couple of less refined sights may prove more memorable. The **Torre di Pulcinella,** in Piazza Michelozzo, is topped by a figure of **Punch** (*Pulcinella* in Italy), who strikes the hour. For seemingly endless **views** ★ over Umbria, scale the Gothic **Palazzo Comunale** (2€; under-12s free) in Piazza Grande. The roof terrace is open 10am to 6pm daily; turn left up the stairs as you enter and pay on the second floor.

The best place in town to be seen sipping an (expensive) *cappuccino* is the Art Deco **Caffè Poliziano** (☎ *0578 758615. **www.caffepoliziano.it***), at Via di Voltaia nel Corso 27. But forget their ice cream; across the street and just downhill at no. 14, **Il Capriccio** is better.

A steep 20-minute downhill walk from Porta dei Grassi takes you to the photogenic **Tempio di San Biagio,** a travertine Renaissance church designed to a Greek cross plan, like St Peter's in Rome. Don't attempt the trek with a buggy.

Cattedrale di Santa Maria Assunta ★ ALL AGES

Piazza Grande. No phone.

Montepulciano's outstanding work of art, a dazzling **Assumption of the Virgin** (1401) altarpiece by Sienese **Taddeo di Bartolo,** is in the town's distinctly unfinished Duomo. The rather dark Renaissance interior also hides a painted terracotta frieze (c. 1512) by Andrea della Robbia known as the **Gigli altar,** in the Baptistery on your immediate left as you enter.

Time *30 min.* ***Open*** *All day except during Mass (noon–1pm).* ***Adm*** *Free.*

TIP Tasting in Montepulciano

It was the Etruscans who first spotted Montepulciano's unique geographical adaptation to the cultivation of wine. Our favourite *cantina* in town is **Gattavecchi** ★★ (*0578 757110. **www.gattavecchi.it***. Daily 9am–7pm Apr–Oct; 10am–1pm and 2–6pm Nov–Mar), at Via di Collazzi 74. This is perhaps Tuscany's best crack at a **child-friendly winery,** with something to really pique their interest: cellars (which you're free to poke around) that have been in use since before 1200, originally by the friars of adjacent **Santa Maria dei Servi.** Older still is the tiny room at the bottom chiselled from the rock; it was probably an Etruscan tomb.

As you'd expect from one of Montepulciano's pioneering wine families, Gattavecchi's **Vino Nobile** is top-notch; even better is the brand-new, 100% Sangiovese **Parceto.** Tasting is free. **Contucci** ★ (*0578 757006. **www.contucci.it***), in a historic palace in Piazza Grande, has a fine range of Vino Nobile wines grown on four soil types, all between the magical numbers of 200m (656 ft) and 400m (1,312 ft) altitude. According to winemaker Adamo Pallecchi, this is crucial. The *cantina* is open for (free) tasting every day of the year.

Opposite the Duomo, the **Palazzo del Capitano del Popolo** is another stop for the wine buffs. Turn right from the corridor for the **Consorzio del Vino Nobile di Montepulciano** ★ (*0578 757812. **www.consorziovinonobile.it***. 11:30am–1:30pm and 2–6pm Mon–Fri, 2–6pm Sat from week after Easter–Oct), which offers a rotating menu of tastings for a small fee. Local wineries without a shop in town also sell by the bottle here, and if you're heading into the country for some wine touring, staff can provide maps and ideas—as can the **Strada del Vino Nobile** office (*0578 717484. **www.stradavinonobile.it***) across the corridor, who are the people to speak to if you want to arrange a local wine itinerary.

PIENZA

South of Siena perched above the Val d'Orcia, **Pienza** ★ was created in the mid-15th century by humanist Pope Pius II and architect Bernardo Rossellino to be the ideal Renaissance town. Rossellino's budget was 10,000 florins and he spent 50,000, but Pius was so pleased he scrapped the old name of Corsignano and named it after himself.

In spite of being heavily frequented by tourists, this remains a delightful place, famous for its sheep's milk cheese, *pecorino di Pienza*.

Visitor Information

Information Centres

The **tourist office** (*0578 749071*. Daily 10am–1pm and 3–7pm 15th Mar–Oct, rest of year Sat and Sun) is in the courtyard at Corso Rossellino 30. Other useful trip-planning resources are ***www.pienza.info*** and ***www.portalepienza.it***.

A Winemaker's Year

The busiest time for any vintner is the **harvest,** usually in September. You might find some vineyards less than excited to see you if you arrive during picking period: check first. That's not to say the rest of the year's quiet, mind you...

Jan/Feb: vines pruned, and barrels kept topped up to stop air getting in.

Mar: new vines planted; last year's young-drinking wine bottled.

Apr/May: barrels racked to separate sediment, and vines pruned to concentrate flavour in a few shoots.

June/July: vines trained so that they get as much sun as possible, then sprayed.

Aug: excess bunches of under-ripe grapes cut away and the winery prepares for harvest.

Sept/Oct: the *vendemmia* (the harvest) and the start of the fermentation to turn grape juice into wine.

Nov/Dec: early tastings of this year's young wine, then cracking open a good bottle for Christmas dinner.

Arriving

For **drivers,** Pienza is 14km (9 miles) west of Montepulciano, 55km (34 miles) southeast of Siena down the SS2 and then the SS146. It's usually easy to find a place in the (free) **car park** beside the Agip garage on the road to or from Montepulciano, from where it's 5 minutes to the centre. There are five daily **TRA.IN buses** (1¼ hr, 3.60€) from Siena on weekdays.

What to See & Do

Pienza is mercifully **flat.** Most sights are crammed into the splendid **Piazza Pio II** ★★, the squashed Renaissance set-piece

The town of Pienza looks down on the Val d'Orcia.

TIP A Little Shopping

Pienza is a compact place with tons of browsing potential, mostly along Corso Rossellino. Among dozens of friendly *tipico* shops, **Marusco e Maria** (*0578 748222*), at 15–21, stands out with its 23 varieties of local **pecorino** and salami made from Cinta Senese pigs. Crafting beautiful but useful objects from iron has been in the **Biagiotti** family, whose shop is at no. 67 (*0578 748027. www.biagiottipienza.com*), for more than a century. Little girls will love the dolls, trinkets and sparkly paraphernalia at **Estetica Silvia** (no. 89)—you might want to set a spending ceiling before letting them inside. **Enoteca di Ghino** ★ (*0578 748057. www.enotecadighino.it*) is a serious wine shop, usually with an impromptu tasting table set up, at Via del Leone 16.

You'll also find **the best ice cream** away from the main drag: Snoopy's **Punto Gelato** ★ is across the road from Piazza Dante.

---

that is as far as Pope Pius's town-planning dream reached; it's like a Matchbox version of architectural perfection. Of the standing follies, the highlight is the **Duomo** ★. Its light-drenched interior was part of Pius's brief to his builders, so visitors could see the four Sienese altarpieces properly. Almost uniquely in Tuscany, they're all still in the spot they were designed for. But the fine monument, built on a precipice, is slowly cracking.

Palazzo Piccolomini (*0578 748392. www.palazzopiccolominipienza.it*) is only accessible via a half-hour (Tues–Sun 10am–6pm, mid-Mar–mid-Oct; 10am–4pm rest of year) **guided tour** (regularly given in English), but unless you and your children have a special interest in Renaissance interiors, you'll be bored rigid. On the other hand, it's almost worth the 7€ (5€ children) to catch the devastating **view** ★★ south over the Val d'Orcia from the *palazzo*'s hanging garden and triple-decked *loggia* (although you can get *almost* the same view for **free** anytime by walking down the steps between the Duomo and the Palazzo on to the old walls). Note that the palace is closed for the second half of both February and November.

The third of Rossellino's triumvirate, the **Palazzo Vescovile,** houses the tourist office (above) and a small **Museo Diocesano.**

Monte Oliveto Maggiore

AGE 8 & UP

9km (6 miles) northeast of Buonconvento. www.monteolivetomaggiore.it.

The most famous of Tuscany's rural **monasteries** is among the loveliest. Set in the scarred hills of the *Crete Senesi* (p. 91) and offering glorious views, Monte Oliveto Maggiore was founded in 1319 by a Sienese nobleman who renounced his wealth to live as a hermit. It owes its fame to the **Chiostro Grande** ★, painted with frescoes begun by Luca

Signorelli in 1497 and completed by Sodoma in 1508. As frescoes go, these are easy to follow, recounting events in the life of **St. Benedict.** Start in the back-left corner as you walk in, with the young Benedict leaving home on horseback, and run clockwise. Sodoma painted the first and last of Benedict's deeds and miracles (a self-portrait with pet badger adorns panel 3); the change of style as Signorelli takes over, for nine panels from God punishing Florenzo onwards, is visible.

The friars ask that you **dress appropriately** (no strappy tops or shorts) and respect their **silence**—so this isn't a place to bring boisterous youngsters. The gatehouse restaurant, **La Torre** (☎ *0577 707022*), has a shaded terrace—and positively encourages talking.

Time *1 hr.* ***Open*** *9:15am–noon and 3:15–6pm daily (until 5pm in winter).* ***Adm*** *Free.* ***Amenities***

MONTALCINO

If you know anything about wine, you don't need us to introduce **Montalcino**—the word comes with its own fanfare. There are few wines that match the intensity of a fine **Brunello di Montalcino.**

The origins of this delightful hilltop town, where modern life ebbs and flows to the rhythm of its red grape, go back to Etruscan times. It isn't an obvious destination for children; there's *just* enough to occupy them while you knock back a few samples of the great wine.

Less well known is the town's reputation for **honey,** which should be added to your tasting list. And remember, that for all its pomp, Montalcino is still rustic at heart—two streets back from the *tipico* food and wine shops, you'll find a ragged olive grove and someone's washing out to dry.

Visitor Information

Information Centres

The **tourist office** is at Costa del Municipio 1 (☎ *0577 849331. **www.prolocomontalcino.it***. 10am–1pm and 2–5:40pm daily, exc. Mon Nov–Mar), up a ramp in the shadow of the bell-tower. There's a **cashpoint** around the other side of the tower.

Arriving

Montalcino, 43km (27 miles) southeast of Siena, is easily reached by **car.** The most reliable place for **parking spaces** (1.50€/hr) is the town's western edge, along Viale Strozzi.

From Siena, Montalcino is also served by regular **TRA.IN buses** (☎ *0577 204246. **www.trainspa.it***), taking 1¼ hr (line 114).

Family-Friendly Festivals

Montalcino's festivals revolve around hunting and are inevitably food-and-wine affairs. Most interesting is the **Sagra del**

Tordo (last Sun in Oct), which 'celebrates' the thrush by spit-roasting the songbirds by the thousand.

What to See & Do

If you parked in Viale Strozzi, continue along the old walls; the best spot to gulp down the panorama is the **Santuario della Madonna del Soccorso.** Continue to Piazza Cavour and turn into Via Mazzini. From there walk the length of the *passeggiata* to the **Fortezza** (see below). Along the way, stop in at **Il Ranocchio** (no. 13; *347 9527882.* Usually 9:30am–1pm and 4:30–7:30pm) for funky (if pricey) children's clothes.

Abbazia di Sant'Antimo

AGE 5 & UP

Castelnuovo dell'Abate. 0577 835659. ***www.antimo.it.*** *9km (6 miles) south of Montalcino.*

Should the urge ever strike, you'd be hard-pressed to find a better place to be a monk—the serene setting of Sant'Antimo, among vines at the foot of Castelnuovo dell'Abate, lends this exquisite Romanesque abbey a serenity rarely found on the tourist trail. Its semi-circular apse shows pure French influence (which probably flowed down the Via Francigena pilgrimage route to Rome). The followers of St. Augustine who reside here worship in Gregorian chant—after a service (which precedes visiting hours), the smell of incense wafts across the surrounding fields.

Abbazia di Sant' Antimo

There's a well-marked **hiking trail** to the monastery from Montalcino, good for fit families (3 hr); ask for the **Camminare Montalcino** map (2€) and a return bus timetable at Montalcino's tourist office.

Time *1 hr.* ***Open*** *10:30am–12:30pm and 3–6:30pm Mon–Sat; 9:15am–12:45pm and 3–6pm Sun.* ***Adm*** *Free.* ***Amenities***

La Fortezza ★ ALL AGES

Piazzale Fortezza. 0577 849211. ***www.enotecalafortezza.it.***

Of the 1,001 places to go to taste wine in and around Montalcino, only one has ramparts. Built in 1361, this castle's moment arrived when the Sienese holed up here for 4 years after their city's final defeat by Florence in 1555. You and the children can walk round the pentagonal walls and scale a ladder to the highest turret. On a

Orcia Meanders

Follow signposts for the village of **Bagno Vignoni** from the main SS2 for a pool like nothing your children have ever seen—for starters, you can't swim or splash in it. More remarkable is its Renaissance *loggia*, that it's where the village's **piazza** should be, and that it was frequented by **St Catherine of Siena** (p. 89). Beware: it is a tour bus favourite, so arrive early; there's a café–*gelateria* opposite.

Nearby **San Quirico d'Orcia** ★ is a tiny place with flattish streets and formal gardens (the 1540 **Horta Leonini**) that are a delight to wander. Its hugely impressive Collegiata dedicated to mother-and-son martyrs Julietta and Quiricus is hewn from honey-coloured travertine, and has notable arched Romanesque portals decorated with all manner of stone-carved birds and beasts. The town's **Birrificio** (*0577 898193.* ***www.birrificiosanquirico.it***), at Via Dante Alighieri 93a, produces and sells artisan beers brewed on site, with free tastings.

clear day, you'll see Siena. Just don't look down.

Inside the keep, the **Enoteca La Fortezza** stocks a range of **Brunello di Montalcino** ★★, carefully selected from 205 registered producers in the DOCG (p. 32). If you know Brunello, ask the knowledgeable, English-speaking staff to pour you something from the southern area; you'll get a fruitier surprise. Apart from 2002, every vintage since 2001 has been excellent or even better. Two tasting samples cost 9€, three 12€, five 19€; a plate of salami or local cheese to complement them costs 8€. Youngsters tearing round the castle for free? Priceless.

If this is your only stop in Montalcino, you can **park** right outside (1.50€/hr).

Time *45 min.* ***Open*** *Daily 9am–8pm Apr–Oct, 10am–6pm Nov–Mar.* ***Adm*** *4€, 2€ under-12s (to walls).* ***Amenities***

Museo di Montalcino ★

AGE 8 & UP

Via Ricasoli 31. 0577 846014.

This slightly stern museum in the cloisters of the church of **Sant'Agostino** is dedicated largely to Sienese works, including a panel by Ambrogio Lorenzetti and four extraordinary carved **Crucifixions** ★ from the 1300s. One of the best small-town collections in Tuscany, it's been supplemented by an archaeological section displayed in an atmospheric vault. As well as prehistoric finds from the area's many digs, children usually love the life-sized model of an Etruscan warrior.

Time *1¼ hr.* ***Open*** *10am–1pm and 2–5:40pm Tues–Sun.* ***Adm*** *4.50€, children 3€. Joint ticket with Fortezza saves 2.50€.*

CHIUSI

The Etruscan city of Camars, or Clevsin, now **Chiusi,** doesn't leave quite the same aesthetic impression as its neighbours. Architecturally, it's a bit of a mish-mash; artistic highs are relatively lacking. But there are three things (mostly Etruscan) that make a short visit worthwhile: tunnels, towers and tucker. For the last, see p. 187; for the rest, read on.

Visitor Information

Information Centres

The **tourist office** is at Via Porsenna 79 (☎ *0578 227667. **www.prolocochiusi.it***. Daily 10am–1pm and 3–6pm Apr–Sept; 10am–2pm Oct, 9:30am–12:30pm Nov–Mar), opposite the campanile. It sells a **combined ticket** for all central sights for 8€.

There's a **cashpoint** uphill from the tourist office, on the corner of Via Porsenna and Via Petrozzi.

Arriving

Chiusi is easily reached from just about anywhere in Italy: it's a major **rail** hub on the Florence–Rome line, with hourly direct trains from **Siena** (1¼ hr, 5.70€) and **Arezzo** (45 min, 4.60€).

By **car,** it's on the **A1**, 80km (50 miles) southeast of Siena and 50km (31 miles) from Perugia. The best spot to **park** (for free) is off Via Pietriccia; follow the 'P' to the right at the T-junction by the *centro storico*.

There's a **playground** and **views** ★ to Umbria and Lazio in the Giardini Pubblici above the car park.

What to See & Do

The **Etruscans** (p. 171) are almost the only game in town; Chiusi's major attractions revolve around them. But before you head for Etruria, check out the town's Romanesque **Duomo** ★. This church designed in the ancient Roman basilica style has roots in the 6th century; dazzling mosaics including a giant *Assumption* appear to rise up behind the altar (0.50€ coin for lights). In fact, these are **frescoes** painted in a 'mock-Byzantine' style between 1887 and 1894 by Arturo Viligiardi.

Chiusi's museum set-piece is its **Museo Archeologico Nazionale** (☎ *0578 20177.* Daily

TIP Rome for the Day

A day trip to Italy's capital is easily done from almost anywhere in southern Tuscany—just make for the railway station in **Chiusi Scalo.** Trains to **Roma Termini** station (1–2 hr) run roughly hourly from 4am. A single costs from 13.10€, depending on the speed of the train, with 4- to 12-year-olds travelling for half price.

9am–8pm. Adm 4€, 2€ ages 18–25), at Via Porsenna 93, housing local finds from the Bronze Age on. Most of the collection is Etruscan, including intricately painted ceramics and a 6th-century B.C. funerary **sphinx.** There's English signage all the way round.

Your ticket is good for entry to two Etruscan tombs 3km (2 miles) north of Chiusi: the **Tomba del Leone** and **Tomba della Pellegrina.** Tell the staff when you leave the museum and they'll make sure someone's there to unlock the tombs for you. Hours are the same as the museum.

The nearby frescoed **Tomba della Scimmia** ★ is visitable Tuesday, Thursday and Saturday only (11am and 4pm, or 2:30pm winter). Book a place at the museum desk (2€ extra).

If the children are getting history-fatigue, carry on past the tombs for 2km (1 mile) to **Lago di Chiusi,** for free swimming (without a beach), row-boat hire, and a lakeside bar–café and picnic area.

Labirinto di Porsenna ★

AGE 5 & UP

Museo della Cattedrale, Piazza Duomo. ☎ *0578 226490.*

Whether this subterranean labyrinth cut from the sandstone had anything to do with **Porsenna,** the Etruscan king who attacked Rome, isn't really the point. The 120-m (394-ft) section open to guided tours is part of a system of defensive tunnels and aqueducts that underpin the entire town. An atmospheric **half-hour tour** leads you through the ancient Etruscan cave system before arriving at a giant Roman cistern, 6m (19 ft) high with a vaulted ceiling right under Chiusi's Piazza Duomo. The tunnel was once used by a private fire brigade who demanded payment before dousing your house. Tours are in **Italian,** with an English handout.

To top the visit off, you're free to climb the 140 steps inside the **campanile of San Secondiano** for **views** ★ over Chiusi and 360° of Tuscan and Umbrian countryside.

Time *1 hr.* ***Guided tours*** *Every 40 min. 10:10am–12:10pm and 4:10–6:10pm daily June–Sept; 10:10am–12:10pm Mon–Sat and 4:10–6:10pm Sun Oct–Dec, Apr and May; Tues, Thurs and Sat 10:10am–12:10pm Jan–Mar.* ***Adm*** *3€ (4€ with Museo della Cattedrale).*

SARTEANO

Escape from high-season hordes for the day to the walled town of **Sarteano** 9km (6 miles) west of Chiusi—a serene little place hiding a couple of under-visited gems. To catch the town's blockbuster (see below), visit on a **Saturday;** at other times, you'll have this pleasant little hill-town, dotted with post-Renaissance *palazzi*, mostly to yourself.

Visitor Information

The tiny **tourist office** (☎ *0578 269204.* ***www.prolocosarteano.it.***

TIP Eating in Sarteano

The best meal in town is to be had at Osteria Da Gagliano ★ (Via Roma 5. *0578 268022;* Thurs–Mon, or Sat and Sun only out of season), a tiny dining room specialising in regional classics such as rabbit stewed in Chianti, and *stringozzi* pasta with a sauce of tomatoes, garlic and porcini mushrooms. Book ahead to be sure of a table in high season.

Alternatively, you'll find everything you need for a **top-notch picnic** just uphill at the *alimentari* store with its superb deli counter, at Via Roma 18. Our favourite extra-virgin olive oil in these parts is sold at **Tistarelli**'s roadside shop (*0578 265425.* ***www.tistarelli.it***), just outside Sarteano on the road to Chianciano.

Wed, Sat and Sun 10am–12:30pm) is at Corso Garibaldi 9, close to **Piazza Giugno XXIV.**

What to See & Do

Sixteenth-century Palazzo Gabrielli is home to Sarteano's **Museo Civico** (2.50€; 10:30am–12:30pm and 4–7pm Tues–Sun May–Oct, Sat and Sun rest of year; see below), with a small collection featuring local Etruscan finds.

Continue uphill into Piazza San Martino for the **Chiesa di San Martino** ★ with its boxy interior and three *Madonnas* from the 14th and 15th centuries. Best of the lot is Domenico Beccafumi's Mannerist 1546 **Annunciation** ★, swept by light and shadow with a stormy landscape out the window. Random winter closures are not uncommon.

For youngsters, the preserved **Castello** (3€ adults, 2€ children) is usually open daily (including evenings) in July and August, or weekends only (10:30am–12:30pm and 3–6pm) the rest of the year, but see ***www.clanis.it*** for variations. You'll probably all enjoy browsing the handmade gifts and linens at **Anna Romagnoli** at Piazza XXIV Giugno 22 (closed Mon).

To cool down, there's the large swimming pool at **Parco delle Piscine** (p. 190).

Tomba della Quadriga Infernale ★★ FIND AGE 3 & UP

c/o Museo Civico, Via Roma 24. 0578 269261. ***museo@comune.sarteano.siena.it.***

Hands-down the best Etruscan attraction in the area, the **Tomb of the Chariot from Hell** is one part of a complex of at least 14 excavated in 2003. Inside, guarding the entrance to the Underworld, are four vivid **frescoes** dating from around 330 B.C. The most striking shows a **demon charioteer** driving two lions and two griffins—the only known image of its kind in Etruscan art.

After the short tour, you're free to explore other tombs on the necropolis, all open, which extend for 1km (half a mile) on a ridge with stupendous **views** ★★ over the Valdichiana.

Visits are limited to 40 people per week, on **Saturdays only.** In summer, e-mail a few weeks in advance to book; otherwise a few days' notice usually suffices. The tour is in **Italian,** with English handouts. You need a car to drive the 2km (just over 1 mile) to the site.

Even if it's not Saturday, the necropolis is great fun and easy to find (make for Cetona and turn left at the 'Pianacce' sign as you leave Sarteano), with 13 other tombs to scramble around.

***Time** 1 hr. **Guided tours** Sat only. **Adm** 5€, inc. Museo Civico.*
***Amenities** P*

PITIGLIANO & THE FAR SOUTH

It's a fair old diversion from the main sights of Tuscany to **Pitigliano** ★★, but you won't regret it—even devoted beach-hounds and jaded hill-town veterans won't be prepared for the almost Transylvanian sight of a town seemingly growing out of a volcanic tufa perch. Look closely: it's impossible to see where rock ends and houses start. Silhouetted against the Tuscan sky, or—even better—illuminated against the inky night, it's unforgettable.

Visitor Information

Information Centres

The **tourist office** (☎ *0564 617111. **www.comune.pitigliano.gr.it***. Tues–Sun 9am–1pm and 3:30–7pm Easter–Sept; 9:30am–12:30pm and 3–6pm rest of year) is at Piazza Garibaldi 51.

There's a **cashpoint** behind the ilex trees in Piazza della Repubblica, and a park with **swings** and **slides** outside the historic centre on Via Ugolini.

Arriving

A long haul from Florence and Siena, Pitigliano is an easy day trip by car from the southern coast or Val d'Orcia, both about 60km (40 miles) away. It's also straightforward if you're staying near **Orvieto** (p. 223), 50km (30 miles) away in southern Umbria.

Wherever you come from, **enter the town from the west,** from Manciano, for that **view** ★★★. **Park for free** just outside the centre: uphill from the arched viaduct over the road,

TIP Sweet as Cherry Wine

If you're in a wine shop around Pitigliano, you might spot a red you've never heard of, even if you're a buff—one made from the **Ciliegiolo** ('cherry-like') grape grown only in the Maremma and areas of southern Umbria. Fortunately, it doesn't taste much like cherries. The excellent wine and local produce shop **Ghiottornia** ★ (☎ *0564 616907. **www.ghiottornia.com***), at Via Roma 111, stocks it.

The impressive sight of Pitigliano

take the right fork marked *cimitero*, and park anywhere on the left along there.

Family-Friendly Festival

The highlight of Pitigliano's festival year is the **Torciata di San Giuseppe** ★, on 19th March. This fire festival to welcome spring includes a torchlit procession along an ancient *vie cave* (see below), climaxing in the burning of a wicker man, symbolic of winter, in Piazza Garibaldi. It's never uncomfortably packed.

What to See & Do

Pitigliano's twisted alleys and gnarled stone staircases make for pleasant strolling, and it's largely navigable with a buggy. For local wine, basic groceries, ceramics or even *Hello Kitty* merchandise, browse the small shops along **Via Roma** ★. Follow this street all the way to its end at the town's oldest church, **San Rocco:** its Romanesque interior has an ancient feel, with a nave and side aisles supported by travertine columns.

Our favourite stop for coffee and a panorama is the outdoor tables at **Caffe degli Archi** (closed Wed) close to the aqueduct at Piazza della Repubblica 267.

Jewish Museum, Synagogue & Ghetto ★★ AGE 7 & UP

Vicolo Marghera (off Via Zuccarelli). 📞 *0564 616006.* ***www.lapiccolagerusalemme.it.***

If your children have an interest in what happened to Europe's Jews, this will be the family highlight of Pitigliano. It was the Jewish community that gave Pitigliano its nickname **La Piccola Gerusalemme** ('Little Jerusalem'). The maze-like museum, built into the ghetto to which the town's Jews were banished by the Medici rulers, is fascinating. The

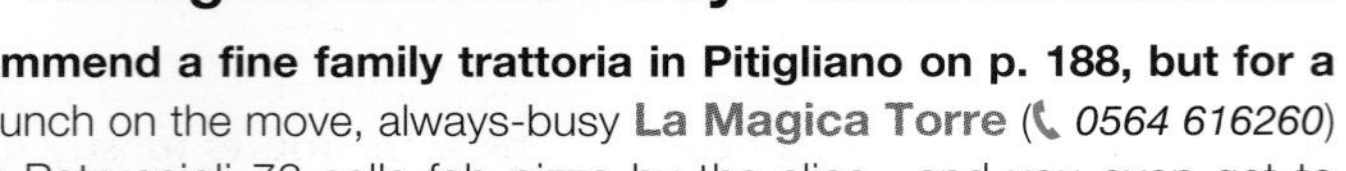

TIP Taking Lunch Both Ways

We recommend a fine family trattoria in Pitigliano on p. 188, but for a cheaper lunch on the move, always-busy **La Magica Torre** (*☎ 0564 616260*) at Piazza Petruccioli 73 sells fab pizza by the slice—and you even get to choose the size of your slice!

Taking eating in the upscale direction, local staples are given a fine-dining flourish at **Tufo Allegro** ★ (*☎ 0564 616192.* Closed Tues, plus Wed lunch) in Vicolo della Costituzione, an atmospheric staircase in the former Jewish quarter. Mains cost 13.50€ to 17.50€.

ritual baths, *matzo* oven (last used for Passover in 1939) and kosher wine cellars are carved into the tufa that underpins the town. The synagogue, built in 1598, not long after Jews were banished from Rome and in disrepair by 1960, is a sombre reminder of how first Christian Europe, then the Nazis and Fascists, treated people they didn't like.

Bits of the trail are **steep,** so hold children's hands—and don't bring buggies. Note that it gets busy on Sundays.

Time *45 min.* ***Open*** *Sun–Fri 10am–12:10pm and 3–5:40pm Mar–May, Oct and Nov; 10am–12:10pm and 3:30–6:10pm June–Sept, 10am–12:10pm and 3–5:10pm Dec–Feb.* ***Adm*** *3€, 2€ children 6–12.* ***Amenities***

INSIDER TIP

If you're interested in more Jewish sights in Tuscany, ask at the *biglietteria* for the free, English-language **Jewish Tours in Tuscany** guide.

Saturnia Hot Springs ★

ALL AGES

1km (about half a mile) south of Saturnia; as road bends left 500m (1,640 ft) after public Terme di Saturnia, turn right, park and walk (1 min).

There are more Etruscan remains at Saturnia, but the place is on the map for something different altogether: the waterfall of **thermal springs** just outside town off the road to Montemerano. This cascade of swirling, steaming, slightly stinky sulphur water at a constant 37°C is a surreal place for a family dip. It's free, it's an oddity—and it's stunning. On a sunny day the cataract cascade reflects an intense cobalt blue, looks like nothing so much as an oversized ornamental water feature and takes a great snap.

The springs get busy at weekends, even way out of season, with a mix of splashing tots, preening teens and older folk taking the supposed medicinal benefits of the mineral-rich waters.

Time *At least 30 min.* ***Adm*** *Free.* ***Amenities***

Tomba Ildebranda ★ AGE 3 & UP

☎ 0564 614074. 2km (just over 1 mile) west of Sovana. www.leviecave.it.

Weirdly, the most important Etruscan site in southern Tuscany, **Hildebrand's Tomb,** was (in its 3rd-century B.C. heyday) decorated with vivid pictures of vegetables. It's now an evocative ruin and just one part of a network of open-air Etruscan burial sites and *vie cave* (below) that you could spend a few hours exploring. The English-language signage on the way round is so good that by the time you're all done, you'll know more about Etruscan funerary architecture than anyone could ever need to. Or, with appropriate footwear, you could just run around the place: the **Via Cava di Poggio Prisca** is especially cool.

Time *1½ hr.* ***Open*** *10am–7pm daily late Mar–Sept; 10am–5pm Sat and Sun Oct.* ***Adm*** *5€, free under-12s.* ***Amenities***

INSIDER TIP

The pretty little village of **Sovana,** near the Tomba, is also worth a stop, with a picnic area at the entrance under the ruined fortress and an ancient, pedestrianised centre ideal for a family mooch.

Vie Cave AGE 3 & UP

Between Pitigliano and Sovana. www.leviecave.it.

You can just about imagine Etruscans processing along these ancient subterranean walkways hollowed from volcanic rock, or perhaps driving livestock along them. In fact, nobody knows what they did with them—maybe it was something to do with magic. But they're great: you can walk for miles in the hidden channels up to 7m (23 ft) deep. You'll need a map (ask at Pitigliano tourist office), decent trainers and plenty of puff. Even in summer, you'll have the routes mostly to yourself; best of the bunch is the **Via Cava di San Giuseppe** ★, 1km (about half a mile) out of Pitigliano towards Sovana.

Time *At least 1 hr.* ***Open*** *Always.* ***Adm*** *Free.*

INSIDER TIP

More structured for youngsters, with an educational bent, the **Museo Archeologico all'Aperto 'Alberto Manzi'** (*0564 614067.* Adm 4€, children 2.50€), on the SS74 just outside Pitigliano, has some real *vie cave* plus reconstructions of Etruscan homes.

FAMILY-FRIENDLY DINING

Acquacheta ★★★ GRILL

Via del Teatro 22, Montepulciano. 0578 717086. www.acquacheta.eu.

This outstanding cellar eatery is one for the carnivores of the family: '*bistecca numero uno*' is how Adamo, the winemaker at Contucci, describes it. But if a plate of cow isn't for you, there's a lengthy specials list, too, plus three pastas and five sauces to combine any way you please. The style is informal and rustic—in fact, fussily so (you drink water and red wine from the same beaker). But staff take the produce seriously: meat is brought to your table for approval before it goes on the grill, briefly (if you like your steak anything but rare, holler). Pasta and bread are made on site, and everything is local so oozes flavour. Eating is a squeeze, but you won't regret or forget a meal here. Reservations are essential.

Open** Noon–3pm and 7:30–10:30pm Wed–Mon exc. mid-Jan–mid-Mar. **Main courses** 5.50€–18€. **Credit** MC, V. **Amenities

Da Gagliano, Sarteano, see p. 183.

Fattoria Pulcino ★ SOUTHERN TUSCAN/GRILL

0578 758711. www.pulcino.com. 1½km (nearly 1 mile) south of Montepulciano on SS146, direction Chianciano.

If you could mark a spot for a perfect Montepulciano panorama, your X would come down somewhere near the **terrace** at Pulcino (don't forget your camera). This former monastery is now the HQ of a *tipico* empire selling Vino Nobile, organic olive oil and salami *della casa* from the roadside. The large restaurant's cooking is almost beside the point, but pasta and grilled meats are perfectly executed, albeit part of a limited menu. The 'local' choice is *pici di Montepulciano*, a thick, handmade spaghetti. Ordering from the grill (free-range chicken, beef, veal) means a longer wait; it's all cooked from scratch.

Open** Noon–10pm daily; call ahead in winter as hours can vary. **Main courses** 9€–16€. **Credit** AE, MC, V. **Amenities

Il Grillo VALUE MAREMMAN

Via Cavour 18, Pitigliano. 0564 615202.

This traditional wood-beamed trattoria right on the aqueduct has become a Pitigliano institution. The short, rustic menu includes Maremma classics such as *acquacotta* (a farmers' soup) and local flourishes such as veal braised in *bianco di Pitigliano* wine or liver with wild fennel (as well as the standard pasta *primi*, of course). Service can be haphazard but is always warm and welcoming, and this is spectacular value: a family of four can eat heartily, drink a little, finish with a *caffè*, and keep change from 50€.

Open** 12:30–2:30pm and 7:30–9:30pm Wed–Mon. **Main courses** 6.50€–9€. **Credit** MC, V. **Amenities

La Botte Piena ★★★ SOUTHERN TUSCAN

Piazza Dionisa Cinughi 12, Montefollonico. 0577 669481. www.labottepiena.com.

Sitting upstairs under the eaves of this *osteria*-cum-*enoteca*, browsing a leather-bound wine list that's as hefty as a Bible, is Tuscan heaven for us. The atmosphere is intimate without being intimidating if you have tots in tow, while the refined rustic food has the Val d'Orcia drizzled all over it (the pasta is *pici*, the cheese is pecorino and the salami is made from Cinta Senese pigs or boar). The menu caters as well to bruschetta snackers as sit-down diners. There are no particular concessions to children, but locals bring theirs and that's good enough for us.

***Open** 7:30–10pm Thurs–Tues, 12:30–2pm and 7:30–10pm Sat and Sun. **Main courses** 7€–12€. **Credit** AE, MC, V.*

La Locanda nel Loggiato ★ TUSCAN

*Piazza di Pescheria 3, Cortona. ☎ 0575 630575. **www.locandanelloggiato.it**.*

Okay, so it's touristy, but this has the **best perch** in Cortona: above Piazza della Repubblica looking right at the Palazzo Comunale. Stop by as soon as you hit town to reserve a lunchtime seat under the *loggia* (3€ p.p. cover charge). The menu is solid rather than spectacular but dishes are much better than you'd expect given the location, especially since pizzas were dropped so chefs could focus on the rest. The pasta is especially tasty, from basic ravioli with porcini mushrooms to inventive flourishes such as *fettuccine* with cabbage and truffles.

Open** 12:15–2:30pm and 7:15–9:30pm Thurs–Tues. **Main courses** 7€–15€. **Credit** MC, V. **Amenities

INSIDER TIP

For fewer tourists and better value but no view, head uphill from La Locanda to **Trattoria Dardano** ★ (☎ *0575 601944.* Closed Wed) at Via Dardano 24.

Latte di Luna TUSCAN

Via San Carlo 2–4, Pienza. ☎ 0578 748606.

This much-recommended trattoria is the standout for families within Pienza's walls. Choose between the small street-front terrace or a traditional dining room with a terracotta tile floor and browse a menu based around freshly prepared Tuscan classics including four kinds of pasta with meat or vegetarian sauces or grilled meats such as boar. Your children will love the parrot, who greets arrivals with a polite '*buonasera*'.

Open** 12:30–2pm and 7:30–10pm Wed–Mon. **Main courses** 8€–16€. **Credit cards** MC, V. **Amenities

Re di Macchia ★ MONTALCINESE

Via Saloni 21, Montalcino. ☎ 0577 846116.

Aside amply loaded bruschetta, *tagliolini* and a soup or two, it's **meat** all the way at this backstreet restaurant; you're in hunting country, remember. The poor old **wild boar** in particular gets it: he's in salami *antipasto*, served with *pinci* (squat, hand-rolled spaghetti) and even pops up in a stew.

Open** Noon–2pm and 7–9pm Fri–Wed. **Main courses** 9€–16€. **Credit** MC, V. **Amenities

INSIDER TIP

If Re di Macchia is a bit hardcore Tuscan, an alternative across the street, with a less refined version of similar dishes plus two pages of pizzas, is **Ristorante San Giorgio** (☎ *0577 848507*).

Ristorante Zaira ★★

SOUTHERN TUSCAN/ETRUSCAN

*Via Arunte 12, Chiusi. ☎ 0578 20260. **www.zaira.it**.*

In a town with a reputation for great eating, this revamped dining room stands out for its 'Etruscan' dishes offered alongside regular southern Tuscan food such as speciality *pasta del Lucumone* (baked, with pecorino, parmesan and ham). For children, the chefs will cook up pasta with a simple sauce, or the *coniglio* (rabbit) *al limone* is delicate enough not to offend (depending on what pets you have at home). Pop down to see the **wine cellar:** 20,000 bottles stored in Etruscan tunnels and wells.

Open** Noon–2:30pm and 7–9:30pm Tues–Sun (plus Mon in summer). **Main courses** 6€–14.50€. **Credit** MC, V. **Amenities

> **INSIDER TIP**
>
> An equally tasty alternative to Zaira is **La Solita Zuppa** ★★ (☎ *0578 21006.* Closed Tues), at Via Porsenna 21, where mains cost from 10.50€.

Tufo Allegro, Pitigliano, see p. 186.

FAMILY-FRIENDLY ACCOMMODATION

APARTMENTS, VILLAS & FARM-STAYS

Le 7 Camicie ★

*Strada Provinciale di Sant'Antimo, km 10+200. ☎ 335 6363730. **www.le7camicie.it**. 1km (about half a mile) south of Castelnuovo dell'Abate.*

If the vines grew any closer to this spot, they'd be in the swimming pools. The converted farm complex could hardly be better sited as a family-friendly base for some southern Tuscan wine tourism. The apartments are simply decorated, with cool tile floors and exposed beams; kitchenettes and bathrooms are adequate if unspectacular. The views towards Monte Amiata are something else, but note that the pools (one kept at an all-year 40°C (104°F) by a thermal spring) aren't fenced off.

***Apartments** 15. **Rates** 1-bed 400€–700€/wk, 2-bed 750€–1200€/wk, 3-bed 1100€–1500€/wk. Daily bookings accepted exc. summer, Christmas and Easter (from 70€/night).Cot 15€/wk. **Credit** MC, V. **Amenities** P **In room** A/C*

CAMPSITES

Parco delle Piscine

*Via del Bagno Santo 29, Sarteano. ☎ 0578 26971. **www.parcodellepiscine.it**. 9km (6 miles) from A1 Chiusi–Chianciano Terme exit.*

In a corner of Tuscany not blessed with many campsites or holiday parks, this place in Sarteano makes an ideal family base: Montepulciano, Chiusi and Lago Trasimeno are within half an hour. The setting is a shade unspectacular, but facilities aren't: the usual ping-pong and playground are joined by tennis courts, a floodlit five-a-side pitch and high-season child and adult entertainment. The three swimming pools are heated by a **thermal spring** so never budge from 24°C.

The well-equipped mobile homes sleep four or six but without much room to spare. In July there are discounts for stays of five nights and over. **Keycamp** and **Eurocamp** both offer bookings here.

Pitches *509 inc. mobile homes (open Apr–Sept).* ***Rates*** *adults 9€–15.50€, 6€–10€ children 3–10, pitch 9€–15.50€.* ***Mobile homes*** *for four 45€–120€/night, for six 55€–150€/ night. Cot 1€/night.* ***Credit*** *MC, V.* ***Amenities*** ***In mobile homes***

HOTELS/BED & BREAKFASTS

B&B Porta Castellana FIND

Via Santa Lucia 20, Montalcino. 0577 839001. ***www.portacastellana.it.***

This has two things you almost never find within the walls of a Tuscan hill-town: **parking** and a **garden.** The former palazzo's old storehouses have been converted into two fine rooms with exposed stone, stylish antiques and new bathrooms. One can accommodate an extra bed; the other can be opened up into a separate adjoining room, making a small 'apartment' for up to five. The constant gentle breeze keeps it all cool. In good weather breakfast is served outside under the gazebo as the mists slowly lift from the Val d'Orcia below. It's magical, 'run for love, not money'. You have to bring your own cot, and there's no TV—all the better to enjoy the silence.

Rooms *2.* ***Rates*** *Double 75€ (extra bed 20€), adjoining rooms for up to five 130€. Breakfast included.* ***Credit*** *MC, V.* ***Amenities*** ***In room***

Hotelito Lupaia ★★

Località Lupaia 74, Torrita di Siena. 0577 668028. ***www.lupaia.com.*** *10km (6 miles) northeast of Pienza.*

The ultimate in quirky luxury and romantic rural seclusion, these eight rooms built imaginatively into a traditional farm complex combine the best of the B&B and *agriturismo* ethos: intimacy complements authenticity. They're spectacularly decorated in an eclectic hippy-chic meets country-manor style, making full use of architectural details, soothing colours and natural fabrics. Standard rooms have space for a third bed; with more than one little one in tow, pick a deluxe or a suite with extra beds (all bar the Blue Suite have a terrace or mini-garden). There's lunch and two or three weekly dinners all summer.

Rooms *8.* ***Rates*** *Standard double 270€, Deluxe 320€, Suite 360€. Extra bed 65€.* ***Credit*** *AE, MC, V.* ***Amenities*** ***In room*** A/C

Terme di Saturnia Spa & Golf Resort ★★

0564 600111. ***www.termedisaturnia.it.*** *1½km (nearly 1 mile) south of Saturnia, direction Montemerano.*

The **luxury** choice among southern Tuscany's spa hotels, this is strictly for the flush. Although the ambience may be a little corporate for some, the quality of service on every level stands out—as you'd expect from a place that's won readers' awards from *Condé Nast Traveller* and *Spafinder*. Various stay-and-spa packages are available: check the website. The pools and tennis make this a great place to treat older children (interconnecting rooms are available)—and so it should be at these prices.

Rooms** 140. **Rates** Double 420€–800€. Breakfast included. Cot 30€. **Credit** AE, MC, V. **Amenities ***In room***

Villa di Piazzano FIND

Località Piazzano, Cortona. 075 826226. www.villadipiazzano.com. 6km (4 miles) southeast of Cortona.

Set among lush hills, this fabulous property combines **historic character** (it dates back to 1464) with plenty of child-friendly touches and modern amenities. There's lots of choice for families: several rooms connect to make de facto **apartments,** while the superior twin can take an extra bed to hold up to three children, or the junior suite comes with a double sofabed for up to two little ones. The **second-floor** rooms have the best views.

The hotel, managed by an Italian-Australian family, has a large pool and gardens to run around in. **Breakfast** comprises a huge spread of homemade cakes, fresh fruit and baked goods, served on a sunswept terrace. Children up to 1 year old stay free; ages 2–12 pay 30€/night when they share with two adults. You'll need to bring your own cot.

Rooms** 18. **Rates** Double 205€–285€, Junior suite 340€. **Credit** AE, MC, V. **Amenities ***In room***

8 Perugia, Assisi & Northern Umbria

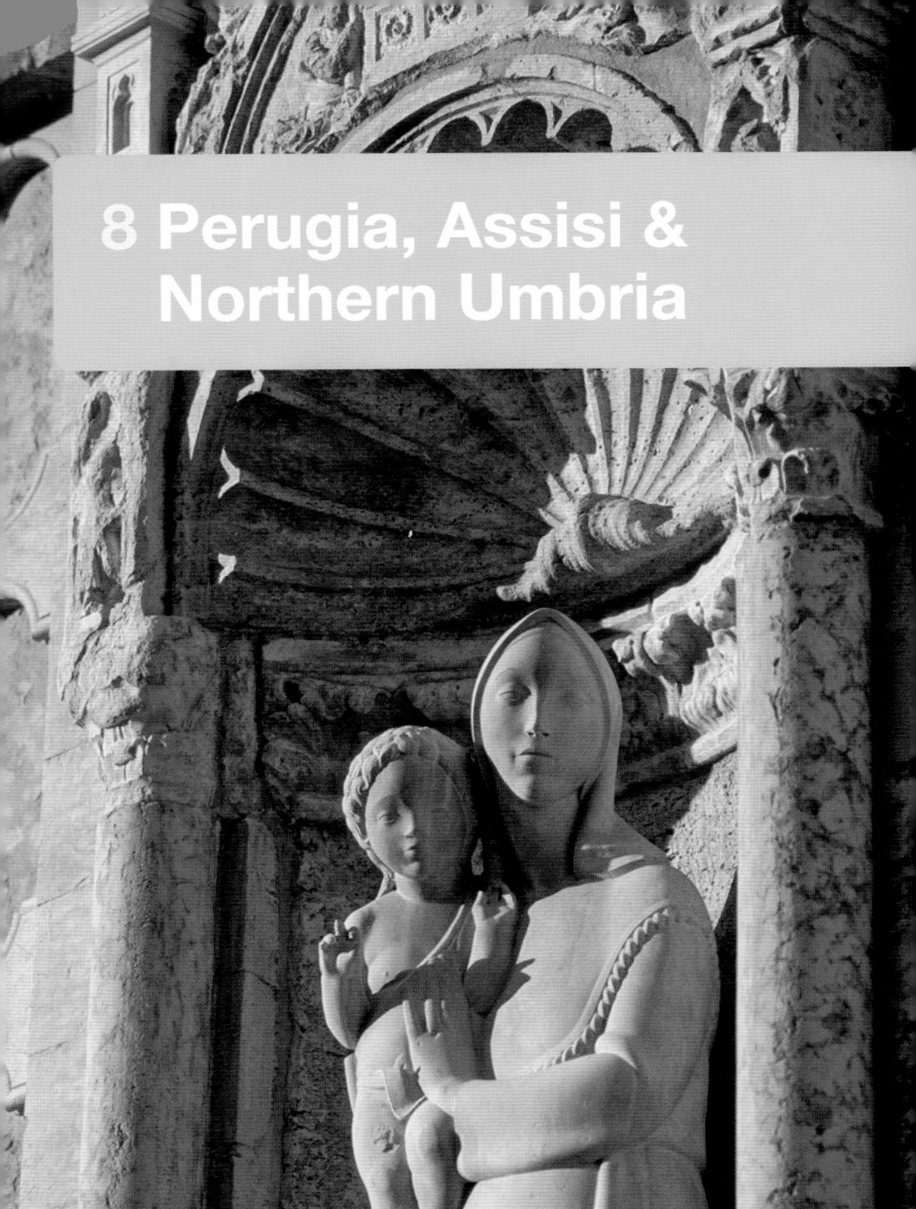

NORTHERN UMBRIA

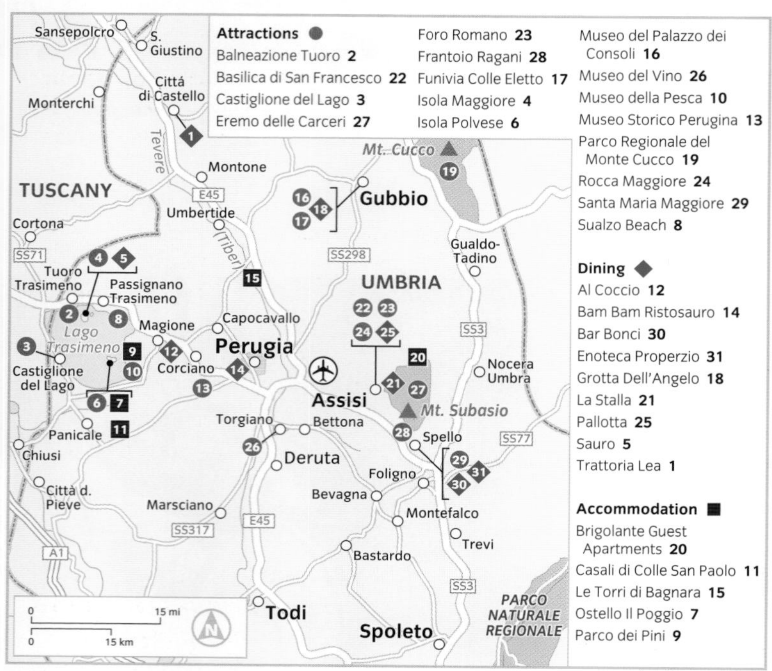

Consistently overshadowed by its culturally mega-rich neighbour, Umbria nevertheless brims with gorgeous medieval hill-towns, plenty of art treasures of its own and an olive-growing industry that's been thriving for thousands of years. There's no Florence, but what it does have is **peace.** This is a place to get away from it all in a farmhouse or villa, eat well, relax by the pool and breathe deeply.

Umbria's spiritual heart is **Assisi,** a place of pilgrimage second only to Rome—not just the birthplace of Italy's patron saint but also of Western art in the form of Giotto's frescoes covering the Basilica di San Francesco. **Perugia** is altogether different: young, fashionable and quite un-Umbrian. There's art, naturally, but the city is also at the centre of attractions designed to appeal to local and visiting families, with young, hip shopping options unique in the region. Elsewhere in the north, Umbria's sort-of-seaside, **Lago Trasimeno,** offers action on, in and above the water; and pretty hill-towns such as **Spello** and **Gubbio** cater for days when you just feel like a mosey.

Fast Facts: Perugia & Northern Umbria

Banks There are **banks** and ATMs along Corso Vannucci, Perugia.

Hospitals & Emergencies 24-hour A&E is provided by **Santa Maria della Misericordia** (or 'Silvestrini'. ☎ *075 5781. **www.ospedale.perugia.it***) in San Sisto, southwest of Perugia's centre. In a medical emergency, call ☎ *118*.

Internet & Wi-Fi It's easiest to find this in Perugia: try **Internet Corner** (☎ *075 5720901. **www.internetcorner.it***. 9:30am–midnight Mon–Sat, noon–midnight Sun) at Piazza Danti 5/b, behind the cathedral (beyond Rocchi, entrance at no. 4); Internet access is 4.5 euro cents/min: Wi-Fi is 2€/day.

Pharmacies There are plenty in the centre of Perugia: try **Farmacia Andreoli** (☎ *075 5720915.* Daily 9am–1pm and 4–8pm) next to the Collegio del Cambio at Corso Vannucci 27.

Post Office Perugia's central **post office** is at Piazza Matteotti 1 (Mon–Fri 8am–6:30pm and Sat 8am–1:15pm).

PERUGIA

This medieval metropolis high above the River Tiber takes an ancient hill-town and adds a dash of cosmopolitan youth. The shops that line **Perugia's** ★ Corso Vannucci are the height of Umbrian and international chic, while the **students** of the town's two universities keep the place jumping at night during term-time. Other notable residents (now former) are Renaissance artists **Pinturicchio** and **Perugino;** as well as achieving acclaim in his own right, the latter taught Raphael to paint.

Visitor Information

Information Centres

Perugia's helpful **tourist office** (☎ *075 5736458. **turismo.comune.perugia.it**.* 8:30am–6:30pm daily) is at Piazza Matteotti 18.

There are plenty of **web resources** for those planning a trip to Umbria, even Perugia specifically. The best are highlighted on p. 10; solely for Perugia, see ***www.perugiaonline.com***.

Pick up a copy of monthly listings magazine **Viva Perugia** ★ (0.80€) at news-stands across the city, which includes public-transport schedules for Umbria and a children's section.

Arriving

By Car Despite lacking a motorway, Perugia is bisected by three fast, and **free**, roads. The **Raccordo Autostradale Perugia-A1** runs east–west between the A1, Lago Trasimeno and Perugia,

Children's Top Attractions of Northern Umbria

- Feeling the **wow** factor at the Basilica di San Francesco, Assisi, p. 207.
- Meeting the art of **Giotto,** Cimabue, Lorenzetti and Martini, p. 207.
- **Windsurfing and canoeing** the placid waters of Lago Trasimeno, p. 203.
- Diving into the **art treasure hoard** in the Collegio del Cambio, Perugia p. 201.
- Scaling Monte Ingino in a **metal cage,** p. 213.
- Stocking up on cocoa and sugar at Perugia's **Eurochocolate,** p. 197.
- DIY **flamegrilling** at Assisi's La Stalla, p. 217.

bypassing the city to link with the **E45** *superstrada*. This heads north to Città di Castello and south to Todi and Terni. Heading southeast, the **SS75b** connects the E45 at Perugia with Assisi and Spoleto.

The best way into the town is via the *raccordo* **Perugia Prepo** exit: to park, follow the 'P' signs for **Europa** or **Partigiani,** next to each other south of the centre. The latter (1.35€ first hour, 1.70€/hr thereafter; 8pm–2am 2€; daily 15€) is handier for the escalators—*scale mobili*—up to Corso Vannucci. Europa is 0.95€ first hour, 1.35€/hr thereafter or 15€/day.

By Bus Perugia's **bus station,** above Partigiani car park, has seven daily services to/from **Assisi** (3.20€), as well as buses to Siena, Florence, Castiglione del Lago and Gubbio.

By Air Five weekly **Ryanair** (☎ *0871 246 0000. www.ryanair.com*) flights connect London Stansted with Perugia's **Aeroporto Internazionale dell'Umbria** (☎ *075 592141. www.airport.umbria.it*), 10km (6 miles) east of the city at San Egidio. It has an ATM, café and four **car rental** desks: **Europcar** (☎ *075 6920615*), **Hertz** (☎ *075 5928590*), **Maggiore** (☎ *075 6929276*) and **Avis** (☎ *075 6929796*). Those on Ryanair flights are usually met by a **minibus** outside the terminal, taking you to the train station and **Piazza Italia** (30–40 min; 3.50€), but heading back there are just five buses per day, so check times in advance. **Taxis** are around 25€.

By Train Two railways serve Perugia. The **state railway** (☎ *892021. www.trenitalia.it*) station serves **Rome** (10.50€–24€, 2–3 hr; most trains require a change at Foligno) and **Florence** (10.10€, 2¼ hr; most trains require a change at Terontola) every couple of hours. There are also hourly trains to **Assisi** (€2.05, 25 min), **Spello** (2.65€, 35 min) and **Spoleto** (4.15€, 1 hr). The station is a few kilometres southwest of the centre but is well served by buses to/from Piazza Italia, at the foot of Corso Vannucci (1€). Taxis are at least 10€. **Europcar** (☎ *075 5018115*) and **Hertz** (☎ *075 5002439*) are near the station.

The station for the private **FCU railway** (☎ *075 575401*. ***www.fcu.it***), Sant'Anna, is closer, in Piazzale Bellucci (by the bus station). These tiny trains serve **Città di Castello** (3.05€) and **Todi** (2.55€) every couple of hours.

Family-Friendly Event

The city's most famous family *festa* is **Eurochocolate** ★ (***www.eurochocolate.com***) each October, when 150-plus exhibitors pitch their tents on Corso Vannucci, the heart of Italy's cocoa capital. *Pesto alla cioccolata*, anyone?

> **INSIDER TIP**
> For events and services for children in Perugia and all over Umbria, bookmark ***www.infobambini.net***. Baby and toddler specialist **Prénatal** (☎ *075 5724382*) has a branch at Via Marconi 75 near Partigiani.

What to See & Do

The best way into Perugia is via the escalators (6:15am–1:15am daily) from Partigiani's car park and bus station, which drill you into the subterranean vaults of the **Rocca Paolina** ★ (☎ *075 5725778*). This fortress and symbol of Papal authority was built after a brief war in 1531 between Pope Paul III and the Perugians over a tax on salt—to this day, Perugian bread is salt-free. After Italian unification in 1860, locals ripped the castle to pieces and built Piazza Italia on top. Today the vaults (which include the remains of medieval dwellings that were smothered by the fort) serve as dimly lit space for temporary exhibitions interspersed with the escalators; 'Rocca Paolina and the city', chronicling the history of the fort and Perugia (Tues–Sun 10:30am–1pm and 2:30–5pm; some seasonal variations), will probably be permanent.

You'll eventually emerge at Plaza Italia and the city's flat main drag, sophisticated **Corso Vannucci** ★. Follow it past the massive **Palazzo dei Priori** ★ to Piazza IV Novembre and the Gothic **Fontana Maggiore** ★★ in front of the cathedral. The fountain's decorative sculpture was added in the late 1200s by the Pisanos.

Dominating the piazza is the massive hulk of the **Cattedrale**

> **TIP** **Take a Tour**
>
> **The Perugia City Tour (☎ *075 5757*) open-top minibus (seven times** daily end of Mar–early Nov, 9:40am–6pm) can be an easy way to see the city for those with tired feet. A full circuit takes around 50 minutes and costs 13€ for adults, 7€ for children 3 to 12 (there's commentary in English). Book ahead.

PERUGIA

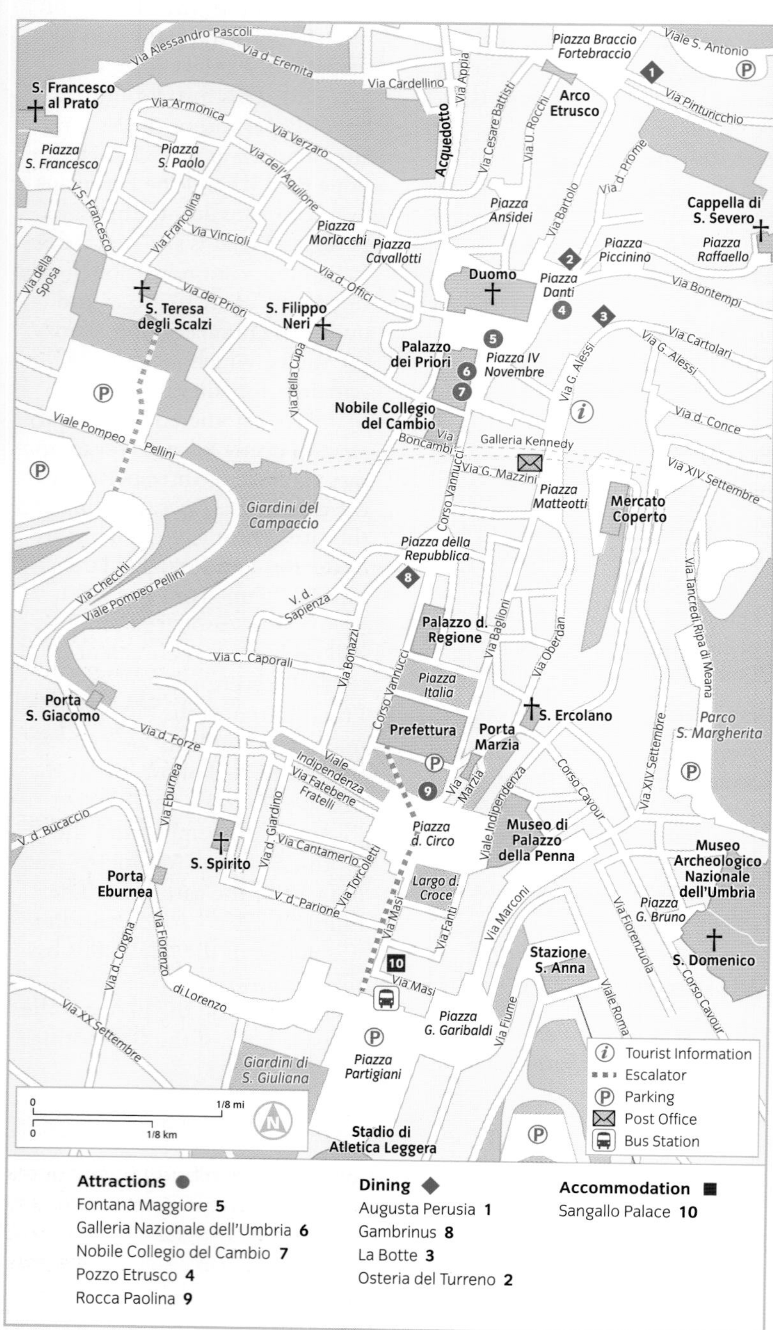

Attractions ●
Fontana Maggiore **5**
Galleria Nazionale dell'Umbria **6**
Nobile Collegio del Cambio **7**
Pozzo Etrusco **4**
Rocca Paolina **9**

Dining ◆
Augusta Perusia **1**
Gambrinus **8**
La Botte **3**
Osteria del Turreno **2**

Accommodation ■
Sangallo Palace **10**

Palazzo dei Priori, Perugia

di San Lorenzo (10am–1pm and 3–6pm daily)—worth a quick peek to take in the vast interior space, vaulted ceiling and giant, veined marble pillars. Opposite, at the end of a narrow lane, the town's water supply came for hundreds of years from a 6th-century B.C. well, known as the **Pozzo Etrusco** (Piazza Danti 18. ☎ *075 5733669*). If echoey, wet, 37-m (121-ft) deep holes in the ground appeal, it's open 10am–1:30pm and 2:30–6pm Tues–Sun Apr–Oct, 11am–1:30pm and 2:30–5pm the rest of the year (adm 3€, 1€ children 7–14).

Galleria Nazionale dell'Umbria AGE 12 & UP

*Palazzo dei Priori, Corso Vannucci. ☎ 075 5741410. **www.gallerianazionaleumbria.it.***

Like most galleries in Tuscany, Umbria's premier art museum is heavy on religious iconography and paintings between the 13th and 16th centuries, though later works are also included. You'll have to be blessed with **very patient children** to get the most out of it. The galleries run chronologically; a highlights tour should start with a *Madonna* by Sienese master **Duccio di Buoninsegna** in Room 2, painted around 1310 for Perugia's San Domenico church. Look out next for

TIP Pick up a Pass

The Città Museo (☎ *075 5772805. www.perugiacittamuseo.it*) pass covers 12 of Perugia's cultural attractions, including **all** those reviewed here, and gives discounts at shops and the Partigiani car park. Visiting any five within a 48-hour period costs 10€ (plus free entry for one child under 18). Buy the pass from any participating sight and many hotels.

TIP Perugia's Sweet Treats

You don't have to visit the Baci museum (p. 201) to enjoy Perugia's famed chocolate: **Perugina** ★ (☎ *075 5734760;* 2:30–7:45pm Mon, 9:30am–7:45pm Tues–Sat, 10:30am–1:30pm 3–8pm Sun) has a shop selling all the major chocolate products at Corso Vannucci 101, while children also love the handmade chocolates and sensational *gelato* from **Augusta Perusia** ★ at Via Pinturicchio 2 (☎ *075 5734577. www.cioccolatoaugustaperusia.it*. 10:30am–8:30pm Mon–Sat; 10:30am–1pm and 4–8pm Sun). More convenient for *gelato* is **Gambrinus** at Via Luigi Bonazzi 3 (just off the Corso).

Taddeo di Bartolo's 1403 **Pentecost** ★ (Room 5) and Iacopo Salimbeni's monochrome 1420 **Crucifixion** ★ (both Room 6), the first for its radical composition, the second for a display of facial emotion that wouldn't become the norm for decades.

By **Piero della Francesca's** polyptych in Room 11 we've moved on to 1468: look at his command of perspective in the top panel, an **Annunciation** ★★. Room 15 has Perugino's **Adoration of the Magi** ★★: Joseph is represented with intense feeling, and there was no better Renaissance **landscape painter.** The expansion downstairs has allowed the gallery to show a raft of his work to best effect.

Time *2 hr.* ***Open*** *8:30am–7:30pm Tues–Sun, 9:30am–7:30pm Mon.* ***Adm*** *6.50€, 3.25€ EU citizens 18–25, EU citizens under 18 free.* ***Amenities***

Museo del Vino AGE 10 & UP

Corso Vittorio Emanuele 31, Torgiano. ☎ *075 9880200.*

These 19 rooms dedicated to the grape, eschew the usual 'here's a barrel, there's a label' approach; Italy's **best wine museum** looks at the history of winemaking and at its impact on Mediterranean civilisation. You need an audioguide (free) or the **guidebook** (8€) to get the most out of the superb expositions of the importance of wine to the Etruscans, Romans and Christians. There is a giant beam wine press, ancient amphora and an unrivalled collection of 13th- to 17th- century **majolica** art. Photographic displays show how the technology of wine-making hardly changed in Umbria from the 2nd century B.C. until 4 decades ago.

There's no actual wine here. For that, go next door to the **Lungarotti**-owned **Osteria del Museo** (8am–1pm and 2–7:30pm daily), where everything from the basic, slightly fizzy white **Brezza** (4.68€ bottle, 1.70€ glass) to the **San Giorgio** (20.88€ bottle, 5.50€ glass) is good.

Time *2 hr.* ***Open*** *9am–1pm and 3–7pm daily summer, 9am–1pm and 3–6pm winter.* ***Adm*** *4.50€, 2.50€ children/students (7€ and 4.50€ with Museo dell'Olivo).* ***Amenities***

INSIDER TIP

The **Museo dell'Olivo e dell'Olio** (Via Garibaldi 10. *075 9880300. www.olio.lungarotti.biz*), in the next street to the Museo del Vino (it opens 1 hr later), continues the agricultural theme; displays include an illuminating collection of ancient olive oil lamps.

Museo Storico Perugina

AGE 3 & UP

*San Sisto. 075 5276796. **www.perugina.it**. 3km (2 miles) southwest of Perugia on Raccordo Autostradale Perugia, A1 exit Madonna Alta.*

If we have to hard-sell a trip to Perugia's iconic **chocolate factory,** you've probably bought the wrong guidebook. The home of *Baci* ('kisses') started out in 1907, selling sugared almonds, and now pumps out 120 tonnes of the brown stuff a day, including 1½ million gianduja-and-hazelnut kisses. Unfortunately, it's a few Oompa-Loompas short of a tourist attraction: the educational video and exhaustively documented 20th-century ads are dull for children. The world's biggest chocolate, the BaciOne (5,980kg/943 stones) might get a satisfying gasp; the **factory tours** (book ahead) are better but tend to run in winter only. On the upside, there's a **free tasting** selection and the best kind of souvenir shop: one full of things to eat.

Time** 30 min. **Open** 9am–1pm and 2–5:30pm Mon–Fri (factory tour by request during opening hours; call 075 5276796 in advance) **Adm** Free. **Amenities

Nobile Collegio del Cambio ★★

AGE 6 & UP

Corso Vannucci 25. 075 5728599.

Behind an unassuming door on the side of the Palazzo dei Priori is Perugia's greatest **art** treasure. The **Moneychanger's Guild** commissioned **Perugino** to fresco their **Sala delle Udienze** in 1496; the chosen subject was the supposed harmony between Christian faith and humanism that typified Renaissance thinking. Socrates, Cato and Pericles, by the entrance, share billing with a *Nativity* on the far wall, each figure sporting the blank serenity that was the Umbrian master's trademark.

Though mostly painted by his students rather than Perugino, the **ceiling** ★★ steals the show, with a vibrant Apollo flanked by allegories of the planets. Tell your children to look closer: can they spot all 12 **zodiac** signs?

***Time** 30 min. **Open** 9am–12:30pm and 2:30–5:30pm Mon–Sat,*

TIP The Finest Plonk Money Can Buy

To stock the fridge with everyday wines, forget the supermarkets or *enoteche* and head for the local cooperative, **Sasso dei Lupi** ★. Its handiest outlet is at Via di Vittorio 14 (9am–1pm and 3:30–7:30pm Mon–Fri, 9am–1pm Sat), on the right-hand side heading out of Ellera towards Corciano.

9am–1pm Sun. ***Adm*** *4.50€, 5.50€ with Collegio della Mercanzia, free under-12s.*

LAGO TRASIMENO

Don't despair: even landlocked Umbria has a **seaside**—or sort of. The flat, calm expanses of **Lago Trasimeno** ★ are only interrupted by the reflections of rolling green hills or the occasional ferryboat plying between the shores and one of the picture-perfect islands that float at its centre.

Right on Umbria's Tuscan border, Italy's **fourth largest lake** offers camping, kayaking, windsurfing and kite-surfing opportunities. Blockbuster sights are thin on the ground, but the water's clean, the sun usually shines, and **Castiglione del Lago** has enough to burn a morning away.

Visitor Information

Information Centres

The lake's main **tourist office** (☎ *075 9652484.* ***www.lagotrasimeno.net***. Mon–Fri 8:30am–1pm and 3:30–7pm, Sat 9am–1pm and 3:30–7pm, Sun 9am–1pm and 4–7pm; Oct–Mar closed Sat afternoon and Sun) is in Castiglione del Lago's Piazza Mazzini, at no. 10. Further planning resources include ***www.trasinet.com***.

Arriving

By Car Lago Trasimeno is less than 1 hour from Orvieto, Perugia, much of southeastern Tuscany, Todi and Assisi.

By Public Transport Perugia's regular **train** link (☎ *892021.* ***www.trenitalia.it***) with Terontola runs along the north shore to **Magione** (2.05€; 25 min), **Passignano** (2.65€; 30 min) and **Tuoro** (2.95€; 40 min). At a push, 5–7 daily **APM buses**

Lago Trasimeno

Lakeside Action

The lakeside's largely gentle gradients make it ideal for a family bike ride. **Marinelli** (☎ *075 953126;* 9am–1pm and 4:30–8pm Mon–Sat), at Via Buozzi 26 in Castiglione del Lago, has mountain-bikes from age 6-ish up for 2€/hr or 10€/day; Passignano's **Sualzo Beach** (p. 203) has children's bikes from age 8 at the same price. The **Lake Trasimeno Cycling Trail** currently links Castiglione with Torricella (24km/15 miles), via Passignano, and is well marked with arrows.

Upping the action ante a little, rent **canoes** from Spiaggia di Tuoro at **Balneazione Tuoro** (☎ *334 9794208.* ***www.laspiaggiadituoro.it***), Tuoro's beachfront (6€/hr single, 8€/hr tandem. Ages 8 and over can hire **windsurfs** 8€/hr from the same place).

The lake was once famed for its carp, eel, tench, perch and pike, but **fishing** here is highly controlled these days and foreigners need a permit; if you don't mind the hassle (and cost—around 30€), contact the provincial office at Via Palermo 21 in Perugia (☎ *0753 681258*) or the Ispettorato di Porto in Passignano (☎ *0758 298808*). You can always visit the **Museo della Pesca** instead (p. 205).

(☎ *075 506781.* ***www.apmperugia.it***) connect **Castiglione del Lago** with Perugia (5.10€; 1¼ hr).

Getting Around

The lake's **ferry** (*traghetti*) service is also run by **APM** (☎ *075 827157*). Summer and winter schedules differ sharply; three main routes link Passignano (6.20€ return), Tuoro (5€) and Castiglione (6.80€) to **Isola Maggiore,** and San Feliciano to **Isola Polvese** (5€). You can buy a day pass for 12.20€ (6.20€ for under-12s) for island-hopping (the islands are also connected by ferry in summer). All journeys take 10 to 30 minutes.

Family-Friendly Events

Castiglione del Lago hosts one of Umbria's most colourful **festivals:** at the end of April, hundreds of kites and hot-air balloons ascend for **Coloriamo i Cieli** ('Let's Colour the Skies') ★ (☎ *075 9652484.* ***www.coloriamoicieli.com***).

What to See & Do

Don't get too excited about **beach life:** Elba (p. 153) this ain't. Best of a mediocre bunch is Passignano's public beach (*spiaggia comunale*), just east of town, known as **Sualzo Beach** (☎ *329 2736840.* ***www.trasinet.net/sualzo.*** Daily 8:30am–8pm Apr–Sept). Two sunbeds and an umbrella cost 10€ to 15€/day. The **playground, swimming pool** and sand are free; there's

Trasimeno's most visited island, Isola Maggiore

also a bar/café and bike hire. **Passignano** itself, on the north side of the lake, is touristy but makes a pleasant lakeside base, with cafés and hotels right on the water.

Castiglione del Lago ALL AGES

www.comune.castiglione-del-lago.pg.it.

The 'capital' of Lago Trasimeno is a handsome medieval town perched high above the lake. Once a wheat-growing area and defensive outpost of the Duchy of Perugia, the place is fuelled by tourism these days. From the **quaint piazza** flanked by *tipico* shops to the fine views of Castiglione's promontory from the ferry, it's (almost) all here because you are. You'll lose the crowds by paying 4€ (3€ ages 6–14; 12€ family ticket for four) for a joint ticket for the **Palazzo della Corgna** (*075 951099*) and 13th-century **Rocca del Leone** ★ (both 9:30am–1pm and 3:30–7pm daily).

Highlight of the spartan *palazzo* is the Sala delle Gesta d'Asciano, frescoed in 1575 by Niccolo Circignani with scenes of battles from Lepanto to Montalcino. The palace is linked by a 186-m (550-ft) covered walkway to the *rocca* or **'Lion Castle'**. From the pentagonal walls an entire lake is laid out below like a magnificent turquoise carpet. Make sure to hold your little ones' hands up there.

Isola Maggiore ALL AGES

Passignano: 20 minutes by ferry; Castiglione: 30 minutes by ferry.

Trasimeno's most-visited island is famous for the fact that St. Francis spent Lent there in 1213, and for a lace-making reputation that stretches back 100 years. This vanishing craft is remembered in a one-room **Museo del Merletto** (Lace Museum; *075 8254233.* Daily 10am–1pm and 3–5:45pm. Adm 3€, 2€ children) opposite the quay. Signposted outside is the island's historical trail, an occasionally steep track to Maggiore's **308-m (1,010 ft) summit,** crowned by olive groves and the 12th-century church of **San Michele Arcangelo.** Check with the museum that it's open if you want to go in to see the medieval frescoes by the Umbrian School. An alternative route down takes in the even more ancient **San Salvatore** (always closed).

The best thing to do before getting the ferry back is eat: **Sauro** ★ (*075 826168.* Closed Wed) serves a fine selection of lake fish (eel, perch, trout) at reasonable prices (7€–13 €) in a pleasant garden on Via Guglielmi. Take the *filetto di persico* (perch), add *patate fritte*, squeeze a lemon and you've got... **fish and chips.** Book ahead in summer.

Isola Polvese ★ GREEN ALL AGES

*075 9659546. **www.polvese.it.** San Feliciano: 10 minutes by ferry.*

While Maggiore looks back, Trasimeno's largest island thinks about the future: the whole place is an **environmental education centre** and **nature reserve.** It's not without history, though: there's evidence of habitation dating as far back as the Etruscans. In medieval times, 88 fishing families lived on the 70-hectare (173-acre) island, and they built the impressive **castle** to protect against constant Tuscan raids.

Traces of the past remain in a ruined Olivetan monastery and a church dedicated to the island's protector, San Giuliano. Pietro Porcinai's swimming pool of 1959 was built inside a sandstone quarry; it's now the island's **aquatic plant garden.** The best bits are only visitable as part of a good 1-hour **guide** (*075 9659546.* Hourly during Infopoint opening. Adm 2€), available in English. Elsewhere on the island is room to roam along panoramic paths and through holm oak and olive groves. If you fancy a quiet night, there are four basic family rooms (with bathrooms; cots not available) at the island's former farmworkers' accommodation, now the 76-bed **Ostello Il Poggio** (*075 9659550.* ***www.fattoriaisolapolvese.com***). High-season prices are 28€ pp including breakfast and Wi-Fi; a two-bedroom apartment (for up to six) with kitchen and Wi-Fi is 110€. Tots stay free. You can also rent **canoes** here, for 6€/half-day, or 12€ for 2–3 people.

Infopoint *Open 10am–1pm and 3–6pm daily July and Aug, Sun only Apr–June and Sept.* ***Amenities***

Museo della Pesca ALL AGES

Via Lungolago 20, San Feliciano. 075 8479261.

This small but illuminating fishing museum makes for a pleasant change from all the outdoor activity, with a decent hands-on section for children, games, displays and activities documenting the lake's history.

Time *30 min.* ***Open*** *10:30am–1pm and 4–7pm Tues–Sun July and Aug; 10am–12:30pm and 3–6pm Tues–Sun Apr–June and Sept; 10:30am–1pm and 3–5:20pm Sat and Sun Oct–Mar.* ***Adm*** *3€, 1.50€ children/students.*

ASSISI

If you drive up early in the morning, you'll soon see that **Assisi** ★★★ is a special place—the rising sun behind Monte Subasio cuts massive silhouettes behind this medieval city of miracles. A peculiar blend of romance, architecture and devotion makes it the quintessential Umbrian hill-town—*the* essential stop on any Umbrian tour.

FUN FACT **Say It So**

While you're here, remember: it's *a-see-zee* not *a-see-see*.

The region's most popular spot has a magic that isn't all about its most famous resident, **St. Francis.** The biggest draw is the giant Basilica di San Francesco, built to honour him after his death but now almost as much a temple to pre-Renaissance painter **Giotto.** The rest is an ideally sited hill-town, hardly spoiled by its pesky traffic and tat shops, and absorbing its millions of annual tourists and pilgrims with a quiet ease.

Visitor Information

Information Centres

The **tourist office** (☎ *075 812534. www.assisionline.com*. 8am–2pm and 3–6pm Mon–Sat, 9am–1pm Sun) is at the western end of Piazza del Comune, no. 22. Banca dell'Umbria has an **ATM** nearby on the piazza.

There's a dedicated resource for disabled visitors: *www.assisiaccessibile.com*.

Arriving

By Car Assisi is 18km (11 miles) east of Perugia, off the **SS75b.** Driving the centre's steep streets is forbidden to tourists. The best strategy is to park in **Piazza Matteotti** (1.15€/hr), keep walking west and finish at the basilica; it's all downhill. Below the basilica, in **Piazza Giovanni Paolo II** (formerly Piazza Unità d'Italia), catch the half-hourly bus (Line C) back to Piazza Matteotti. The adjacent tabacchi sells tickets (1€; 1.50€ if you pay on the bus).

A dependable alternative is the Mojano multi-storey (1.05€ first 2 hours, 1.45€/hr thereafter) halfway up the hill from Piazza Giovanni Paolo II to Porta Nuova. Escalators whisk you into the centre of town.

INSIDER TIP

There's a map of Assisi's car parks at *www.assisi.com/parcheggi.htm*.

By Public Transport The **APM bus** (☎ *075 506781. www.apmperugia.it*) from Perugia (3.20€; 4€ if you pay on the bus) stops in Piazza Matteotti (7 daily Mon–Fri). The **train** is more frequent (2.05€) but drops you at the foot of the hill, from where you'll need to take a bus (1€) or taxi (12€).

Family-Friendly Events

Unless you have a religious motive, with children in tow the big dates in Assisi's calendar are best avoided. The **Festa di San Francesco** (3rd–4th Oct) and **Easter Week** are packed.

What to See & Do

In a **UNESCO World Heritage** town dominated by one man and his story (see 'The Life of Saint Francis', p. 208), there's a surprising amount of secular interest to see here. The geographical and civic heart is **Piazza del Comune** with its 13th-century **Palazzo del Capitano** and the stately Corinthian columns of the Roman **Tempio di Minerva** ★ (7:15am–7:30pm daily) guarding its northern fringe. The most atmospheric route to the basilica goes downhill along medieval **Via Portica** ★, which becomes Via Fortini and Via San Francesco before arriving at the main event.

Basilica di San Francesco

★★★ **AGE 6 & UP**

Piazza di San Francesco. ☎ 075 819001. ***www.sanfrancescoassisi.org.***

Although Assisi's basilica is known for its **art,** it's first of all a masterpiece of medieval **architecture.** The almost simultaneous construction of huge Lower (1228) and Upper (1230) Churches in contrasting Romanesque and Gothic styles had no peer or precedent. Franciscan **Brother Elias,** the probable architect, invites contemplation downstairs while upstairs the grand Gothic vaults set up a gawp at **Giotto.**

It was in the Basilica's **Upper Church** that Giotto became the greatest single influence on Western art, though the attribution of his most famous frescoes is challenged by some modern scholars. What is possibly his 28-part fresco cycle on the **Life of St. Francis** ★★★ was painted in the 1290s, pre-dating what is certainly his work in Florence's **Santa Croce** (p. 56). Start in the nave's far right, with the *Homage of a Simple Man*, and read clockwise. The famous *Sermon to the Birds* is behind you on your left as you enter, but the next two panels show what Giotto (or whoever) was about; both are full of tension, emotion, narrative detail and an

Basilica di San Francesco, Assisi

The Life of Saint Francis

1182 Francis is born in Assisi, son of a rich cloth merchant and his French wife. As he grows up, Francis is said to become increasingly disillusioned with his materially wealthy life.

1201 Francis joins the army and is captured in battle by the Perugians.

1206 Francis claims that a vision of Jesus commands him to rebuild the Church of San Damiano outside Assisi.

1209 Pope Innocent III approves Francis's religious order, the Frati Minori, after seeing him in a dream.

1211 Francis receives Clare of Assisi, and the Order of the Poor Dames is founded.

1219 Francis appears before Sultan Melek-el-Kamel of Egypt and proposes trial-by-fire to test the true religion; the Sultan declines.

1220 Francis builds the first Christmas crib in Greccio.

1226 Francis dies in the Porziuncola, a small church in Santa Maria degli Angeli, 4km (2½ miles) from Assisi.

1228 Pope Gregory IX canonises St. Francis and lays the first stone of the Basilica di San Francesco. Francis is buried here in 1230.

1939 St. Francis is named Italy's patron saint.

attempt at perspective that had never been seen before. At a time when plain representation of devotional icons was the norm, he painted people with real faces.

Downstairs in the **Lower Church** are further wonderful murals; pause especially for Simone Martini's 1317 **Cappella di San Martino** ★★ (first chapel on the left) and Pietro Lorenzetti's 1315 **Crucifixion** ★★ and 1320 **Deposition** ★★★ in the left transept near the main altar. The crypt below houses the chokingly atmospheric **Tomb of St. Francis** ★ and four of his followers, so well hidden it wasn't rediscovered until 1818.

Some planning hints. First, the basilica's **dress code**—no short skirts, shorts, sleeveless tops or low-cut dresses—is enforced. Ditto the *silenzio*: don't bring a tantrum-prone toddler. And while access to the churches is fine with **buggies,** you won't be able to get to the cloister or shop.

Time *1 hr.* ***Open*** *Lower: 6am–6:45pm daily. Upper: 8:30am–6:45pm daily.* ***Adm*** *Free.* ***Amenities***

Eremo delle Carceri AGE 4 & UP

075 812301. ***www.eremocarceri.it.*** *4½km (3 miles) northeast of Assisi (taxi 075 813100).*

In theory, St. Francis's mountain retreat is a place of sanctuary and **silence**—a spot for contemplation wedged into a ravine on the wooded slopes of Monte

Subasio. Despite the polite signs, though, there isn't much chance of quiet. Yet despite being overrun with tourists, the tiny rooms of the hermitage itself remain atmospheric, especially the rock 'bed' where St. Francis slept (remember to duck).

You'll find more peace and plenty of shade in the tracked **woodlands** ★ behind the monastery, where Francis preached to the birds.

Time *1 hr.* ***Open*** *6:30am–6:45pm daily, Easter–Oct, rest of year 6:30am–6pm.* ***Adm*** *Free.* ***Amenities***

Foro Romano ★ AGE 7 & UP

Via Portica 2. 075 813053. ***www.sistemamuseo.it****.*

Central Assisi's secular highlight is a little underwhelming for non-history buffs, but this **Roman forum** can still hold some magic for youngsters. An entrance room (the old crypt of San Niccolò Church) houses inscribed tablets and headless statues, but the main passage leading off from here preserves a tiny piece of 2nd-century B.C. **Asisium**—a slice of the old forum right below 21st-century Piazza del Comune. There isn't much to see beyond more tablets and the foundations (with English labels) of what would've been grand Roman buildings, but it'll stir a curious imagination.

Time *30 min.* ***Open*** *10am–1pm and 2:30–7pm daily June–Aug, 10am–1pm and 2:30–6pm Mar–May, Sept and Oct, 10:30am–1pm and 2–5pm Nov–Feb.* ***Adm*** *4€, 2.50€ ages 8–17; joint ticket with Rocca Maggiore and Pinacoteca Comunale 8€ and 5€.* ***Amenities***

Rocca Maggiore AGE 7 & UP

075 813053/812033. ***www.sistemamuseo.it****.*

The semi-ruined 14th-century **Rocca Maggiore** crowns a *very* steep hill behind the town—a stunning location that rewards the climb up with gasp-inducing views (don't attempt the relentless climb with a buggy or young children). Inside, the castle is a warren of rooms and halls highlighting costumes, arms and festivals of medieval Assisi. The note warning **claustrophobes** and **vertigo-sufferers** only refers to the tower section, accessed via a very narrow, very steep spiral staircase—most children will love this, though.

Time *1 hr.* ***Open*** *8:30am–6:30pm daily.* ***Adm*** *4€, 2.50€ ages 8–17; joint ticket with Foro Romano and Pinacoteca Comunale 8€ and 5€.* ***Amenities***

SPELLO

A little balcony above the checkerboard plains of the Vale of Spoleto, **Spello** with its warm-pink glow is visible for miles. The former Roman retirement town of Hispellum caught the tourism bug late—even in high season you'll find a quiet backwater or a corner with a measure of peace. It's an essential half-day for **art-lovers,** with the best Pinturicchio you can see for free, and hosts one of Umbria's most charming **festivals.**

Spello isn't easy to visit with a **buggy:** streets are steep and mostly cobbled, and there are no pavements, making car-dodging a full-time job.

Visitor Information

Information Centres

The **tourist office** (☎ *0742 301009. **http://turismo.comune.spello.pg.it**.* 9:30am–12:30pm and 3:30–5:30pm daily) is at Piazza Matteotti 3.

Arriving

Spello is 28km (17 miles) south-east of Perugia, on the SS75 just short of Foligno. The **parking** spaces immediately on your right as you drive in may be taken; if so, make for the three signposted (and free) car parks on the other side of town as you approach from the SS75.

Trains (☎ *892021. **www.trenitalia.it***) run hourly from Perugia (2.65€, 35 min); town is a 10-minute walk from the station.

Family-Friendly Event

Each Corpus Christi, 60 days after Easter, the streets are carpeted in murals made with fresh petals for the **Infiorate** ★ (***www.infioratespello.it***), literally 'flower decorations'. Come by train.

What to See & Do

The best route for a cobblestoned mooch is up Via Garibaldi and Via San Severino to the foot of the ruined **medieval Rocca** (now the Capuchin monastery of San Severino). You can't get in, but the views ★ over the pancake-flat Vale of Spoleto, back to Assisi and what's left of a Roman amphitheatre, are worth the climb. It's **nigh impossible** with a buggy, however.

Spello is a treat for fans of **religious art** (see below), but the renovated **Pinacoteca Civica** (☎ *0742 301497;* 10:30am–1pm and 3–6:30pm Tues–Sun Apr–Oct, 10:30am–12:30pm and 3:30–5:30pm rest of year. Adm 5€, 4€ for children 7–14) next

Spello carpeted in flower petals

TIP Spello's Top Shops

You might baulk at the relentless self-promotion at the door, but the hype is almost justified at **Enoteca Properzio** ★ (Piazza Matteotti 8, ☎ *0742 301521.* ***www.enoteche.it***. 10am–10pm daily). Wines by the glass, wine tastings and even wine courses are the prelude to selecting a serious bottle. There's also decent food (plus seating on the piazza) to please non-connoisseurs: plates of ham, cheese and bruschetta with truffle from 10€.

For quirky **art** to remember Spello by, visit **Bottega d'Arte di Michela Parroni** (Via Consolare 46; most days 9:30am–1pm and 3:30–7pm), which sells the medieval-style paintings, cards, prints and bookmarks (1€–15€).

to Santa Maria Maggiore is strictly for hardcore fans. More enticingly for children, perhaps, your ticket includes entry to the **Mosaici Villa Romana** (10:30am–12:30pm and 3–5pm Tues–Sun), a group of delicate Roman mosaics protected by a futuristic dome on the outskirts of the old town, at Via Porta Consolare. Finish your tour at the excellent **playground** nearby, wedged between Piazza Kennedy and Via Centrale Umbria.

Frantoio Ragani ★ ALL AGES

Via degli Ulivi 8. ☎ *0742 301156.* ***www.olioragani.com****. 2km (just over 1 mile) from Spello, direction Assisi; follow signs from Assisi road.*

For *degustazione* with a difference—one that everyone can get into—stop in at this family *frantoio* (olive press). It's actually little more than a house with a shop in the garage, but conditions 350m (1,148 ft) up the slopes of Monte Subasio ensure that its **first cold-pressed olive oil** from November's harvest is among Umbria's best. The regular *extra vergine* (13€ for 750ml) is smooth and slightly sweet; strictly regulated **DOP Umbria** ★★ (15€ for 750ml), made with at least 70% green fruit, has a distinct olive aroma and a peppery bite. For the full flavour experience, **drink** the oil when you taste instead of dipping bread—it sounds a bit grim, but you'll notice the difference.

Time *15 min.* ***Open*** *9:30am–7pm daily.*

Santa Maria Maggiore

AGE 5 & UP

Piazza Matteotti.

Don't be distracted by the showy Baroque interior; this church is a major spot for Umbrian **Renaissance** painting. To the left and right of the altar a *Madonna and Child* and a *Pietà* by Perugino neatly bookend the life of Christ. The highlight is the **Cappella Baglioni** ★, frescoed like Siena's **Piccolomini Library** (p. 85) by Pinturicchio. It's on the left as you walk in; bring 1€ for lights.

The vaulted ceiling depicts four sibyls (pre-Christian prophetesses). The three main panels read left to right: an *Annunciation* (p. 53), followed by a *Nativity*

TIP A Bite on the Go

It looks ordinary from the outside, but the large panoramic garden at **Bar Bonci** (*0742 651397.* Thurs-Tues 7am–10pm, or until midnight Mar–Oct) at Via Garibaldi 10 is an ideal spot to take a break in Spello. Forget the pizza and pasta dishes and share plates of local salami (6.50€), cheeses (7€), mixed bruschetta (3€) and *torta al testo* (flatbread; 5€).

and *Christ's Dispute with the Doctors*. At the far end of the first panel, a Pinturicchio self-portrait 'hangs' on the wall. When the lights run out, you'll get a better view of the **ceramic floor** laid by craftsmen from Deruta, just south of Perugia.

Time *30 min.* ***Open*** *8:30am–noon and 3–7pm daily.* ***Adm*** *Free.* ***Amenities***

GUBBIO

The hazy hills of the Umbrian north stretch from Perugia's suburbs to Sansepolcro. The major town in an otherwise sleepy region is **Gubbio;** its *centro storico* is one of the most picturesque in Umbria, with an enchanting ensemble of medieval limestone buildings overlooking an undulating valley.

Visitor Information

Information Centres

The **tourist office** (*075 9220693.* ***www.gubbioaltochiascio.umbria2000.it.*** 8:30am–1:45pm and 3:30–6:30pm Mon–Fri, 9am–1pm and 3:30–6:30pm Sat, 9:30am–12:30pm and 3:30–6:30pm Sun Mar–Oct; rest of year 8:30am–1.45pm and 3–6:30pm Mon–Fri, 9am–1pm and 3–6:30pm Sat, 9:30am–12:30pm and 3–6:30pm exc. Jan and Feb, Sun) is at Via della Repubblica 15. There's an **ATM** opposite.

Arriving

By Car To park in **Gubbio,** follow the 'P' signs on the road from Perugia: turn left at the second mini-roundabout and right at the next two to reach the **Teatro Romano** free car park (with a great **playground** ★ behind). Marginally closer, at **Piazza 40 Martiri,** is some pay parking (0.80€/first hour, then 0.30€/20 min; Gubbio hotel guests pay 8€/24 hr).

By Public Transport There are around 8 daily **APM buses** (*075 506781.* ***www.apmperugia.it***) from Perugia (4.60€; 5.50€ if you pay on board) to Piazza 40 Martiri. Forget the wilds farther north, east or west without a car.

Family-Friendly Event

Thousands pile in every 15th May for the **Festa dei Ceri** ★, when giant candles (*ceri*) bearing images of St. Ubaldo, St. George and St. Anthony are raced from the town to the Basilica di Sant'Ubaldo on the mountain above.

What to See & Do

Your likely entry point is **Piazza 40 Martiri,** named after 40 locals murdered by the Nazis for assisting partisans; they're remembered every 22nd June.

The quickest route uphill follows **Via della Repubblica** past the tourist office; the **Via dei Consoli** is a gentler climb. Both get you to **Piazza Grande** ★, dominated by the fortress-like Palazzo dei Consoli, built in the 1330s.

Funivia Colle Eletto ★ AGE 3 & UP

Via San Girolamo. ☎ 075 9273881.

This 'cable car' with a difference will either thrill or terrify young ones. The 'car' is actually a metal cage, with standing room for two adults and two tots, just (no room for buggies). The 5-minute trip to the top of **Monte Ingino** (908m/2,980 ft) isn't as scary as it might seem, though, as you're never very far from the ground. As well as **views** ★ of the valley spread below, the top station has shady tables for a panoramic picnic.

Five minutes up the path, the **Basilica di Sant'Ubaldo** is dedicated to a 12th-century bishop who saved the town from marauding German 'Holy Roman' Emperor Barbarossa. Aside from his desiccated (and venerated) remains, check out the huge 'Ceri' carried up here during Gubbio's iconic *festa* (above).

On the way back into town, fans of Umbrian painting shouldn't miss **Ottaviano Nelli's** outstanding 1420 **Life of St. Augustine** ★ covering the apse of **Sant'Agostino** (☎ *075 9273814. **www.santagostino.net***), outside the Porta Romana (a short trot down from the Funivia); there's an explanatory leaflet and light-switch right of the altar. It's often open all day, but come before noon or after 3:30pm to be sure.

Time *2 hr.* ***Open*** *10am–1:15pm and 2:30–6:30pm Mon–Fri; 9:30am–1:15pm and 2:30–7pm Sat and Sun.* ***Adm*** *5€, 4€ children 4–14.* ***Amenities***

Museo del Palazzo dei Consoli ★★ AGE 5 & UP

Piazza Grande. ☎ 075 9274298.

Once the home of the town government, this *palazzo* now houses an enjoyable history museum best known for its 3rd-century B.C. **Eugubine Tablets**—the only existing record of the Umbri language transposed in Etruscan and Latin letters: ancient Umbria's Rosetta Stone. It's more fun exploring the old palace than examining the exhibits (an odd mish-mash of coins, pottery and paintings): don't miss the **secret corridor** ★ from the back of the majolica ceramics room to the Pinacoteca upstairs (via the medieval toilets—for looking only). Don't let tots run up the main staircase with its **dangerously low handrail.**

FUN FACT **Crazy World**

Gubbio's Fontana dei Matti or 'fountain of madmen' is in the tiny piazza known as Largo del Bargello. Run round it three times, get yourself baptised with its water, and you're officially entitled to hold a 'nutter of Gubbio' licence.

Time** 1 hr. **Open** 10am–1pm and 3–6pm daily Apr–Oct, 10am–1pm and 3–6pm rest of year. **Adm** 5€, 2.50€ ages 7–25. **Amenities

Parco Regionale del Monte Cucco ★ AGE 3 & UP

*075 9170400. **www.discovermontecucco.it.***

Gubbio's tourist office (p. 212) should be your first stop if you plan to trek, spelunk (cave) or mountain-bike in the pristine wildernesses of the **Parco Regionale del Monte Cucco;** there's generally a list of guided excursions you can join May to September. If your children are aged 10 or older, consider the **Caves of Monte Cucco** ★ (*075 9171046.* Hourly 8am–around noon daily July and Aug, Sat and Sun Apr–June and Sept–Nov. Adm 20€, 12€ children 10–14), a mesmerising 4-hour, 800-m (2,624 ft) amble through huge caverns and grottos glistening with stalactites. Tours begin at Costacciaro.

CITTÀ DI CASTELLO

Up in the far north of Umbria, the main point of interest is **Città di Castello,** a working place quite unlike the hill-towns elsewhere on the tourist trail. In the Middle Ages it was known as *Castrum Felicitatis*, the 'Town of Happiness'. More recently, as a tobacco, printing and textile centre, it developed an **artisan** aura that's only reluctantly fading. There's no distinguished piazza and little medieval masonry, so you'll have to settle for enough art treasures to satisfy an expert, and perhaps the **ugliest cathedral** in Umbria—a magnificent pile that has to be seen to be believed. The town is untainted, authentic and best of all flat: buggy-pushers can give weary forearms a time-out.

Visitor Information

Information Centres

The helpful **tourist office** (*075 8554922;* 8:30am–1:30pm and 3:30–6:30pm Mon–Fri, 9:30am–12:30pm and 3:30–6:30pm Sat, 9:30am–12:30pm Sun) is under the Logge Bufalini at Piazza Matteotti 8. There's an **ATM** opposite.

For online trip planning, try ***www.cdcnet.net***.

Arriving

Northern Umbria is sliced in two by the E45 *superstrada*, making access to **Città** very easy: from Perugia, exit the E45 at *Città di Castello* (not the first *Sud* exit) and turn right at the

Città of Art

Città's galleries are all of the serious variety. Best known is the **Pinacoteca Comunale** (*075 8520656. **www.cdcnet.net/pinacoteca***. Tues–Sun 10am–1pm and 2:30–6:30pm Apr–Oct, 10am–1pm and 3–6pm rest of year), Umbria's second gallery after Perugia, in a fine Renaissance *palazzo* on Via della Cannoniera, with 30 rooms tracing the development of Umbrian art from its early roots to the 1900s. Sadly, despite **Raphael** and **Luca Signorelli** both being active in Città, only one work from each remains: a damaged *Holy Trinity* by Raphael and Signorelli's 1498 *Martyrdom of St. Sebastian* (not one of his classics). Best of the rest is Room 16, dedicated to **Raffaellino dal Colle** ★. Ask for the English-language handout.

An otherwise dry **Museo del Duomo** in Piazza Gabriotti (*075 8554705.* Tues–Sun 10am–1pm and 3–6pm) is enlivened by an embossed, 12th-century **silver altar-front** ★ with scenes from the *New Testament* and **Rosso Fiorentino's** oh-so-dark *Christ in Glory*.

Completing the trinity is (shock, horror) a modern art museum, the **Collezione Burri** (*075 8554649. **www.fondazioneburri.org/***. 9am–12:30pm and 2:30–6:30pm Tues–Sat, 10:30am–12:30pm and 3–7pm Sun), in the Palazzo Albizzini on Via Albizzini. Burri's home town has an unmatched collection of his textured, abstract art, including his 1963 *Grande Plastica*—not something Raphael could have dreamed up.

Admission to any of the three galleries is 6€, children 4€.

first roundabout and you'll eventually pass the free **Parcheggio Ferri** car park, 3 minutes from the Duomo via the *scala mobile* over the road.

If you're using public transport, the hourly **FCU train** from Perugia (*075 5754034. **www.fcu.it***. 3.05€) takes 1¼ hours.

What to See & Do

It's a feature of Città that most of its medieval buildings were fitted with later **facades**. At the **Palazzo del Podestà,** facing the tourist office across Piazza Matteotti, spot the obvious 'new' (1687) front stuck on an old (1368) palace. Keep walking along Corso Cavour for an unmissable **Duomo:** its cylindrical campanile seems lifted from a Breton château and grafted onto an architectural mess. On Thursday and Saturday mornings the local **market** fills the streets around here; be sure to grab a luscious ***porchetta* panino** ★ (2.50€) from the stalls by the Duomo.

If your Italian's up to it, the best way to pass 45 minutes is a guided tour of **Tipografia Grifani-Donati** ★ (*075 8554349*; 9am–12:30pm and 3–7pm Mon–Fri, 9am–1pm Sat. Adm 10€) at Corso Cavour 4. This family printer has occupied the old church of San Paolo since 1799; you'll see lithographs and engravings printed in the original workshops still in use, and your souvenir is made in front of you on 19th-century printing machines. You can also visit the site on your own (3€), or just pop into the shop across the street (no. 5b; closed Mon) for a postcard (1.25€) with a difference: *ex-libris* images designed by Grifani over the centuries.

There's a **playground** opposite the Duomo, and a second behind Parcheggio Ferri.

FAMILY-FRIENDLY DINING

Al Coccio ★★ FIND UMBRIAN

Via del Quadrifoglio 12/a, Magione. ☎ 075 841829. ***www.alcoccio.it.***

This **local hangout** in a plain side-street just outside Magione isn't the kind of place you find on your own (we didn't either). The ambience is typical *ristorante*, with ceiling fans blowing strong, hams hanging and walls decked with red wines, especially the **Montefalco DOC.** It's all *tipico Umbra* in the true sense—a place where a serious attitude to food doesn't crowd out the family welcome. Children can eat pasta and plain grills or join in with a tour of Umbrian specialities: pecorino cheese cooked in the oven for starters, followed by *umbrichelli* pasta with truffles and juicy rabbit *della Nonna* (roasted with rosemary and leeks, like 'granny' used to make). Even the soufflé's local: the chocolate is **Perugina,** made down the road.

Open *12:15–3:30pm and 7:30–11pm Tues–Sun.* ***Main courses*** *7€–18€.* ***Credit*** *AE, MC, V.* ***Amenities***

Bar Bonci, Spello, see p. 209.

Enoteca Properzio, Spello, see p. 211.

Grotta Dell'Angelo ★ UMBRIAN/ ITALIAN

Via Gioia 47, Gubbio. ☎ 075 9271747. ***www.grottadellangelo.it.***

There's plenty of gourmet choice in Gubbio; this appealing trattoria is one of the best, tucked away down a narrow street in the heart of the old town. The speciality is meats roasted over a wood fire; think whole roast chicken, duck and rabbit stuffed with wild fennel (10€–14€). Plenty of pastas grace the menu, but you should also consider the high-quality *menù turistico* for 15€. The leafy garden terrace has plenty of space for big groups and energetic children.

Open *12:15–2:30pm and 7:30–10pm Wed–Mon exc. Jan.* ***Main courses*** *6€–14€.* ***Credit*** *AE, MC, V.*

INSIDER TIP

Hardcore foodies may prefer to book ahead for the medieval basement at **Osteria del Re** (☎ *075 9222504*), Piazza Busone 17, where you might expect platters of traditional 'Eugubina' food such as tripe, salt cod, and *polenta* (13€ pp).

La Stalla ★★★ VALUE

SELF-SERVICE GRILL

*Via Eremo delle Carceri 24, Assisi. ☎ 075 812317. **www.fontemaggio.it**. 1½km (less than 1 mile) from centre, direction Eremo.*

There aren't many restaurants where you can feed the whole family healthily for **less than 20€,** but here, four huge bowls of spaghetti plus a litre of water and a ¼ litre of house red will leave you change from that. The outdoor flamegrill has more: steak, pork and sausage skewers, chicken, even barbecued potatoes. Grab a tablecloth and cutlery, find a spot under the large pergola and order at the till, relaxed in the knowledge that whatever happy chaos your youngsters create won't match what's already going on. While you're waiting (it's all cooked from scratch), don't miss the world's best *bruschetta al pomodoro* and ask yourself how they get so much flavour into tomatoes on toast.

It can be a pleasant **walk** up here from Assisi, although with young ones it's best to come by car.

Open *12:30–2:30pm and 7:30–10pm Tues–Sun.* ***Main courses*** *4.50€–12€.* ***Amenities***

Osteria del Turreno ★ VALUE

SELF-SERVICE

Piazza Danti 16, Perugia. ☎ 075 5721976.

This *tavola calda* diner opposite the cathedral has been serving **basic lunches** with a Perugian twist for decades. The day's dishes are displayed canteen-style; pick what you fancy, pay at the till and take it to your table, inside or out. Options always include simple pasta, grilled meats and plenty of salad and veg. Desserts are a bit scarce—but beer and wine (3€ for ¼ litre) aren't! There are no highchairs but there's (just) enough room inside and out for a buggy.

Open *Noon–3pm Sun–Fri.* ***Main courses*** *3.60€–6.70€.*

Pallotta ★ UMBRIAN/CLASSIC ITALIAN

*Vicolo della Volta Pinta, Assisi. ☎ 075 812649. **www.pallottaassisi.it**.*

You don't have to veer far from the **tourist traps** ringing Assisi's Piazza del Comune to find good food; this much-recommended trattoria lies through the medieval arch on the south side. The exposed-beams-and-stone dining room works well with the **traditional menu** and old-fashioned dessert cabinet. Food is simple, seasonal and well cooked: Umbrian *antipasti*, local and classic Italian pastas, and plain grills served without fuss. For children, there are veal escalopes or plain pasta 'n' sauce, which staff are happy to cook right away and serve first. There is also a decent *menù turistico* (16€) with wine, tasting menus for **vegetarians** (24€) and gourmets (25€), and 14 wines by the glass, ¼ or ½ a litre. It's rightly popular, so **book ahead** or arrive early.

Open *12:15–2:30pm and 7:15–9:30pm Wed–Mon.* ***Main courses*** *7.50€–16€.* ***Credit*** *AE, MC, V.* ***Amenities***

TIP Lunch Alternatives in Perugia

The Flintstones, Umbrian-style? It may sound very un-Italian, but Bam Bam Ristosauro (☎ *075 5173315.* ***www.bambamristosauro.it***, noon–2:30pm and 7pm–midnight Wed–Mon), just west of the city at Strada Trasimeno Ovest 159/z, is a Stone-Age themed restaurant guaranteed to amuse children of all ages—think cartoonish dino plate settings and lots of leopard-skin drapes. The food *is* Italian, though—plenty of pizzas and pastas (albeit with the obligatory *primitivo* and *broccosauro* labels). You'll need a car to get here; take the Ferro di Cavallo exit off the *raccordo*, then turn left towards Corciano at the main road—it's up ahead on the right.

La Botte (☎ *075 5722679.* ***www.ristorantelabotte.com***, noon–2:30pm and 7:30–10:30pm Mon–Sat), at Via Volte della Pace 31, is rather more local and central, with a good reputation and a vast menu that includes pizzas. Its 11.50€ *menu turistico* has a long list of options.

Sauro, Isola Maggiore, see p. 204.

Trattoria Lea ★ VALUE

UMBRIAN/CLASSIC ITALIAN

Via San Florido 38a, Città di Castello. ☎ *075 8521678.*

This cosy, traditional restaurant down a back-street not far from the Duomo has a decent menu of all the favourites and plenty of local Umbrian ingredients. There's no menu here (there are few tourists), but pastas (4€–6€) include a very tasty ravioli (4.50€), or there's a magnificent *gnocchi ai funghi porcini* (6€). *Secondi* cost 5€–13€, but do leave room for the cheese plates (3€) and some tiramisù (5€).

Open *12:30–3pm and 7:30–10pm Tues–Sun.* ***Main courses*** *4€–13€.* ***Credit*** *AE, MC, V.*

FAMILY-FRIENDLY ACCOMMODATION

For more accommodation ideas, see p. 220.

APARTMENTS, VILLAS & FARM-STAYS

Brigolante Guest Apartments ★

Via Costa di Trex 31, 6km (4 miles) east of Assisi. ☎ *075 802250.* ***www.brigolante.com.***

Skip Assisi's overpriced central hotels in preference for this rural gem only 5 minutes' drive from town in the foothills of Monte Subasio. The 16th-century *agriturismo*, once part of a castle, offers three self-catering apartments featuring terracotta floors, hand-painted tiles, antiques and period furniture. Host Rebecca and her family are very welcoming; your children are guaranteed plenty of attention and outdoor space with a sandpit and playground. There's mountain-bike loan, and cots, highchairs, toys and plastic tableware.

Apartments** 3. **Rates** 475€–550€/wk; daily rates available Nov–Mar (exc. Christmas). Cots free. **Credit** AE, MC, V. **Amenities ***In apartment***

Casali di Colle San Paolo ★ FIND

*Località Muserale 8, Colle San Paolo, Tavernelle di Panicale. 075 832030. **www.collesanpaolo.it.** 25km (16 miles) southwest of Perugia off SS220.*

If it's **rural** you're after, this *agriturismo* in a magical landscape of olive trees in the hills overlooking Lake Trasimeno has three stone farmhouses (*casali*) built in the 17th century. Fontanelle offers unique views of the Nestore Valley, while Molinella is connected to an old water-mill (three buildings surrounded by oak woods). Each complex contains several apartments and a shared swimming pool, panoramic terracotta terraces equipped for alfresco eating, outside showers and barbecues. Poderaccio, the best for families, also has an outside play area (including a sandpit and small pools).

Apartments** 12. **Rates** 600€–1000€/wk. Cot free. **Amenities ***In apartment***

INSIDER TIP

Note that San Paolo itself hosts the well-respected **Arte al Sole summer art programme** for children aged 6 to 12, usually lasting a week at the end of June.

Le Torri di Bagnara FIND

*Strada della Bruna 8, Località Pieve San Quirico, 335 6408549. **www.letorridibagnara.it.** 18km (11 miles) north of Perugia.*

One of Umbria's most popular and romantic *agriturismo* options is also a fabulous choice for families. The grounds are gorgeous, featuring stunning views, ancient towers, herb gardens and a **saltwater pool** (where adults can enjoy a glass of wine). Children are sure to fall in love with the cat. The apartments are spacious, have stupendous views and are well equipped for families of up to five; all are within the **medieval tower** (the other rooms occupy the 11th-century **abbey** nearby). There's mountain-bike loan if required. It's a 20-minute drive from central Perugia, 4km (2½ miles) from the E45 'Resina' exit.

Apartments** 4. **Rooms** 4 doubles; 3 luxury suites. **Rates** Doubles 130€–200€/night. Apartment for four 790€–1290€/wk; for five 850€–1390€. Cots 10€–30€. **Credit** AE, MC, V. **Amenities ***In apartment***

CAMPSITES & HOSTELS

Ostello Il Poggio, Isola Polvese, see p. 20.

Parco dei Pini

*Via Gandhi 1, San Feliciano. 075 8476270. **www.villaggioparcodeipini.it.***

This intimate **campsite** offers something different to the supersites that circle Lago Trasimeno: its roadside location under the

Your Own Umbrian Retreat

It could only be Umbria: almost-deserted hill-towns and epic views under the midday sun, long lunches of the finest ingredients cooked simply, a flash of sunflower yellow and the aroma of olives. Just don't limit yourselves to spectating: renting a secluded villa, *agriturismo* or farmhouse enables you to *truly take part* in Umbria. Buy ham cured and hung on a local farm, pan-fry a lake fish picked up at the morning market, barbecue a *bistecca alla Fiorentina* (T-bone-like steak) and wash it down with a neighbour's robust red. Eat seasonally and sustainably: asparagus in late spring, wild *porcini* mushrooms as summer turns to autumn. You're **living local**—it's what Umbria does best.

More prosaically, a farmhouse or villa rental is also a **practical** choice for families. It supplies the flexibility to come and go as you please, and to feed little ones at times that suit. Splash around in your own pool, rent bikes and take long walks in the early evening before having dinner together on the terrace.

As well as the 'Family-friendly Accommodation' recommendations here and in Chapter 9, there's plenty of choice at ***www.invillas.com***, ***www.tuscanestates.com***, ***www.perugiarentals.com*** and ***www.hostedvillas.com***. For more on *agriturismo* holidays, see p. 29.

pines just north of San Feliciano gives it views of Isola Polvese and Castiglione in the distance, and some pitches, the common area and the pool are on the **lakeside.** Its mobile homes are of the usual compact design (they're said to be for 5/6 but really fit 4 maximum) and a little close together but are newly refitted and well kitted out. They're also rentable by the night year-round.

Pitches *75 (+ 7 mobile homes).* ***Rates*** *Camping: adults 6€–7€, 4€–5€ children 4–10, pitch 6€–7€. Mobile homes: 45€–85€/night, 12€ final cleaning charge, plus 2€ per car per night.* ***Credit*** *MC, V.* ***Amenities*** ***In mobile home***

HOTEL

Sangallo Palace ★★

Via L. Masi 9, Perugia. 075 5730202. ***www.sangallo.it.***

If you fancy a few nights in the city, this smart, reliable choice is easy to drive to (right next to Partigiani car park) yet a pleasant walk from the centre of town. It has a decent indoor pool and plenty of **triple rooms** that can accommodate extra beds: comfy but fairly standard four-star affairs with the usual amenities. Service is excellent.

Rooms *93.* ***Rates*** *doubles 90€–120€; triples 110€–145€, extra bed 40€ (5.50€ discount for child under 12).* ***Amenities*** ***In room***

9 Orvieto & Southern Umbria

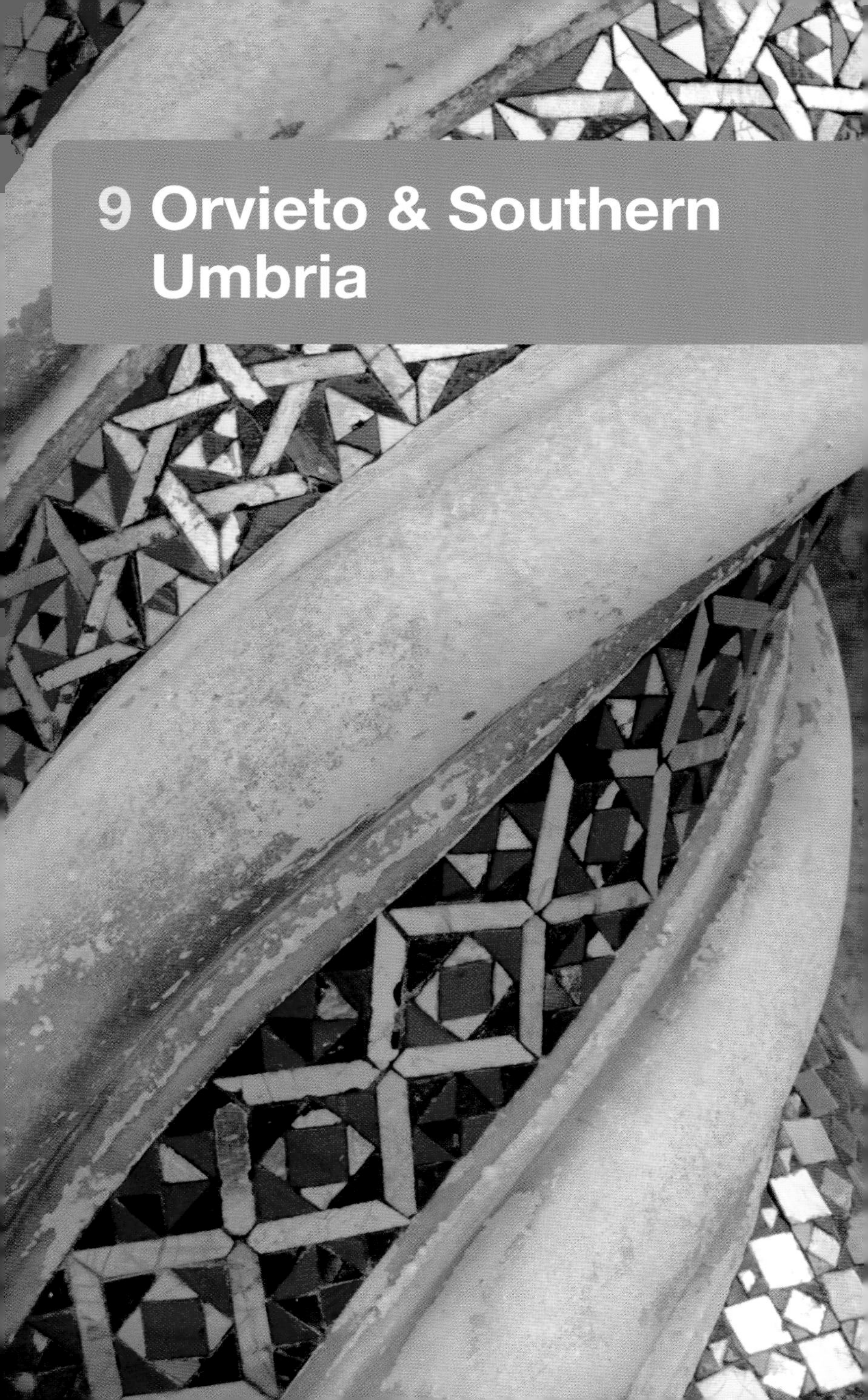

CENTRAL & SOUTHERN UMBRIA

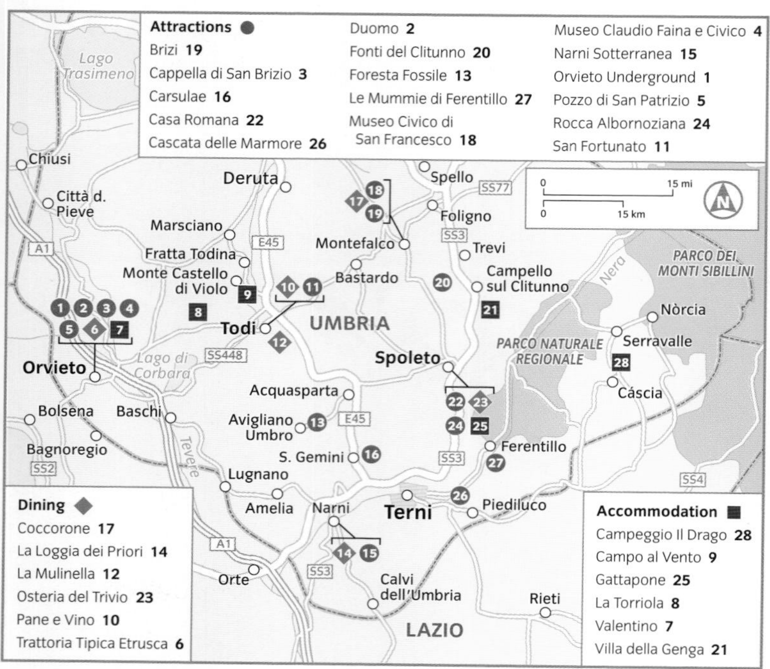

More than anywhere else in the region, southern Umbria remains governed by the rhythms of the sun and the path of the seasons. This is a land of historic villages, family vineyards and sunny slopes thick with olive groves—ideal territory for escaping to a secluded villa or farmhouse. The food is richer, the traffic slower, and life in general much more laid-back.

From a sightseeing point of view, it's a little trickier. Etruscan **Orvieto**—the pearl of the south, and Umbria's magnificent cathedral *città* and wine centre at the meeting point of Lazio and Tuscany—isn't a place you'd fancy making a day trip of from **Norcia;** it's too far, and roads round here don't oblige if you want to get anywhere fast. Plan to stay around the centre if you can; the sleepy towns of **Todi, Spoleto** and **Montefalco** are quintessential Umbria with sights and views that children love. All three are within reach of the white waters of the **Valnerina,** the ruins at **Carsulae** and the hidden world of the Dominican Inquisition below **Narni**—each a great spot for burning off the calorific local food, considered among Italy's best **cuisine** by those who love wild mushrooms and truffles.

Fast Facts: Orvieto & Southern Umbria

Banks Orvieto is the best place to find major retail banks, with most branches on **Corso Cavour** or **Via Garibaldi.** Most close at 1:30pm for lunch and only open for an hour or so in the afternoon.

Hospitals & Emergencies The **Ospedale Santa Maria della Stella** is at Località Ciconia, just outside Orvieto (*0763 3071*). The nearest A&E department to Orvieto is at the **Ospedaliera Santa Maria di Terni,** Viale Tristano di Joannuccio, Terni (*0744 2051*). In a medical emergency, call *118*.

Internet & Wi-Fi **Montanucci** (7am–midnight daily) at Corso Cavour 23 in Orvieto is a café with free terminals at the rear (buy a coffee).

Pharmacies **Farmacia Gammarota,** Corso Cavour 33, Orvieto, is the most central (*0763 341726,* 9am–1pm and 4–8pm Mon–Sat). On Sundays and holidays pharmacies take turns opening; you can find out which by checking a notice outside this one.

Post Offices Orvieto's post office is at Largo M. Ravelli 4 (*0763 398349*, 8am–6:30pm Mon–Fri, 8am–12:30pm Sat).

ORVIETO

The defining feature of southern Umbria's most touristy town is its cathedral with its sparkling facade fronting on the massive piazza: day-trippers come to see **Orvieto** ★★ from as far as Florence and Rome. The rest of town looks much as it did 500 years ago—a preserved medieval centre stuck high on a volcanic plug, visible for miles in every direction. This impenetrable perch ensured that Etruscan *Velzna* was among the most powerful members of the *dodecapoli* (p. 171); its Etruscan heritage has left an **underground** world as much fun to explore as the one above.

Visitor Information

Information Centres

Orvieto's **tourist office** (*0763 341772. www.orvieto.umbria2000.it.* open 8:15am–1:50pm and 4–7pm Mon–Fri, 10am–1pm and 3–6pm Sat and Sun) is at Piazza del Duomo 24.

Arriving

By Car Orvieto is easy to reach by **car,** especially from southern Tuscany: it's by the **A1.** The main link to the rest of Umbria is the **SS448** to Todi (40 min). There's pay **parking** (0.80€ first hour; 1€/hr thereafter) in Piazza Cahen, the first major square as you arrive in town, opposite the Pozzo di San Patritio. An alternative is the multi-storey west of town, **Ex-Campo della Fiera**

Children's Top Attractions in Southern Umbria

- Riding the **rapids** on an inflatable raft in the Valnerina, p. 236.
- Getting grisly with the **gruesome mummies** of Ferentillo, p. 236.
- Meeting the **Etruscans** at Orvieto's Museo Claudio Faina, p. 226.
- **Exploring** another world below Orvieto, p. 227.
- Digging in to **Umbria's tastiest ice cream** at Colder, p. 234.
- **Hanging out** at the Hotel Gattapone in Spoleto, p. 240.
- Sampling wonderful **cuisine** in a laid-back setting at Coccorone, p. 237.

(0.55€/hr, 6.20€/24 hr); from there, take an escalator up to the old centre. The Carta Unica (p. 225) gives you 5 hours of free parking at the latter.

By Train **Orvieto Scalo** is on the fast Rome–Florence train line (✆ *892021*. *www.trenitalia.it*). **Chiusi–Chianciano Terme,** the main station for southern Tuscany, is 25–35 minutes. **Perugia** (1½ hr) requires a change at Terontola. From Orvieto Scalo, take the 100-year-old **funicular** (1€) to Piazza Cahen (every 10 min, 7:20am–8:30pm). For the *centro storico*, walk 10 minutes uphill (on buggy-unfriendly cobblestones) or take **Bus A** or B (every 10 min, 7am–8pm) for the Duomo (a funicular ticket is valid on the bus, otherwise it's also 1€; accompanied under-10s ride free).

Family-Friendly Events

Along with Spello's **Infiorate** (p. 210), Orvieto is the best place to experience the annual festival of **Corpus Domini** (or 'Corpus Christi'), culminating in an elaborate parade through the streets of the old town.

What to See & Do

It's quaint, for sure, but **Orvieto's** cobbled alleys and streets retain a lived-in feel: even along **Corso Cavour** there are butchers and barbers besides the wine-tasting, ceramics and *tipico* shops. Next to the funicular terminal, Orvieto's semi-ruined 14th-century **Rocca** (8am–7:30pm daily May–Sept, rest of year 8am–4:30pm) houses the **Giardino Comunale,** with a small **playground.** The mighty ramparts afford the best **view** ★ of Orvieto Scalo below—one from a distance.

FUN FACT **4 x 4**

Orvieto is divided into four ancient *quartiere:* Corsica, Olmo, Stella and Serancia. Ask your children to spot signs marking all four as you walk round.

TIP A Super Saver

The best cumulative ticket in Umbria is the Orvieto Unica Card (*www.cartaunica.it*): 18€ (15€ students; under-10s free) gets you into **everything** mentioned below, as well as the **Museo Archeologico Nazionale.** It includes 5 hours' parking at Ex-Campo della Fiera, a return-trip on the funicular and bus, and discounts at hotels, shops and restaurants. Buy the ticket from the **funicular car park** (*0763 302378*) in Orvieto Scalo, any participating sight, or the **Carta Unica office** (10am–6pm daily in summer, shorter hours in winter) next to the tourist office. It's valid for a year.

More fine **views** ★ are to be had from the top of the **Torre del Moro** (*0763 344567;* 10am–8pm daily May–Aug, 10am–7pm Mar, Apr, Sept and Oct, 10:30am–4:30pm Nov–Feb) at Corso Cavour 87, Orvieto's clock tower, with a bell that has been ringing since 1313. If you don't fancy climbing all **236** steps, a lift whizzes you up the first 100 or so. Tickets are 2.80€, 2€ students; under-10s go free.

For sweet treats, try **Montanucci** at Corso Cavour 23 (7am–midnight daily), with a tempting range of cakes and chocolate to take out or eat in, plus a tranquil garden, lots of cosy rooms and free Internet. **Pasqualetti** (*0763 341034*) at Piazza del Duomo 14 is the best *gelato* stop.

Duomo ★★ AGE 7 & UP

Piazza del Duomo. 0763 342477. www.opsm.it.

Nothing you've yet seen in Tuscany or Umbria prepares you for a first encounter with **Orvieto's Duomo,** the **Cathedral of Santa Maria Assunta:** the 'Golden Lily of Cathedrals' is either the height of garish ostentation or a masterpiece. The attention-grabbing **facade** ★★, restored and glowing in Gothic glory, is grafted on to a Romanesque body originally planned in 1290—the whole thing took 300 years to complete. Of Lorenzo Maitani's four **reliefs** ★★★ carved on exterior columns, look out for a brutal *Last Judgement* on the lower right: as the dead rise from their graves, demonic torturers look delighted, and the damned a touch concerned.

Inside, as well as the Cappella di San Brizio (see below) and the Gothic frescoes behind the altar (dedicated to the life of Mary and created around 1370 by Ugolino di Prete Ilario), check out Ugolino's frescoes in the **Cappella del Corporale** ★ (left of the altar). These tell the story of the **Miracle of Bolsena:** a young German priest was saying Mass nearby when blood dripped from the Host on to the altar cloth (the *corporale*). The cloth is kept inside, and memory lives on in the annual festival of **Corpus Domini** (above).

Time *45 min.* ***Open*** *9:30am–7pm Mon–Sat, 1–5:30pm Sun Apr–Oct; 9:30am–7pm Mon–Sat, 1–6:30pm Sun July–Sept; 9:30am–1pm and*

TIP Stick to the Classics

Just as in Chianti, the *classico* in Orvieto Classico signifies that white grapes come from the original growing area only (p. 32). Look out for uncommon Orvietan versions, such as off-dry (neither dry nor sweet) *abboccato*. **Enoteca Duomo** at Via Pedota 2, just off Via Maitani (usually 9am–7pm daily), is one of the best places to buy wine around Piazza del Duomo.

2:30–5pm Mon–Sat, Sun 2:30–5:30pm Nov–Mar. ***Adm*** *2€; 3€ with Cappella di San Brizio; 5€ with Museo dell'Opera del Duomo (☎ 0763 343592.* ***www.opsm.it****); under-6s free.*

Cappella di San Brizio ★★ AGE 7 & UP

Inside Duomo.

If you've come to Orvieto to see the frescoes in the Duomo, you're in good company: **Michelangelo** made sketches of them on his way south to paint the Sistine Chapel. Luca Signorelli's 1499 **Last Judgement** is considered a masterpiece of the early Renaissance, on a subject clearly close to Orvietan hearts. There's no real order; all depict our anticipated final reckoning with varying degrees of gore. Compare the faces of **The Saved** and **The Damned** on either side of the altar; above your head, **The End of the World** ★ drips with blood. Easily the most striking image in the chapel is the glazed preacher and his demonic companion in **The Rule of the Antichrist** ★★★. The two robed figures on the far left are Signorelli and Fra' Angelico (p. 59), who painted **Christ Judge** and **The Prophets** on the ceiling vaults.

Time *15 min.* ***Open*** *Same hours as Duomo.* ***Adm*** *3€ with Duomo; 5€ with Museo dell'Opera del Duomo; under-6s free.*

Museo Claudio Faina e Civico ★ AGE 7 & UP

Piazza Duomo 29. ☎ 0763 341511. ***www.museofaina.it****.*

Two cheers for the only museum in Etruria that makes the Etruscans come alive for **children**—including English-speaking ones. There are some rare finds on display, mainly from digs around Orvieto. Notable are the striking 6th-century B.C. black-figure vases painted in Attic style by renowned Ancient Greek vase-painter Exekias, and Room XVI's **tiny bronze warriors,** horses and goddesses from 100 years earlier.

Star of the show is the **Museo dei Ragazzi** ★, where child-oriented displays help youngsters interact with the exhibits by prompting 20 questions (and answers) in English and Italian—what did Etruscans eat? How does an archaeologist work? What is a sarcophagus? Each room has its own discussion point to help you all round.

Time *45 min.* ***Open*** *9:30am–6pm daily Apr–Sept, 10am–5pm daily Oct and Mar, 10am–5pm Tues–Sun*

Nov–Feb. ***Adm*** *4.50€, 3€ children 7–12, those with bus/funicular ticket, or anyone with family.* ***Amenities***

Orvieto Underground ★

AGE 8 & UP

c/o Piazza del Duomo 23. 0763 340688. ***www.orvietounderground.it.***

The real history of Orvieto is the almost 3,000-year story of its caves: more than 1,200 artificial and natural caverns have been found in the pozzolana and tufa rock that the city sits on. Regular guided tours take in just two, under Santa Chiara convent, that have variously been used as Etruscan houses, water wells, ceramic ovens, pigeon coops, quarries and natural fridges. Most recently they were employed, unwisely, as shelters from Allied bombing of Orvieto Scalo station; a direct hit would have obliterated the soft rock.

The tour is fine for children who can climb a few steep steps **(don't bring buggies)**. Bring sweatshirts as it's always 15°C (59°F) down here.

Time *1 hr.* ***Guided tours*** *(1 hr) 11am, 12:15pm, 4pm, 5:15pm daily (only Sat and Sun in Feb).* ***Adm*** *5.50€, 4.50€ students.*

Pozzo di San Patrizio **AGE 4 & UP**

Viale Sangallo. 0763 343768.

As a feat of Renaissance engineering, there's no doubting **St. Patrick's Well** is impressive. Designed by Antonio da Sangallo the Younger in 1527, it took 10 years of digging, a 62-m (203-ft) hole and the destruction of an Etruscan tomb to strike water. Just as well no one was thirsty. The **double-helix** stairways never intersect, so that donkeys bringing water up avoided donkey down-traffic; whether any admired the dizzy view through one of the 72 internal windows isn't documented.

Time *30 min.* ***Open*** *9am–7:45pm daily May–Aug, 9am–6:45pm Mar, Apr, Sept and Oct; 10am–4:45pm Nov–Feb.* ***Adm*** *5€, 3.50€ students.*

INSIDER TIP

Better set up for impatient youngsters as it involves less walking and takes only about 10 minutes to get round, the **Pozzo della Cava** ★ (0763 342373. ***www.pozzodellacava.it***. 9am–8pm Tues–Sun. Adm 3€, 2€ children 6+ or those with funicular ticket) is another Etruscan well at Via della Cava 28.

Pozza di San Patrizio

TODI

It may be a concept your children struggle with, but **Todi ★** is a great place in which to simply *be*, not necessarily to *see*. Its sedate rhythm was hardly dented by the waves of publicity it received when chosen by University of Kentucky researchers as the planet's model sustainable city in 1991 (and after it was subsequently dubbed 'the world's ideal city' by the Italian press). In reality, it's a small hilltop town perched perfectly above the Tiber Valley, with a history stretching back beyond Rome, superb 360° views, the best piazza in Umbria—and not an Internet café to be had for love or euros.

Visitor Information

Information Centres

The **tourist office** (*075 8945416. www.comune.todi.pg.it/fap/.* 9:30am–1pm and 3–6pm Mon–Sat, plus 10am–1pm Sun in winter) is at Piazza del Popolo 38.

Arriving

By Car Todi is 40km (25 miles) south of Perugia, off the E45 *superstrada*. For the quickest route into town, take the 'Todi-Orvieto' exit and turn right by the orange building immediately after Ponterio; it heads straight up to Todi's Porta Perugiana. **Don't park** here: turn right again for the **Porta Orvietana** car park (0.90€ first hour, 0.60€/hr thereafter; 6.60€/day). A single-car funicular whizzes you up to Via Ciuffelli.

By Public Transport The **APM bus** (*075 506781. www.apmperugia.it*) stops in the centre, on Piazza Jacopone; the only useful link is with **Perugia** (1½ hr, 4.60€).

What to See & Do

Built on top of a Roman temple, Todi's **Piazza del Popolo ★★** is Umbria's most majestic medieval square, with a subtle grandeur deriving from several buildings preserved in harmony: the south side is enclosed by the **Palazzo dei Priori** (1334) with its curious trapezoidal tower; to the east stands the **Palazzo del Popolo** of 1213 and the **Palazzo del Capitano** (above the tourist office), built 30 years later. Best of the lot, Todi's **Duomo ★★** is a study in classy simplicity: its square bell-tower and plain facade draw the eye towards the rose window, added to the 12th-century structure in 1500.

Art pilgrims should make for the **Purgatorio di San Patrizio** (9–11am daily Sun–Fri. Adm free) at the Monastero di San Francesco, Via Borgo Nuovo 20. This 14th-century fresco was among the first depictions of the circles of Hell envisaged by Dante's *Divine Comedy*. Alas, it isn't possible to get really close. Signposted opposite the tourist office are the **Cisterne Romane** (*075 8944148.* 10am–1:30pm and 3–6pm Tues–Sun Apr–Oct; rest of year 10:30am–1pm and

TIP Eating Out Near Todi

For a rustic lunch break, drive down the slopes south of Todi to La Mulinella at Ponte Naia 2 (Thurs–Tues 12:30–2:30pm and 7:30–11:30pm), an exceptional restaurant set within a lovely Umbrian house and garden full of blossoms. There's a small swing, lots of room to run around, stunning views back up to the town and a menu of hearty Umbrian classics.

2:30–5pm Sat and Sun. Adm 2€, 1.50€ ages 6–25)—old water cisterns that form part of 5km (3 miles) of tunnels under Todi.

Uphill and right of San Fortunato (see below) is Todi's **Parco della Rocca,** a ruined fort with far-reaching views and a decent **playground.**

INSIDER TIP

If you're planning to stay in Todi a few days to complete the *circuito museale* (all the sights mentioned here plus the Pinacoteca), consider getting a **cumulative ticket** (7.50€, 6€ ages 15–25, 5€ children 6–14).

Foresta Fossile FIND AGE 10 & UP

Dunarobba. 0744 940348. ***www.forestafossile.it****. 14km (9 miles) south of Todi.*

A pleasant 20-minute drive from Todi lies this curious phenomenon commonly (and wrongly) called a **'petrified forest'**. In fact, these are the preserved, *not* fossilised, remains of an ancient Sequoia forest on what was once the shore of Lago Tiberino. It's **wood** of 3-million-year vintage, mummified in grey clay and only found when the brickyard next door was digging raw materials for its ovens. The 50 giant stumps, some more than 4m (13 ft) in diameter, are all inclined at a 30° angle to the east, resulting from tectonic movements in prehistory. The **Palaeontology Centre** at the entrance provides a basic introduction and tours in either Italian or English if you book ahead; otherwise, they'll let you wander around with an English-language leaflet.

Bring **hats** for children: the temperature reaches 40°C (104°F) in summer. The site isn't navigable with a buggy and becomes a clay bog in the rain. And brace yourselves: although it's an intriguing tour, the place is deeply **un-picturesque.**

Time *1 hr.* ***Guided tours*** *(1 hr) hourly; times vary considerably by month—see website for details.* ***Adm*** *5€, 3€ children 6–14.* ***Amenities***

San Fortunato AGE 3 & UP

Piazza Umberto I. 075 8945311. ***www.sistemamuseo.it****.*

Not *another* church, surely? Yes, but we're not here for (what's left of) the art. Instead, climb the 153 stairs of the bell-tower for the best **views ★** in town—into Piazza del Popolo, over the agricultural plains of the Tiber Valley, and best of all to **Santa Maria della Consolazione ★**, a monumental Renaissance church built to a Greek cross plan in perfect proportion.

Time 45 min. Open 10am–1pm and 3–6:30pm Tues–Sun Apr–Oct; 10:30am–1pm and 2:30–5pm rest of year. Adm 2€, 1.50€ ages 6–25.

MONTEFALCO

The journey is almost as much fun as the arriving in **Montefalco:** this 475-m (1,558-ft) 'Balcony of Umbria' surveys a 360° scene of wine trellises, olive groves and arable fields east to Spoleto and west to Todi. It's home to the big exception among Umbria's unheralded wines: the town's **Sagrantino di Montefalco ★★**, made from an indigenous grape and qualifying as a DOCG (p. 32)—it must be matured for 2½ years before release. Truly great years, such as **2003,** can improve in the bottle for a further 15, leaving a rich, velvety wine quite unlike neighbouring Tuscany's robust reds.

Visitor Information

Information Centres

The **Strada del Sagrantino** wine trail office doubles as tourist information (☎ *0742 378490. www. montefalcodoc.it*. 8am–6:30pm Mon–Fri and 10am–6pm Sat and Sun). It's in Piazza del Comune, on the Palazzo's left.

Arriving

Parking is plentiful and free around the walls; just follow them when you drive up. There are three **buses** a day from Perugia (11am, 1:12pm and 2pm; 5.20€).

What to See & Do

The town is anchored by the fine hexagonal **Piazza del Comune** with its 13th-century **Palazzo** tastefully embellished with a simple loggia. Down the Corso at **Sant'Agostino,** the once-extensive frescoes have long been knobbled by damp, but children with a grisly streak should check out the body of the 'Holy Pilgrim' in the right wall—this **mummified corpse** is that of an anonymous Spaniard who came to venerate the holy bones of Beata Chiarella and Beata Illuminata in the adjacent casket but reclined on a pew and died. If that doesn't satisfy youngsters, there's a shady **playground** round the back.

Back uphill in Piazza Domenico Mustafa, the nameless bar (11:30am–7:30pm Wed–Mon) serves yummy **ice cream ★** from 1.50€.

Brizi GREEN ALL AGES

Via Verdi 34–60. ☎ 0742 379165. www.frantoiobrizi.it.

Brizi is a **one-stop shop** for what Montefalco is all about. At the centre of things is an **olive oil ★** business run with passion since 1915. The *frantoio* still uses traditional granite wheels to get a complete cold press and retain the olives' vitamins. Don't be fooled by the price (7.50€ for 500ml): this is a serious oil, made only from hand-picked fruit—it's more labour of love than commercial venture. Brizio also selects small **Sagrantino** wine producers to sell for in its *cantina* (bottles from 7€)—only those whose grapes poke above the spring mists that make pesticides necessary farther downhill. Olive oil soaps (2.50€), creams and shampoos (11–13€) complete the experience.

There's also a family **trattoria** ★, where the commitment to seasonal food and simple Umbrian cooking is apparent the second you walk through the door.

Time *15 min.* ***Open*** *Shop: 10am–12:30pm and 2:30–5:30pm daily. Restaurant: 11:30am–2:30pm and 7–10pm Mon–Sat.*

Fonti del Clitunno FIND ALL AGES

0743 521141. ***www.fontidelclitunno.it.*** *1km (about half a mile) north of Campello sul Clitunno.*

The source of the river Clitunno has been a site of ancient pilgrimage and gladiator fights, admired by Pliny and rocked by a massive earthquake in A.D. 444, which reshaped the terrain. Since the 1860s it's been a small **Romantic garden;** a little patch of England on a sunbaked Umbrian plain, with weeping willows, poplars, babbling brook and a couple of swans. Even Byron liked it here. As a peaceful respite, it's only slightly marred by traffic noise and a plastic wire-fence. Don't forget to buy **duck food** (0.50€) on the way in.

Time *1 hr.* ***Open*** *8:30am–8pm daily May–Aug, 8:30am–7:30pm Apr and Sept–Mar, but long lunch closures Oct–Mar.* ***Adm*** *2€, free under-11s.* ***Amenities***

Museo Civico di San Francesco ★ AGE 5 & UP

Via Ringhiera Umbra. 0742 379598. ***www.benozzogozzoli.it.***

If his masterpiece, Pisa's Campo Santo (p. 116), hadn't been razed by Allied firebombs in World War II, **Benozzo Gozzoli** would have a higher profile. The artist's frescoed apse of this former church was his first major commission, completed in 1452; it saw him step from the shadows of Lorenzo Ghiberti (p. 48) and Fra' Angelico (p. 59), with whom he'd long collaborated. The **Life of St. Francis** ★★ will be familiar to people with Assisi (p. 207) already under their belt. To follow the story, start at his birth (lower-left), basically a *Nativity*, and work clockwise; return to the left and work clockwise again, before starting

TIP Wine in Montefalco

As you'd expect, plenty of shops sell the local wine—in fact, most places double as wine bars. **Enoteca L'Alchimista** on Piazza del Comune (*0742 378558;* Thurs–Tues about 9am–11pm) is convenient and friendly with a wide selection. The other safe bet is **Enoteca di Benozzo,** also on the piazza (about 9am–11pm, closed Thursday afternoons in winter).

on the upper-left lunette and clockwise again to Francis's death.

Elsewhere in the cavernous church, Perugino's 1503 **Nativity** ★, as much an Umbrian landscape as a devotional work, shows his mastery of skin tone and composition. Downstairs is the archaeological collection, including a reconstructed traditional wine *cantina*.

Time *45 min.* ***Open*** *10:30am–1pm and 3–7pm daily June–Aug, 10:30am–1pm and 2–6pm Mar–May, Sept and Oct, 10:30am–1pm and 2:30–5pm Tues–Sun Nov–Feb.* ***Adm*** *5€, 3€ 18–25s, 2€ 11–18s.* ***Amenities***

SPOLETO

Provincial backwater for 11 months of the year, **Spoleto** ★ is centre of the Italian arts world for the other. Though largely without the medieval air that wafts about Assisi and Todi, it was once the seat of a Duchy that ruled central Italy as far south as Naples. The **Duomo** is the equal of Todi's, and the town itself trumps anywhere in Umbria for **Roman heritage.** Though arty, it has a welcoming feel and a fair degree of accessibility, even with young children. Its crooked streets and hidden corners are ideal for getting pleasantly lost.

Visitor Information

Information Centres

Spoleto treats its guests well: the huge, helpful **tourist office** (*0743 238920.* ***www.comune.spoleto.pg.it***. 8:30am–1:30pm and 4–7pm Mon–Sat, 9:30am–12:30pm and 4–7pm Sun Apr–Sept; rest of year 8:30am–1:30pm and 3:30–6:30pm Mon–Sat, 9:30am–12:30pm and 3:30–6:30pm Sun) is at Piazza della Libertà 7. Independent ***www.prospoleto.it*** is also useful.

Arriving

By Train If you're based close to a station, Spoleto is a great place to visit by **rail** (*892021.* ***www.trenitalia.it***). Hourly services from **Perugia** (via Foligno; 1¼ hr, 4.15€) stop here. From outside the station, take bus A, B or C to Piazza Carducci on the edge of the Old Town (it has plenty of room for buggies). Don't try to walk up (20–30 min) with young children. Bus tickets (1€) are sold at the **Centro Servizi Stazione** on the platform.

TIP Spoleto Discounted

If you plan to see everything in town, the Spoleto Card can make it cheaper, allowing free access to public buses and seven museums (including all those listed here). One-day cards are 12€, 8€ for 6–25s; 2 days costs 16€ and 12€ for 6–25s.

A Walk in the Woods

There's plenty to explore on foot or by mountain-bike on the wooded slopes of **Monteluco,** but it's just as easy to dip your toe in with a 1-hour circuit starting by the gatehouse of the **Rocca Albornoziana** in Piazza Campello. From the piazza walk up Via del Ponte and buy water from **Bar La Portella** as you pass—it's your last chance. Round the bend, you'll catch a first (and best—snap now) view of the 14th-century **Ponte delle Torri** ★, 236m (774 ft) long, with nine pillars, standing 90m (295 ft) above the Tessino river. It has become the emblem of Spoleto. Unbelievably, it was built on top of a Roman aqueduct. Exactly how *that* was engineered remains a mystery.

Once you're over the bridge, drink in the silence, birdsong and views back to Spoleto from the woods; **Michelangelo** came here to chill out, too. Turn right and continue on the road parallel to the river as far as **San Pietro** church, with its facade **reliefs** ★ ranking second only to Orvieto's (p. 225). They narrate obscure medieval allegories, although (as in Orvieto) demons torturing sinners are rendered with particular relish.

From the church, cross the busy road and take the second right. Straight ahead (5 min) is **Piazza della Libertà;** the park on your left has a shaded **playground** for children who need more action.

By Car The town sits on top of the old Roman Via Flaminia, now the **SS3,** 26km (16 miles) north of Terni. There's usually plenty of **parking,** but the easiest option is to make for the **Spoletosfera** car park signposted from the SS3 *Spoleto sud* exit (0.80€/hr). It's a 5–10-minute (flat) walk to Piazza della Libertà via underground moving walkways.

Family-Friendly Events

If it's culture you're after, come in late June: the **Spoleto Festival** (*www.spoletofestival.it*), now one of Europe's leading arts and music festivals, hosts classical music, dance and opera in unique settings around town. Book months in advance and expect to pay... well, more than you'd expect (hotels here have three seasons: low, high and Festival).

What to See & Do

A ramp down into Piazza del Duomo makes for a suitably grand prelude to Spoleto's architectural highlight, the **Cattedrale di Santa Maria dell'Assunta** ★★ (✆ *0743 231063.* Daily 8:30am–12:30pm and 3:30–7pm), which although obviously built in stages retains a harmony equalled only by Todi's Duomo (p. 228). Even the addition of a Renaissance balcony and portico to the 12th-century structure managed not to mess up the facade. Inside, the apse is covered with **frescoes** ★

tracing the life of the Virgin Mary, begun by **Filippo Lippi** (p. 62) and completed by assistants after he died.

Children might prefer the spooky crypt of **Sant' Isacco** ★ beneath 11th-century **Sant'Ansano** (8am–noon and 3–6:30pm daily in summer, 8am–noon and 3–5:30pm rest of year). The sarcophagus allegedly contains the body of Sant' Isacco, who died in 552. The church is by the Roman **Arco del Druso:** look how much the street level has risen since that was built.

Its location at the Piazza Vittoria end of Viale Trento e Trieste (no. 29) isn't exactly convenient, but don't miss **Colder Gelateria** ★★ (12:30pm–midnight daily), whose ice cream (notably 'bread and chocolate' flavour; 1.50€–3€) is the best we've found in Umbria.

Casa Romana AGE 3 & UP

Via di Visiale. ✆ 0743 234250. ***www.sistemamuseo.it.***

Spoletium had a strong Roman heritage and an especially brutal reputation for martyring Christians—its amphitheatre needed an ingenious drainage system to whisk away the blood. This fantastically preserved **Roman house** beneath Piazza del Comune obviously belonged to someone rich, though there's little evidence that that someone was Emperor Vespasian's *mamma*, as previously claimed. What's left of the frescoed plaster gives an idea of how it was decorated 2,000 years ago.

Time *30 min.* ***Open*** *11am–6pm Mon–Thurs, 10:30am–7pm Fri–Sun.* ***Adm*** *2.50€, 2€ 15–25s, 1€ 7–14s.* ***Amenities*** 🛍

Rocca Albornoziana AGE 5 & UP

Piazza Campello. ✆ 0743 224952.

The most fierce-looking castle in Umbria was built in the 14th century for the papal governors of Spoleto; Lucrezia Borgia lived here (1499–1502), and Mussolini used it as a prison. Much of the interior is now occupied by the **Museo Nazionale del Ducato di Spoleto** (*✆ 0743 223055*), which chronicles the history of the city from Roman times to the Renaissance, with an ensemble of richly inscribed sarcophagi, mosaics and plenty of religious art and statuary.

Exploring the battlements of the *rocca* itself will appeal more to children, though don't miss the **frescoes** in the Camera Pinta, in the **Torre Maestra.** Uncovered during recent restoration, they were commissioned by governor Marino Tomacelli around 1400—the artist is unknown.

Time *2 hr.* ***Open*** *10am–6pm Mon, 9am–6pm Tues–Sun; museum open 9am–1:30pm Tues–Sun.* ***Adm*** *6€, 5€ 15–25s, 2.50€ 7–14s; museum 6€, 3€ children; castle and museum 7.50€, 6.50€ 15–25s, 3.50€ 7–14s.*

THE FAR SOUTH

Economically, the south of Umbria is dominated by **Terni.** This industrial town, in a bowl of rolling agricultural plains, isn't somewhere you'll want to linger, but it's at the centre of some attractions that escape the art-heavy bias. The rugged **Valnerina** is Umbria's action-holiday capital—with white water, quiet campsites and remote hillsides ideal for family outdoor fun. Archaeological sites at **Narni** and **Carsulae,** meanwhile, are intriguing enough to be accessible for all bar the very youngest.

Carsulae ★ ALL AGES

San Gémini Fonte. ☎ 0744 334133.

Tourists have been coming to this windswept hill for more than 2,000 years: Umbria's largest **Roman** site was once a popular resort with the Empire's wealthy. Although some of the monumental blocks were recycled to build the 11th-century church of **San Gemini,** much of what remains is easily identifiable. You can walk right into the **amphitheatre,** just as gladiators did when Carsulae was an important town in the 3rd century B.C. Best of all, stroll along the ancient high street, on the limestone flagstones of the **Via Flaminia,** past the Forum and Temple of Gemini and out of the main gate to the necropolis. One circuit is an easy hour.

Strictly speaking, there's **no picnicking,** but if you sneak in a roll for the children and dispose of litter properly, you'll probably be spared jail.

Time *1 hr.* ***Open*** *8:30am–7:30pm daily Apr–Sept, 8:30am–5:30pm rest of year.* ***Adm*** *5€, 3.50€ ages 18–25, 2.50€ under-18s.* ***Amenities***

Cascata delle Marmore

ALL AGES

☎ 0744 62982. 6km (4 miles) east of Terni on SS209.

You don't come across a waterfall that runs to a timetable very often, but the 165-m (541-ft) **Marmore Falls** aren't quite what they seem. The problem of what to do about regular flooding on the Rieti plain above was first tackled by the Romans in 271 B.C.: they cut a channel to create an **artificial cascade** into the River Nera. Patchy success was followed by inevitable local squabbles until the falls took their current shape, in 1786.

The whole area is now a **landscaped park,** with four marked trails up and around the roaring water, of varying degrees of difficulty; with a **buggy,** you're limited to standing at the bottom getting sprayed (it's just 250m/ 820 ft to the lower viewpoint). Because the water now powers a hydroelectric station, it isn't always going when you want it to, but the **timetable** (see ***www.marmore.it*** or any Umbrian tourist office) accommodates visitor demands—there's more action Saturdays and Sundays and in summer.

Cascata delle Marmore

Wild Rides

Just over the hills from Spoleto, the Valnerina is Umbria's white-water rafting ★★ capital. The following outfits run three to four trips a day; book ahead and take clothes that you don't mind getting wet. There's no need for special skills (or even to understand Italian).

Pangea (*☎ 348 7711170.* ***www.pangea-italia.com***), based in Scheggino, caters for children aged 3 and up: a half-day session is 45€ for adults, 35€ for under-18s (1-hr trips are 15–25€).

Gaia (*☎ 338 7678308.* ***www.asgaia.it***) charges 22€ (17€ for under-12s) for 1 hr and 33€ (22€ for under-12s) for 2 hr from its base 6km (4 miles) outside Norcia.

Rafting Umbria (*☎ 348 3511798.* ***www.raftingumbria.it***) runs 2-hr trips along the Corno from Serravalle di Norcia; it's 35€ for adults, 25€ for children 4 to 14.

Finally, **Activo Park** (*☎ 0743 618005.* ***www.activopark.com***), also in Scheggino 12km (7 miles) south of Spoleto, acts as a one-stop shop for the area's extreme sports, with 'full' tickets (25€, 15€ children) including tubing, canopy walking, archery and even zorbing. A two-bedroom wooden chalet at **Campeggio Il Drago** (*☎ 0743 751070.* ***www.campeggioildrago.it***) makes a suitably adventurous base for budding rafters. Prices are 70€ to 90€ per night.

Time *1 hr.* ***Open*** *10am–10pm Mon–Fri, 9am–10pm Sat and Sun June–Sept; 10am–7pm Mon–Fri, 9am–10pm Sat and Sun Apr and May; 10am–6pm Mon–Fri, 10am–10pm Sat and Sun Mar; 11am–5pm Mon–Fri, 10am–6pm Sat and Sun Feb; 11am–5pm Sat and Sun Jan; 10am–6pm Mon–Fri, Sat and Sun 10am–8pm Oct; 11am–5pm Mon–Fri, 1am–5pm Sat and Sun Nov and Dec.* ***Adm*** *5€, 2.50€ children 6–12.* ***Amenities***

Le Mummie di Ferentillo ★

AGE 10 & UP

Chiesa di Santo Stefano, Ferentillo. ☎ 0743 54395. 17km (11 miles) northeast of Terni on SS209.

In the jagged shadows of the Valnerina (the valley of the Nera river) is a phenomenon usually linked with the Egyptian desert: **mummies.** For centuries, the dusty crypt of Santo Stefano was also Ferentillo's graveyard. Dry air, porous soil and a fungus that ate organisms causing putrefaction, mummified several corpses. It's a **gruesome** roll-call of desiccated death: French soldiers tortured and hanged during the Napoleonic wars; Chinese 'honeymooners' (more likely Christian pilgrims) dead from cholera; a lawyer stabbed 27 times; even a bell-ringer who fell from his tower. All died here, and each remains frozen in a final agony: this ghoulish sight **absolutely isn't a place to bring young or sensitive children.**

Repeated thefts mean visits are by **guided tour** only, but they run regularly and are pretty loose. You may be given an English handout and left to it.

Time *30 min.* ***Open*** *9am–12:30pm and 2:30–7:30pm daily Apr–Sept, 9am–12:30pm and 2:30–6pm daily Mar and Oct; 9:30am–noon and 2:30–5pm Nov–Feb; regular guided tours (15 min).* ***Adm*** *3€.*

Narni Sotterranea AGE 12 & UP

Via San Bernardo 12, Narni. ☎ 0744 722292. ***www.narnisotterranea.it.***

When the Romans arrived here, they scrapped the town's ancient name and gave it 'Narnia'—perhaps later nicked by **C. S. Lewis.** The highlights of its eerie 'underground' tour have a more recent vintage: the tiny frescoed church of **Sant' Angelo,** carved from rock and hidden until 1979, was already here when the Dominicans arrived in 1303. They found a more sinister use for other passageways and cellars: the **torture** room used by their Holy Inquisition is under the abbey altar. An adjacent cell, covered in 18th-century **graffiti,** is one for family cryptographers: spot masonic and Jesuit symbols, the 14 Stations of the Cross, and the repetitive numeric palindrome '07 24 42 70'. Weird.

It's a fascinating historical tour but one without concessions to young ones; there's a **playground** by the entrance if you want to operate split-shifts.

Time *1 hr.* ***Guided tours*** *(1 hr) 10am, 11:15am, 12:30pm, 3pm, 4:15pm and 5:30pm Sun, 3pm and 6pm Sat Apr–Oct; 11am, 12:15pm, 3pm and 4:15pm Sun Nov–Mar.* ***Adm*** *5€, free under-14s.*

FAMILY-FRIENDLY DINING

Brizi, Montefalco, see p. 230.

Coccorone ★★ VALUE UMBRIAN

Largo Tempestivi (behind Palazzo del Comune), Montefalco. ☎ 0742 379535. ***www.coccorone.com.***

We dread to think how much a dining experience of this **quality** would cost back home: the Umbrian and local dishes are cooked and presented perfectly, the service is attentive without being annoyingly hovering, and the wine list would make a Michelin-starred restaurant proud. At no point are you made to feel unwelcome or intimidated, even with noisy children. Little ones can play it safe with *pasta al pomodoro* (with tomato sauce) or veal cutlets. For the daring there's beef in Sagrantino wine, lamb with truffles or snail kebabs. The outdoor cover charge (3€pp) is a bit steep but beneath the parasols on the terrace is the best spot.

Open *12:30–3pm and 7–10pm Thurs–Tues (plus Wed in summer).* ***Main courses*** *8€–22 €.* ***Credit*** *MC, V.* ***Amenities*** *⛩*

La Loggia dei Priori ★★

SOUTHERN UMBRIAN

Vicolo del Comune 4, Narni. ☎ 0744 726843. ***www.loggiadeipriori.it.***

The **oldest restaurant** in Narni's old town is also the best, with a vaulted, dark interior complemented by a rear terrace that makes up in cool shade for what it lacks in panorama. The short, classy menu screams 'proper restaurant'. Adventurous eaters might fancy start-to-finish black truffles: *crostini* to *tagliolini* or *gnocchi* to fillet steak with shavings on top. There are **no half-portions,** but staff are happy for you to order a selection of pasta and meat and split it up (if you do, note that *secondi* portions aren't huge).

Open *12:30–3pm and 7:30–9:30pm daily.* ***Main courses*** *8€–11€.* ***Credit*** *MC, V.*

Osteria del Trivio UMBRIAN/ITALIAN

Via del Trivio 16, Spoleto. ☎ 0743 44349. ***www.osteriadeltrivio.it****.*

It's worth the trek down steep streets and steps for this taste of lunch in a proper Umbrian trattoria. The menu changes daily, but if you can, try the stuffed artichokes or divine *funghi sanguinosi* pasta (with 'bloody mushrooms', named after their bright-red colour and usually served in autumn). Whenever you visit, you'll have a choice of hearty plates of homemade gnocchi, tagliatelle and ravioli, and plenty of rich, filling mains such as *pollo alla cacciatore* (chicken stew).

Open *12:30–2:30pm and 5–10pm Wed–Mon.* ***Main courses*** *6€–16€.* ***Credit*** *AE, MC, V.*

Pane e Vino PIZZA & PASTA/UMBRIAN

Via Ciuffelli 33, Todi. ☎ 075 8945448. ***www.panevinotodi.com****.*

This exceptional spot for lunch or dinner, just 50m (164 ft) or so from the top of Todi's funicular, is tucked away in a lovely nook between two medieval stone buildings. You'll find all the basics here but the specialty is black Noria **truffles:** thick, Umbrian *strangozzi* pasta with truffles (10€) and beef or lamb with truffles for 15€ to 16€ are our faves. **Vegetarians** shouldn't miss the pumpkin risotto (9.50€).

Open *Noon–2:30pm and 7–10pm Thurs–Tues.* ***Main courses*** *8€–15€.* ***Credit*** *MC, V.*

Trattoria Tipica Etrusca ★ ORVIETAN

Via Maitani 10, Orvieto. ☎ 0763 344016.

In a town full of self-service joints, the Etrusca offers a bite with a bit of **class.** Its location within sight of the Duomo doesn't preclude a commitment to quality food and attentive service—and the **air-con** sure helps in summer. Tuscan classics such as *pappardelle* with hare sauce, grilled sausages, wild boar, pigeon, spring lamb and lashings of truffles (even in the ice cream) are served with a smile, *especially* to picky youngsters.

Open *Noon–3pm and 7:15–10pm daily (exc. Mon in winter).* ***Main courses*** *7€–15€.* ***Credit*** *AE, MC, V.*

INSIDER TIP

For something quicker in Orvieto (but not necessarily cheaper; main dishes 9€–14€), the oft-recommended self-service **Al San Francesco** (*0763 343302. www.ristorantealsanfrancesco.it*) opposite Trattoria Tipica Etrusca at Via B. Cerretti 10 does fine, as long as there isn't a tour bus in.

FAMILY-FRIENDLY ACCOMMODATION

The **Spoleto Festival** skews prices and availability across Umbria's central belt from mid-June into July: book ahead. For more ideas on hotels and accommodation, see p. 27.

APARTMENTS, VILLAS & FARM-STAYS

Campo al Vento ★★ FIND

*Voc. Coste Faena 61, 3km (2 miles) south of Monte Castello di Vibio. 075 8796044. **www.campoalvento.it**. 20km (12 miles) north of Todi; take Fratta Todina–Montecastello di Vibio exit off E45.*

You're never far from the middle of nowhere in Umbria, and this *agriturismo*'s breezy hillside 20 minutes from Todi certainly qualifies. The **18th-century stone farmhouse,** converted into three apartments and four double/twin B&B rooms in 2007, has new wooden furniture in sympathy with the exposed beams and tiled interiors. The effect is airy, stylish but still rustic. The owner will book your family excursions with a local riding school and also give cooking lessons and teach you how to make soap (he produces organic olive oil, chickens and wine). In August, it's weekly (Sat–Sat) bookings only.

Apartments** 3. **Rooms** 4. **Rates** Double 60€, apartment 120€. **Credit** MC, V. **Amenities** **In room

La Torriola

*Pian di San Martino, Todi 333 4950860. **www.torriola.com**. 2km (just over 1 mile) from E45 Todi-Orvieto exit via SS448.*

This gorgeous farmhouse west of Todi houses five apartments comfortably sleeping six on a farm that still produces its own wine and cold-pressed extra-virgin olive oil. Children are well catered for with plenty of open space, gardens, table tennis, a pool and a small playground, all with fabulous views of Todi. Apartments are normally available on a weekly basis (Sat–Sat) but exceptions can be made if you book well in advance (especially off-season).

***Apartments** 5. **Rates** 100€–240€/night. **Credit** MC, V. **Amenities** **In apartment** A/C*

Villa della Genga ★ GREEN

*0743 521186. **www.leterrediporeta.it**. 2km (just over 1 mile) south of Campello del Clitunno.*

At the centre of a sustainable, organic olive oil estate, this complex of 17th-century country houses is a grand base within 20 minutes of Spoleto, Spello and Montefalco. The spacious, well-equipped country kitchens match the terracotta-tiled living

Villa della Genga

areas and cool bedrooms—even the pool is **stylish.** Outside, manicured grounds look out over the Vale of Spoleto without even the sound of a Vespa to disturb your slumber. If the mood grabs you, there are truffle-hunting and horse-riding treks.

Apartments *6.* ***Rates*** *750€–1650€/wk.* ***Credit*** *MC, V.* ***Amenities*** ***In apartment***

CAMPSITE

Campeggio Il Drago, Cascia, see p. 236.

HOTELS/BED & BREAKFASTS

Gattapone ★★

Via del Ponte 6, Spoleto. 0743 223447. www.hotelgattapone.it.

If you don't pay 200€ a night very often, this is one place you'll probably be happy to do so. It's terraced into the precipice below Spoleto's castle, and its silent setting gives guests the sensation of **countryside serenity** just 2 minutes uphill from the Duomo. This is simultaneously a chic rural retreat and a modern, stylish urban hotel. The three family rooms for up to four are all suites with a simple, tasteful but compact main room with a raised double-bed area, and extra sleeping in the annex room, where there is a TV. Each suite has a spectacular panorama of the **Ponte delle Torri;** bathrooms have tubs. You'll need to bring your own travel cot.

Rooms *15.* ***Rates*** *Double 120€–170€, suite 170€–230€, extra beds 30€. Breakfast included.* ***Credit*** *AE, MC, V.* ***Amenities*** ***In room***

INSIDER TIP

If the Gattapone's full, or too expensive, the 21-room **Hotel Charleston ★** by San Domenico (*0743 220052. www.hotelcharleston.it*) is a great second choice in Spoleto, with triples and quads from 99€ and 105€.

Valentino VALUE

Via Angelo da Orvieto 30–32, Orvieto 0763 342464. www.valentinohotel.com.

A few nights in Orvieto can have lots of appeal as a prelude to—or a splurge after—staying in the Umbrian countryside. This friendly, great-value **hotel** in a restored Renaissance palace is conveniently located just off the main drag and a 15-minute walk from the funicular; its comfy triples are big enough for a family of four. You also get free Wi-Fi—not so common around these parts.

Rooms *19.* ***Rates*** *Double 80€–95€, triple 95€–120€, extra bed 30€, cot 10€. Breakfast free if booked online; otherwise 6.50€.* ***Credit*** *MC, V.* ***Amenities*** ***In room***

Index

A

Abbazia di Sant'Antimo (Montalcino), 4, 179
Abbey of San Galgano, 156
Accommodation, 8, 15, 27–31
  central Tuscany, 94, 102, 107, 110–112
  Florence, 76–78
  northern Tuscany, 138–140
  northern Umbria, 205, 218–220
  southern Tuscany, 190–192
  southern Umbria, 239–240
  Tuscan coast, 163–166
Acquario (Porto Santo Stefano), 161
Acquario di Talamone, 160
Active families, activities for, 66–67
Acuto, Giovanni, 50
Adoration of the Magi (Leonardo da Vinci), 53
Adoration of the Magi (Pietro Perugino), 6, 200
Agriturismi (farm-stays), 8, 29
  Tuscany, 110–111, 138, 139, 166, 190
  Umbria, 219, 220, 239
Air travel, 22
alab'Arte (Volterra), 98, 99
Alabaster, 98, 99
Allegories of Good and Bad Government (Ambrogio Lorenzetti), 6, 86
Ammannati, Bartolomeo, 51
Annunciation (Donatello), 56
Annunciation (Fra' Angelico), 59, 170
Annunciation (Leonardo da Vinci), 53
Annunciation (Piero della Francesca), 6, 200
Annunciation (Simone Martini), 52
Anticamera sel Concistoro (Siena), 86
Antiques fairs, 103, 124
Apartment rental, 8
  Florence, 76–77
  Tuscany, 110–112, 138–139, 163–165
  Umbria, 218–220, 239–240
Apuane Alps, 114
Arco del Druso (Spoleto), 233
Arezzo, 80, 103–108
Art museums and galleries, 6–7, 57, 64. *See also specific entries*
Asciano, 89
AS Livorno, 143, 146
Assisi, 4, 194, 205–209, 217–219
Assumption of the Virgin (Taddeo di Bartolo), 174
Astiludio (Volterra), 98
ATMs, 15
Audouin's gull, 145

B

Baby supplies, 15, 17
Bagno Vignoni, 180
Balestro del Girifalco (Massa Marittima), 155
Baptistery
  Pisa, 116, 118, 120
  Pistoia, 128
  Volterra, 98
Barabarca, 153
Bargello, 59
Bar La Portella (Spoleto), 233
Basilica di San Francesco
  Arezzo, 105, 106
  Assisi, 6, 194, 196, 206–208
Basilica di Sant'Ubaldo (Gubbio), 213
Battistero
  Florence, 48–49
  Siena, 88
Bay of Quercetano, 147
B&Bs, 27–29, 78, 191
Beaches, 4
  Tuscany, 132, 147–148, 153, 157, 159–162
  Umbria, 203
Bellini, Giovanni, 53
Benedict (saint), 178
Benicasa, Catherine. *See* Catherine of Siena (saint)
Biblioteca delle Oblate (Florence), 65
Bicycle rides, 4, 27
  Florence, 66
  Tuscany, 121, 125–126
  Umbria, 203, 233
Biduino, 120
Birdwatching, 133, 143, 157–158, 160
Birrificio (San Quirico d'Orcia), 180
The Birth of Venus (Sandro Boticelli), 52, 53
Boboli Garden. *See* Giardino di Boboli (Florence)
Bolgheri, 149
Bonanno Pisano, 120
Books, on Italy, 30, 31
Borgo Medioevale, 157
Botticelli, Sandro, 6, 52, 53
Bravio delle Botti (Montepulciano), 18, 173
Brizi (Montefalco), 230–231
Brunelleschi, Filippo, 48, 49
Buccellato, 125
Burlmacco, 132
Buses, 23, 26
Butteri, 159

C

Cabinovia Marciana (Elba), 152, 154
Calcio, 18, 19, 48, 65–66, 143, 146
Calcio Storico (Florence), 18, 48
Camping, 8, 30, 31
  Florence, 77
  Tuscany, 112, 129, 139, 166, 190–191
  Umbria, 219, 220

Campo dei Miracoli (Pisa), 114–118
Campo Santo (Pisa), 116, 117, 231
Canoeing, 159, 196, 203, 205
Cantiere delle Navi Antiche di Pisa, 3, 115, 118–119
Capella del Tau (Pistoia), 128
Capella di Montesiepi, 156
Capella di Santa Caterina (Siena), 89
Cappella Brancacci (Florence), 61–62
Caravaggio, Michelangelo Merisi da, 54, 161
Carnevale (Viareggio), 17, 115, 131
Carnevale Aretino Orciolaia (Arezzo), 17, 103
Carrara, 134, 135
Car rental, 25
Carsulae, 222, 234, 235
Casa di Santa Caterina (Siena), 89
Casa di Vasari (Arezzo), 105
Casa Napoleone (Elba), 154
Casa Roman (Spoleto), 234
Cascata delle Marmore (Terni), 235, 236
Cascine market (Florence), 68
Casentino, 106
Cashpoints, 15
Castagneto Carducci, 149
Castellina, 101
Castello
  Populonia Alta, 149
  Sarteano, 183
Castello dei Conti Guidi (Vinci), 106, 129
Castiglione del Lago, 204
Castiglione della Pescaia, 157–158, 162
Cathedral of Santa Maria Assunta (Orvieto), 225–226
Catherine of Siena (saint), 89, 180
Cattedrale di San Francesco (Livorno), 145
Cattedrale di San Lorenzo (Perugia), 197, 199
Cattedrale di San Martino (Lucca), 126–127
Cattedrale di Santa Maria Assunta (Montepulciano), 174
Cattedrale di Santa Maria del Fiore (Duomo) (Florence), 7, 39, 49–51
Cattedrale di Santa Maria dell'Assunta (Spoleto), 233
Cattedrale di San Zeno (Pistoia), 128
Cattedrale San Cerbone Vescovo (Massa Marittima), 156
Cavallino Matto Fun Park, 148
Cavoli, 4, 153
Cavriglia Nature Park (Castellina), 101
Cellini, Benvenuto, 51
Cell phones, 33
Central Tuscany, 80–112
  accommodation, 110–112
  Arezzo, 103–107
  dining, 107–110
  San Gimignano, 90–96
  Siena, 80–90
  visitor information, 80–82, 91, 93, 96, 103
  Volterra, 96–102
Certosa di Pisa, 120–121
Chianti, 4, 100–101
Chiesa di San Martino (Sarteano), 183
Children
  inteterested, in Italy, 16
  kit for, 19, 20
Chiosco degli Sportivi (Florence), 66
Chiostro Grande (Pienza), 177–178
Chiostro Verde (Florence), 56
Chiusi, 168, 173, 181–182, 190
Chocolatiers, 73, 200, 201, 225
Christ Judge (Fra' Angelico), 226
Churches, 6, 33. *See also specific churches*
Ciclopìsta dell'Arno (Florence), 66
Ciliegiolo grapes, 184
Cimabue, Cenni di Pepo, 52
Cisterne Romane (Todi), 228, 229
Città di Castello, 214–216, 218
Città Nuova (Massa Marittima), 155
Città Vecchio (Massa Marittima), 156
Climate, 16–17
Collezione Burri (Città di Castello), 215
Colonnata, 135
Coloriamo I Cieli (Castiglione-del-Lago), 18, 203
Consorzio del Vino Nobile di Montepulciano, 107, 175
Contucci (Montepulciano), 175
Corpus Domini (Orvieto), 224, 225
Corridoio Vasariano (Florence), 61
Cortona, 168–171, 189, 192
Cosimo I (Giambologna), 51
Costa degli Estruschi, 147–149
Cowboys, 159
Credit cards, 14–16
Cremí (Arezzo), 105
Crucifixion (Iacopo Salimbeni), 200
Crucifixion (Pietro Lorenzetti), 208
Currency, 14
Customs, 13

D

Dante Alighieri, 56
David, 59
David (Michelangelo Buonarotti), 51, 58–59, 135
Day trips, from Florence, 67
Debit cards, 14–16
Deposition (Fra' Angelico), 59
Deposition (Pietro Lorenzetti), 208
Deposition (Rosso Fiorentino), 6, 99
Diavolino, 158
Dining, 7–8, 15, 31–32
  central Tuscany, 98, 101, 107–110
  Florence, 69, 72–76
  northern Tuscany, 136–138
  northern Umbria, 204–205, 209, 216–218
  southern Tuscany, 183, 186–190
  southern Umbria, 229, 231, 237–239
  Tuscan coast, 149, 162–163
Disabilities, travellers with, 13, 14
Dodecapoli, 171
Donatello, 55, 56
Doni Tondo (Michelangelo Buonarotti), 53
Dress, appropriate, 18–19, 208
Driving, 19, 22–25
Duccio di Buoninsegna, 52, 88, 199
Duomo
  Chiusi, 181
  Città di Castello, 215
  Florence, 7, 39, 49–51

Orvieto, 6, 225, 226
Pienza, 177
Pisa, 116, 117, 119
Siena, 85, 88
Spoleto, 232
Todi, 228, 233
Volterra, 98

E

Easter Week, 206
Ecomuseo dell'Alabastro (Volterra), 99
Effeto Venezia (Livorno), 144
Elba, 142, 149–154, 163–165
Elderly travellers, 13
Elias, Brother, 207
Enoteca del Chianti Classico (Greve), 100
Enoteca della Fortezza (Elba), 152
Enoteca di Benozzo (Montefalco), 231
Enoteca Duomo (Orvieto), 226
Enoteca Italiana (Siena), 86
Enoteca La Fortezza (Montalcino), 180
Enoteca L'Alchimista (Montefalco), 231
Enoteca Properzio (Spello), 211
Enoteca Vanni (Lucca), 125
Enthroned Madonna (Taddeo di Bartolo), 99
Entry requirements, 12, 13
Equestrian shows, 159
Eremo delle Carceri (Assisi), 208–209
Estruscan coast, 147–149
Etruscans, 171, 181
Eugubine Tablets, 214
Eurochocolate (Perugia), 18, 196, 197
Euros, 14
Events, family-friendly, 5, 17, 18
central Tuscany, 82, 83, 93, 98, 103
Florence, 44, 48
northern Tuscany, 117, 124, 131–132
northern Umbria, 197, 203, 206, 210, 213
southern Tuscany, 173, 178–179, 185
southern Umbria, 224, 232, 233
Tuscan coast, 144, 155, 161
Exchange rate, 14
Expulsion from Eden (Masaccio), 61

F

Fabbriche di Careggine, 134
Facciatone (Siena), 88
Fantiscritti, 135
Farm-stays. *See Agriturismi*
Festa dei Ceri (Gubbio), 18, 213
Festa del Grillo (Florence), 18, 48
Festa della Rificolona (Florence), 18, 48
Festa di San Francesco (Assisi), 206
Festa di San Giovanni (Florence), 48
Festa di San Ranieri (Pisa), 18, 117
Festivals. *See* Events, family-friendly
Fetovaia, 4, 143, 152, 153
Field of Miracles (Pisa), 114–118
Fiera delle Messi (San Gimignano), 93
Fiesole, 67
Fiorentina football team, 65–66
Fiorentino, Rosso, 6, 99
Firenze Musei (Florence), 49
Fishing, 132, 203
Florence, 4, 38–78, 80, 173
accommodation, 76–78
for active families, 66–67
day trips, 67
dining, 69, 72–76
events, 44, 48
history, 41
indoor activities, 64, 65
Oltrarno, 60–64
Piazza del Duomo, 48–51
Piazza della Signoria, 51–56
San Marco area, 58–60
Santa Maria Novella area, 56–58
shopping, 67–69
spectator sports, 65–66
visitor information, 38–44
Fontana dei Matti (Gubbio), 212
Fontana di Bacco (Florence), 62
Fontana Maggiore (Perugia), 197
Fontebranda (Siena), 83, 89
Fonte Gaia (Siena), 83
Fonti del Citunno (Montefalco), 231
Food shops, 89–90, 123, 145, 156
Football, 18, 19, 48, 65–66, 143, 146
Foresta Fossile (Todi), 229
Foro Romano (Assisi), 209
Forte di Belvedere (Florence), 67
Fortezza di Santa Barbara (Siena), 5, 85–86
Fortezza Medicea
Arezzo, 104
Elba, 152
Fortezza Medicea Girifalco (Cortona), 5, 171
Fortezza Nuovo (Livorno), 144
Fortezza Vecchio (Livorno), 144
Fountain of Neptune (Bartolomeo Ammannati), 51
Four Slaves (Michelangelo Buonarotti), 59
Fra' Angelico, 59, 170, 226, 231
Francis (saint), 106, 204, 206, 208
Frantoio Ragani (Spello), 211
Free activities, 4, 15
Fresco-painting classes, 55, 56
Funivia Colle Eletto (Gubbio), 213

G

Gaddi, Taddeo, 56
Galeria Palatina (Florence), 63
Galgano Guidotti, 156
Galileo Galilei, 54, 56, 119
Galleria degli Uffizi (Florence), 6, 39, 43, 49, 52–54
Galleria del Costume (Florence), 62
Galleria dell'Accademia (Florence), 39, 44, 49, 58–59, 62
Galleria Nazionale dell'Umbria (Perugia), 6, 199, 200
Garfagnana, 114, 134–136
Gattavecchi (Montepulciano), 175
Gelato, 8, 32, 74
Gelato World Champions, 82
Gentileschi, Artemisia, 54
Ghiberti, Lorenzo, 48, 54, 231
Giambologna, 51
Giardini Pubblici (Chiusi), 181
Giardino Bardini (Florence), 67
Giardino Comunale (Orvieto), 224

Giardino di Boboli (Florence), 4, 39, 43, 62, 63, 66
Giardino Zoologico di Pistoia, 5, 115, 130–131
Gioco del Ponte (Pisa), 18, 117
Giostra del Saracino (Arezzo), 18, 103
Giotto di Bondone, 5, 52, 56, 196, 206–208
"Golden Legend" (Jacopo da Varagine), 105
Golfo di Baratti, 148
Gozzoli, Benozzo, 94, 96, 231
Graffiti, 130, 237
Greve, 100
Grosseto, 157
Grotta del Vento (Vergemoli), 135
Gubbio, 4, 194, 212–214, 216
Guido d'Arezzo, 105

H

Health, 20–21
Hiking, 159–161, 179, 214
Holidays, 17
Honey, 178
Horse racing, 5, 17, 82, 83
Horta Leonini (San Quirico d'Orcia), 180
Hostels, 29, 77, 139
Hotels, 27–29. *See also* Accommodation

I

Ice cream, 8, 32, 74, 82
Il Biancone statue (Florence), 52
Il Porcellino statue (Florence), 52
Indoor activities, 3, 64, 65
Infiorate (Spello), 18, 210, 224
Innamorata, 153
Insurance, 20
Isacco (saint), 233
Isola Capraia, 145
Isola Giglio, 160, 161
Isola Maggiore, 203–205
Isola Polvese, 203, 205

J

Jacopo da Varagine, 105
Jacopo della Quercia, 127
Jewish Museum (Pitigliano), 170, 185, 186
Judith Slaying Holofernes (Artemisia Gentileschi), 54

L

Labirinto di Porsenna (Chiusi), 170, 182
La Bottega dei Ragazzi (Florence), 5, 65
La Bottega del Cioccolato di Andrea Bianchini (Florence), 73
La Caduta delle Foglie (Lodovico Tommasi), 146
La Collegiata (San Gimignano), 86, 94, 95
Lacona, 153
La Fortezza (Montalcino), 179, 180
Lago di Massaciuccoli, 133
Lago di Vagli, 134
Lago Trasimeno, 4, 194, 196, 202–205
La Lizza (Siena), 85
Lamentation over the Dead Christ (Luca Signorelli), 170
Last Judgement (Luca Signorelli), 226
Last Judgement (Taddeo di Bartolo), 95
La Verna, 106
Leaning Tower of Pisa, 7, 115, 118–120
Le Cantine di Greve in Chianti, 100
Le Crete Sensei, 82, 91, 107, 177
Le Dune (Viareggio), 132
The Legend of the True Cross (Piero della Francesca), 6, 82, 105, 106
Le Mummie di Ferentillo, 6, 224, 236–237
Leonardo da Vinci, 53, 129
Life of St. Augustine (Ottaviano Nelli), 213
Life of St. Francis (Benozzo Gozzoli), 231
Life of St. Francis (Giotto de Bondone), 56, 207
Lippi, Filippino, 62
Lirica in Piazza (Massa Marittima), 155
Livorno, 7, 143–147, 164, 165
Loggia dei Lanzi (Florence), 51
Lorenzetti, Ambrogio, 6, 52, 86, 155
Lorenzetti, Pietro, 52, 208
Lorenzini, Carlo, 129, 130
Lorien, 98
Lucca, 4, 123–127, 136–137, 140
Luminara di Santa Croce (Lucca), 18, 127
Lunigiana, 114, 115, 134–136

M

Macchiaioli School (Livorno), 145
Machiavelli, Niccolò, 56
Madonna (Cenni di Pepo Cimabue), 52
Madonna (Giotto di Bondone), 52
Madonna of the Goldfinch (Raphael), 53
Maestà (Ambrogio Lorenzetti), 155
Maestà (Simone Martini), 6, 86
Marble quarries (Carrara), 135
Maremma Pisana, 147–149
Marina di Alberese, 157, 160
Marina di Campo, 152, 153
Marini, Marino, 57
Markets
- Florence, 44, 67, 68, 73
- Tuscany, 85, 123, 128
- Umbria, 215

Martini, Simone, 6, 52, 86, 208
Marzocco, 173
Masaccio, 61
Masolino da Panicale, 61
Massacre of the Innocents (Matteo di Giovanni), 87
Massa Marittima, 142–143, 154–156, 162–163
Matteo di Giovanni, 87
Medical emergencies, 20–21
Medical insurance, 20
Medici family, 48
Mercato Centrale (Florence), 44, 68, 73
Mercato Nuovo (Florence), 52
Michelangelo Buonarotti, 51, 53, 54, 56, 58–59, 135, 226, 233
"Miracle of Bolsena," 225

Mobile phones, 33
Money, 14–16
Montalcino, 168, 178–180, 189, 191
Monte Argentario, 160–162
Monte Capanne (Elba), 4, 143, 152, 154
Montefalco, 222, 230–232, 237
Monte Ingino (Gubbio), 196, 213
Monteluco, 233
Monte Oliveto Maggiore, 4, 91, 107, 168, 177–178
Montepulciano, 4–5, 168, 172–175, 187–188
Monterchi, 106
Monte Subasio, 4
Monti dell'Uccellina, 158
Morcone, 153
Mosaici Villa Romana (Spello), 211
Mummies, 51, 224, 230, 236–237
Museo Archeologico
  - Marina di Cecina, 148
  - Siena, 88

Museo Archeologico all'Aperto 'Alberto Manzi,' 187
Museo Archeologico Nazionale
  - Chiusi, 181–182
  - Orvieto, 225

Museo Civico
  - Sarteano, 183
  - Siena, 6, 86

Museo Civico Archaeologico (Vetulonia), 158
Museo Civico di San Francesco (Montefalco), 231, 232
Museo Civico Giovanni Fattori (Livorno), 145, 146
Museo Claudio Faina e Civico (Orvieto), 226–227
Museo Corboli (Asciano), 91
Museo d'Arte per Bambini (Siena), 7, 87, 88
Museo degli Argenti (Florence), 62
Museo dei Ragazzi (Florence), 53, 226
Museo del Duomo (Città di Castello), 215
Museo dell'Accademia Etrusca e della Città (Cortona), 169, 170
Museo della Marineria (Viareggio), 132
Museo della Miniera (Massa Marittima), 155, 156
Museo della Pesca (Lago Trasimeno), 203, 205
Museo della Tortura (San Gimignano), 95
Museo delle Sinopie (Pisa), 116
Museo delle Statue-Stele Lunigianesi (Pontrémoli), 135–136
Museo dell'Olivo e dell'Olio (Perugia), 201
Museo dell'Opera
  - Florence, 48
  - Siena, 88

Museo dell'Opera del Duomo (Pisa), 116
Museo del Merletto (Isola Maggiore), 204
Museo del Palazzo dei Consoli (Gubbio), 213–214
Museo del Vino
  - Perugia, 200
  - San Gimignano, 94

Museo di Antropologia (Florence), 51
Museo di Arte Sacra
  - Massa Marittima, 155
  - Volterra, 99

Museo di Geologia e Paleontologia (Florence), 60
Museo di Mineralgia e Litologia (Florence), 60
Museo di Montalcino, 180
Museo Diocesano
  - Cortona, 170
  - Pienza, 177

Museo di San Marco (Florence), 7, 59, 60
Museo di Santa Maria Novella (Florence), 56, 57
Museo di Storia Naturale
  - Certosa di Pisa, 120–121
  - Florence, 60, 63
  - Siena, 4, 86–87

Museo di Storia Naturale del Mediterraneo (Livorno), 146–147
Museo Etrusco Guarnacci (Volterra), 99
Museo Galileo (Florence), 3, 39, 42, 54
Museo La Specola (Florence), 6, 63
Museo Leonardiano (Vinci), 129
Museo Marino Marini (Florence), 57–58
Museo Multimediale Casa Rossa Ximenes (Castiglione della Pescaia), 157–158
Museo Nazionale del Bargello (Florence), 54–55
Museo Nazionale del Ducato di Spoleto, 234
Museo Nazionale del Fumetto (Lucca), 127
Museo Piaggio (Pisa), 4, 121, 122
Museo Stibbert (Florence), 3, 39, 60
Museo Storico Perugina, 201

N

Napoleon Bonaparte, 154
Narni, 222, 234, 237–238
Narni Sotterranea, 237
National Curriculum, 42
Nativity (Pietro Perugino), 232
Nelli, Ottaviano, 213
Niccolò di Tommaso, 128
Nicodemus, 126
Nobile Collegio del Cambio (Perugia), 196, 201, 202
Norcia, 222
Northern Tuscany, 114–140
  - accommodation, 138–140
  - dining, 136–138
  - Garfagnana and Lunigiana, 134–136
  - Lucca, 123–127
  - Pisa, 115–123
  - Pistoia, 127–131
  - Viareggio, 131–134
  - visitor information, 115–117, 123, 127–128, 131, 134

Northern Umbria, 194–220
  - accommodation, 205, 218–220
  - Assisi, 205–209
  - Città di Castello, 214–216
  - dining, 204–205, 209, 216–218
  - Gubbio, 212–214
  - Lago Trasimeno, 202–205
  - Perugia, 195–202
  - Spello, 210–212
  - visitor information, 195–197, 202, 203, 206, 210, 212–215

O

Oasi LIPU Massacuiccoli (Viareggio), 132, 133
Olive oil, 149, 201, 211, 230–231
Oltrarno (Florence), 43, 60–64, 75
Open-Air Museo Italo Bolano (Elba), 152
Oratoria di Santa Caterina (Siena), 87
Orbetello, 160
Ornellaia, 32
Orsanmichele (Florence), 64
Orto Botanico
  Florence, 60
  Livorno, 146–147
  Lucca, 126
  Pisa, 122, 123
  Siena, 87
Orvieto, 171, 184, 223–227, 238–240
Orvieto Underground, 3, 222, 227
Ospedale del Ceppo (Pistoia), 128
Osteria del Museo (Perugia), 200

P

Package tours, 24
Painting classes, 55, 56
Palaeontology Centre (Todi), 229
Palazzina Uzielli (Vinci), 129
Palazzo Comunale
  Cortona, 170
  Montepulciano, 174
  San Gimignano, 94, 95
Palazzo dei Priori
  Perugia, 197
  Todi, 228
Palazzo del Capitano
  Assisi, 207
  Todi, 228
Palazzo del Capitano del Popolo (Montepulciano), 175
Palazzo della Corgna (Castiglione del Lago), 204
Palazzo del Podestà (Città di Castello), 215
Palazzo del Popolo (Todi), 228
Palazzo De' Nobili-Tarugi (Montepulciano), 174
Palazzo Medici-Riccardi (Florence), 58
Palazzo Pfanner (Lucca), 126
Palazzo Piccolomini (Pienza), 177
Palazzo Pitti (Florence), 63
Palazzo Pubblico (Siena), 86
Palazzo Vecchio (Florence), 39, 51, 53, 55, 56, 98, 148
Palazzo Vescovile (Pienza), 177
Palio delle Contrande (Siena), 5, 18, 82, 83
Palio Marinaro del Argentario, 161
Panforte, 90
Parco Archeologico (Volterra), 98
Parco Archeologico di Baratti e Populonia, 148, 149
Parco Avventura Fosdinovo, 136
Parco della Rocca (Todi), 229
Parco delle Cascine (Florence), 48, 67
Parco delle Piscine (Sarteano), 183
Parco di Pinocchio (Collodi), 5, 129, 130
Parco Naturale delle Foreste Casentinesi, 106
Parco Naturale di Migliarino San Rossore Massaciuccoli (Pisa), 121, 133
Parco Pitagora (Viareggio), 133, 134
Parco Prehistorico (Volterra), 102
Parco Regionale della Maremma, 3, 143, 158–160, 166
Parco Regionale del Monte Cucco, 214
Parking, 25
Passeggio del Prato (Arezzo), 104
Passignano, 204
Passports, 12–14
Patron saints, 18
Pentecost (Taddeo di Bartolo), 200
Perseus (Benvenuto Cellini), 51
Perugia, 194–202, 217, 218
Perugino, Pietro, 6, 195, 200, 201, 232
Pesto, 115, 138
Petrarch, 105
Pets, vacations with, 13
Piazza del Duomo (Florence), 43, 48–51, 72
Piazza della Signoria (Florence), 43, 48, 51–56, 72, 73
Piazzale Michelangelo (Florence), 39, 40, 43, 44, 48, 67
Piccolomini Library (Duomo of Siena), 85, 212
Pienza, 168, 175–178, 189
Piero della Francesca, 5, 6, 82, 105, 106, 200
Pietera, 158
Pieve di Santa Maria Assunta (Arezzo), 104
Pinacoteca
  San Gimignano, 94
  Volterra, 6, 99
Pinacoteca Civica (Spello), 211
Pinacoteca Comunale (Città di Castello), 215
Pinocchio Park, 31
Pinturicchio, 195, 212
Pisa, 115–123, 136–140
Pistoia, 114, 127–131, 137
Pistoia Zoo, 5, 115, 130–131
Pitigliano, 168–170, 184–188
Poggio Lecci, 158
Ponte delle Torri (Spoleto), 233, 240
Ponte Vecchio (Florence), 43, 61, 106
Pope Leo X with Cardinals Giulio de'Medici and Luigi de'Rossi (Raphael), 53
Populonia Alta, 149
Porsenna, 182
Porta all'Arco (Volterra), 98, 106
Porta San Gervasio (Lucca), 126
Porte Ecole, 161
Porte Santo Stefano, 161
Portoferraio, 152, 164, 165
Pozzo della Cava (Orvieto), 227
Pozzo di San Patrizio (Orvieto), 227
Pozzo Etrusco (Perugia), 199
Pratini, 159
Primavera (Sandro Botticelli), 6, 52, 53
Procchio, 152, 153
The Prophets (Fra' Angelico), 226
Puccini, Giacomo, 133
Puccini e la sua Lucca, 124, 133
Punti Bìciclette (Florence), 66
Purgatorio di San Patrizio (Todi), 228

Q

Quartiere (of Orvieto), 224
Quattro Mori (Pietro Tacca), 144

R

Raffaellino dal Colle, 215
Rafting, white-water, 3, 224, 236
Rape of the Sabine Women (Giambologna), 51
Raphael, 53, 215
Rembrandt van Rijn, 54
Responsible travel, 21, 22
River Arno, 43, 57, 60, 67
Rocca Albornoziana (Spoleto), 233, 234
Rocca del Leone (Castiglione del Lago), 204
Rocca Maggiore (Assisi), 209
Rocca Paolina (Perugia), 197
Roccas
 Orvieto, 224
 San Gimignano, 94
 Spello, 211
Rontini, Andrea, 101
Rossi di Montalcino, 32

S

Sacred Allegory (Giovanni Bellini), 53
Safety, 21
Sagra del Tordo (Montalcino), 18, 178–179
Sagrantino di Montefalco, 32, 231
St. Sebastian (Benozzo Gozzoli), 94
Salimbeni, Iacopo, 200
Salone dei Cinquecento (Florence), 55
San Bernardino oratory (Siena), 88
San Domenico (Siena), 89
San Fortunato (Todi), 229–230
San Fredanio (Lucca), 126
San Gemini (Carsulae), 235
San Gimignano, 4, 80, 82, 90–96
 accommodation, 94, 110–111
 dining, 109–110
San Gimignano 1300 reproduction, 95–96
San Giovanni d'Asso, 91
San Lorenzo market (Florence), 44, 67, 68
San Marco Altarpiece (Fra' Angelico), 59
San Marco area (Florence), 58–60
San Michele Arcangelo (Isola Maggiore), 204
San Michele in Foro (Lucca), 125
San Miniato al Monte (Florence), 39, 64
San Pietro (Spoleto), 233
San Quirico d'Orcia, 180
San Rocco (Pitigliano), 185
San Salvatore (Isola Maggiore), 204
Sansepolcro, 106
Santa Caterina da Siena (Livorno), 144
Santa Croce (Florence), 44, 48, 56, 75, 207
Sant'Agostino church
 Gubbio, 213
 Montalcino, 180
 Montefalco, 230
 San Gimignano, 96
Santa Maria dei Servi (Montepulciano), 175
Santa Maria della Consolazione (Todi), 229–230
Santa Maria della Scalla (Siena), 6–7, 82, 87, 88
Santa Maria Maggiore (Spello), 212
Santa Maria Novella area (Florence), 56–58, 73, 74
Sant'Andrea beach, 4, 153
Sant'Andrea church (Pistoia), 128
Sant'Angelo (Narnia), 237
Sant'Ansano (Spoleto), 233
Sant'Antonio Abate (Pistoia), 128
Santa Trinita (Florence), 64
Santuario della Madonna del Soccorso (Montalcino), 179
San Vicenzo, 147–148, 163
Sarteano, 182–184, 190–191
Sassicaia, 32
Sasso dei Lupi (Perugia), 201
Saturnia Hot Springs, 4, 170, 186
Scenes from the Life of the Virgin (Taddeo Gaddi), 56
Scoppio del Carro (Florence), 44
Seafood, 7, 143, 164, 165
Sebastian (saint), 94, 95
Self-catering, 29, 30
Self Portrait as an Old Man (Rembrandt van Rijn), 54
Severini, Gino, 169
Shopping
 central Tuscany, 89, 90, 94, 99, 104
 Florence, 56, 67–69
 food shops, 89–90, 123, 145, 156
 northern Tuscany, 122, 123, 125
 southern Tuscany, 177
 Tuscan coast, 156
 Umbria, 211
Siena, 80–90, 107–109, 111–112, 173
Signorelli, Luca, 170, 215, 226
Single parents, 12
Soccer, 18, 19, 48, 65–66, 143, 146
Southern Tuscany, 168–192
 accommodation, 190–192
 Chiusi, 181–182
 Cortona, 169–171
 dining, 187–190
 Montalcino, 178–180
 Montepulciano, 172–175
 Pienza, 175–178
 Pitigliano, 184–187
 Sarteano, 182–184
 visitor information, 169, 172, 173, 175, 176, 178, 181–185
Southern Umbria, 222–240
 accommodation, 239–240
 dining, 237–239
 far south, 234–237
 Montefalco, 230–232
 Orvieto, 223–227
 Spoleto, 232–234
 Todi, 228–230
 visitor information, 223–224, 228, 230, 232
Sovana, 187
Spectator sports, 65–66
Spello, 194, 209–212
Spoleto, 4, 222, 232–234, 238, 240
Spoleto Festival, 18, 232, 233, 239
Sports, spectator, 65–66
Strada del Vino Nobile (Montepulciano), 175

Sualzo Beach (Passignano), 203–204
Summer Festival (Lucca), 124
Supermercato il Centro (Florence), 73

T

Tacca, Pietro, 144
Taddeo di Bartolo, 95, 99, 174, 200
Taxis, 27
Tempio di Minerva (Assisi), 207
Tempio di San Biagio (Montepulciano), 174
Terni, 234
Terrazza Mascagni (Livorno), 145
Thermal springs, 4, 170, 186
Tignanello, 32
Tipografia Grifani-Donati (Città di Castello), 215–216
Titian, 53–54
Todi, 222, 228–230, 238, 239
Tomba della Pellegrina (Chiusi), 182
Tomba della Quadriga Infernale (Sarteano), 3, 170, 171, 183–184
Tomba della Scimmia (Chiusi), 182
Tomba del Leone (Chiusi), 182
Tomba Ildebranda, 186–187
Tomb of Ilaria del Carrettol (Jacopo della Quercia), 127
Tomb of St. Francis, 208
Tombolo della Feniglia, 4, 143, 160–162
Tommasi, Lodovico, 146
Torano, 135
Torciata di San Giuseppe (Pitigliano), 18, 185
Torre del Candeliere (Massa Marittima), 155
Torre del Lago, 133
Torre delle Ore (Lucca), 126
Torre del Mangia (Siena), 82, 88
Torre del Moro (Orvieto), 225
Torre del Porcellino (Volterra), 98
Torre di Pulcinella (Montepulciano), 174
Torre Grossa (San Gimignano), 93–94
Torre Guinigi (Lucca), 126
Torre Maestra (Spoleto), 234
Torre Pendente. *See* Leaning Tower of Pisa
Toscana Foto Festival (Massa Marittima), 155
Trains, 23, 26
Travel insurance, 20
Trenonatura (Siena), 89
Tre Stelle (Viareggio), 132
Tuscan coast, 142–166
    accommodation, 163–166
    Castiglione della Pescaia, 157–158
    dining, 162–163
    Elba, 149–154
    Etruscan coast, 147–149
    Livorno, 143–147
    Massa Marittima, 154–156
    Monte Argentario, 160–162
    Parco Regionale della Maremma, 158–160
    visitor information, 143, 144, 147, 151, 152, 154–155, 157–161
Tuscany. *See specific regions*

U

Uccello, Paolo, 56
Umbria. *See* Northern Umbria; Southern Umbria

V

Vada, 147
Valnerina, 3, 222, 224, 234, 236
Vasari, Giorgio, 105
Venezia Nuova quarter (Livorno), 144
Venus of Urbino (Titian), 53–54
Versilian coast, 114
Vetulonia, 158
Via Cava di San Giuseppe, 4, 187
Viareggio, 131–134, 137
Vie Cave, 170, 187
Vignamaggio winery, 100
Villa Mimbelli (Livorno), 145
Villas, 111, 112
Villa San Martino (Elba), 154
Vineyards, 176
Visas, 12
Visitor information, 10, 12
    central Tuscany, 80–82, 91, 93, 96, 103
    Florence, 38–44
    northern Tuscany, 115–117, 123, 127–128, 131, 134
    northern Umbria, 195–197, 202, 203, 206, 210, 212–215
    southern Tuscany, 169, 172, 173, 175, 176, 178, 181–185
    southern Umbria, 223–224, 228, 230, 232
    Tuscan coast, 143, 144, 147, 151, 152, 154–155, 157–161
Vite, Antonio, 128
Volterra, 80, 96–102, 110, 171
Volterra AD1398 festival, 18, 82, 98
Volto Santo (Nicodemus), 126

W

Walking, 27, 66, 67, 82, 121, 233
Weather, 16–19
White-water rafting, 3, 224, 236
Windsurfing, 196, 203
Wine, 32–33. *See also specific enotecas*
    in Bolgheri, 149
    in Chianti, 100
    from Ciliegiolo grapes, 184
    in Florence, 76
    in Montalcino, 178
    in Montefalco, 230, 231
    in Montepulciano, 107, 175
    museums, 94, 200
    in Umbria, 200, 201
    winemaker's calendar, 176

Z

Zuccale, 153